VIBRANT
PUBLISHERS

TEST PREP SERIES

GRE®

WORDS IN CONTEXT:
THE COMPLETE LIST

2022

1500 GRE-level
vocabulary words

THREE to FIVE example
sentences per word

Parts of speech, Synonyms
and Definitions for each word

Fourth Edition

GRE® Words In Context: The Complete List
Fourth Edition

Paperback ISBN-10: 1-63651-051-5
Paperback ISBN-13: 978-1-63651-051-4

E-book ISBN-10: 1-63651-052-3
E-book ISBN-13: 978-1-63651-052-1
Library of Congress Control Number: 2018915127

This publication is designed to provide accurate and authoritative information in regard to the subject matter covered. The Author has made every effort in the preparation of this book to ensure the accuracy of the information. However, information in this book is sold without warranty either expressed or implied. The Author or the Publisher will not be liable for any damages caused or alleged to be caused either directly or indirectly by this book.

Vibrant Publishers books are available at special quantity discount for sales promotions, or for use in corporate training programs. For more information please write to bulkorders@vibrantpublishers.com

Please email feedback / corrections (technical, grammatical or spelling) to spellerrors@vibrantpublishers.com

To access the complete catalogue of Vibrant Publishers, visit www.vibrantpublishers.com

GRE is the registered trademark of the Educational Testing Service (ETS) which neither sponsors nor endorses this product.

Table of Contents

Challenging Word List

Dear Student,

Thank you for purchasing **GRE® Words In Context: The Complete List**. We are committed to publishing books that are content-rich, concise and approachable enabling more students to read and make the fullest use of them. We hope this book provides the most enriching learning experience as you prepare for your GRE exam.

Should you have any questions or suggestions, feel free to email us at reachus@vibrantpublishers.com

Thanks again for your purchase. Good luck for your GRE!

– Vibrant Publishers Team

///////// GRE Books in Test Prep Series //////////

TITLE	PAPERBACK ISBN
6 Practice Tests for the GRE	978-1-63651-090-3
GRE Analytical Writing Supreme: Solutions to the Real Essay Topics	978-1-63651-053-8
GRE Analytical Writing: Solutions to the Real Essay Topics - Book 1	978-1-63651-067-5
GRE Analytical Writing: Solutions to the Real Essay Topics - Book 2	978-1-63651-069-9
GRE Master Wordlist: 1535 Words for Verbal Mastery	978-1-63651-083-5
GRE Quantitative Reasoning Supreme: Study Guide with Practice Questions	978-1-63651-091-0
GRE Reading Comprehension: Detailed Solutions to 325 Questions	978-1-63651-063-7
GRE Text Completion and Sentence Equivalence Practice Questions	978-1-63651-064-4
GRE Verbal Reasoning Supreme: Study Guide with Practice Questions	978-1-63651-057-6
GRE Words In Context: The Complete List	978-1-63651-051-4

For the most updated list of books visit
www.vibrantpublishers.com

How to Get Most Out of this Book

What's in this Book?

This book contains wordlists unlike any you have seen before. A traditional word list offers a vocabulary word, its dictionary definition, and a SINGLE use of the word in a sentence. That is simply not enough for a fully functional understanding of a word in all its complexities. Our Word List takes each vocabulary word through its paces, denoting its part of speech, synonyms for its various contexts, its descriptive meaning, and, most importantly, THREE (3) to FIVE (5) sentences using the word in its varied contexts. When appropriate, those varied contexts include both literal and figurative uses of the word.

The Logic Behind the Division of the 3 Word Lists

In this book, we have divided the Word Lists into three sections- **Word List 1**, **Word List 2**, and **Challenging Word List**. Each section includes **10 chapters** with **500 words** arranged in an alphabetical order throughout the section. It is important to remember that your goal is to be fully conversant in as many of these vocabulary words as possible. Why? You must not only recognize and comprehend the words when you encounter them in GRE test questions, but you must also utilize sophisticated vocabulary to express your own ideas in the Analytical Writing section of the test. It is to your advantage, therefore, to have as many high-level vocabulary words as possible at your disposal. This is especially difficult to do if your preparation time is limited.

The aim of such categorization, therefore, is to facilitate easy studying. Looking at 1,500 words arranged alphabetically from cover to cover can be an overwhelming experience. From a psychological viewpoint, progressing alphabet-by-alphabet (as though you are reading a dictionary) makes the study process seem long and tedious. That's why we've grouped the words into **three sets of alphabetical divisions** to help you fast-track your learning.

Usually, words that begin with alphabets like 'A', 'C', 'D', 'P', and 'S', for example, have long lists (110+ words). On the opposite side of the spectrum are words that begin with 'J', 'K', 'Q' etc. These word lists will have over 10+ words on an average. If the 1,500 words were arranged alphabetically, a significant portion of time would be used up in working through 'A' itself. With 50 words per day, you would have been able to finish only 1 alphabet in a week.

Instead of progressing from words that start with 'A' to words that start with 'B' and so on until 'Z', you will be able to cover words from the whole alphabet in each section. You will be able to cover more than 5 alphabets in the first 5-7 days. In this way, your vocabulary will be enriched by a rich selection of words from across the alphabet. Finishing a series of 5 alphabets will boost your confidence and motivate you to continue your progress through the list.

Once you've made headway through **Word List 1**, you can proceed to **Word List 2**, and finally onto the **Challenging Word List**.

Challenging Word List: After you've mastered the first two lists, you've completed a significant portion of the material and you can move onto the next list. This list is comprised of words that are much more difficult than the words in the previous sections. Pay special attention to these words and keep aside more time to study them.

Eventually, mastering the three Word Lists will refine your vocabulary and give an edge to your writing skills that will help you beyond the GRE.

	Number of Chapters	Number of Words in Each Chapter	Number of Words in the Whole Section
Word List 1 (**Aberration-Zany**)	10	50	500
Word List 2 (**Abbreviate-Zephyr**)	10	50	500
Challenging Word List (**Acclivity-Zeal**)	10	50	500
Total			**1500**

WORD LIST DIVISIONS

How will our Word Lists Help You Prepare for the GRE?

Performing well on the GRE General Test, especially its Verbal Reasoning section, requires a strong working knowledge of the vocabulary that appears in the questions - how those words function both literally and figuratively, how their meanings vary based on context, and how (in many cases) they operate as more than one part of speech.

The following is an example of a question type the GRE refers to as "Sentence Equivalence." The test-taker is instructed to select two (2) answer choices that, when used to complete the sentence, fit the meaning of the sentence as a whole and produce complete sentences that are alike in meaning.

The angry delegates no longer debated the matter with equipoise, and the _____ that ensued prevented any further rational or intelligent discourse.

a) finesse

b) pandemonium

c) pragmatist

d) appellation

e) maelstrom

f) liaison

To perform well on this test question, the test-taker must look beyond the more traditional use (i.e., dictionary definitions) of the vocabulary it contains. The dictionary definition of the word "equipoise," for instance, is not particularly helpful.

a: a state of equilibrium

b: counterbalance

Source: "Equipoise." Merriam-Webster.com. Merriam-Webster, n.d. Web. 20 June 2014. <http://www.merriam-webster.com/dictionary/equipoise>.

The "state of equilibrium" here is not physical (e.g., a gymnast in "equipoise"). Instead, the word is being applied figuratively to a debate or discussion in which the arguments are not in equilibrium - in other words, are not being discussed in an equal and fair manner. By combining the figurative use of "equipoise" with the clues that the delegates are "angry" and the debate is no longer "rational" or "intelligent," one can conclude the discussion has broken down into mayhem or confusion. The two (2) correct answers signify such a situation. They are: pandemonium (wild chaos or disorder) and maelstrom (a violent whirlpool or, figuratively, a tumultuous situation).

Tips and Strategies for Learning the Vocabulary using the Word List

Activate what you already know.

We recommend progressing in sequence, starting from Word List 1, Word List 2, and then onto the Challenging Word List. Whichever list you've chosen to start out with, five hundred (500) words may seem like a great deal, but it is likely you already know a number of them, in one form or another. Begin by focusing on those you think you may know:

a) Review the example sentences. Is that how you use the word? If not, how is your use different?

b) If you are familiar with a word, check to see that its part of speech on the list is one with which you are familiar. For example, you may be familiar with the use of "sham" as a noun (as in, "The charity fundraiser was a sham."), but you may be unfamiliar with its use as a verb ("The used car salesman tried to sham us.") If the word's use as another part of speech is unfamiliar, familiarize yourself with that new use of the word.

c) Note whether the word can be used both literally and figuratively. For example, the word "dilute" has both a literal use, as in thinning something by adding liquid (e.g., to dilute the chemicals by adding water), and a figurative use in which nothing physical occurs (e.g., to dilute the power of his argument by offering counterarguments). Adjust your understanding of the word to include both its literal and figurative meanings

d) Even if you do not know a particular word, can you connect the word with one that is familiar to you? For example, you may not know the word "dulcet," but you may be familiar with the Spanish word "dulce," which means "sweet." Increasingly, for instance, you can find "dulce de leche" or "sweet milk" ice cream or candies in the store, referring to a sweet caramel flavoring. You learn, from the Word List, that "dulcet" means sweet, especially something that is "sweet" or pleasing to the ear (e.g., the "dulcet" tones of the violin). The connection is, therefore, an easy one!

e) Color-code the words with which you are familiar.

    i) For example, you might highlight in yellow those words that you know outright, without making any adjustments to your understanding.

    ii) Highlight in green those that are functioning as a different part of speech than what you are used to seeing.

    iii) Highlight in blue those words with a literal or figurative use that is unfamiliar to you. Also highlight the example sentence(s) in which that use of the word appears.

    iv) Highlight in pink those words that you do not know, but that you can connect to using related words.

"Chunk" your learning of the remaining vocabulary.

After activating your prior knowledge and weeding out those words you already know or with which you have some familiarity, it's time to focus on those words you don't know. You can "chunk" or group those words into manageable segments for learning.

a) One approach to "chunking" is to group together words that perform as the same part of speech and look for patterns. For instance, words ending in "ous," such as "amorphous," "chivalrous," "dexterous," "ominous," and "vacuous," all function as adjectives.

b) Another approach to "chunking" is to group words that primarily pertain to certain subject areas. For example, "avalanche," "arid," "navigable," and "glacial" are primarily geographic terms, while "cognitive," "debunk," "muse" and "paradigm" are terms that relate to the act of thinking.

c) A final approach to "chunking" might be personal to you: divide the words into groups based on how difficult or easy they are to you.

d) However you "chunk" your words, you can then design a schedule for working with the words, taking on no more than 4-5 words at a time before moving on to another "chunk."

Have fun with the words as you make them your own!

Never lose sight of your ultimate goal: to incorporate these words into your personal vocabulary. The Word List example sentences will give you a solid foundation for how the word is used - an excellent launching pad for using that word appropriately in your own world.

a) Enliven your family dinner conversations with words from the Word List. Doing so helps you, but also challenges your family and creates a "vocabulary-rich" environment from which every family member can learn. You might even hold a contest to see if your family members can guess the vocabulary from the Word List you are adding to that night's dinner conversation.

b) Challenge yourself to use a word (especially one that you are finding difficult to remember) at least three (3) times in a given day. You might incorporate it, for instance, into an email to a colleague, a conversation with your boss, and a text to your best friend. The more you use the word (appropriately), the more it becomes your own.

c) Make a note of the words from the Word List when you see them elsewhere. You will be pleasantly surprised at how often you encounter them in the reading you do on a daily basis. Whenever you do so, make a note of the word and its use. Doing so reinforces your understanding of the word and its applications.

d) Take every opportunity to practice. Keep your "chunked" lists handy for any time you have a moment: while brushing your teeth in the morning, sitting in traffic, waiting for your daughter's soccer game to start, or even standing in line in the grocery store. The greater exposure you have to the words and their uses, the more you will become comfortable with them and make them your own.

How Can Our Word Lists Help You Beyond the GRE?

The goal of entrance exams, like the GRE, is to anticipate the test-taker's likelihood of success in the field into which they seek entry. Thus, the "long view" of mastering sophisticated vocabulary is that doing so will not only help you prepare for the GRE, but will simultaneously prepare you for what lies ahead: comprehending, analyzing, and evaluating graduate-level materials and writing with the complexity and sophistication expected of a graduate-level student. To put it simply: a fully-functioning, high-level vocabulary is the key to success in your graduate experience.

Prepare for success NOW!

Word List 1

This page is intentionally left blank

Chapter 1

Aberration – Banal

This chapter covers the following words, each with its part of speech, pronunciation, and descriptive meaning.
Usage of the word is also illustrated in three to five sample sentences.

aberration	agenda	aspirant
abolish	aghast	assay
abominable	agitate	assessment
aboriginal	alienate	assimilate
abortive	amass	astronomical
absolve	amend	avid
abusive	amorphous	bait
abyss	amphibian	balk
accommodate	amputate	balm
acknowledge	anchor	banal
acme	animated	
adherent	annex	
adjacent	anomaly	
adjutant	anthropoid	
adorn	apex	
advent	apologist	
advert	appellation	
affirmation	arbiter	
affront	arrogance	
agape	ashen	

ABERRATION (n)   [ab-*uh*-REY-sh*uh* n]

Meaning: abnormality; the act of departing from the normal

Usage 1: Her willingness to work in a group is an *aberration;* she is usually a loner.

Usage 2: There appears to be an *aberration* in the data that no one can explain.

Usage 3: His course was determined and he would tolerate no *aberration.*

Usage 4: You must order straight from the menu, with no *aberration* or modification.

Usage 5: Can you find the *aberration* in that homogeneous group?

ABOLISH (v)   [*uh*-BOL-ish]

Meaning: cancel; to put an end to

Usage 1: We hope they *abolish* the practice of imprisoning people for their political views.

Usage 2: To *abolish* slavery is an essential requirement of all modern societies.

Usage 3: Some people believe that no form of death penalty is acceptable, and we should *abolish* it entirely.

Usage 4: I advocate that we *abolish* the use of cell phones on all types of public transportation.

Usage 5: If we *abolish* the legal right to own a gun, what will be the effect?

ABOMINABLE (adj)   [*uh*-BOM-*uh*-n*uh*-b*uh* l]

Meaning: detestable; extremely unpleasant; worthy of causing disgust

Usage 1: Her treatment of her younger siblings is *abominable;* there is no way I'd ask her to babysit.

Usage 2: That *abominable* woman rudely interrupted me again!

Usage 3: The conditions at the cabin in the mountains were *abominable;* it hadn't been inhabited for years.

Usage 4: Your snowman is *abominable;* he has no eyes, nose, or mouth!

Usage 5: Don't you agree that the odor of dead fish at the fish market is *abominable*?

ABORIGINAL (adj)   [ab-*uh*-RIJ-*uh*-nl]

Meaning: being the first of its kind in a region; original or earliest known

Usage 1: The pottery of this area's *aboriginal* inhabitants is exquisitely beautiful.

Usage 2: I was fascinated by our study of the island's animals, including those that were *aboriginal.*

Usage 3: The dark jungle looked primeval, filled as it was with *aboriginal* plants and animals.

Usage 4: The *aboriginal* people of the area must have thought the settlers were crazy.

Usage 5: How do their *aboriginal* practices influence their modern customs and traditions?

ABORTIVE (adj)   [*uh*-BAWR-tiv]

Meaning: unsuccessful; fruitless; failing to succeed

Usage 1: There were several *abortive* attempts to start a rocket program, but none was successful.

Usage 2: The rebel insurgence was *abortive* and was quickly brought down.

Usage 3: She refused to believe the student demonstration would be *abortive*, but the rest of us knew it would fail.

Usage 4: After my *abortive* effort to make homemade chocolate truffles, I decided store-bought ones were superior.

Usage 5: I hear you made an *abortive* trip to Alaska; what happened?

ABSOLVE (v)   [ab-ZOLV]

Meaning: pardon (an offense); exonerate; exculpate; to pronounce free from guilt or blame

Usage 1: One goal of confession is to allow a priest to *absolve* a sinner from his/her sins.

Usage 2: I refuse to *absolve* you for the hurtful comments you made.

Usage 3: You think your good deeds will somehow *absolve* you from all your misdeeds, but you're wrong.

Usage 4: There would be no need to *absolve* you if you didn't do anything wrong in the first place.

Usage 5: Did she finally *absolve* him of the accusations that he was unfaithful?

ABUSIVE (adj)   [*uh*-BYOO-siv]

Meaning: coarsely insulting; physically harmful; harsh or injurious; using harsh language

Usage 1: Her *abusive* behavior towards her peers ended in a fight.

Usage 2: I know you are angry, but please refrain from using *abusive* language.

Usage 3: That use of power is *abusive*; surely we can find another way to accomplish our goals.

Usage 4: Chocolate and I have an *abusive* relationship; I can't resist its decadence.

Usage 5: Is she afraid because he has been an *abusive* husband?

ABYSS (n)   [*uh*-BIS]

Meaning: enormous chasm; a deep, immeasurable space

Usage 1: The earthquake caused the ground to separate and form an *abyss*.

Usage 2: The volcano experts crept towards the edge of the opening and stared down into the *abyss*.

Usage 3: He has fallen into an *abyss* of sadness.

Usage 4: I am not only out of money; my wallet has become a gaping *abyss*.

Usage 5: Is that *abyss* bottomless?

ACCOMMODATE (v)   [*uh*-KOM-*uh*-deyt]

Meaning: oblige or help someone; to provide suitably

Usage 1: We hope they can *accommodate* this request, even though it is an unusual one.

Usage 2: I fail to see why we need to *accommodate* their interests; they are not even trying to compromise.

Usage 3: The hotel is happy to *accommodate* the special needs of its guests.

Usage 4: Please tell him my minivan was designed to *accommodate* seven passengers, not twenty.

Usage 5: Did you leave enough room in the jar to *accommodate* two crickets?

ACKNOWLEDGE (v)   [ak-NOL-ij]

Meaning: recognize; to admit to be real or true

Usage 1: He refused to *acknowledge* that he'd cheated on that test.

Usage 2: Those experts must *acknowledge* the possibility that global warming is a reality.

Usage 3: To *acknowledge* one may be wrong is often difficult.

Usage 4: The annoying thing about moms is that you must *acknowledge* they have your best interests at heart.

Usage 5: When did world leaders *acknowledge* there was an economic crisis?

ACME (n)   [AK-mee]

Meaning: top; pinnacle; highest peak or point of achievement; zenith; the highest point

Usage 1: With this scandal, I believe he has reached the *acme* of his political career.

Usage 2: When the hikers reached the *acme* of the rugged peak, they collapsed in exhaustion.

Usage 3: Nothing could compare to the view from the mountain's *acme*.

Usage 4: I realized I'd reached the *acme* of embarrassing moments when I burped during the job interview.

Usage 5: Which play would you say represents the *acme* of Shakespeare's career?

ADHERENT (n)   [ad-HEER-*uh* nt]

Meaning: supporter; follower, one who follows or upholds another person, a cause, a belief, etc.

Usage 1: She was an *adherent* of a new school of thought about recycling.

Usage 2: I enjoy attending the meetings, but I am not an *adherent* to their beliefs.

Usage 3: Which of those nations is an *adherent* to the treaty?

Usage 4: As an *adherent* to the cause of laziness, I plan to do absolutely nothing today.

Usage 5: Is he a strict *adherent* to the rules and principles that govern the organization?

ADJACENT (adj)   [*uh*-JEY-s*uh* nt]

Meaning: adjoining; neighboring; close by; lying near; next to

Usage 1: In this classroom you will don your costume, and in the *adjacent* classroom you will perform your skit.

Usage 2: The last I recall, my keys were *adjacent* to the telephone on the desk.

Usage 3: The state map is on this page, and on the *adjacent* page are maps of the state's major cities.

Usage 4: Whatever you do, don't put Tamryn *adjacent* to Raymond.

Usage 5: What parking lot is *adjacent* to that building?

ADJUTANT (n/adj)   [AJ-*uh*-t*uh* nt]

Meaning: staff officer assisting the commander; assistant; one of lower rank who assists one of high rank

Usage 1: He says his *adjutant* keeps his schedule, and we need to go through her. (n)

Usage 2: My goal is to move quickly beyond the *adjutant* position to which I've been assigned. (adj)

Usage 3: Let my *adjutant* know your answer, and he'll pass it on to me. (n)

Usage 4: I was sick and tired of him treating me like an *adjutant;* we both operated at the same level! (n)

Usage 5: If we can't reach the officer, should we try her *adjutant?* (n)

ADORN (v)   [*uh*-DAWRN]

Meaning: decorate; to make more pleasing or attractive

Usage 1: We will *adorn* the house with pastel colors during the Easter celebration.

Usage 2: Soft dew glistened on every blade of grass, which only served to *adorn* the meadow even more.

Usage 3: During graduations we always *adorn* the cars of the new graduates with shaving cream and aluminum cans.

Usage 4: The newly-wealthy woman sought to *adorn* herself with priceless jewelry.

Usage 5: Why do we *adorn* ourselves so completely, thereby masking our natural beauty?

ADVENT (n)   [AD-vent]

Meaning: arrival; the coming of

Usage 1: After a devastatingly hot summer, we were relieved at the *advent* of fall.

Usage 2: Her *advent* as a university guest lecturer was a source of great excitement.

Usage 3: With the *advent* of my position as director came a surprisingly large salary.

Usage 4: I do not welcome the *advent* of my senior years.

Usage 5: How does the *advent* of spring usually affect you?

ADVERT (v)   [ad-VURT]

Meaning: refer to; to call attention to

Usage 1: During the press conference, do not *advert* to the ethics investigation unless you are prepared to talk about it fully.

Usage 2: Be sure to *advert* to the fact that many of our members made generous contributions to the sponsored charity.

Usage 3: At the faculty meeting, the principal will *advert* to opportunities for professional learning this summer.

Usage 4: I feel the need to *advert* to the fact that we haven't had lunch, and I am weak with hunger.

Usage 5: Did you notice he did not *advert* to the allegations of fraud made against him?

AFFIRMATION (n) [af-er-MEY-sh*uh* n]

Meaning: positive assertion; confirmation of the truth; praise; a truthful statement

Usage 1: His compliments of my work were an incredible *affirmation.*

Usage 2: The congregation's *affirmation* made the new members feel welcome.

Usage 3: With her *affirmation* regarding the events of that day, the case against him was looking grim.

Usage 4: I don't know why I fish for compliments; I don't need that kind of *affirmation.*

Usage 5: Was your *affirmation* accepted into evidence at trial?

AFFRONT (n) [*uh*-FRUHNT]

Meaning: insult; offence; intentional act of disrespect; a deliberately rude act or word

Usage 1: The lawyer took it as an *affront* that I wanted a second opinion.

Usage 2: The look on her face confirmed she felt the *affront.*

Usage 3: She promised her fiancé not to give *affront* to her prospective in-laws.

Usage 4: The apartment's tacky wallpaper and 70s carpeting was an *affront* to my senses.

Usage 5: Are you sure that email will not give *affront* to its recipients?

AGAPE (adj) [*uh*-GEYP]

Meaning: with mouth wide open because of surprise or wonder

Usage 1: The students were *agape* with wonder at the milky-white Beluga whales.

Usage 2: It is no help whatsoever when drivers passing an accident are distracted and *agape* with horror.

Usage 3: Please don't stand there with your mouth *agape*; help me!

Usage 4: My mouth stood *agape* when the clerk finally punched the rude customer.

Usage 5: Didn't the sight of the Aurora Borealis leave you *agape* with astonishment?

AGENDA (n) [*uh*-JEN-d*uh*]

Meaning: items of business at a meeting; a list of things to be done

Usage 1: Each student will be provided with an *agenda* so that they may keep track of their classroom assignments.

Usage 2: Today's *agenda* is filled to the brim; we will have to save new items for tomorrow.

Usage 3: Please refer to your *agenda* as the conference progresses.

Usage 4: There are three items on my *agenda* today: sleep, turn over, sleep some more.

Usage 5: What is on the *agenda* for tonight's meeting?

AGHAST (adj) [*uh*-GAST]

Meaning: horrified; struck with overwhelming shock

Usage 1: The interviewers were *aghast* at the sloppy clothing worn by the interviewees.

Usage 2: The crowd at the air show was *aghast* when the stunt plane fell from the sky.

Usage 3: As the wildfire destroyed home after home, residents stood *aghast.*

Usage 4: I tried not to look *aghast* when my mother-in-law wiped my husband's chin.

Usage 5: Were you as *aghast* as I at her rudeness?

AGITATE (v) [AJ-i-teyt]

Meaning: stir up; disturb; to excite emotion

Usage 1: The editorial was designed to *agitate* local citizens and cause more controversy.

Usage 2: You have no idea how that tiger will respond if you *agitate* him.

Usage 3: It is about time we *agitate* that championship team; they've become too complacent in their victories.

Usage 4: Hearing any more about their stupidity will only *agitate* me further.

Usage 5: Why does she *agitate* him again right after he calms down?

ALIENATE (v) [EYL-y*uh*-neyt]

Meaning: make hostile; separate; to make unfriendly; estrange

Usage 1: The new, stringent rules will certainly *alienate* our long-standing members.

Usage 2: I don't want to *alienate* anyone, but I am determined to speak my mind.

Usage 3: The fundraisers cannot afford to *alienate* even a single contributor.

Usage 4: I am convinced that my natural, wholesome beauty will *alienate* me, making every woman at the party jealous.

Usage 5: Will my decision *alienate* me from the rest of the committee?

AMASS (v) [*uh*-MAS]

Meaning: collect; to gather

Usage 1: To *amass* a collection of classic cars from the 1930s has always been my dream.

Usage 2: The general's plan to *amass* a large battalion at the bridge was thwarted by a powerful storm.

Usage 3: The goal of a flash mob is to *amass* a large number of people at the same time at the same location to witness or participate in a particular event.

Usage 4: One of my goals in life is to *amass* as much knowledge as my brain can handle.

Usage 5: How could he *amass* such a fortune legally?

AMEND (v) [*uh*-MEND]

Meaning: correct; change, generally for the better; to improve

Usage 1: The president has decided to *amend* the company's position.

Usage 2: There is no way to *amend* your wrongdoing; you must simply learn from your mistakes.

Usage 3: Let me *amend* my speech so that my argument is clear.

Usage 4: Believe me; you will want to *amend* your rude behavior when you appear in front of the judge.

Usage 5: Will they *amend* the law or leave it as it stands?

AMORPHOUS (adj) [*uh*-MAWR-f*uh* s]

Meaning: formless; lacking shape or definition

Usage 1: That movie monster was totally unbelievable; it was a *amorphous* mass of goo.

Usage 2: Those minerals lack internal structure and are regarded as *amorphous.*

Usage 3: My feelings about the project were *amorphous;* I wasn't sure how I felt.

Usage 4: I accidentally put the ice cream cake in the fridge and it came out a chunky, *amorphous* mass.

Usage 5: Are her plans still undefined and *amorphous*?

AMPHIBIAN (adj)   [am-FIB-ee-*uh*n]

Meaning: possessing the qualities of *Amphibia,* including the ability to function on land and water

Usage 1: The *amphibian* characteristics of frogs and toads allow them to live in both land and water.

Usage 2: Watching those *amphibian* planes land on water is fascinating.

Usage 3: The *amphibian* nature of those vehicles made them invaluable during the Korean and Vietnam Wars.

Usage 4: She must have thought her car was an *amphibian* because she ran it into the lake.

Usage 5: Will this terrarium work for *amphibian* inhabitants?

AMPUTATE (v)   [AM-py*oo*-teyt]

Meaning: cut off part of body; to cut off, usually by surgery, or to prune

Usage 1: When growing roses, it is best to *amputate* dead branches regularly.

Usage 2: The gangrene has set into the ankle, and they will need to *amputate* it from the knee down.

Usage 3: The goal is to avoid the need to *amputate* the limbs.

Usage 4: I would rather *amputate* my right arm than lend her a hand.

Usage 5: Should we *amputate* the last two sentences of the third paragraph?

ANCHOR (v)   [ANG-ker]

Meaning: secure or fasten firmly; to hold in place

Usage 1: We need to *anchor* the base of the windmills firmly into the mountainside.

Usage 2: When you visit us at the lake, simply *anchor* your boat at our dock.

Usage 3: I want to *anchor* this discussion in concern for what is best for the children.

Usage 4: You can *anchor* yourself in the belief that no one saw your embarrassing moment.

Usage 5: Did you *anchor* the edges of the tent so that it doesn't blow away?

ANIMATED (adj)   [AN-*uh*-mey-tid]

Meaning: lively; spirited; vivacious; brought to life

Usage 1: Her discussion about her day was *animated* and entertaining.

Usage 2: I am always *animated* when I talk; I gesture with my hands the whole time.

Usage 3: In her art video, Milly allowed an *animated* necktie and scarf to tell her story.

Usage 4: My polychromatic outfits made me feel like an *animated* character from a children's cartoon.

Usage 5: You are not very *animated* today; are you feeling okay?

ANNEX (v)   [*uh*-NEKS]

Meaning: attach; take possession of; to add or incorporate

Usage 1: The city will *annex* the land and will assume responsibility for the residents who live there.

Usage 2: We are hoping they *annex* the new room at the museum so that we will have additional room for display.

Usage 3: Let's *annex* our efforts to see if, together, we can produce an even better product.

Usage 4: If you keep buying junk, we will have to *annex* the next building in order to store it all.

Usage 5: Does one country have the right to *annex* portions of another without the approval of the citizens?

ANOMALY (n)   [*uh*-NOM-*uh*-lee]

Meaning: irregularity; a deviation from normal

Usage 1: The weather pattern this past winter was an *anomaly*; our winters here are usually mild.

Usage 2: I could not explain the *anomaly* in the results of my science fair project.

Usage 3: The nebula you are viewing is considered a space *anomaly*; it shouldn't be there.

Usage 4: I don't want my wardrobe at the reunion to be an *anomaly*; I want to fit in with everyone else.

Usage 5: Do you have a theory that explains the *anomaly* we are seeing right now?

ANTHROPOID (adj/n)   [AN-thr*uh*-poid]

Meaning: manlike; having the characteristics of a human

Usage 1: You can easily see from a chimpanzee's *anthropoid* appearance why chimpanzees and humans share the designation of primates. (adj)

Usage 2: That robot's *anthropoid* face gives me the creeps; it's too lifelike! (adj)

Usage 3: An *anthropoid* appearance is no guarantee of human-like intelligence. (adj)

Usage 4: He is, arguably, merely an *anthropoid*; I don't think there's truly a man inside of him. (n)

Usage 5: Do you think if we encounter aliens in space that they will be *anthropoids*? (n)

APEX (n)   [EY-peks]

Meaning: tip; summit; climax; the highest point

Usage 1: We were elated when we reached the dormant volcano's *apex* and could peer directly into it.

Usage 2: It seemed the closer we approached, the more distant the mountain's *apex* was.

Usage 3: When the moon reaches its *apex,* the initiation ceremony will begin.

Usage 4: The *apex* of my career as a dancer occurred when I was at my two-year-old birthday party, and I danced atop my grandfather's shoes.

Usage 5: Have the climbers reached the *apex* yet?

APOLOGIST (n)   [*uh*-POL-*uh*-jist]

Meaning: one who writes in defense of a cause or institution; a person who offers a defense or argument in support

Usage 1: He has become an *apologist* for the misdeeds of the church.

Usage 2: You sound like an *apologist* arguing from a position of weakness.

Usage 3: The company spokeswoman served as an *apologist* for the poor handling of the matter.

Usage 4: I refuse to be an *apologist* for the behavior of my insane family.

Usage 5: Why have you assumed the role of *apologist* for decisions over which you had no control?

APPELLATION (n)   [ap-*uh*-LEY-sh*uh* n]

Meaning: title; a name or designation

Usage 1: "Cruel" would be the *appellation* I would use for the team owner's firing of the coach.

Usage 2: It wasn't until the *appellation* of her son that his existence became real to her.

Usage 3: Another *appellation* would not suit her; the name fit.

Usage 4: My *appellation* signifies nothing; wait until you meet me in person.

Usage 5: By what *appellation* will you answer when you become a grandmother?

ARBITER (n)   [AHR-bi-ter]

Meaning: a person with power to decide a dispute; judge; a person authorized to decide; an arbitrator

Usage 1: The decision in the case will be left to the *arbiter.*

Usage 2: He believes he is the sole *arbiter* of what is morally correct, but that simply isn't the case.

Usage 3: With her fashion sense, she is always held out as the *arbiter* of good taste.

Usage 4: I am perpetually the *arbiter* of disputes between my cat and my goldfish.

Usage 5: Who is the *arbiter* assigned to decide this case?

ARROGANCE (n)   [AR-*uh-guh* ns]
Meaning: pride; haughtiness; self-importance
Usage 1: I find her *arrogance* annoying; she is not the only authority in this matter.
Usage 2: His *arrogance* as a competitor was not justified; he wasn't evena skilled player.
Usage 3: Such *arrogance* in one so young and inexperienced is rare.
Usage 4: Only my innate *arrogance* made me foolishly believe I could prepare a meal for twenty with minimal cooking experience.
Usage 5: Was her *arrogance* the only reason you refused to go out with her?

ASHEN (adj)   [ASH-*uh* n]
Meaning: ash-colored, deathly pale
Usage 1: When she heard the verdict, her face became *ashen*.
Usage 2: I hate when my skin becomes *ashen* because it is so dry.
Usage 3: The tree leaves appeared *ashen* in the intense sunlight.
Usage 4: Your legs and arms appear tanned and healthy; mine are *ashen*.
Usage 5: Wasn't that purple house originally supposed to be *ashen* gray?

ASPIRANT (n)   [AS-per-*uh* nt]
Meaning: seeker of position or status; one who seeks a higher position
Usage 1: He was not the only *aspirant* for the lead in the Broadway show; there were many others.
Usage 2: As an *aspirant* in the field of professional golf, his long hours of practice were essential.
Usage 3: The *aspirant* who demonstrates the best understanding of what we do here will have a tremendous advantage.
Usage 4: I hate to admit it, but I am the *aspirant* they are interviewing to take your position.
Usage 5: Are you an *aspirant* for a career in space travel?

ASSAY (v)/ (n)   [a-SEY/ AS-ey]
Meaning: analyze; evaluate; examine/examination
Usage 1: The tailor must *assay* his client to determine the measurements for the handmade suit. (v)
Usage 2: The tailor will make an *assay* of his client to determine the measurements for the handmade suit. (n)
Usage 3: To *assay* the components of the compound, the students subjected it to varying degrees of heat. (v)
Usage 4: The alchemist attempted to *assay* items that could be turned to gold. (v)
Usage 5: What does your *assay* reveal about the chemical components of that liquid? (n)

ASSESSMENT (n)   [*uh*-SES-m*uh* nt]
Meaning: evaluation; the act of making a judgment
Usage 1: In my *assessment*, the umpire made the wrong call.
Usage 2: We asked for an expert *assessment* of the situation.
Usage 3: At this point we are in the *assessment* phase of the project.
Usage 4: When I saw my jewels were gone from the safe, I made an immediate *assessment* that I had been burgled.
Usage 5: Is our final exam our last *assessment* of the school year?

ASSIMILATE (v)   [*uh*-SIM-*uh*-leyt]

Meaning: absorb; cause to become homogeneous; to become like others

Usage 1: Many immigrants struggle to *assimilate* when they move to a new country.

Usage 2: It is important that you *assimilate* into the corporation's culture so that you can work well with others.

Usage 3: Some argue that the desire to *assimilate* can cause individuals to forget their own, unique heritage.

Usage 4: Don't try to *assimilate*; instead, be the original that you are.

Usage 5: Can you *assimilate* new knowledge as quickly as you would like?

ASTRONOMICAL (adj)   [as-tr*uh*-NOM-i-k*uh* l]

Meaning: enormously large or extensive; inconceivably large

Usage 1: My migraine is reaching *astronomical* proportions, and I desperately need peace and quiet.

Usage 2: The distances across the universe are so *astronomical,* we cannot begin to understand them.

Usage 3: Her *astronomical* rise from an unknown to a superstar still astonishes me.

Usage 4: He was going to fly her to the moon, but the cost of the trip was *astronomical.*

Usage 5: Can you believe the *astronomical* rise in housing prices?

AVID (adj)   [AV-id]

Meaning: greedy; eager for; enthusiastic

Usage 1: I have been an *avid* reader for years.

Usage 2: As an *avid* scholar, he thoroughly researched every paper he wrote.

Usage 3: He was an *avid* keeper of the meeting notes; not a statement was made without his recording it.

Usage 4: I am not sure there is a difference between and *avid* fan and a fanatic.

Usage 5: Are you an *avid* poker player or a casual one?

BAIT (v)   [beyt]

Meaning: harass; tease; purposely seek a response from (usually negative)

Usage 1: Don't *bait* your little brother; leave him alone.

Usage 2: A bully depends on his or her ability to *bait* you into action.

Usage 3: In an effort to *bait* the teacher, the students stood on their desks.

Usage 4: I think he's trying to *bait* me into doing something I will regret.

Usage 5: Did you *bait* the hook?

BALK (v)   [bawk]

Meaning: foil or thwart; stop short; refuse to go on; obstruct; impede; prevent; frustrate; object to vigorously

Usage 1: If you try to feed the baby mashed spinach, he will *balk* at it.

Usage 2: I tried not to *balk* at his ridiculous opinions.

Usage 3: The horse will *balk* at any attempt to bring him into the ring.

Usage 4: I reserve the right to *balk* at the price tag of whichever suit you choose.

Usage 5: Wouldn't you *balk* at what amounts to prison food?

BALM (n)   [bahm]

Meaning: something that relieves pain; an ointment designed to soothe

Usage 1: My mother always had one *balm* or another for aching muscles.

Usage 2: His kind words were a *balm* to my increasing anxiety.

Usage 3: The warm rain was a *balm* to my winter-weary body.

Usage 4: My plans tonight include a long, hot bath in an aromatic *balm*.

Usage 5: Would this *balm* help the sores on her feet?

BANAL (adj)   [b*uh*-NAL]

Meaning: hackneyed; trite; lacking originality; boring and commonplace

Usage 1: His tone indicated he felt the conversation was *banal*.

Usage 2: These *banal* expressions get on my nerves.

Usage 3: Her paintings of fruit bowls were *banal* and uninteresting.

Usage 4: Modern gargoyles are *banal* when compared to medieval ones.

Usage 5: Didn't you find your conversation with the celebrity surprisingly *banal*?

This page is intentionally left blank

Chapter 2

Barrister – Conveyance

This chapter covers the following words, each with its part of speech, pronunciation, and descriptive meaning.

Usage of the word is also illustrated in three to five sample sentences.

barrister	caprice	coercion
beget	casualty	collateral
beneficial	cataract	collusion
berserk	cavalier	commiserate
besiege	censor	compliance
blanch	cerebration	complicity
blare	chaff	concave
bleak	champion	conclusive
bloated	chasm	conservatory
blowhard	chasten	consistency
bluff	chisel	contend
bogus	chivalrous	contest
brittle	choreography	contravene
broach	circuitous	contrived
brochure	circumspect	conventional
calamity	cloying	conveyance
canine	coalition	

BARRISTER (n)   [BAR-*uh*-ster]

Meaning: counselor-at-law; a lawyer authorized to appear in court

Usage 1: In America, a courtroom lawyer is a litigator, but in England he or she is known as a *barrister*.

Usage 2: Her *barrister* knew all the judges on the circuit, which gave her a distinct advantage.

Usage 3: Many attorneys avoid the role of the *barrister*, and they never appear in court.

Usage 4: You don't have to be a *barrister* to know that arguing with a judge never helps your case.

Usage 5: Has your *barrister* practiced your testimony with you?

BEGET (v)   [bih-GET]

Meaning: father; produce; give rise to; to give birth to; prompt

Usage 1: One good deed can *beget* another.

Usage 2: Poor reasoning will *beget* poor judicial decisions.

Usage 3: Careful following of the recipe will *beget* the perfect cheese soufflé.

Usage 4: I had the chance to *beget* children, but I chose to adopt a puppy.

Usage 5: Who knew that he would *beget* such beautiful offspring?

BENEFICIAL (adj)   [ben-*uh*-FISH-*uh* l]

Meaning: helpful; useful; producing a good result

Usage 1: Eating vegetables and fruit is *beneficial* to your health.

Usage 2: It isn't *beneficial* for you to spend money on that right now.

Usage 3: Arguing with him will not result in a *beneficial* outcome.

Usage 4: It would be *beneficial* for you to take your foot out of your mouth.

Usage 5: Do you think exercising the leg would be *beneficial* at this point?

BERSERK (adj)   [ber-SURK]

Meaning: frenzied; wild and destructive

Usage 1: The director went *berserk* when his star actor did not show up.

Usage 2: Don't go *berserk*; it will all work out in the end.

Usage 3: Some shoppers have gone *berserk* over the latest smartphone.

Usage 4: To go *berserk* is sometimes a luxury and sometimes a necessity.

Usage 5: Are you confused or have you simply gone *berserk*?

BESIEGE (v)   [bih-SEEJ]

Meaning: surround with armed forces; put under attack

Usage 1: The peasants made plans to *besiege* the castle during the night.

Usage 2: The spring pollen will *besiege* my senses.

Usage 3: Whether there were plans to *besiege* the embassy is still under investigation.

Usage 4: If I ever win the lottery, my family will *besiege* me with requests for loans.

Usage 5: When will they *besiege* the capital and end the dictator's rule?

BLANCH (v)   [blahnch]

Meaning: bleach; whiten; drain the color from

Usage 1: These doilies have turned gray with age; I will need to *blanch* them.

Usage 2: Those acids are used to *blanch* the surround metallic surfaces and enhance the stenciled words.

Usage 3: We must *blanch* the cloth so that its dyeing will come out even.

Usage 4: The long, hard winter had managed to *blanch* my cheeks and dry my skin.

Usage 5: Did her face just *blanch* when you mentioned her old boyfriend's name?

BLARE (n)   [blair]

Meaning: loud, harsh; an intense sound or image

Usage 1: The *blare* of the trumpets announced the arrival of the king.

Usage 2: The crash of colors on the canvas was a *blare* to my senses.

Usage 3: You will likely experience a *blare* of car horns when you make that U-turn.

Usage 4: If you don't shut down that *blare* of music, I am going to shut down the circuitry to your bedroom.

Usage 5: When did restaurants exchange elevator music for the *blare* of hard rock?

BLEAK (adj)   [bleek]

Meaning: cold or cheerless; unlikely to be favorable; not hopeful

Usage 1: After serving time in prison my job prospects were *bleak*.

Usage 2: The long, *bleak* winter in Russia made the spring that much more enticing.

Usage 3: The disastrous quarterly report made his continuing career as a corporate executive appear *bleak*.

Usage 4: The house seemed *bleak* after the parade of visitors left.

Usage 5: Have you ever experienced such a *bleak* winter day?

BLOATED (adj)   [BLOH-tid]

Meaning: swollen or puffed as with water or with air; over-sized or over-extended

Usage 1: The treasury coffers were *bloated* with illegal tax dollars.

Usage 2: The corpse was *bloated* after nine days in the river.

Usage 3: The *bloated* air balloon lifted gently into the sky.

Usage 4: My wallet is *bloated* with one-dollar bills; I wish they were twenties.

Usage 5: How can a *bloated* body look so different?

BLOWHARD (n)   [BLOH-hahrd]

Meaning: talkative boaster; one who brags (generally on himself/herself)

Usage 1: I always suspect a *blowhard* of actually being the most insecure person in the room.

*Usage 2:*What a *blowhard*; she didn't stop bragging about her accomplishments even for a second.

Usage 3: No coach seeks a *blowhard* to join his or her team.

Usage 4: He is such a *blowhard*; I can't remember why I married him.

Usage 5: Have you ever met a *blowhard* with so little to brag about?

BLUFF (n)   [bluhf]

Meaning: pretense (of strength); deception; an attempt to fool others with a lie; a cliff

Usage 1: He was a master at the *bluff* in poker.

Usage 2: It was all a *bluff*; he did not have a gun in his pocket.

Usage 3: We stood on the *bluff* above Puget Sound and enjoyed the view.

Usage 4: The wind whipped the hat right off my head and it went sailing down the *bluff*.

Usage 5: Was that a *bluff*, or did you really mean what you were saying?

BOGUS (adj)   [BOH-g*uh* s]

Meaning: counterfeit; not authentic; fake; not real

Usage 1: These twenty dollar bills are *bogus*.

Usage 2: The results of that study are *bogus*, and we should not base our decisions on them.

Usage 3: Mom gave me ten *bogus* reasons I cannot go to the movies with my friends.

Usage 4: I think of *bogus* checks as an opportunity for creative writing.

Usage 5: Do you think these credit cards are *bogus* or are they the real thing?

BRITTLE (adj)   [BRIT-l]

Meaning: easily broken; difficult; fragile; frail

Usage 1: Her illness made her bones *brittle*.

Usage 2: The wind was so cold, my fingers felt *brittle*.

Usage 3: The frozen grass was too *brittle* even for the cows to eat.

Usage 4: The peace between us could be described as *brittle*.

Usage 5: Is the antique stained glass *brittle*?

BROACH (v)   [brohch]

Meaning: introduce; open up; bring up for discussion

Usage 1: I did not want to *broach* the matter of money owed; he was already upset.

Usage 2: Please *broach* the topic of counseling with her; it would do her some good.

Usage 3: We cannot even *broach* the idea of raising the necessary funds through taxation.

Usage 4: I hate to *broach* the subject, but your house is on fire.

Usage 5: How can we *broach* the topic of their wedding plans when they aren't even talking to each other?

BROCHURE (n)   [broh-SHOO R]

Meaning: pamphlet; an informational leaflet

Usage 1: In our social studies class, we prepared a *brochure* about a country we wanted to visit.

Usage 2: You can download a *brochure* that contains a side-by-side comparison of these SUVs.

Usage 3: As a service project, we can produce a *brochure* with information about easy exercises for the elderly.

Usage 4: With the *brochure* in hand, I made my purchase and was confident it was the best one.

Usage 5: Did the *brochure* give you more information than the travel agent?

CALAMITY (n)   [kuh-LAM-i-tee]

Meaning: disaster; misery; a mishap or catastrophe

Usage 1: What a *calamity*; the pigs are routing through the garden.

Usage 2: Don't act as if this is a *calamity*; you wanted this outcome all along.

Usage 3: The organization always helps its members when there is a *calamity*.

Usage 4: They thought of it as a *calamity*; I thought of it as an insurance claim.

Usage 5: When *calamity* strikes, will you be ready?

CANINE (adj)   [KEY-nahyn]

Meaning: related to dogs; dog-like

Usage 1: The veterinarian's *canine* practice is more profitable than her feline one.

Usage 2: He had an almost- *canine* sense of smell.

Usage 3: Those are *canine* toys, not human ones.

Usage 4: I tend to prefer *canine* company over almost any other.

Usage 5: Why can't all fidelity be like *canine* fidelity?

CAPRICE (n) [kuh-PREES]

Meaning: sudden, unexpected fancy; whim; an action taken on impulse

Usage 1: On the *caprice* of the moment, we hopped on a flight to Italy.

Usage 2: Greek myths reinforce the belief that we live at the *caprice* of the gods.

Usage 3: It wasn't merely *caprice*; I was making a fully-thought-out change in mylife.

Usage 4: Some find her sense of *caprice* charming; I find it annoying.

Usage 5: Is the committee operating at the *caprice* of the legislature?

CASUALTY (n) [KAZH-oo-uh l-tee]

Meaning: serious or fatal accident; an accident or one who is harmed in an accident

Usage 1: I object to your claiming him as a *casualty* of war; his death was unrelated to the war.

Usage 2: This *casualty* could easily have been avoided if the driver had followed safety precautions.

Usage 3: Using your cell phone while driving is inviting a *casualty*.

Usage 4: The only *casualty* when we were hiking through the mud was my sandals; I lost both of them in the muck.

Usage 5: Is their loss of customers a *casualty* of tougher economic times?

CATARACT (n) [KAT-uh-rakt]

Meaning: great waterfall; downward rush of water; eye abnormality; opacity in the eye

Usage 1: The railroad trip took us past the most astonishing *cataract* above the fjords of Norway.

Usage 2: My last eye test revealed the early formation of a *cataract* on my left eye.

Usage 3: The *cataract* was not only a tourist attraction, but the rushing water generated enough electricity to power a small town.

Usage 4: I wish I'd never had the *cataract* removed; once it was gone, I could clearly see all my wrinkles.

Usage 5: Does having a *cataract* in both eyes significantly affect your vision?

CAVALIER (adj) [kav-uh-LEER]

Meaning: offhand or casual; haughty; thoughtless

Usage 1: The first sign of trouble was his *cavalier* handshake.

Usage 2: There is no need for the *cavalier* attitude; we are co-workers on this project.

Usage 3: I get so tired of his *cavalier* approach to training employees.

Usage 4: You might think you're appearing brave and daring, but you're coming off as *cavalier*.

Usage 5: Will I come off as *cavalier* if I don't follow the new procedures?

CENSOR (n) [SEN-ser]

Meaning: overseer of morals; person who reads to eliminate inappropriate remarks; person in charge of removing inappropriate items from public view

Usage 1: It was the job of our *censor* to monitor content on the webpage.

Usage 2: In the experience of the *censor*, the parameters of what was deemed morally wrong were ever- changing.

Usage 3: The *censor* was fired for allowing the newspaper to print an article that even mildly criticized the government.

Usage 4: I am my teenager's cell-phone-text *censor*; nothing gets by me.

Usage 5: Can we count on the *censor* to catch every bit of foul language in the music?

CEREBRATION (n)   [ser-*uh*-brey-sh*uh* n]

Meaning: thought; the act of thinking

Usage 1: He may not be strong in the area of *cerebration*, but he is a loyal friend.

Usage 2: It would take some deep *cerebration*, but I was confident we could solve the problem.

Usage 3: His parents worry that the music he listens to encourages dark *cerebration*.

Usage 4: They say broccoli promotes efficient *cerebration*.

Usage 5: Have you considered the extent to which the lesson promotes student *cerebration*?

CHAFF (n)   [chaf]

Meaning: worthless products of an endeavor; husks of grain disposed of during processing; unused items

Usage 1: It is imperative that we separate the wheat from the *chaff* during the interview process.

Usage 2: I was treated like *chaff* disposed of with little concern for my well-being.

Usage 3: Once you remove the *chaff* from the mix, the beauty of the project shines through.

Usage 4: At the discount clothing store I spend hours sifting through *chaff* to find a single piece of wheat.

Usage 5: After removing the *chaff*, were there any kernels of wheat left?

CHAMPION (v)   [CHAM-pee-*uh* n]

Meaning: support militantly; defend or support with fervor

Usage 1: Once I married her, she expected me to *champion* all her charitable causes.

Usage 2: To *champion* the political views of his party was the wisest way to obtain early support.

Usage 3: It would *champion* the cause of justice if he were to win this battle in court.

Usage 4: I refuse to *champion* any group that won't allow me to be a member.

Usage 5: Did he *champion* for the cause of freedom?

CHASM (n)   [KAZ-*uh* m]

Meaning: abyss; a deep, immeasurable space

Usage 1: The deep *chasm* narrowed to a tiny, swift-moving stream.

Usage 2: They will search every *chasm* for the missing rafters.

Usage 3: There was a *chasm* between the positions of the two warring nations.

Usage 4: I hoped a *chasm* would suddenly open up, and my boss would fall into it.

Usage 5: Have they measured how deep that *chasm* is?

CHASTEN (v)   [CHEY-s*uh* n]

Meaning: discipline; punish or correct in order to cause improvement; chastise

Usage 1: You do not need to *chasten* me; I know my job.

Usage 2: The ridiculous principal did not feel the need to *chasten* either the students or the teachers.

Usage 3: If I *chasten* you, it is only because I want you to improve your performance.

Usage 4: She was the last person who had any right to *chasten* me.

Usage 5: Did you duly *chasten* the miscreants for their inappropriate conduct?

CHISEL (n)   [CHIZ-*uh* l]

Meaning: wedge like tool for cutting; a tool with a sharp, cutting edge

Usage 1: The sculpture in the rock was created using a hammer and *chisel*.

Usage 2: The marks of the *chisel* were evident in the poorly-crafted headstone.

Usage 3: Some wood carvings are created using a heated *chisel* that burns and seals the wood.

Usage 4: I can't remember if I used the hammer or the *chisel* to leave a message in the side of his sports car.

Usage 5: Is that *chisel* sharp enough for someone sculpting a marble statue?

CHIVALROUS (adj) [SHIV-*uh* l-r*uh* s]

Meaning: courteous; faithful; brave; gracious and honorable

Usage 1: His *chivalrous* defending of my honor endeared him to me immediately.

Usage 2: The *chivalrous* knight turned out to be a chivalrous princess disguised as a knight.

Usage 3: She made a *chivalrous* attempt to ignore her partner's rudeness to the crowd.

Usage 4: There is nothing that makes me more hopeful than a *chivalrous* teenager.

Usage 5: What *chivalrous* acts brought him to your attention?

CHOREOGRAPHY (n) [kawr-ee-OG-r*uh*-fee]

Meaning: art of representing dances in written symbols; arrangement of dances; art of arranging dance steps

Usage 1: The student-led *choreography* was even better than that devised by the teacher.

Usage 2: Her *choreography* does not match the rhythm of the music.

Usage 3: He loves to dance, but he discovered that his true talent lies in *choreography*.

Usage 4: If I had done the *choreography*, the dancers would have staged a mutiny.

Usage 5: What did you think of the ultra-modern *choreography* in that new musical?

CIRCUITOUS (adj) [ser-KYOO-i-t*uh* s]

Meaning: Roundabout; traveling in circles

Usage 1: The taxi driver took us on a ridiculously *circuitous* route to downtown.

Usage 2: We didn't realize the path was *circuitous*, and soon we were back where we started.

Usage 3: Such reasoning seems awfully *circuitous*; whichever path we take, we're wrong.

Usage 4: Your *circuitous* argument is giving me a headache.

Usage 5: Has the walkway through the gardens always been *circuitous*?

CIRCUMSPECT (adj) [SUR-k*uh* m-spekt]

Meaning: prudent; cautious; looking at the entire situation before acting

Usage 1: Before commenting on the disputed issue, he was notably *circumspect*.

Usage 2: I urge you to be more *circumspect* in your dealings with the police.

Usage 3: Being *circumspect* prevented me from making another foolhardy decision.

Usage 4: It is wise to be *circumspect* before approaching the beehive.

Usage 5: Does his tendency to be *circumspect* clash with your tendency to be impulsive?

CLOYING (adj) [KLOI-ing]

Meaning: distasteful (because excessive); excessively sweet or sentimental; so sweet it overrides the senses

Usage 1: I like brownies, but these triple-chocolate brownies are unappetizingly *cloying*.

Usage 2: I could not bear their *cloying* endearments, especially since I knew they were divorcing.

Usage 3: I use artificial sweetener instead of honey because I find the taste of honey *cloying*.

Usage 4: She found my husband's flattery sweet; I found it *cloying*.

Usage 5: At what point does my praise of her in my introduction become *cloying*?

COALITION (n) [koh-*uh*-LISH-*uh* n]

Meaning: partnership; league; a group of entitles acting in cooperation

Usage 1: In many countries the various political parties form a *coalition* government.

Usage 2: It was a *coalition* to end childhood diseases.

Usage 3: I flip-flopped from one *coalition* to another, never forming a true allegiance.

Usage 4: If the cats in my neighborhood ever form a *coalition*, my cat-harassing dogs are in deep trouble.

Usage 5: Have the *coalition* forces entered the disputed territory?

COERCION (n)　[koh-UR-sh*uh* n]

Meaning: use of force to get someone to obey; using force to intimidate

Usage 1: The officers have a reputation for exerting unnecessary *coercion*.

Usage 2: I wanted to resist such obvious *coercion*, but I didn't have the strength.

Usage 3: They now realize that *coercion* and torture are ineffective.

Usage 4: Clearly I needed to teach my third-grader about resisting the *coercion* of bullies.

Usage 5: Were you able to ignore her clear attempt at *coercion*?

COLLATERAL (n)　[k*uh*-LAT-er-*uh* l]

Meaning: security given for loan; items pledged as security for repayment of a loan

Usage 1: He took out a loan and used his new yacht as *collateral*.

Usage 2: If you do not repay your loan, the repossession men will seize your car as *collateral*.

Usage 3: He expected his good name, alone, to serve as *collateral*.

Usage 4: I said I'd take his two, beastly children as *collateral* for the twenty dollars he owed me; then I realized how insane that was.

Usage 5: Don't you need *collateral* to secure even a small bank loan?

COLLUSION (n)　[k*uh*-LOO-zh*uh* n]

Meaning: conspiring in a fraudulent scheme; working together secretively to commit wrongdoing

Usage 1: There was clearly *collusion* among the workers; this was a well-executed company takeover.

Usage 2: You are working in *collusion* with their representatives to demand bribes from government officials.

Usage 3: Proof of their *collusion* was in their cell phone records; they acted together when they threatened us.

Usage 4: There is no way I'd work in *collusion* with my supervisor to defraud the public.

Usage 5: Was this the product of people working in *collusion* or was it mere coincidence?

COMMISERATE (v)　[k*uh*-MIZ-*uh*-reyt]

Meaning: feel or express pity or sympathy for; empathize with

Usage 1: When we have time, let's *commiserate* with each other about our tough, new jobs.

Usage 2: I wish I had time to *commiserate* with you, but I am late for a meeting.

Usage 3: We will *commiserate* with him over the loss of his brother.

Usage 4: I could do something productive, or I could stay here and *commiserate* with you.

Usage 5: Did it help to *commiserate* with others who struggle with addiction?

COMPLIANCE (n)　[k*uh* m-PLAHY-*uh* ns]

Meaning: readiness to yield; conformity in fulfilling requirements; acting in accordance with

Usage 1: Make sure all your equipment is in *compliance* with safety regulations.

Usage 2: Your *compliance* with these new requirements is essential to the success of this venture.

Usage 3: The officer demanded the visitors' strict *compliance* with all prison rules.

Usage 4: A little *compliance* with figures in authority goes a long way.

Usage 5: Are these packages in *compliance* with postal regulations?

COMPLICITY (n)   [k*uh* m-PLIS-i-tee]
Meaning: participation; involvement; acting in concert in wrongdoing
Usage 1: Her *complicity* in the crime was evident on the video tapes.
Usage 2: With your *complicity*, we can drive them from the neighborhood.
Usage 3: The political leaders hid their *complicity* in defrauding the public.
Usage 4: His *complicity* was evident when he joined the posse.
Usage 5: Do his actions demonstrate a *complicity* in their illegal plan?

CONCAVE (adj)   [kon-KEYV]
Meaning: hollow; inward-sinking
Usage 1: The lenses were *concave* so that they easily fitted to the eye.
Usage 2: The volcanic eruption left a *concave* depression at the top of the mountain.
Usage 3: The dough should be slightly *concave* when you place it on the pan.
Usage 4: I missed the *concave* depression in the ground and fell headlong into the hedge.
Usage 5: Does the fact that his cheeks look *concave* mean that he is ill?

CONCLUSIVE (adj)   [k*uh* n-KLOO-siv]
Meaning: decisive; ending all debate; serving to settle or close a discussion
Usage 1: We have *conclusive* evidence that a tornado did touch down in that area.
Usage 2: The jury believed the evidence was *conclusive* and the defendant was guilty on all counts.
Usage 3: His *conclusive* remarks rankled many in the audience who expected to be part of the debate.
Usage 4: You may think your position is *conclusive*, but I am reopening the debate.
Usage 5: Do we have *conclusive* proof that the disease is spreading?

CONSERVATORY (n)   [k*uh* n-SUR-v*uh*-tawr-ee]
Meaning: school of the fine arts (especially music and drama); school of music; a greenhouse
Usage 1: Next fall, she will attend the *conservatory* in Savannah.
Usage 2: After training at a *conservatory* in New York City, he appeared in his first play on Broadway.
Usage 3: During your time at the *conservatory*, you will receive music lessons from one of our masters.
Usage 4: Lacking any talent in art or drama, I found it ironic I was now working at a *conservatory*.
Usage 5: Did those years at the *conservatory* contribute to your later success in the theater?

CONSISTENCY (n)   [k*uh* n-SIS-t*uh* n-see]
Meaning: absence of contradictions; dependability; uniformity; degree of thickness; firmness; reliability
Usage 1: The *consistency* of this cheese is perfect for making a sauce.
Usage 2: Her *consistency* is never in question; she's completely reliable.
Usage 3: I would question the *consistency* of your arguments.
Usage 4: The instructor said our clay needed to be the *consistency* of mud, but mine was the *consistency* of soapy water.
Usage 5: Has his *consistency* changed over the course of the years?

CONTEND (v)   [k*uh* n-TEND]
Meaning: struggle; assert earnestly; compete against; take a position in support of

Usage 1: She is one of two archers who will *contend* for the grand prize.

Usage 2: I cannot *contend* to be an expert in this matter.

Usage 3: They cannot *contend* with such stupidity.

Usage 4: Don't even try to *contend* that you are innocent; we both know better.

Usage 5: Does he *contend* that he will win the race?

CONTEST (v)   [k*uh* n-TEST]

Meaning: dispute; argue for or against

Usage 1: The lawyer will *contest* at trial that both defendants were at fault.

Usage 2: We *contest* the findings of the committee because it did not act independently.

Usage 3: You have every right to *contest* these results through the appeal process.

Usage 4: I *contest* that drinking water makes me hungry, but drinking coffee has the opposite effect.

Usage 5: Will the parents *contest* the new school district lines?

CONTRAVENE (v)   [kon-tr*uh*-VEEN]

Meaning: contradict; oppose; infringe on or transgress; to go against

Usage 1: He never *contravenes* his mother.

Usage 2: Her words often *contravene* her actions; they don't go together.

Usage 3: The candidates may *contravene* one another, but behind the scenes they are good friends.

Usage 4: I'd like to *contravene* every assertion she made, but it just isn't worth it.

Usage 5: Did you ever *contravene* a direct order given to you by your commanding officer?

CONTRIVED (adj)   [k*uh* n-TRAHYVD]

Meaning: forced; artificial; not spontaneous; made up or manufactured

Usage 1: Her smile at the reunion appeared forced and *contrived*.

Usage 2: The *contrived* nature of our meeting was evident because he had no reason to be anywhere near here.

Usage 3: The first act of his new play was *contrived* and difficult to watch.

Usage 4: My *contrived* laughter couldn't hide the fact that I was miserable.

Usage 5: Did you think the plot of the film was *contrived*?

CONVENTIONAL (adj)   [k*uh* n-VEN-sh*uh*-nl]

Meaning: abiding by accepted standards; ordinary

Usage 1: It was *conventional* wisdom that he was searching for another job.

Usage 2: In a *conventional* sense, they were like every other family in America.

Usage 3: A *conventional* view of the matter would tell us it boils down to what is right or wrong.

Usage 4: I wouldn't say his views are *conventional*; they're simply boring.

Usage 5: Is his approach to problem-solving *conventional* or out-of-the-ordinary?

CONVEYANCE (n)   [k*uh* n-VEY-*uh* ns]

Meaning: vehicle; transfer from one location to another

Usage 1: The airport uses shuttles, trains, and moving sidewalks for *conveyance* of passengers.

Usage 2: Upon the *conveyance* of the documents to our office, the money will be placed in your account.

Usage 3: Transport on charter buses is the primary mode of *conveyance* for student field trips.

Usage 4: The snarl on your face serves as the *conveyance* of your feelings in the matter.

Usage 5: What is your plan for *conveyance* of the new zoo animals?

Chapter **3**

Conviction – Drone

This chapter covers the following words, each with its part of speech, pronunciation, and descriptive meaning.

Usage of the word is also illustrated in three to five sample sentences.

conviction	decoy	dexterous
cornice	defamation	dictum
corrugated	defer	dilate
coup	defiance	dilatory
cower	deft	disavowal
coy	dehydrate	discourse
credence	demean	disembark
credulity	demographic	disgorge
crescendo	denizen	disinter
crevice	deplore	distortion
criteria	deranged	divergent
cryptic	descry	diversity
culmination	despotism	dogged
curtail	destitute	don
decant	detraction	douse
decelerate	devoid	drone
deciduous	devout	

CONVICTION (n)   [k*uh* n-VIK-sh*uh* n]

Meaning: judgment that someone is guilty of a crime; a negative result in court; a firm belief in something

Usage 1: His *conviction* at trial was no surprise; the evidence against him was convincing.

Usage 2: Their *conviction* that the world would end in 2012 never wavered for a moment.

Usage 3: The chance of *conviction* was great, so my lawyer advised that I settle out of court.

Usage 4: I argued with *conviction* that my cannoli had very few calories.

Usage 5: Did his *conviction* when he was twenty prevent you from considering him for the job?

CORNICE (n)   [KAWR-nis]

Meaning: projecting molding on building (usually above columns); molding decorating a building

Usage 1: The raven sat on the edge of the roof above the building's *cornice* and cawed loudly.

Usage 2: The building's ornate *cornice* and exquisitely-shuttered windows made it a classic.

Usage 3: The building's elaborate terra-cotta *cornice* looked as if it had been made from fine lace.

Usage 4: I'd hang a sign from the building's *cornice* if I thought it would get his attention.

Usage 5: Do you see the drain running from the building's *cornice* to the street?

CORRUGATED (adj)   [KAWR-*uh*-GEY-tid]

Meaning: wrinkled; having ridges, usually appearing as waves

Usage 1: The rain pattered against the *corrugated* tin roof.

Usage 2: That *corrugated* cardboard box is strong enough to hold these books.

Usage 3: The walls of the small greenhouse were *corrugated* plastic.

Usage 4: I like my potato chips with *corrugated* ridges.

Usage 5: Is that roof made of *corrugated* metal?

COUP (n)   [koo]

Meaning: highly successful action or sudden attack; quick, decisive action (successful)

Usage 1: They staged a small *coup* at the board meeting.

Usage 2: The *coup* brought down a duly- elected government.

Usage 3: There were rumors that the military intended to stage a *coup*.

Usage 4: The rookie's award was a *coup* against the power of the old cronies in the group.

Usage 5: Was your dinner tonight a *coup* against those who claimed you had no cooking talent?

COWER (v)   [KOU-er]

Meaning: shrink quivering, as from fear; make oneself small out of fear

Usage 1: At the animal shelter, I tend to choose the animals that *cower* in the corner.

Usage 2: I hate to see him *cower*, rather than to stand up to that bully.

Usage 3: We will not *cower* in the face of injustice; we will fight against it.

Usage 4: I thought it best to *cower*, rather than to explain to the bear that I was higher up the food chain.

Usage 5: Did you tell him to *cower* behind that wall when the police arrived?

COY (adj)   [koi]

Meaning: modest; coquettish; unconvincingly shy

Usage 1: Don't be fooled by her *coy* manners; she's actually an extrovert.

Usage 2: The celebrity was *coy* when they asked him if he was seeing anyone.

Usage 3: Being *coy* may sound like a good idea, but they will learn not to trust you.

Usage 4: Her *coy* response got on my nerves; I wanted her to be herself for once.

Usage 5: Do you think a *coy* response is appropriate in this situation?

CREDENCE (n)   [KREED-ns]

Meaning: belief; acceptance of something as true

Usage 1: I cannot give any *credence* to his claim that he had no knowledge of the crime; he was definitely present when it happened.

Usage 2: The results of the study lend *credence* to the belief that young people are at greater risk of diabetes than ever before.

Usage 3: If you give *credence* to every idea espoused on television, you will soon be thoroughly confused.

Usage 4: The extra-large footprint in the snow in my back yard gave *credence* to the existence of the abominable Snowman.

Usage 5: Has your research leant further *credence* to your hypothesis?

CREDULITY (n)   [kr*uh*-DOO-li-tee]

Meaning: gullibility; naiveté; belief in something too easily

Usage 1: Movie-makers depend on audience *credulity* when it comes to unlikely plot lines.

Usage 2: Their *credulity* in the other side's commitment to peace was touching.

Usage 3: The street magician heavily depended on the *credulity* of a less-than-sober audience.

Usage 4: I don't think I ever possessed *credulity* because I never believed in anything.

Usage 5: Doesn't a belief in aliens hiding in the sewers strain your *credulity*?

CRESCENDO (n)   [kri-SHEN-doh]

Meaning: increase in the volume or intensity, as in a musical passage; climax

Usage 1: The music slowly reached a *crescendo* until the audience was virtually in tears.

Usage 2: The early buds bloomed until late spring when the flowering reached a *crescendo*.

Usage 3: Her performance reached a *crescendo* in the third act, during which her character went mad.

Usage 4: My impatience with his inattention reached a *crescendo* last August, and we separated.

Usage 5: Did you notice the *crescendo* ending in the music of a single flute?

CREVICE (n)   [KREV-is]

Meaning: crack; fissure; an opening in something

Usage 1: My keys had fallen into the *crevice* between two rocks, and there was no way to get them out.

Usage 2: After the earthquake, building inspectors found *crevices* in most of the city's older buildings.

Usage 3: We searched every crack and *crevice* for the engagement ring, but it was nowhere to be found.

Usage 4: I told her to crawl back into her *crevice* like any common rat.

Usage 5: How could that tiny stream of water form such a deep *crevice* between the rocks?

CRITERIA (n)   [krahy-TEER-ee-*uh*]

Meaning: standards used in judging; principles used to judge an outcome (especially test results)

Usage 1: We needed test preparation materials that used similar *criteria* for assessing the outcome.

Usage 2: The company has posted a list of *criteria* for any applicant seeking the position.

Usage 3: At the top of the list of *criteria* is a Ph.D. in microbiology.

Usage 4: My *criteria* for the perfect man were impossible for any man to match; that's why I'm single.

Usage 5: By what *criteria* are they judging the dogs in the contest?

CRYPTIC (adj)   [KRIP-tik]

Meaning: mysterious; hidden; secret; difficult to understand or figure out

Usage 1: The symbols on the stone were *cryptic*, but we were sure they meant something.

Usage 2: Based on his *cryptic* text message, I thought he was in trouble.

Usage 3: There was no map, only a *cryptic* list of directions to her house.

Usage 4: I hadn't the foggiest idea what her *cryptic* remark signified.

Usage 5: Why must you always be so *cryptic* about how you feel?

CULMINATION (n)   [kuhl-m*uh*-NEY-sh*uh* n]

Meaning: attainment of highest point; gathering of all the elements of effort

Usage 1: Her Olympic medal was the *culmination* of years of hard work and practice.

Usage 2: The monument was the *culmination* of ten years of planning and fundraising.

Usage 3: Her perfect English accent was the *culmination* of weeks of practice with the trainer.

Usage 4: I couldn't help but wonder about the *culmination* of all her efforts to conspire against me.

Usage 5: What do you think will be the *culmination* of our many attempts to explore space?

CURTAIL (v)   [ker-TEYL]

Meaning: shorten; reduce; put a quick end to

Usage 1: We will need to *curtail* the actions of the aggressors in the territorial dispute.

Usage 2: The new manager was determined to *curtail* the high absenteeism the company was experiencing.

Usage 3: If you *curtail* the relief efforts, many refugees will suffer.

Usage 4: I must remember to *curtail* my acceptance speech when I receive my Oscar on Sunday night.

Usage 5: After learning what it does to your lungs, don't you want to *curtail* your smoking?

DECANT (v)   [dih-KANT]

Meaning: pour off gently; pour off liquid

Usage 1: As oil is released from the cooking meat, be sure to *decant* it.

Usage 2: The wine seller advised that we *decant* these bottles before we taste the wine inside them.

Usage 3: When you get a moment, please *decant* the can of coconut milk to separate out the coconut solids.

Usage 4: It was as if I needed to *decant* the conversation and skim off her preliminary nonsense.

Usage 5: Do you know how to *decant* that bottle of wine?

DECELERATE (v)   [dee-SEL-*uh*-reyt]

Meaning: slow down; decrease in speed

Usage 1: Do not *decelerate* on the curve or you will lose control of the car.

Usage 2: There was a clear need to *decelerate* tensions between the two religious leaders.

Usage 3: Economic growth has clearly begun to *decelerate* in the fourth quarter of the year.

Usage 4: I felt we needed to *decelerate* the relationship; it was moving far too fast.

Usage 5: What factors do you believe will *decelerate* this path to civil unrest?

DECIDUOUS (adj)   [dih-SIJ-oo-*uh* s]

Meaning: shedding; falling off (as of leaves); shedding leaves annually

Usage 1: The mountain's *deciduous* trees turned brilliantly red and yellow in October.

Usage 2: This is a *deciduous* forest, rather than an evergreen one.

Usage 3: I want *deciduous* shrubs for the front and sides of the house and a flowerbed in the back.

Usage 4: My costume kept falling off in clumps; I felt like a *deciduous* tree.

Usage 5: Don't you love the beauty of the *deciduous* trees reflected off the surface of the lake?

DECOY (n)   [DEE-koi]

Meaning: lure or bait; attention-grabber for purposes of distraction

Usage 1: The unarmed surface vessel was a *decoy* to protect the submarine.

Usage 2: I am not interested in serving as a *decoy* for your pursuit of my cousin.

Usage 3: What I thought was a beautiful and rare duck was actually a well-crafted *decoy*.

Usage 4: I didn't mind serving as a *decoy* as long as I wasn't the target.

Usage 5: Isn't this filibuster a *decoy* to prevent consideration of important legislation?

DEFAMATION (n)   [def-*uh*-MEY-sh*uh* n]

Meaning: harming a person's reputation; false claims designed to harm one's reputation

Usage 1: There is no need to resort to *defamation*; we simply disagree with one another.

Usage 2: If you continue to tell those lies to the press, I will haul you into court for *defamation*.

Usage 3: Defamation was the least of her concerns; she was arrested for murder.

Usage 4: I'd love to claim *defamation*, but everything he said was true.

Usage 5: Do you understand that your lies will result in a conviction for *defamation*?

DEFER (v)   [dih-FUR]

Meaning: give in respectfully; to delay; to submit to the opinion or expertise of another

Usage 1: Please *defer* all applause to the end of the award presentation.

Usage 2: I *defer* to your expertise on the Siberian white tiger.

Usage 3: As a servant in this house, you must *defer* to the instructions of all members of the family.

Usage 4: There was no way I would *defer* to her knowledge in this matter; I knew more than she did, anyway.

Usage 5: Will he *defer* his entry into college in order to earn money to buy a car?

DEFIANCE (n)   [dih-FAHY-*uh* ns]

Meaning: refusal to yield; open contempt; a resistance to authority

Usage 1: Her *defiance* against the police officers was a surprise; she was usually so docile.

Usage 2: In an act of *defiance* against company policy, they picketed outside the company's headquarters.

Usage 3: The rebels chanted their *defiance* and refused to yield to the government's soldiers.

Usage 4: Your *defiance* of every single rule I set in this house is wearing on my nerves.

Usage 5: Do you consider it an act of *defiance* to protest against the government?

DEFT (adj)   [deft]

Meaning: Adroit; neat; dexterous; skilled

Usage 1: He was *deft* at avoiding answering any questions about himself.

Usage 2: Your carving skill is *deft*, indeed; I wish mine were half so good.

Usage 3: With one last, *deft*, tug, he secured the knot.

Usage 4: It was a *deft* answer to a tricky question.

Usage 5: How *deft* are you at driving in a hurricane?

DEHYDRATE (v)   [dee-HAHY-dreyt]

Meaning: remove water from; dry out; to dry by removing the water from

Usage 1: Be careful not to exercise too much in the heat, or you will *dehydrate* yourself.

Usage 2: To *dehydrate* fruits, you can set them out in the sun, covered in cheese cloth.

Usage 3: The chemicals they use tend to *dehydrate* the cells and kill them.

Usage 4: I drank extra water to make sure that I did not *dehydrate*.

Usage 5: Is there a more efficient way to *dehydrate* apples than this?

DEMEAN (v)   [dih-MEEN]

Meaning: degrade; humiliate; debase; lower in standing

Usage 1: It was not enough for her to beat her competition; she also sought to *demean* them.

Usage 2: I think it will *demean* you to perform a job for which you are so clearly overqualified.

Usage 3: I don't want to *demean* the situation, but we have more important concerns.

Usage 4: To *demean* others is the surest way to demean yourself.

Usage 5: Will it *demean* her if I ask her for identification?

DEMOGRAPHIC (adj)   [dem-*uh*-GRAF-ik]

Meaning: related to population balance; human statistics

Usage 1: For what *demographic* group have you written this story?

Usage 2: There's been a *demographic* shift in our district.

Usage 3: The report found a distinct *demographic* change in the city.

Usage 4: If the *demographic* breakdown in this group were analyzed, we would still all be old.

Usage 5: What is the *demographic* history of the population of your county?

DENIZEN (n)   [DEN-*uh*-zuh n]

Meaning: inhabitant or resident; regular visitor; a person who regularly visits a place or who resides there

Usage 1: My uncle proved to be the *denizen* of every bar in the small town in which he lived.

Usage 2: As a *denizen* of the world, he knew surprisingly little about other cultures.

Usage 3: The waiter knows me; I am a *denizen* of this restaurant.

Usage 4: If I had the money, I'd be a *denizen* of a Greek island in winter and a Swedish island in summer.

Usage 5: When did you become a *denizen* of Portland, Oregon?

DEPLORE (v)   [dih-PLAWR]

Meaning: regret; disapprove of; to hate

Usage 1: I *deplore* people who pretend to be one thing when they are actually another.

Usage 2: It is hard not to *deplore* the hot, humid summers.

Usage 3: They had started to *deplore* the conditions under which they were working.

Usage 4: I *deplore* your tendency to take advantage of every situation.

Usage 5: Don't you *deplore* people who talk loudly on their cell phones in public places?

DERANGED (adj)   [dih-REYNJD]

Meaning: insane; mentallyunstable

Usage 1: Your plan to rob the bank and live out your years in Mexico is *deranged*.

Usage 2: There was a *deranged* look in his eyes that told me I had crossed the line.

Usage 3: I wouldn't want to share a cell with that convicted killer; she appeared *deranged*.

Usage 4: Don't tell me my life is *deranged*; take a look at your own first.

Usage 5: Is he *deranged*, or will this plan actually work?

DESCRY (v) [dih-SKRAHY]

Meaning: catch sight of; to see by looking carefully

Usage 1: If you *descry* the crowd on the Megatron, you will see me among the Mariners fans.

Usage 2: All that he was able to *descry* was a single swatch of fabric on a low-hanging tree limb.

Usage 3: Through the murky water, he was able to *descry* the outline of the sunken vessel.

Usage 4: Looking at my checking account statements, I failed to *descry* a single deposit over the last three months.

Usage 5: Using the binoculars, can you *descry* their location in the water?

DESPOTISM (n) [DES-p*uh*-tiz-*uh* m]

Meaning: tyranny; the exercise of absolute power or control

Usage 1: The *despotism* of the small country's government was so pervasive that every citizen felt it at every moment.

Usage 2: If we don't step in and fight for freedom, *despotism* will soon prevail.

Usage 3: The threat of *despotism* could not be ignored.

Usage 4: Of course *despotism* reigns in my classroom; I am the despot.

Usage 5: Why do democratically-elected rulers resort to *despotism* in order to retain power?

DESTITUTE (adj) [DES-ti-toot]

Meaning: extremely poor; poverty-ridden

Usage 1: If she keeps spending like this, she will be *destitute* within a month.

Usage 2: After so many failed attempts, I was *destitute* of ideas.

Usage 3: So many government policies are geared for those who are *destitute*, that we ignore the middle class.

Usage 4: I don't want my former business partners to be *destitute*; I just don't want them to have any money.

Usage 5: Was your family left *destitute* after the crash on Wall Street?

DETRACTION (n) [dih-TRAK-sh*uh* n]

Meaning: slandering; aspersion; taking away by discrediting

Usage 1: His *detraction* of the athletes who won awards demonstrated what a bad sport he was.

Usage 2: There were those who busied themselves with *detraction* against her large body of work.

Usage 3: Television news these days is all about pumping yourself up through the *detraction* of others.

Usage 4: If I believed the *detraction*, I would never purchase another item that company produced.

Usage 5: Does such criticism and *detraction* really lead to the truth?

DEVOID (adj) [dih-VOID]

Meaning: empty; lacking; marked by an absence of

Usage 1: After the pollutants were released into the water, the river became virtually *devoid* of life.

Usage 2: I find this situation to be completely *devoid* of humor.

Usage 3: His privileged background left him *devoid* of any understanding of those who had grown up in poverty.

Usage 4: I have a treasure chest, but it is *devoid* of treasure.

Usage 5: Why are his words so *devoid* of meaning?

DEVOUT (adj) [dih-VOUT]

Meaning: pious; someone devoted to an idea or religion

Usage 1: He is a *devout* Catholic, even though his parents were non-Catholics.

Usage 2: Devout leaders of churches across the country objected to the government's position on public prayer.

Usage 3: He was a *devout* believer in humans as protectors of the environment.

Usage 4: I am *devout* in my belief that cheese should never be "fat free."

Usage 5: As a *devout* Christian, do you believe violence is ever warranted?

DEXTEROUS (adj)   [DEK-str*uh* s]

Meaning: adroit; skillful; having the ability or skill to perform

Usage 1: Her *dexterous* hands didn't miss a single stroke as she cut the diamond.

Usage 2: It takes a *dexterous* player to pull off that shot.

Usage 3: This job requires a *dexterous* hand with children.

Usage 4: I have never been *dexterous*, just lucky.

Usage 5: Is he *dexterous* with a knife?

DICTUM (n)   [DIK-t*uh* m]

Meaning: authoritative and weighty statement; saying; maxim; powerful words or statements; adage

Usage 1: The Supreme Court judges, in *dictum*, revealed that they had reached the same decision, but for different reasons.

Usage 2: The old *dictum* that "the squeaky wheel gets the grease" certainly applies here.

Usage 3: Does the *dictum* about the early bird come to mind when we review our delayed response?

Usage 4: There is a reason that a *dictum* often rings true; it is usually based in well-worn reality.

Usage 5: Isn't the court's discussion in *dictum* as important here as the actual decision?

DILATE (v)   [dahy-LEYT]

Meaning: expand; make larger

Usage 1: I can't drive home alone; they will *dilate* my eyes at the optometrist's office.

Usage 2: The camera shutter doesn't *dilate* properly.

Usage 3: The medications are designed to *dilate* the blood vessels and improve the flow of blood.

Usage 4: If her eyes *dilate*, you know you've angered her.

Usage 5: Why do our eyes *dilate* when we experience surprise?

DILATORY (adj)   [DIL-*uh*-tawr-ee]

Meaning: delaying; not on time; not meeting deadlines

Usage 1: I know I was *dilatory* in my response, but I needed more time to think.

Usage 2: His *dilatory* nature is about to get him fired.

Usage 3: I cannot be *dilatory* for even one more session with my parole officer.

Usage 4: I guess I've been *dilatory* about throwing you out of my house; you can go now.

Usage 5: Do you understand you will be evicted if you continue to be *dilatory* in paying your rent?

DISAVOWAL (n)   [dis-*uh*-VOU-*uh* l]

Meaning: disclaiming; a denial of any connection with

Usage 1: Her *disavowal* of any knowledge of the law does not protect her.

Usage 2: I had no idea that our disagreement would result in his *disavowal* of our most basic beliefs.

Usage 3: The thief's *disavowal* of being in the house that night is contradicted by the video.

Usage 4: I attempted a *disavowal* of any connection with my children, but they keep showing back up.

Usage 5: Did you expect his *disavowal* of any association with you?

DISCOURSE (n)   [DIS-kawrs]
Meaning: formal discussion; conversation; communication (primarily by words)
Usage 1: It was a disappointment that during the *discourse* on the treaty, war broke out.
Usage 2: According to the *discourse* in the newspapers, there were strong feelings on both sides of the case.
Usage 3: If we don't keep the *discourse* going, we will never come to an agreement.
Usage 4: Even his normal *discourse* involved shouting.
Usage 5: Couldn't we have a regular *discourse* on the issue, rather than wailing and tears?

DISEMBARK (v)   [dis-em-BAHRK]
Meaning: go ashore; unload cargo from a ship; to get off a ship
Usage 1: They just called for all visitors to *disembark* the vessel.
Usage 2: I could see we had reached America, but I could not bring myself to *disembark* from the ship.
Usage 3: When they *disembark* the boxes of crystal, they need to take extra care.
Usage 4: It would be wise to *disembark* before I throw you over the side.
Usage 5: Will he be ready to *disembark* on a career in the military?

DISGORGE (v)   [dis-GAWRJ]
Meaning: surrender something; eject; vomit; discharge from the mouth by force
Usage 1: Our pet cat could do little but *disgorge* the tainted meat.
Usage 2: It was the goal of the doctors to *disgorge* the contents of his stomach.
Usage 3: This is not the time or place to *disgorge* the details of my latest crisis.
Usage 4: I wanted to *disgorge* every reminder of those horrible years.
Usage 5: Was the oil company forced to *disgorge* its profits to pay the claimants?

DISINTER (v)   [dis-in-TUR]
Meaning: dig up; unearth; to remove (especially from a grave); to bring to light
Usage 1: They had no right to *disinter* my uncle, even if they did suspect homicide.
Usage 2: The newspaper reporter was determined to *disinter* every bit of scandal from her past.
Usage 3: Their object was to *disinter* the criminal practices of the manufacturers along the river.
Usage 4: Are you sure you want to *disinter* every grievance we've ever had against each other?
Usage 5: Is there any way to *disinter* a casket that is buried in frozen ground?

DISTORTION (n)   [dih-STAWR-sh*uh* n]
Meaning: a twisting out of normal shape; a falsehood
Usage 1: His lies are a complete *distortion* of the truth.
Usage 2: The mirror in the Fun House created a hysterical *distortion* of my body and head.
Usage 3: With the *distortion* of the facts in this manner, we cannot make a well-informed decision.
Usage 4: I am not sure where or how the *distortion* of your memory occurred.
Usage 5: Has his *distortion* of the facts had an impact on how the jury views him?

DIVERGENT (adj)   [dih-VUR-j*uh* nt]
Meaning: differing; deviating; moving off the main direction
Usage 1: The goals of the group soon splintered and became *divergent* from the original purpose.

Usage 2: Strangely, their *divergent* paths lead them back to each other, eventually.

Usage 3: A little bit of *divergent* thinking led us to a much more productive approach.

Usage 4: I am accused of being *divergent*, but I think of myself as an original.

Usage 5: Does the fact that the scores are dramatically *divergent* bolster the view that some students cheated?

DIVERSITY (n)   [dih-VUR-si-tee]

Meaning: variety; dissimilitude; state of being unlike one another

Usage 1: It was a relief when my all-white school became one steeped in *diversity*.

Usage 2: The *diversity* of his opinions made it hard to keep up with the position he was taking.

Usage 3: Such *diversity* in flora and fauna is rarely seen in a desert.

Usage 4: I enjoy eating a *diversity* of fish, from sushi to Southern fried catfish.

Usage 5: How does our *diversity* strengthen our corporate culture?

DOGGED (adj)   [DAW-gid]

Meaning: determined; stubborn; persistent

Usage 1: She was *dogged* in her attempts to pin the blame on me.

Usage 2: Such a *dogged* pursuit of wealth and power surely erases something from the soul.

Usage 3: I loved her *dogged* attempts to swim the fastest; she was a fighter.

Usage 4: You could say they are *dogged* in pursuit of the "Best in Breed" award at this canine extravaganza.

Usage 5: Does it always require *dogged* pursuit of our goals for us to meet them?

DON (v)   [don]

Meaning: put on; to clothe oneself in

Usage 1: Did you *don* that top hat just for the performance?

Usage 2: The stage manager ordered the actors from the first act to *don* their costumes.

Usage 3: The forest will *don* itself in red and yellow leaves come this fall.

Usage 4: My pet ferret objected to my plan to *don* him in a beaver costume.

Usage 5: Will you *don* your Santa suit this year?

DOUSE (v)   [dous]

Meaning: plunge into water; drench; extinguish; cover with liquid

Usage 1: Don't forget to *douse* the campfire with water before you go to bed.

Usage 2: *Douse* the cooked potatoes in cool water before proceeding to the next step.

Usage 3: If they *douse* us with work, we can always quit.

Usage 4: I was sure to *douse* the cooked eggs in cold water, but they were still difficult to peel.

Usage 5: Why did you *douse* this pasta in hot sauce?

DRONE (n)   [drohn]

Meaning: idle person; male bee; someone who lives off another's labor or efforts

Usage 1: As a *drone*, the male bee does not contribute to the vital role of making honey.

Usage 2: I would not be satisfied to be a *drone*, living off the hard work of others.

Usage 3: Although originally ambitious, she has steadily declined until now she is nothing more than a *drone*.

Usage 4: She doesn't have a partner; she has a *drone*.

Usage 5: Have you noticed how the other bees seem to have little respect for a *drone*?

Chapter **4**

Ecstasy – Gait

This chapter covers the following words, each with its part of speech, pronunciation, and descriptive meaning.

Usage of the word is also illustrated in three to five sample sentences.

ecstasy	equipoise	feign
eerie	equitable	felon
effigy	espouse	feral
effusion	estranged	ferment
ejaculation	ethnology	filing
elaboration	evince	finesse
elusive	exasperate	fitful
embed	execrate	flay
embrace	exemplary	flick
emulate	expedient	flinch
endorse	expurgate	foray
endue	exult	fortitude
energize	factitious	fraught
enigmatic	fancied	friction
enrapture	fanfare	fruition
enterprising	farce	gait
entity	fatalism	

ECSTASY (n)   [EK-st*uh*-see]

Meaning: rapture; joy; any overpowering emotion; extreme happiness or satisfaction

Usage 1: Her *ecstasy* at getting her first book published was obvious.

Usage 2: It was a long, hard battle, which made her *ecstasy* at the outcome that much more well-earned.

Usage 3: I never felt such *ecstasy* until I held my baby nephew in my arms.

Usage 4: Many believe in the *ecstasy* of love, but I am not so sure.

Usage 5: Was his graduation a mix of both *ecstasy* and sorrow?

EERIE (adj)   [EER-ee]

Meaning: weird; strange; inspiring fear or superstition

Usage 1: I had an *eerie* feeling that I'd been there before.

Usage 2: The deserted town was filled with ramshackle, *eerie* buildings.

Usage 3: The howling wind and clattering bells made the scene that much more *eerie*.

Usage 4: It was *eerie* that no one realized I was wearing a mask.

Usage 5: Doesn't that *eerie* music give you the creeps?

EFFIGY (n)   [EF-i-jee]

Meaning: dummy; a representation of something hated

Usage 1: It was a gruesome sight until I realized they were only burning him in *effigy*.

Usage 2: The queen knew her time was limited when the peasants hanged her in *effigy*.

Usage 3: In some cultures, burning a deceased person's photograph in *effigy* is a tribute to that person.

Usage 4: As tempted as I was to burn his photographs in *effigy*, I threw them away, instead.

Usage 5: Do you want to stay and watch them dance with an *effigy* of our fearless leader?

EFFUSION (n)   [ih-FYOO-zh*uh* n]

Meaning: pouring forth; the act of flowing out

Usage 1: There was an *effusion* of support for the families after their homes were destroyed.

Usage 2: An *effusion* of outrage greeted the judge when she left the courtroom.

Usage 3: The rose beds were blooming with an *effusion* of color.

Usage 4: That kind of an *effusion* of emotion from strangers always makes me uncomfortable.

Usage 5: Have you ever seen such an *effusion* of sympathy?

EJACULATION(n)   [ih-jak-y*uh*-LEY-sh*uh* n]

Meaning: exclamation; interjection; expression of surprise, horror, or wonder

Usage 1: It was only when I heard his *ejaculation* that I realized he was hurt.

Usage 2: She gave such an *ejaculation* that I knew the sleeping body wasn't actually sleeping.

Usage 3: It was with an *ejaculation* of wonder that we watched the amazing display of flying birds

Usage 4: If an *ejaculation* is required to get your attention, then that's what I'm going for.

Usage 5: Did that *ejaculation* come from him or from someone else in the crowd?

ELABORATION (n)   [ih-lab-*uh*-REY-sh*uh* n]

Meaning: addition of details; intricacy; expanding upon with details

Usage 1: Elaboration of your ideas must occur in every paragraph.

Usage 2: He ordered us to our rooms without further *elaboration*.

Usage 3: Without *elaboration*, it is difficult to tell exactly what she means.

Usage 4: As they get older, my children demand greater *elaboration* on the instructions I give them.

Usage 5: Will *elaboration* help you understand our reasoning?

ELUSIVE (adj)   [ih-LOO-siv]

Meaning: evasive; baffling; hard to grasp; difficult to conceive of or understand

Usage 1: Alice found the white rabbit to be *elusive*.

Usage 2: His *elusive* comments about the training program made me distrust him.

Usage 3: For an animal weakened by hunger, the prey can be much more *elusive*.

Usage 4: Happiness is *elusive*; don't expect it to be around forever.

Usage 5: How could the answer to this simple question be so *elusive*?

EMBED (v)   [em-BED]

Meaning: enclose; place in something; incorporate inside a larger object

Usage 1: Ancient civilizations did not hesitate to *embed* statues with precious stones.

Usage 2: We must *embed* the video file into your presentation.

Usage 3: Even when I treat them with tick repellant, those nasty bugs *embed* themselves inside my dogs' ears.

Usage 4: He plans to *embed* her engagement ring inside a cream-filled doughnut.

Usage 5: Where will they *embed* the file when they transfer it to our database?

EMBRACE (v)   [em-BREYS]

Meaning: hug; adopt or espouse; to take in one's arms; to support

Usage 1: I couldn't wait to *embrace* my parents at the airport.

Usage 2: He would not *embrace* that line of thinking because he deemed it unproductive.

Usage 3: After he made sure to *embrace* me, I was no longer convinced he was my enemy.

Usage 4: My once-abused dog showed great progress when she allowed me to *embrace* her.

Usage 5: Will you finally *embrace* the notion that I have your best interests at heart?

EMULATE (v)   [EM-*yuh*-leyt]

Meaning: imitate; to copy in an effort to equal or improve

Usage 1: My niece flatters me every time she tries to *emulate* my wardrobe.

Usage 2: I don't have to *emulate* her cooking; mine is better than hers.

Usage 3: There is no need to *emulate* our approach; it was a disaster.

Usage 4: To *emulate* is one thing; to destroy the original is another.

Usage 5: Does the championship team, in your opinion, *emulate* the moves of last year's champions?

ENDORSE (v)   [en-DAWRS]

Meaning: approve; support, sustain

Usage 1: I simply cannot *endorse* your charity; I suspect it is bogus.

Usage 2: We will *endorse* the candidate who best addresses our concerns.

Usage 3: To *endorse* that line of thinking would send us on a path of self-destruction.

Usage 4: I had no desire to *endorse* his proposal because my feelings were exactly the opposite.

Usage 5: Did you need me to *endorse* that check for you?

ENDUE (v)   [en-DOO]

Meaning: provide with some quality; endow; to put on

Usage 1: A careful study of the subject will *endue* you with the knowledge needed to move forward.

Usage 2: The award -winning actress has the ability to *endue* every character with her unique sensibility.

Usage 3: My goal as a teacher is to *endue* each student with a basic understanding of my subject.

Usage 4: If I can *endue* my children with an unwavering sense of right and wrong, then my job is done.

Usage 5: How do you *endue* the characters you portray so completely?

ENERGIZE (v)   [EN-er-jahyz]

Meaning: invigorate; make forceful and active; give energy to

Usage 1: I want to *energize* my colleagues with a new exercise program.

Usage 2: I depend on caffeine to *energize* me in the morning.

Usage 3: The young runner's enthusiasm could not help but *energize* the crowd.

Usage 4: My all-vegetable diet did little to *energize* me.

Usage 5: Did the performers at the concert *energize* the audience?

ENIGMATIC (adj)   [en-ig-MAT-ik]

Meaning: obscure; puzzling; difficult to understand

Usage 1: His response was *enigmatic*; I didn't know what it meant.

Usage 2: It was an *enigmatic* end to a day already fraught with confusion.

Usage 3: The *enigmatic* clues at the crime scene made the investigation even more difficult.

Usage 4: If I see one more of his *enigmatic* expressions when I ask him to dance, I am going to throw my shoe at him.

Usage 5: Does that *enigmatic* letter reveal anything about her motives?

ENRAPTURE (v)   [en-RAP-cher]

Meaning: please intensely; enthrall; delight

Usage 1: The orchestra made every effort to *enrapture* us with its music, and it succeeded.

Usage 2: For a comedian to *enrapture* an audience so consistently and so completely is rare.

Usage 3: The young actor will *enrapture* us with her performance as Ophelia in *Hamlet.*

Usage 4: I did not need to *enrapture* him, but I did want him to have a good time.

Usage 5: To further *enrapture* the crowd on the street, the magician levitated.

ENTERPRISING (adj)   [EN-ter-prahy-zing]

Meaning: full of initiative; ambitious

Usage 1: He was an *enterprising* young man, but I didn't trust him.

Usage 2: Such an *enterprising* nature will surely lead to success in life.

Usage 3: *Enterprising* workers understand that every task becomes part of their resume.

Usage 4: I need to find a way to be *enterprising* without actually doing much work.

Usage 5: Does her *enterprising* approach to selling Girl Scout cookies work?

ENTITY (n)   [EN-ti-tee]

Meaning: real being; something with a real existence

Usage 1: Under the law, this is a new *entity*, somewhere between a corporation and a sole proprietorship.

Usage 2: The alien *entity* spoke to us without moving what appeared to be its lips.

Usage 3: The three organizations will come together as a single *entity*.

Usage 4: They created in the laboratory a new cellular *entity* that would be free from disease.

Usage 5: Do they expect us to believe that such a strange *entity* could really exist?

EQUIPOISE (n) [EE-kw*uh*-poiz]

Meaning: equilibrium; counterbalance; equal distribution of weight

Usage 1: The stork stood with one leg in perfect *equipoise*.

Usage 2: The *equipoise* of the gymnasts on the balance beam was extraordinary.

Usage 3: The animal kingdom generally requires *equipoise*; without it some animals flourish and others are extinguished.

Usage 4: Lacking *equipoise*, as soon as I crossed the narrow bridge I landed in the water.

Usage 5: Do you see how that boulder appears in perfect *equipoise* on the edge of that cliff?

EQUITABLE (adj) [EK-wi-t*uh*-b*uh* l]

Meaning: fair; just; impartial; treating equally

Usage 1: We are hoping for an *equitable* decision that recognizes the interests of both sides.

Usage 2: It is hard to be *equitable* when dealing with an employee you like and one that you don't.

Usage 3: She was *equitable* in her response to all three children; she told them all "no."

Usage 4: I don't mind being turned down, as long as the decision-making is *equitable*.

Usage 5: Do judges find it hard to be *equitable* when dealing with such a quantity and variety of cases?

ESPOUSE (v) [ih-SPOUZ]

Meaning: adopt; support; speak in support of

Usage 1: He seems to *espouse* a new position at every speech he makes.

Usage 2: It seems hypocritical for him to *espouse* the dangers of tobacco he himself smokes.

Usage 3: I plan to *espouse* the many benefits of contributing money to your cause.

Usage 4: I refused to *espouse* the position of the "other woman" in an affair.

Usage 5: What if I were to *espouse* the theory that the world is flat, after all?

ESTRANGED (v) [ih-STREYNJD]

Meaning: separated; alienated; turned away in feeling or regard

Usage 1: The homeless man had *estranged* himself from his family for fifteen years.

Usage 2: The tension between them had so *estranged* her that she'd reached a point of no return.

Usage 3: We'd been *estranged* for years after the death of our youngest child.

Usage 4: I felt that his decision to choose his career over mine *estranged* us.

Usage 5: Has moving to another state *estranged* me from my dearest friends?

ETHNOLOGY (n) [eth-NOL-*uh*-jee]

Meaning: study of mankind; study of man's historical, cultural, or racial development

Usage 1: After years of working in the field of *ethnology*, she retired and studied her neighbors.

Usage 2: Several studies in *ethnology* reveal that folk stories played a pivotal role in contributing to cultural norms.

Usage 3: He was always a student of human nature, and, therefore, he has chosen to study *ethnology*.

Usage 4: What does *ethnology* reveal about those who, historically, never learn from their mistakes?

Usage 5: Isn't his position that *ethnology* answers all questions pertaining to mankind erroneous?

EVINCE (v)   [ih-VINS]

Meaning: show clearly; make evident; prove

Usage 1: Her teaching methods *evince* her understanding of current research on metacognition.

Usage 2: You could at least *evince* some concern for the disaster you created.

Usage 3: The happy warble of the birds may *evince* their awareness that spring will soon be upon us.

Usage 4: I tried to *evince* a sudden interest in photography, but my pretense didn't work.

Usage 5: Does he *evince* any knowledge of what happened in the past?

EXASPERATE (v)   [ig-ZAS-p*uh*-reyt]

Meaning: vex; annoy; frustrate

Usage 1: Clearly your words are meant to *exasperate* me.

Usage 2: If you don't want to *exasperate* her any further, perhaps you should stop talking.

Usage 3: Asking him if he needs help will only *exasperate* him.

Usage 4: Her obsession with eating only organic foods is beginning to *exasperate* me.

Usage 5: Doesn't her habit of talking without thinking *exasperate* you?

EXECRATE (v)   [EK-si-kreyt]

Meaning: curse; express abhorrence for; to detest or denounce

Usage 1: To *execrate* injustice and inequality is a sign of strength.

Usage 2: It makes no sense to *execrate* an entire nation of people.

Usage 3: I know her style; she will *execrate* the government and all of its officials.

Usage 4: It is pointless to *execrate* the situation; you created it.

Usage 5: Must you *execrate* daily every one of your enemies, past and present?

EXEMPLARY (adj)   [ig-ZEM-pl*uh*-ree]

Meaning: serving as a model; outstanding, setting a positive example

Usage 1: Her dignified behavior, in the face of such rudeness, was *exemplary*.

Usage 2: The award for the most *exemplary* business project went to our company.

Usage 3: The pasta dishes at the new bistro are *exemplary*; you must try them.

Usage 4: These sugar-free brownies would be *exemplary* if they had some sugar in them.

Usage 5: Do you think those athletes are *exemplary* role models?

EXPEDIENT (adj)   [ik-SPEE-dee-*uh* nt]

Meaning: suitable; practical; appropriate; efficient

Usage 1: Surely this is the most *expedient* course of action.

Usage 2: It would be more *expedient* if I take her to the airport, rather than you.

Usage 3: He gave me an *expedient* answer, but I am not sure it was the correct one.

Usage 4: Isn't it more *expedient* simply to sign over my paycheck to the IRS?

Usage 5: How *expedient* would it be to take a shortcut through the city?

EXPURGATE (v)   [EK-sper-geyt]

Meaning: clean; remove offensive parts of a book; purge off offending items

Usage 1: Her redactions were designed to *expurgate* all references that might offend a conservative audience.

Usage 2: When you *expurgate* the script, don't take out any of the funny bits.

Usage 3: I can't believe they are requiring us to *expurgate* all references to unhealthy eating habits.

Usage 4: After you *expurgate* all the objectionable parts of the speech, the speaker is left with only two words.

Usage 5: Do we really need to *expurgate* a song that was written for children?

EXULT (v)   [ig-ZUHLT]

Meaning: rejoice; take pleasure or joy in

Usage 1: She will *exult* when she learns she made a positive difference in your life.

Usage 2: However much he deserved it, they couldn't bring themselves to *exult* in his misfortune.

Usage 3: She will *exult* when she learns they are publishing her story.

Usage 4: To truly *exult* at the extreme good fortune of a friend is a sign of a deep and lasting friendship.

Usage 5: You were fired, too; what on earth do you have to *exult* about?

FACTITIOUS (adj)   [fak-TISH-*uh* s]

Meaning: artificial; sham contrived; not real

Usage 1: The food on display in that gourmet magazine is *factitious*; they have to enhance it so that it photographs correctly.

Usage 2: The department head's response to employee concerns about safety sounded *factitious*; I don't think they're going to do anything.

Usage 3: In a moment of *factitious* friendliness, she made a show of kissing him on the cheek.

Usage 4: We were truly miserable, and any laughter you heard was *factitious*.

Usage 5: Do you think her tears at the funeral were real or *factitious*?

FANCIED (adj)   [FAN-seed]

Meaning: imagined; unreal; illusory; fictitious

Usage 1: The adoration of her employees was *fancied*; they couldn't wait for her to resign.

Usage 2: Her memories of their times at the lake, more *fancied* than real, sustained her through the tough days of rehabilitation.

Usage 3: His *fancied* climb up the corporate ladder led to a crashing fall last week.

Usage 4: My *fancied* skills at dog training led to a trip to the emergency room for treatment of a dog bite.

Usage 5: Was her crisis, as usual, more *fancied* than real?

FANFARE (n)   [FAN-fair]

Meaning: call by bugles or trumpets; an elaborate celebration

Usage 1: A five-minute *fanfare* announced the arrival of the princess and her entourage.

Usage 2: All this *fanfare* makes me impatient; let's just get to the point.

Usage 3: Amidst all the *fanfare* of her birthday party, Jessie collapsed in tears.

Usage 4: Don't let the *fanfare* fool you; it's still a used car lot.

Usage 5: What is all the *fanfare*—did someone win the sweepstakes?

FARCE (n)   [fahrs]

Meaning: broad comedy; mockery; a silly or foolish showing

Usage 1: It took me a moment to realize the puppet show was a *farce* that ridiculed the current political situation.

Usage 2: What a *farce* his displays of wealth were; in reality he was bankrupt.

Usage 3: Once you understood how the winners were chosen, it was impossible not to view the award ceremony as a *farce*.

Usage 4: My attempts to behave in a more sophisticated manner were a *farce*; it just wasn't me.

Usage 5: Do you agree that these legislative attempts to improve education are a *farce*?

FATALISM (n)   [FEYT-l-iz-*uh* m]

Meaning: belief that events are determined by forces beyond one's control; submission to the power of fate

Usage 1: When all their efforts to improve the situation were ineffective, they were reduced to *fatalism*.

Usage 2: Her *fatalism* was no help to the situation; we still believed we could make a difference.

Usage 3: It was with a sense of *fatalism* that we listened to continuing reports about the rescue operations.

Usage 4: I tried to treat my disastrous marriage choices as mere *fatalism*.

Usage 5: Was it an end to all hope, or *fatalism*, that most contributed to the outcome?

FEIGN (v)   [feyn]

Meaning: pretend; to make believe; to represent fictitiously

Usage 1: Please do not *feign* surprise; I know they told you about your birthday party.

Usage 2: An animal under attack will often *feign* death to prevent further harm.

Usage 3: The fact that he could *feign* a Scottish accent put him at the top of the list for the part.

Usage 4: If you *feign* ignorance, I will show you the video that confirms you were there.

Usage 5: Should humans *feign* death when being chased by a bear?

FELON (n)   [FEL-*uh* n]

Meaning: criminal; person convicted of a grave crime; a convict

Usage 1: I simply refused to allow my daughter to date a *felon*.

Usage 2: As a *felon*, he had tremendous difficulty finding employment.

Usage 3: The mentoring program gave him the opportunity to work with a young *felon*.

Usage 4: My last date was arrested during dinner; it turned out he was a *felon*.

Usage 5: Does he realize that after his stupid teenage prank he is now a *felon*?

FERAL (adj)   [FEER-*uh* l]

Meaning: not domestic; wild; untamed

Usage 1: They had one house cat and one feral cat, but the *feral* cat was the sweeter of the two.

Usage 2: Do not underestimate a *feral* creature.

Usage 3: After years in the jungle, she was more *feral* than human.

Usage 4: My new son-in-law's manners could be described as *feral*.

Usage 5: Have they warned us that *feral* animals are a problem thisyear?

FERMENT (n)   [FUR-ment]

Meaning: agitation; commotion; unrest

Usage 1: The rebel forces were in a state of *ferment* immediately before the attack.

Usage 2: The political rally was a *ferment* of angry voices.

Usage 3: The planning session was an exciting *ferment* of enthusiasm and creativity.

Usage 4: I avoid any *ferment* that arises when the two families get together.

Usage 5: Did you enjoy the *ferment* of juices in the punch at the wedding?

FILING (n)   [FAHY-ling]

Meaning: particle removed by a file a fragment rubbed off with a file

Usage 1: When we sifted the cereal, we found pieces of iron *filing*.

Usage 2: Collect the pieces of *filing* and send them off for analysis.

Usage 3: The little bits of *filing* won't hurt you.

Usage 4: I was tempted to put more than one *filing* in her morning coffee.

Usage 5: Is an iron *filing* magnetic?

FINESSE (n)   [fi-NESS]

Meaning: skill in handling

Usage 1: Her *finesse* in handling temperamental clients was clearly called for here.

Usage 2: With a little bit of *finesse*, he was able to coax the two pieces of wood to interlock with one another.

Usage 3: It will take considerable diplomatic *finesse* to get these two parties to talk with one another.

Usage 4: In the oyster-shucking contest, he couldn't match her *finesse*.

Usage 5: Did you see the *finesse* with which he handled the basketball?

FITFUL (adj)   [FIT-*fuh* l]

Meaning: spasmodic; intermittent; occurring in irregular spells

Usage 1: After the automobile accident, he had months of *fitful* sleep filled with nightmares.

Usage 2: Her violin practice has become inconsistent and *fitful*, and it's showing in her performances.

Usage 3: There were *fitful* attempts to remedy the situation, but none of the attempts succeeded.

Usage 4: My bouts of productive writing were *fitful* and depended on the weather and the quantity of coffee in my system.

Usage 5: Has the baby's sleeping been *fitful*?

FLAY (v)   [fley]

Meaning: strip off skin; plunder; to strip away from; criticize severely

Usage 1: After an afternoon of catching fish, it was time to *flay* them.

Usage 2: She will *flay* you alive if she ever hears you swear.

Usage 3: The punishment for mutiny was to *flay* the ringleader.

Usage 4: I was so angry, I was ready to *flay* him the moment he came in the door.

Usage 5: How did you learn how to *flay* a quail so quickly?

FLICK (n)   [flik]

Meaning: light stroke as with a whip; a rapid movement of an item

Usage 1: With a *flick* of his wand, the magician made the rabbitre appear.

Usage 2: The *flick* of the whip startled me.

Usage 3: With several *flicks* of the wrist, he finished the carving.

Usage 4: I know I'm in trouble when my cat gives a *flick* of its tail.

Usage 5: Did you see how the *flick* of a switch changed everything?

FLINCH (v)   [flinch]

Meaning: hesitate; shrink; move away from in fear

Usage 1: That owl swooping down on the crowd made us all *flinch*.

Usage 2: When I accidentally threw the javelin at him, he did not even *flinch*.

Usage 3: I try not to *flinch* when she misuses the English language, but it's hard.

Usage 4: What makes me *flinch* is the thought that I am twenty years away from retirement, and I'm already counting down the days.

Usage 5: Did his in-your-face screaming make you *flinch*?

FORAY (n) [FAWR-ey]

Meaning: raid; a sudden attack; an initial venture

Usage 1: After years of being the victims of broken promises, the angry tribe members made a *foray* on the encroaching settlers.

Usage 2: Her first *foray* as a corporate executive was seen as a disaster.

Usage 3: I am considering a *foray* into politics, but I lack the necessary funds.

Usage 4: As desperate as I am to start dating again, I have not been tempted to make a *foray* into online dating.

Usage 5: How successful was your first *foray* into competitive biking?

FORTITUDE (n) [FAWR-ti-tood]

Meaning: bravery; courage; strength in the face of adversity

Usage 1: It took *fortitude* for those young, black students to face the angry, white mob.

Usage 2: He lacks the *fortitude* required to make this project a success.

Usage 3: Handling the crisis was going to take months of *fortitude*.

Usage 4: Every time you fail, it's a chance to prove *fortitude*.

Usage 5: Was it, do you think, a lack of strength or a lack of *fortitude*?

FRAUGHT (adj) [frawt]

Meaning: filled; full of; accompanied by

Usage 1: The plan was *fraught* with flaws; there was no way it would work.

Usage 2: She was *fraught* with confusion over how to shut off the water to the house.

Usage 3: Her comments, *fraught* with bitterness, revealed her true feelings towards her colleagues.

Usage 4: As I entered the cave, *fraught* with fear over being attacked by bears or bats, I wondered how I'd gotten myself into this mess.

Usage 5: Don't you think skydiving is *fraught* with too many possibilities of something going wrong?

FRICTION (n) [FRIK-sh*uh* n]

Meaning: clash in opinion; rubbing against; resistant to a sliding or rolling motion; dissension

Usage 1: The *friction* of our shoes on the new carpet created tons of static electricity.

Usage 2: The tractor trailer came to a stop because the *friction* of the gravel slowed the movement of the tires.

Usage 3: I don't want to cause any *friction* between you, but one of the two of you is not being honest.

Usage 4: The *friction* between my teenagers will end when I stop feeding them, and they unite in an effort to survive.

Usage 5: Have you noticed any *friction* between the newlyweds?

FRUITION (n) [froo-ISH-*uh* n]

Meaning: bearing of fruit; fulfillment; realization; attainment of a desired object

Usage 1: All their efforts had come to *fruition*: the opening of the restaurant was a huge success.

Usage 2: We must move this venture from preliminary planning to *fruition*.

Usage 3: Through their efforts, they brought to *fruition* the foundation for deeper space exploration.

Usage 4: My hopes of winning the lottery did not come to *fruition*, especially since I did not purchase a ticket.

Usage 5: Have their efforts to devise artificial fuel sources come to *fruition*?

GAIT (n)   [geyt]

Meaning: manner of walking or running; speed; the style or manner of walking, especially of a horse

Usage 1: You could see in the horse's *gait* that she had thrown a shoe.

Usage 2: During the show, all of the horses must maintain the same *gait*.

Usage 3: The marathon runners needed to make their *gait* more efficient.

Usage 4: With back problems and a sore knee, of course my *gait* looked strange.

Usage 5: Will the knee operation affect his *gait*?

This page is intentionally left blank

Chapter **5**

Gale – Initiate

This chapter covers the following words, each with its part of speech, pronunciation, and descriptive meaning.

Usage of the word is also illustrated in three to five sample sentences.

gale	hatch	importunate
gall	herbivorous	imposture
gaunt	heresy	incarnate
gazette	hibernal	incense
genre	hinterlands	incentive
germane	holster	incisive
gist	hubris	inclined
gossamer	idiosyncrasy	incoherent
gourmet	igneous	incredulity
graphic	ignominious	incubate
grill	illusion	indenture
grisly	immune	indisputable
grueling	immure	ineffectual
hale	impale	inept
harass	impeach	infallible
hardy	impecunious	initiate
harry	imply	

GALE (n) [geyl]

Meaning: windstorm; gust of wind; strong wind; eruption

Usage 1: It wasn't a soft, refreshing wind; it was a *gale*.

Usage 2: A *gale* of snickers and snorts greeted the strange-looking visitor.

Usage 3: We are due for a *gale* tonight, and we must cover the plants.

Usage 4: The niece that visited me was a *gale* of energy and noise.

Usage 5: Have you witnessed the power of a *gale* to bring down trees and electric lines?

GALL (n) [gawl]

Meaning: bitterness; nerve; impudence; rancor

Usage 1: What *gall* it must have taken to contend that they were exempt from the law.

Usage 2: Her *gall* at the situation had her almost spitting at me in anger.

Usage 3: The *gall* it takes to seek such revenge is beyond me.

Usage 4: It was hard to miss the *gall* in her tone when her colleague corrected her.

Usage 5: Can you believe the *gall* of that woman when she demanded that she be seated without a reservation?

GAUNT (adj) [gawnt]

Meaning: lean and angular; barren; thin and haggard

Usage 1: You can tell he's been ill; he is clearly *gaunt*.

Usage 2: Some who lived in the besieged city survived, but they were *gaunt* and hollow-faced.

Usage 3: The forest in winter appeared *gaunt* and lifeless.

Usage 4: How she could prize her *gaunt* appearance was beyond me; she looked emaciated.

Usage 5: Don't many of the older buildings in Russia appear *gaunt* and unfriendly?

GAZETTE (n) [*guh*-ZET]

Meaning: official publication; an official journal or newspaper

Usage 1: I read about the charity fundraiser in this morning's *gazette*.

Usage 2: They say the *gazette* has fallen on hard times with the rise of internet news sources.

Usage 3: The senior center publishes a *gazette* each month listing the upcoming events at the center.

Usage 4: I don't want to read about your antics in the *gazette*.

Usage 5: Has the *gazette* verified the story with multiple sources of information?

GENRE (n) [ZHAHN-*ruh*]

Meaning: particular variety of art or literature; class or category of writing or art

Usage 1: Every *genre* of literature has distinctive characteristics.

Usage 2: Some *genres*, like fantasy, have more of a following among younger readers than older ones.

Usage 3: The *genre* known as magic realism intertwines elements of magic and real life.

Usage 4: During my painting class, the professor accused me of creating a new and disturbing art *genre*.

Usage 5: Isn't it a bad sign when you cannot even determine the *genre* in which a story might be placed?

GERMANE (adj) [jer-MEYN]

Meaning: pertinent; bearing upon the case at hand; relevant to

Usage 1: Your comments are simply not *germane* to the issue at hand.

Usage 2: His prior experience is not *germane* to the new project.

Usage 3: The judge allowed the attorney's line of inquiry because she found it *germane* to the case.

Usage 4: I felt my questions about his motives were certainly *germane* to his proposal to my daughter.

Usage 5: Isn't the issue of whether the project will produce revenue *germane* to the committee's evaluation?

GIST (n)   [jist]

Meaning: essence; the essential elements of

Usage 1: The *gist* of the story is that every life has a value, and we must never forget that.

Usage 2: The basic *gist* of the report is that the railroad company was at fault.

Usage 3: I couldn't get the *gist* of what he was saying; what does he want from us?

Usage 4: My Spanish is mediocre, but I understand the *gist* of what she's saying.

Usage 5: Even though you are having trouble hearing, are you getting the *gist* of their discussion?

GOSSAMER (adj)   [GOS-*uh*-mer]

Meaning: sheer; like cobwebs; diaphanous; transparent

Usage 1: The butterfly's *gossamer* wings made it even more delicate.

Usage 2: Her favorite birthday present was a colorful, *gossamer* scarf from her aunt.

Usage 3: The artist's *gossamer* paintings of elephants made them appear magical.

Usage 4: The pirate's costume included a *gossamer*-sleeved white shirt and a lethal-looking scabbard.

Usage 5: Have you seen the *gossamer* ghosts at the haunted house?

GOURMET (n)   [g*oo* r-MEY]

Meaning: one who enjoys good food or wine

Usage 1: When it came to wine and desserts, she was a *gourmet*.

Usage 2: Like any good *gourmet*, he chose only the freshest ingredients at the market.

Usage 3: They appreciated the artistry and ability of the *gourmet* chef who had prepared their dinner.

Usage 4: I dabble in *gourmet* preparations, but I have no formal training.

Usage 5: Do you aspire to be a *gourmet* cook?

GRAPHIC (adj)   [GRAF-ik]

Meaning: pertaining to the art of delineating; vividly described; producing mental images

Usage 1: His description of the execution was so *graphic*, I almost fainted.

Usage 2: She has a degree in *graphic* design from some famous art school.

Usage 3: There is no need to be so *graphic*; I get the picture.

Usage 4: Her *graphic* illustrations brought the designs to life.

Usage 5: Have you ever heard such a *graphic* description of what happens in battle?

GRILL (v)   [gril]

Meaning: question severely; interrogate

Usage 1: We will *grill* every member of the group until we get to the truth.

Usage 2: The mediator will *grill* both sides during the television debate.

Usage 3: The police will *grill* those they suspect participated in the crime.

Usage 4: I hated to *grill* the clerk for information, but she was the only witness I could find.

Usage 5: If I don't know anything, how can it help you to *grill* me?

GRISLY (adj)   [GRIZ-lee]

Meaning: ghastly; horror-producing

Usage 1: The crime scene was particularly *grisly*, with blood everywhere.

Usage 2: It was a *grisly* showdown between the forces of good and evil.

Usage 3: The effects of the flesh-eating bacteria on his internal organs were *grisly*.

Usage 4: My attempts at creating a beautiful piece of pottery resulted in *grisly*, misshapen blobs of clay.

Usage 5: Will the world ever fully comprehend the *grisly* scenes from the concentration camps?

GRUELING (adj)   [GROO-*uh*-ling]

Meaning: exhausting; extremely difficult

Usage 1: Rescuing the birds from the massive oil slick was a *grueling* task.

Usage 2: The audition process is a *grueling* one and occurs over a course of ten days.

Usage 3: The experts warned them that hiking over the mountains would be a *grueling* experience.

Usage 4: The project that she grossly underbid was *grueling*, to say the least.

Usage 5: Is her lacrosse practice schedule as *grueling* as the one for soccer?

HALE (adj)   [heyl]

Meaning: healthy; vigorous; free from disease

Usage 1: She was a young girl, *hale* and hearty in spite of her illnesses earlier in life.

Usage 2: It takes a *hale* and hearty young man to chop his way through this pile of wood.

Usage 3: She watched the *hale* and hearty sailors as they prepared the vessel for its voyage.

Usage 4: Even after months of working out, I didn't feel *hale* or hearty in the least.

Usage 5: Are you feeling *hale* and hearty for the tug-of-war competition?

HARASS (v)   [h*uh*-RAS]

Meaning: annoy repeatedly

Usage 1: I don't mean to *harass* you, but the deadline is quickly approaching.

Usage 2: Creditors do not have the right to *harass* you each day over the telephone.

Usage 3: If they *harass* you at work, you can notify your representative.

Usage 4: As your father, only I am allowed to *harass* you; everyone else has to answer to me.

Usage 5: Do you mind if I *harass* you for a little bit?

HARDY (adj)   [HAHR-dee]

Meaning: sturdy; robust; able to stand inclement weather; able to withstand adverse conditions

Usage 1: Those rose bushes are *hardier* than they look.

Usage 2: He is a *hardy* young man and will outperform us all.

Usage 3: It was a *hardy* crop of watermelon this year, notwithstanding the hard frost.

Usage 4: After playing weekend warrior, my husband wasn't feeling too *hardy*.

Usage 5: Is the wheat grown here a *hardy* variety?

HARRY (v)   [HAR-ee]

Meaning: annoy, torment; raid; ravage, devastate or harass

Usage 1: We must not allow soldiers to *harry* local residents after we invade the city.

Usage 2: There is no need for us to *harry* the oxen; they are doing the best they can.

Usage 3: If they keep sounding the alarm, it will *harry* the workers.

Usage 4: Don't allow my criticism to *harry* you; I rarely mean what Isay.

Usage 5: Was it his intent to *harry* every one of the project'sparticipants?

HATCH (n)   [hach]

Meaning: deck opening; lid covering a deck opening; a doorway to a lower portion of a ship

Usage 1: A lower *hatch* on the ship was left open, allowing rain to fall in the storage areas below.

Usage 2: When the crew members tried the *hatch*, it was stuck, and they were unable to escape.

Usage 3: Those coffee tables are made from *hatch* covers that were once aboard U.S. Navy vessels.

Usage 4: Close the *hatch* or you'll sink the ship!

Usage 5: Has anyone considered that a defective *hatch* was the reason the vessel took on water?

HERBIVOROUS (adj)   [hur-BIV-er-*uh* s]

Meaning: grain-eating; plant-eating (as opposed to meat-eating)

Usage 1: It is mind-boggling to me that enormous dinosaurs were *herbivorous*.

Usage 2: It's a good thing that whale is *herbivorous*; it could swallow us in one bite!

Usage 3: Many *herbivorous* creatures must eat plants and grains constantly in order to stay alive.

Usage 4: She experimented with being *herbivorous* when she was in college, but she missed eating meat too much.

Usage 5: Is there such a thing as an *herbivorous* Venus Flytrap?

HERESY (n)   [HER-*uh*-see]

Meaning: opinion contrary to popular belief or religion; a belief or opinion that is not accepted

Usage 1: Her views about women and the priesthood were considered *heresy* by many in the church.

Usage 2: After being accused of *heresy*, the alleged witch was burned at the stake.

Usage 3: I get weary of their accusations of *heresy* every time we don't agree with them.

Usage 4: I know some would consider this *heresy*, but I don't see the point of owning expensive jewelry when the fake stuff is beautiful.

Usage 5: Do you believe mere consideration of the law to be *heresy*?

HIBERNAL (adj)   [hahy-BUR-nl]

Meaning: wintry; occurring in winter

Usage 1: Their *hibernal* home is half a world away from their summer residence.

Usage 2: Florida is filled with those seeking shelter from *hibernal* conditions in the north.

Usage 3: My dog's *hibernal* coat is coarser than her summer coat.

Usage 4: The *hibernal* beauty of the mountains was lost on me; I was freezing.

Usage 5: Is the *hibernal* season the most profitable for tourist shops?

HINTERLANDS (n)   [HIN-ter-lands]

Meaning: back country; around the edges of settled land

Usage 1: He claimed to be from the *hinterlands*, where the rules of civilization were different.

Usage 2: Defending the *hinterlands* was often a concern for western towns.

Usage 3: She threatened to move to the *hinterlands* in order to get away from her family.

Usage 4: Don't go running off to the *hinterlands* before dinner.

Usage 5: Have you visited the *hinterlands*, or have you always stayed in the city?

HOLSTER (n)   [HOHL-ster]

Meaning: pistol case; a sheaf for storing a gun or other weapon

Usage 1: The gunslinger returned the pistol to its *holster*.

Usage 2: The sheriff demanded that the vigilante put his weapon in its *holster*.

Usage 3: My machete *holster* is made of heavy canvas.

Usage 4: Even though the bear had been subdued by animal control, I was reluctant to put the cleaver I was wielding in its *holster*.

Usage 5: Could you return your rifle to its *holster* before someone gets shot?

HUBRIS (n)   [HYOO-bris]

Meaning: arrogance; excessive self-conceit; pride; self-importance

Usage 1: It was the *hubris* of the designers of the *Titanic* that prevented them from assessing the vessel's vulnerabilities.

Usage 2: His *hubris* was evident when he talked about himself incessantly.

Usage 3: Too often it is *hubris* that gets in the way and the result is a calamity.

Usage 4: Pride is one thing, but hers rises to the level of *hubris*.

Usage 5: Are you sure it is not your *hubris* talking?

IDIOSYNCRASY (n)   [id-ee-*uh*-SING-kr*uh*-see]

Meaning: individual trait usually odd in nature; eccentricity; peculiarity

Usage 1: His little sister has explored every *idiosyncrasy* in an effort to establish her identity.

Usage 2: I guess my only *idiosyncrasy* is that I eat a piece of pizza for breakfast every morning.

Usage 3: It is an *idiosyncrasy* of nature that the scorpions which are the most harmless- looking are also the most lethal.

Usage 4: It was an *idiosyncrasy* of that government that, although founded on principles of freedom, it allowed slavery.

Usage 5: Is it possible to enter old age without having at least one *idiosyncrasy*?

IGNEOUS (adj)   [IG-nee-*uh* s]

Meaning: produced by fire; volcanic; produced under conditions of intense heat

Usage 1: My sixth grader keeps grilling me on the types of rock: *igneous*, metamorphic, and sedimentary.

Usage 2: The area was strewn with what turned out to be *igneous* rock, indicating one-time volcanic activity.

Usage 3: The expert specialized in *igneous* petrology, the study of rocks forged by fire (most often by volcano).

Usage 4: When magma, or liquid rock, seeps into cracks and crevices under the earth's crust, then cools and turns into rock, the resulting rock formations are called "*igneous* intrusions."

Usage 5: Have you seen the museum's excellent display of *igneous* rocks?

IGNOMINIOUS (adj)   [ig-n*uh*-MIN-ee-*uh* s]

Meaning: disgraceful; marked by disgrace or dishonor

Usage 1: His arrest for armed robbery at the age of 17 was *ignominious*.

Usage 2: She tried to hide from the *ignominious* revelations of her abuse of power.

Usage 3: Because he felt his work as a custodian was *ignominious*, he hid it from us.

Usage 4: It was an *ignominious* battle between self-control and the absence of self-control.

Usage 5: What *ignominious* actions would prompt him to consider committing suicide?

ILLUSION (n**)**   [ih-LOO-zh*uh* n]

Meaning: misleading vision; something that appears different from its reality

Usage 1: His dream of making it to the NFL proved to be a heartbreaking *illusion*.

Usage 2: The crowd was awed by the last of the magician's *illusions*.

Usage 3: By cheating on the tests, they gave the *illusion* that they understood the material.

Usage 4: I hope you are not under the *illusion* that you are welcome in my house.

Usage 5: Is a mirage considered an optical *illusion*?

IMMUNE (adj)   [ih-MYOON]

Meaning: resistant to; free or exempt from; protected from

Usage 1: No one is *immune* to the wrath of our evil employer.

Usage 2: Not a single seaside town will be *immune* to the effects of this hurricane.

Usage 3: The response of his *immune* system to the new medication is crucial at this point.

Usage 4: I hoped that I was *immune* to the body's typical response to sudden and vigorous exercise, but I was not.

Usage 5: Does he really believe he is somehow *immune* from punishment?

IMMURE (v**)**   [ih-MY*OO* R]

Meaning: imprison; shut up in confinement; close within walls

Usage 1: To *immure* the protestors cannot be the solution.

Usage 2: The mountaineers were forced to *immure* themselves in ice caves to protect themselves from the storm.

Usage 3: They might *immure* his body, but they cannot contain his thoughts.

Usage 4: While visiting my in-laws, I was careful to *immure* my true thoughts and feelings about the entire family.

Usage 5: Isn't it clear that the regime simply wants to *immure* anyone who opposes it?

IMPALE (v**)**   [im-PEYL]

Meaning: pierce; to thrust through something with a pointed object

Usage 1: The medieval king ordered his soldiers to *impale* the heads of his enemies and place them on display above the castle wall.

Usage 2: The tornado-torn fence posts had become sharp spikes that could *impale* those who were careless crossing over them.

Usage 3: The wasp has the ability to *impale* its victims with its stinger repeatedly.

Usage 4: You are supposed to gently pierce my ears, not *impale* them with that needle.

Usage 5: Can you believe the power of the rushing water to *impale* objects against the splintered spikes of the wreckage?

IMPEACH (v**)**   [im-PEECH]

Meaning: indict; challenge the credibility of; charge with crimes

Usage 1: The prosecutor will *impeach* our witness next.

Usage 2: His misdeeds are such that the committee plans to *impeach* him.

Usage 3: The decision to *impeach* her is now out of our hands; it is up to the district attorney.

Usage 4: My old lawyer instincts kicked in, and I couldn't help but *impeach* my granddaughter's new boyfriend.

Usage 5: How will a vote to *impeach* her affect her aspirations for higher public office?

IMPECUNIOUS (adj)   [im-pi-KYOO-nee-*uh* s]

Meaning: without money; poor

Usage 1: After the young girl bragged to a friend that she was wealthy, her father reminded her that *he* was wealthy and *she* was *impecunious*.

Usage 2: When the recession hit and tax revenue dried up, previously- wealthy governments found themselves *impecunious*.

Usage 3: The Baltic cruise was fabulous, but it left me decidedly *impecunious*.

Usage 4: It is the *impecunious* student who learns to love boxed macaroni and cheese.

Usage 5: After paying off the individual bequests, will the estate be left *impecunious*?

IMPLY (v)   [im-PLAHY]

Meaning: suggest a meaning not expressed; signify; indicate without explicitly stating

Usage 1: She tried to *imply* that you were the one at fault.

Usage 2: I didn't mean to *imply* that I was opposed to the plan.

Usage 3: Those angry citizens may *imply* that our town leaders are corrupt, but I don't think that's the case.

Usage 4: Do you mean to *imply* that I'm a rotten mother?

Usage 5: Did he just *imply* that I care only about myself?

IMPORTUNATE (adj)   [im-PAWR-ch*uh*-nit]

Meaning: urging; demanding; annoyingly persistent

Usage 1: His *importunate* need for attention wears on my nerves.

Usage 2: The new mother seems to be ignoring her infant's *importunate* cries to be fed.

Usage 3: I think she's crossed the line; she is no longer persistent but *importunate*.

Usage 4: I could no longer ignore the *importunate* call of the luscious chocolate brownies.

Usage 5: Do you feel the latest demands of the workers have become *importunate*?

IMPOSTER (n)   [im-POS-cher]

Meaning: assuming a false identity; masquerade; the act of deceiving, especially by assuming the identity of another

Usage 1: The circus clown was an *imposter*; he was only some guy dressed in a clown suit.

Usage 2: The *imposter*, posing as a bank executive, convinced my grandfather to give him his personal banking information.

Usage 3: She wasn't the caring colleague she pretended to be, and I was disappointed to realize she was an *imposter*.

Usage 4: I felt like an *imposter* dressed in that fancy ball gown and wearing those fancy shoes.

Usage 5: When you give those inspirational talks, do you sometimes feel like an *imposter*?

INCARNATE (adj)   [in-KAHR-nit]

Meaning: endowed with flesh; personified; in concrete form

Usage 1: I did not care if the devil *incarnate* told me to do it; I was not going to cheat on my exam.

Usage 2: The orphanage's benefactor was good will and generosity *incarnate*.

Usage 3: Their god *incarnate* appeared in the form of a shining globe of light.

Usage 4: I don't mind living in a haunted house as long as the ghosts are not *incarnate*.

Usage 5: Don't you think the killer in that movie is evil *incarnate*?

INCENSE (v)   [IN-sens]
Meaning: enrage; infuriate; make angry
Usage 1: Failing to tell him the truth will only further *incense* him.
Usage 2: If you *incense* her, there is no way she will allow you to go to the beach.
Usage 3: I needed to tell her "no," but I didn't want to *incense* her.
Usage 4: It takes very little to *incense* me on days like this.
Usage 5: Is it wise to *incense* your supervisor like that?

INCENTIVE (n)   [in-SEN-tiv]
Meaning: spur; impetus; an offering to entice; a reward
Usage 1: What *incentive* do I have to tell the truth?
Usage 2: The hotel coupon offers an *incentive* if you stay more than three days.
Usage 3: Without a tax break, the factory has no *incentive* to relocate here.
Usage 4: I hate that I always have to offer her an *incentive* to help him with his homework.
Usage 5: Are they offering any other *incentive* to retire early?

INCISIVE (adj)   [in-SAHY-siv]
Meaning: cutting; sharp; clear and direct; biting
Usage 1: Her *incisive* comments on my research paper proved extremely useful.
Usage 2: I am sure his *incisive* manner will step on toes.
Usage 3: They are not used to such *incisive* interactions; it will take them time to adjust.
Usage 4: I no longer cared if my tone of voice was *incisive*; we needed to improve our performance.
Usage 5: Isn't his *incisive*, no-nonsense approach refreshing?

INCLINED (adj)   [in-KLAHYND]
Meaning: tending or leaning toward; bent; disposed to; having a tendency to
Usage 1: I am *inclined* to say no because the venture is too risky.
Usage 2: The data indicates customer preferences are *inclined* to change over time.
Usage 3: We are having the trees that are *inclined* towards the west side of the house removed for safety's sake.
Usage 4: After they failed to invite her to their party, she was *inclined* to destroy their invitations to her party.
Usage 5: Are you *inclined* to have a cup of tea with me this afternoon?

INCOHERENT (adj)   [in-koh-HEER-*uh* nt]
Meaning: unintelligible; muddled; illogical; not making sense
Usage 1: After the blow to his head, the prize fighter was *incoherent* for several minutes.
Usage 2: She was under such stress that her speech had become *incoherent*.
Usage 3: Your arguments are *incoherent* and have no basis in reality.
Usage 4: My son loves that music, but I find the lyrics completely *incoherent*.
Usage 5: Don't you find it *incoherent* that we are spending more money than we have?

INCREDULITY (n)   [in-kri-DOO-li-tee]
Meaning: a tendency to disbelieve; inability to believe
Usage 1: We watched the horrific scene, filled with *incredulity*.

Usage 2: She stared at the pink slip in her hand with shock and *incredulity*.

Usage 3: I didn't want to treat her claims of suffering with *incredulity*, but I really didn't believe her.

Usage 4: I gasped with *incredulity* when I saw the rope of the acrobat's trapeze snap.

Usage 5: Was that expression on your face one of belief or *incredulity*?

INCUBATE (v)   [IN-ky*uh*-beyt]

Meaning: scheme; produce by hatching; give form to

Usage 1: The hen will *incubate* the eggs to ensure that every one of them hatches.

Usage 2: It appeared his plan for revenge began to *incubate* at the picnic last summer.

Usage 3: I need to let the idea sit and *incubate* for a while before I act on it.

Usage 4: It does not surprise me that, in nature, it generally falls to the females to *incubate* any offspring.

Usage 5: Can we *incubate* these eggs artificially?

INDENTURE (v)   [in-DEN-cher]

Meaning: bind as servant or apprentice to master; to commit to service by formal agreement

Usage 1: To come to this country, my ancestors were forced to *indenture* themselves.

Usage 2: Volunteering is one thing, but you don't want to *indenture* yourself.

Usage 3: He resisted the temptation to *indenture* himself simply to gain work experience.

Usage 4: I refuse to *indenture* myself and become a slave to house-cleaning.

Usage 5: Was the requirement to *indenture* oneself pervasive in all of the colonies?

INDISPUTABLE (adj)   [in-di-SPYOO-t*uh*-b*uh* l]

Meaning: too certain to be disputed; undeniable

Usage 1: Her win at the competition was decisive and *indisputable*.

Usage 2: Many argue that the signs of global warming are *indisputable*.

Usage 3: He wisely took the *indisputable* position that he and his team were at fault in the matter.

Usage 4: After missing two deadlines, my inability to multi-task was *indisputable*.

Usage 5: Why does she treat those facts as *indisputable* when they are still being questioned?

INEFFECTUAL (adj)   [in-i-FEK-choo-*uh* l]

Meaning: not effective; weak; not working; futile

Usage 1: Her *ineffectual* response to the situation got her fired.

Usage 2: Adding vegetable oil to the chocolate was *ineffectual*; it remained a massive clump.

Usage 3: The survey revealed that the program had been *ineffectual* in educating the public.

Usage 4: My efforts to clean the house were *ineffectual* because the mud-ridden soccer team soon undid them.

Usage 5: Won't this plan be *ineffectual* unless all parties actively participate?

INEPT (adj)   [in-EPT]

Meaning: lacking skill; unsuited; incompetent; not capable

Usage 1: We cannot tolerate another *inept* handling of this crisis.

Usage 2: Without proper training, their actions will repeatedly be judged as *inept*.

Usage 3: His response to the public about the scandal was completely *inept*.

Usage 4: Because I completely lacked musical talent, I felt *inept* to judge the singing competition.

Usage 5: Would that candidate be competent or *inept* at handling this difficult situation?

INFALLIBLE (adj)   [in-FAL-*uh*-b*uh* l]

Meaning: unerring; unable to make mistakes

Usage 1: Notwithstanding common misconceptions, even a robot is not *infallible*.

Usage 2: You set yourself up for disaster if you take the position that your invention is *infallible*.

Usage 3: His performance on the ice at the Olympics was utterly *infallible*.

Usage 4: I don't claim to be *infallible*; I just claim to be right all of the time.

Usage 5: Doesn't the mere fact that you think you are *infallible* make you fallible?

INITIATE (v)   [ih-NISH-ee-eyt]

Meaning: begin; originate; receive into a group; to start

Usage 1: It is important that you be the one to *initiate* the conversation.

Usage 2: We will *initiate* new members in the fall.

Usage 3: I want to *initiate* this discussion with our areas of agreement, not those of discord.

Usage 4: I can't believe they are asking me to *initiate* this plan of action.

Usage 5: Did you *initiate* the argument or did she?

This page is intentionally left blank

Chapter 6

Insightful – Monetary

This chapter covers the following words, each with its part of speech, pronunciation, and descriptive meaning.

Usage of the word is also illustrated in three to five sample sentences.

insightful	languish	manifest
insolence	leaven	manipulate
insolvent	leery	marred
intellect	liaison	maul
inverse	ligneous	mauve
invoke	limpid	maxim
irreparable	lineage	mentor
isotope	linguistic	merger
jettison	litotes	methodical
jocose	low	migratory
jostle	luminary	millennium
jurisprudence	lurk	minuscule
ken	maelstrom	miscellany
kindred	magnate	missive
laborious	magnitude	molecule
laity	malign	monetary
lancet	mammoth	

INSIGHTFUL (adj) [IN-sahyt-*fuh* l]

Meaning: displaying discernment

Usage 1: The children's responses were surprisingly *insightful*.

Usage 2: Even though this is not your expertise, your opinion on these matters is always *insightful*.

Usage 3: Her newspaper editorial was praised as an *insightful* foray into the heart of the matter.

Usage 4: I am feeling less than *insightful* today; tell me again what it is that you want.

Usage 5: Will your poetry be brilliant and *insightful* as usual?

INSOLENCE (n) [IN-*suh*-*luh* ns]

Meaning: impudent; haughtiness; brazenly rude or disrespectful

Usage 1: Her *insolence* to the judge did not go unnoticed.

Usage 2: Such *insolence* in one so young is difficult to comprehend.

Usage 3: If it were not for his *insolence*, I would have been happy to help him out.

Usage 4: Some people call it *insolence*, but I think of it as in-your-face self-confidence.

Usage 5: Will his *insolence* affect his scoring by the gymnastics judges?

INSOLVENT (adj) [in-SOL-v*uh* nt]

Meaning: bankrupt; unable to repay one's debts; having more debt than money to pay the debt

Usage 1: The bank regulators realized that many of the banks were hiding the fact that they were *insolvent*.

Usage 2: When the company admitted it was *insolvent*, hundreds lost their jobs.

Usage 3: The government is spending so much more than it receives in taxes that soon it will become *insolvent*.

Usage 4: My goal is not to become *insolvent* during the first month of my freshman year in college.

Usage 5: Will the fact that she is *insolvent* affect the closing on the house?

INTELLECT (n) [IN-tl-ekt]

Meaning: higher mental powers; mental ability

Usage 1: It wasn't his good looks that attracted me, but his *intellect*.

Usage 2: With such an *intellect*, she will not want for college scholarship offers.

Usage 3: The power of his *intellect*, alone, was persuasive.

Usage 4: It was a case of my emotions overpowering my *intellect*.

Usage 5: Is he lacking in *intellect*, or was this simply an unwise decision?

INVERSE (adj) [in-VURS]

Meaning: opposite; reversed in position or direction

Usage 1: The answer you got for number two on your math worksheet is the *inverse* of the correct answer.

Usage 2: My position on this issue is not what she described, but is the *inverse*.

Usage 3: The correlation is not a positive one but an *inverse* one

Usage 4: My desire to eat was in *inverse* proportion to my desire to be unemployed.

Usage 5: Her exultation at our increased profitability was *inverse* to mine; I wanted to leave the business.

INVOKE (v) [in-VOHK]

Meaning: call upon; ask for; petition or seek

Usage 1: The elders will *invoke* the wisdom of their ancestors during the ceremony.

Usage 2: If you don't leave me alone, I will *invoke* the aid of the police.

Usage 3: We don't hire moving companies; we *invoke* the assistance of our friends.

Usage 4: I will *invoke* the first rule of motherhood: whatever the situation, Mom is always right.

Usage 5: How can they *invoke* the new rules without having them approved by the membership?

IRREPARABLE (adj)   [ih-REP-er-*uh-buh* l]

Meaning: not able to be corrected or repaired; incapable of being repaired or rectified

Usage 1: The damage to her reputation after she was found to have lied to the public was *irreparable*.

Usage 2: If you take this course of action, the damage you cause will be *irreparable*.

Usage 3: Her grandmother's antique cookie jar was *irreparable* after if fell off the fridge and broke into hundreds of pieces.

Usage 4: I am done with women; being abandoned at the altar has left me with a credit card bill that is enormous and a heart that is *irreparable*.

Usage 5: Were you aware that smoking does *irreparable* damage to the lungs?

ISOTOPE (n)   [AHY-s*uh*-tohp]

Meaning: varying form of an element; a form of a chemical element whose atoms contain the same number of protons but a different number of neutrons

Usage 1: Today we will be studying radioactive *isotopes* and their use to create energy.

Usage 2: An element and its *isotope* react very similarly in the laboratory.

Usage 3: It is not unusual, even in modern times, for a new chemical *isotope* to be discovered.

Usage 4: The twins were like *isotopes* of one another; they were similar in many ways, but in one or two ways completely different.

Usage 5: What is the difference between uranium and its *isotopes*?

JETTISON (v)   [JET-*uh-suh* n]

Meaning: throw overboard; throw away from

Usage 1: The ship was sinking, and the crew had to *jettison* the passenger's luggage.

Usage 2: The spaceship was on a regular schedule to *jettison* refuse into what amounted to space garbage trucks.

Usage 3: Don't throw out the entire agreement; simply *jettison* the objectionable parts.

Usage 4: I told my son that if he didn't straighten up, I would *jettison* his personal belongings out his bedroom window.

Usage 5: Is it standard procedure for a plane to *jettison* fuel before a crash?

JOCOSE (adj)   [joh-KOHS]

Meaning: given to joking; a joking manner

Usage 1: His *jocose* manner made me believe that the matter was not too serious.

Usage 2: Don't be fooled by his *jocose* demeanor; he is deadly serious.

Usage 3: Her *jocose* personality made her popular with little children.

Usage 4: It is hard to be *jocose* when the world is falling around your ears.

Usage 5: Is her personality somber or *jocose*?

JOSTLE (v)   [JOS-*uh* l]

Meaning: bump; a light shoving

Usage 1: Be careful not to *jostle* the baby; she's just eaten.

Usage 2: The children tend to play and *jostle* one another in the back seat of the car.

Usage 3: If you *jostle* his headphones, he'll know you're talking to him.

Usage 4: The microwave works as long as you *jostle* the handle and punch each of the buttons twice.

Usage 5: Could someone *jostle* the plastic keys above the infant's head to distract him?

JURISPRUDENCE (n)   [j*oo* r-is-PROOD-ns]

Meaning: a system of laws; the science or study of law

Usage 1: His long career in *jurisprudence* told him that this was no way to run a country.

Usage 2: Under the commonly accepted principles of *jurisprudence*, ignorance of the law is no defense.

Usage 3: We will introduce a new *jurisprudence* to the countries that were once ruled by dictators.

Usage 4: Without knowing the *jurisprudence* on the issue, I was terrified of the legal ramifications of her acts.

Usage 5: Does your knowledge of *jurisprudence* help you as you decide disputes during the soccer matches?

KEN (n)   [ken]

Meaning: range of knowledge; one's mental perception

Usage 1: The citified ways of the visitor were beyond her countrified *ken*.

Usage 2: Criminal law is outside of my *ken*; I was a corporate lawyer.

Usage 3: In my *ken*, cheating one's neighbor is simply wrong.

Usage 4: My husband always pretended that using a toilet brush was out of his *ken*.

Usage 5: Is building a campfire within your *ken*?

KINDRED (adj)   [KIN-drid]

Meaning: related; belonging to the same family; bearing a familial relationship or some sort of affinity

Usage 1: We had a *kindred* affiliation; he was my cousin.

Usage 2: I could tell she was a *kindred* spirit; she loved animals, too.

Usage 3: I had no idea we had a *kindred* connection until we shared our family photographs.

Usage 4: As *kindred* souls, being miles apart did not affect their friendship.

Usage 5: Even though they are different breeds, don't the dogs look enough alike to be *kindred*?

LABORIOUS (adj)   [l*uh*-BAWR-ee-*uh* s]

Meaning: demanding much work or care; tedious; requiring extra effort or care

Usage 1: The process of writing can be *laborious*, depending on the task.

Usage 2: Decorating the cake was *laborious*; each rose petal and stem had to be hand-crafted.

Usage 3: Painting the outside of the old house was *laborious*; the shingles absorbed the first two coats of paint.

Usage 4: I find housework *laborious*; just when you finish, you need to start all over again.

Usage 5: Was milking the cows by hand *laborious*?

LAITY (n)   [LEY-i-tee]

Meaning: laypersons; persons not connected with the clergy; church members who are not the preacher or priest; people outside a profession

Usage 1: It was the *laity* of the church that initiated the fundraiser for the steeple.

Usage 2: The priest felt it was a question, not for the clergy, but for the *laity*.

Usage 3: I was a member of the *laity* on this issue; oil drilling was completely outside my area of expertise.

Usage 4: When it came to raising children, my husband was a member of the *laity*.

Usage 5: Should we consult the *laity* on the plans for our Easter celebration?

LANCET (n) [LAN-sit]

Meaning: small surgical tool for making incisions; small, sharp instrument used for cutting into skin

Usage 1: He needed a *lancet* to pierce his finger so that he could check his blood sugar levels.

Usage 2: Please make sure you sterilize the *lancet* before we use it again.

Usage 3: You could use a sewing needle, but a *lancet* is preferable.

Usage 4: I was going to draw his blood, whether it was with a *lancet* or a lance.

Usage 5: Have you ever used a *lancet* to draw blood?

LANGUISH (v) [LANG-gwish]

Meaning: to become languid or sluggish; to exist unproductively; be ignored

Usage 1: After she was indicted on the fraud charges, she chose to *languish* under house arrest.

Usage 2: He meant to *languish* by the pool throughout the seven days on the cruise.

Usage 3: We need to make sure the legislation does not *languish* in committee; get a vote on it.

Usage 4: I'd love to *languish* for three days in the swimming pool, except we don't have a swimming pool.

Usage 5: Why are you allowing those electric generators to *languish* in the warehouse?

LEAVEN (v) [LEV-*uh* n]

Meaning: cause to rise or grow lighter; enliven; to make something less serious; lighten up

Usage 1: We can *leaven* the bread now that it is no longer Passover.

Usage 2: We need to *leaven* the mood in the boardroom; it is grim in there.

Usage 3: Her barrage of silly comments could not help but *leaven* everyone's mood.

Usage 4: I tried to *leaven* the dough by pumping it with air; that didn't work.

Usage 5: Isn't yeast usually used to *leaven* bread?

LEERY (adj) [LEER-ee]

Meaning: suspicious; cautious; wary

Usage 1: I was *leery* of buying a house immediately after the housing bubble burst.

Usage 2: His run-in with the stampeding horses made him *leery* of ever riding again.

Usage 3: It is wise to be *leery* of getting into debt.

Usage 4: Don't be *leery* of asking questions; it's the best way to learn.

Usage 5: The bears looked cuddly; what was there to be *leery* of?

LIAISON (n) [LEE-*uh*-zon]

Meaning: contact keeping parts of an organization in communication; secret love affair; a go-between to ensure cooperation; a secret sexual relationship

Usage 1: They asked him to be a *liaison* between the townspeople and the railroad company.

Usage 2: As a *liaison* between homicide and vice, I don't see any reason the two groups can't work together.

Usage 3: His *liaison* with those women cost him an election.

Usage 4: It turned out his alibi was his *liaison* with my best friend.

Usage 5: Have you met the *liaison* between the U.S. scientists and the Canadian ones?

LIGNEOUS (adj) [LIG-nee-*uh* s]

Meaning: like wood; resembling wood

Usage 1: The canoe felt *ligneous*, but it was actually made from a plastic composite.

Usage 2: The stones were *ligneous*, their striations looking like grains in the wood.

Usage 3: The product of the 3D printer was at least *ligneous*, even though it was not made of wood.

Usage 4: She carves *ligneous* material, not wood.

Usage 5: Did you see the *ligneous* sculpture that looks like a wooden statue?

LIMPID (adj)   [LIM-pid]

Meaning: clear; transparent

Usage 1: He stared down into her *limpid* green eyes and instantly fell in love.

Usage 2: The waters of Crescent Lake were refreshingly blue and *limpid*; you could see the lake bottom.

Usage 3: Her true meaning is *limpid*; she does not agree with our position.

Usage 4: The play's dialogue was surprisingly effective: both short and *limpid*.

Usage 5: Can you see the wispy clouds, almost *limpid* in their appearance?

LINEAGE (n)   [LIN-ee-ij]

Meaning: descent; ancestry; line of family ancestors

Usage 1: The *lineage* of the kings and queens of Europe was far from clear.

Usage 2: She comes from a *lineage* of talented musicians.

Usage 3: He is the latest in a *lineage* steeped in contributors to the arts.

Usage 4: I get confused about my *lineage* because no one will admit that I am his or her offspring.

Usage 5: Have you tried to trace your *lineage* using online resources?

LINGUISTIC (adj)   [ling-GWIS-tik]

Meaning: pertaining to language; language-related

Usage 1: She was unable to come up with an appropriate *linguistic* response, so she flapped her arms.

Usage 2: As a student of *linguistic* science, she catches nuances in the way we speak.

Usage 3: My son has become fascinated with *linguistic* research, and he will pursue that field in college.

Usage 4: I'm not sure if it was my *linguistic* emphasis or my body language that conveyed the message: go away.

Usage 5: What are a chimpanzee's *linguistic* capabilities?

LITOTES (n)   [LAHY-t*uh*-teez]

Meaning: understatement for emphasis; understatement (usually in the negative)

Usage 1: I prefer *litotes*, rather than hyperbole, when I am creating dialogue that is not unfunny.

Usage 2: When I asked him what he thought of my *litotes*, he replied, "not bad."

Usage 3: She thought a more frequent use of *litotes* was not unwelcome.

Usage 4: It was my use of sarcastic *litotes* that got me into a "not good" situation with my professor.

Usage 5: Is it "not wrong" to think of the *litotes* frequently appearing as double negatives?

LOW (v)   [loh]

Meaning: moo; to make a deep sound (as in the sound a cow makes)

Usage 1: We figured out where the escaped cows had gone because we heard them *low*.

Usage 2: What causes a cow to *low*?

Usage 3: When cows *low*, it can indicate that they are fearful.

Usage 4: The cattle *low* every time we approach them.

Usage 5: Do blue whales *low*?

LUMINARY (n) [LOO-m*uh*-ner-ee]

Meaning: celebrity; dignitary; enlightening person

Usage 1: She was a *luminary* in the field of aeronautics.

Usage 2: His world travels gave him wisdom beyond his year; he was a *luminary*.

Usage 3: Because he was a *luminary* of both the stage and screen, we were honored to have him as a drama teacher.

Usage 4: Some consider me a *luminary* in the field of cleaning products.

Usage 5: Isn't he a *luminary* in the field of major league baseball?

LURK (v) [lurk]

Meaning: stealthily lie in waiting; slink; exist unperceived; remain in a place secretly

Usage 1: Don't just *lurk* in the shadows; come out and greet our guests.

Usage 2: In our hearts *lurk* many aspirations for wealth and beauty; even if we don't admit it.

Usage 3: I asked the group of teenagers not to *lurk* by the dumpster behind the theater.

Usage 4: I don't want to *lurk* here by the window; he'll think I'm stalking him.

Usage 5: Do you know that water moccasins tend to *lurk* in the tangle of roots along the river banks?

MAELSTROM (n) [MEYL-str*uh* m]

Meaning: a violent whirlpool; a tumultuous situation

Usage 1: We could see the *maelstrom* at the center of the river from where we sat on the raft.

Usage 2: As the roof of the shelter was torn off by the tornado, we could see the *maelstrom* of the storm.

Usage 3: They thrust her into the *maelstrom* of an already- turbulent situation.

Usage 4: I didn't want to tell him about the car accident because I didn't want to experience the *maelstrom* of his temper.

Usage 5: What would happen if our canoe entered that *maelstrom*?

MAGNATE (n) [MAG-neyt]

Meaning: person of prominence or influence; an influential person (often wealthy)

Usage 1: The railroad *magnates* in the early 20th century were some of the wealthiest men of their day.

Usage 2: One of the victims of the small-plane crash was a local real-estate *magnate*.

Usage 3: Upon achieving wealth, many *magnates* seek to exert their influence by supporting charitable causes.

Usage 4: With wealth comes power; with a wealthy *magnate* comes influence.

Usage 5: Would you consider Bill Gates a modern *magnate*?

MAGNITUDE (n) [MAG-ni-tood]

Meaning: extent; greatness of size

Usage 1: The earthquake was small, but of sufficient *magnitude* to rattle our nerves.

Usage 2: The *magnitude* of that star will change over the course of time.

Usage 3: I don't think you realize the *magnitude* of your mistake.

Usage 4: It was the first time he'd witnessed a temper tantrum of this *magnitude*.

Usage 5: How does the *magnitude* of an earthquake affect the amount of damage it does?

MALIGN (v) [m*uh*-LAHYN]

Meaning: speak evil of; bad-mouth; defame; speak badly about; slander

Usage 1: I don't mean to *malign* him, but his workmanship is a disaster.

Usage 2: She couldn't help but *malign* every opposing player on the field.

Usage 3: To *malign* a person just because they won is clearly bad sportsmanship.

Usage 4: I did not need to *malign* her; she was doing a great job of it, herself.

Usage 5: Why do you always *malign* complete strangers who have no connection to you?

MAMMOTH (adj)   [MAM-*uh* th]

Meaning: gigantic; enormous; extremely large

Usage 1: It was a *mammoth* sea creature, and it made an eerie sound.

Usage 2: The *mammoth* tornado was headed straight towards us.

Usage 3: Building the pyramids must have been a *mammoth* undertaking.

Usage 4: In a display of *mammoth* restraint, I kept my opinions to myself.

Usage 5: Did you visit that *mammoth* cave in Kentucky?

MANIFEST (adj)   [MAN-*uh*-fest]

Meaning: understandable; clear; readily perceived; obvious

Usage 1: Her skill at playing the piano was *manifest* at the recital.

Usage 2: His many charms were *manifest* to the young ladies present.

Usage 3: I think the inadequacy of the precautions will become *manifest* once tornado season arrives.

Usage 4: It was *manifest* that she had no intention of going to the prom with me.

Usage 5: Were my instructions *manifest*, or do I need to simplify them for you?

MANIPULATE (v)   [m*uh*-NIP-y*uh*-leyt]

Meaning: operate with one's hands; control or play upon (people, forces, etc.) artfully; handle with the hands; skillfully maneuver or control

Usage 1: This lesson allows the children to *manipulate* the building materials, themselves.

Usage 2: I wish I could *manipulate* the controls on that crane as skillfully as he does.

Usage 3: I'll never learn to *manipulate* the screens on my smartphone properly.

Usage 4: I know her intent was to *manipulate* me into hosting the party, and it worked.

Usage 5: Do you find it difficult to *manipulate* the steering wheel single-handedly?

MARRED (adj)   [mahrd]

Meaning: damaged; disfigured; spoiled; rendered less attractive

Usage 1: His naturally good looks were *marred* by the snarl he always wore on his face.

Usage 2: The surface of the beautiful antique table had been *marred* by the careless movers.

Usage 3: The only thing that *marred* my happiness at winning the race was the sight of his unhappiness at losing it.

Usage 4: Our first day on the Baltic cruise was *marred* by the fact that we were seasick the entire day.

Usage 5: How could they have *marred* the beautiful ocean view by building another ghastly hotel?

MAUL (v)   [mawl]

Meaning: handle roughly; injure or damage through rough treatment

Usage 1: Don't move, or the bear might *maul* you.

Usage 2: You can't let the cats *maul* the living room sofa like that.

Usage 3: Surely your pet ferret did not intentionally *maul* my favorite slippers.

Usage 4: Wait until your grandmother leaves and I'll let you *maul* each other as much as you want.

Usage 5: What possessed you to *maul* my stuffed animals like that?

MAUVE (adj)   [mohv]
Meaning: pale purple; light purple with a bluish tinge
Usage 1: The bridesmaid's dress was a beautiful *mauve* color that matched the floral displays.
Usage 2: The purple ranged from an intensely violet hue to an almost-bluish *mauve* color.
Usage 3: The fall grasses were a delicate *mauve* in the setting sun.
Usage 4: I've never liked that *mauve* dress; it always looked like a faded rag to me.
Usage 5: What colors on the palette do you mix to achieve a *mauve* pigment?

MAXIM (n)   [MAK-sim]
Meaning: proverb; a truth, pithily stated; an adage; the statement of a piece of wisdom
Usage 1: I have a book that contains every *maxim* Mark Twain ever wrote.
Usage 2: Benjamin Franklin's Poor Richard's Almanac contains many a pithy *maxim*.
Usage 3: Taking apart a *maxim* to determine its source is one of my favorite pastimes.
Usage 4: If she spat one more overused *maxim* at me, I was going to throw a book at her.
Usage 5: How true is the *maxim* "with knowledge comes power"?

MENTOR (n)   [MEN-tawr]
Meaning: teacher; counselor; helper; role model
Usage 1: She was a *mentor* to ten former students last summer.
Usage 2: He signed up to be a *mentor* at the youth center, playing basketball with girls and boys from troubled homes.
Usage 3: I cannot thank the *mentor* I had when I was eleven years old for the positive effects he had on my life.
Usage 4: He was both my *mentor* and my friend.
Usage 5: Do you think a *mentor* might help her gain confidence in her skills?

MERGER (n)   [MUR-jer]
Meaning: combination (of two business corporations); a joining together
Usage 1: The *merger* between AT&T and Direct TV is currently being evaluated by the FCC.
Usage 2: We moved to Georgia after the airline in which my dad worked entered a *merger* with another airline.
Usage 3: A *merger* of our efforts here makes perfect sense so that we don't repeat each others' efforts.
Usage 4: I was talking about marriage; he was talking about a business *merger*.
Usage 5: Do you think the *merger* will ultimately result in higher prices for an airline ticket?

METHODICAL (adj)   [m*uh*-THOD-i-k*uh* l]
Meaning: systematic; orderly; slow and deliberate
Usage 1: She *methodically* extracted the slivers of glass that had embedded into his finger.
Usage 2: The study *methodically* analyzes the rate at which the icebergs are melting.
Usage 3: He *methodically* itemized his deductions, including those under a dollar.
Usage 4: I will *methodically* position the pebbles until they form a beautiful mosaic.
Usage 5: Aren't they *methodically* tracking the last movements of the airplane?

MIGRATORY (adj)   [MAHY-gr*uh*-tawr-ee]

Meaning: wandering; roaming; moving from place to place (often with the change in seasons)

Usage 1: Each year we require over two hundred *migratory* workers to pick the grapes.

Usage 2: It was his *migratory* nature that would not allow him to settle down.

Usage 3: Studying the *migratory* patterns of the polar bears was utterly fascinating.

Usage 4: The advantage of being *migratory* is that your creditors have trouble locating you.

Usage 5: Do you enjoy being *migratory*, traveling to Iceland each summer and back to the U.S. each winter?

MILLENNIUM (n)   [mi-LEN-ee-*uh* m]

Meaning: a period of a thousand years; a long period

Usage 1: During my lifetime, we traversed into the second *millennium* on the Julian calendar.

Usage 2: The glory of Camelot is reputed to have lasted for a *millennium*.

Usage 3: We looked back joyfully on a *millennium* of peace, prosperity, and the advancement of knowledge and understanding.

Usage 4: The enchanted prince slept for a *millennium* until the princess took a hammer to his glass coffin.

Usage 5: Do you know where you will be when we cross into the next *millennium*?

MINUSCULE (adj)   [MIN-*uh*-skyool]

Meaning: extremely small; tiny

Usage 1: With a *minuscule* of effort, you could have reached your goal.

Usage 2: The ladybug was a *minuscule*, but welcome, addition to the coloring of the leaf.

Usage 3: I told him I had a *minuscule* problem that was about to become an enormous one.

Usage 4: As my friends pointed out, the diamond in the engagement ring was *minuscule*.

Usage 5: Aren't you tired of our paychecks being *minuscule*?

MISCELLANY (n)   [MIS-*uh*-ley-nee]

Meaning: mixture of writings on various subjects; a group of unrelated items

Usage 1: The hard-bound book my grandmother gave me was filled with *miscellany* on every topic from Greek mythology to science fiction.

Usage 2: The toddler was entertained with *miscellany* from the bedroom closet: a broken telephone, a bean bag chair, and a pack of plastic soldiers.

Usage 3: We searched for dried flowers, ribbon, and other *miscellany* that we could use to dress the tables at Tammy's wedding shower.

Usage 4: I just cleaned out that junk drawer and took out a ton of *miscellany*, ranging from wads of garbage bag ties to packets of Chinese mustard.

Usage 5: Do you have any *miscellany* in your closet that we can donate to the charity shop?

MISSIVE (n)   [MIS-iv]

Meaning: a letter or communication

Usage 1: Her *missive* was on the back of a used envelope.

Usage 2: He sent a handwritten *missive* to the rebel forces in the hopes of spurring peace discussions.

Usage 3: I read your *missive*, but I didn't understand it.

Usage 4: I refuse to accept another *missive* from you; the last one was vile.

Usage 5: What did his *missive* say about the plan for tomorrow?

MOLECULE (n)   [MOL-*uh*-kyool]

Meaning: the smallest particle of a substance that has all the properties of that substance; the smallest unit of a compound; something very small

Usage 1: There are two atoms of hydrogen and one atom of oxygen in a *molecule* of water

Usage 2: In science today, we will study the structure of the *molecule*.

Usage 3: A molecule of sodium chloride differs from a *molecule* of hydrogen fluoride.

Usage 4: With every *molecule* of my body, I hated the situation.

Usage 5: Is that your model of a *molecule*?

MONETARY (adj)   [MON-i-ter-ee]

Meaning: pertaining to money; having to do with money

Usage 1: Our goal is, of course, *monetary* gain in all segments of the company.

Usage 2: My need to change jobs was not a *monetary* issue.

Usage 3: The *monetary* concerns for this project are paramount.

Usage 4: My complaints about him were not *monetary*; he was simply a schmuck.

Usage 5: Have you considered the *monetary* aspects of developing this new technology?

This page is intentionally left blank

Chapter 7

Mortician – Practicable

This chapter covers the following words, each with its part of speech, pronunciation, and descriptive meaning.

Usage of the word is also illustrated in three to five sample sentences.

mortician	omnipresent	penance
multiplicity	omnivorous	perimeter
mutable	onomatopoeia	periphery
mutinous	ordain	perjury
nadir	orient	perpetuate
narrative	outspoken	perturb
novelty	pacifist	pestle
nubile	pacify	phylum
nugatory	palatable	pique
nullify	pallid	pivotal
nuptial	paltry	pluck
oaf	panacea	polarize
obese	pandemic	polemical
oblivion	pandemonium	polity
obsidian	partiality	portent
obsolete	pathos	practicable
ominous	patronize	

MORTICIAN (n)   [mawr-TISH-*uh* n]

Meaning: undertaker; one who arranges funerals; a funeral director

Usage 1: The *mortician* was extremely useful in helping us plan the funeral.

Usage 2: We will need to talk to the *mortician* about options for caskets.

Usage 3: That check should be used to pay the *mortician* and the funeral home.

Usage 4: Given her interest in the color black, I thought a job as a *mortician* would be suitable for her.

Usage 5: Didn't you tell me that your uncle was a *mortician*?

MULTIPLICITY (n)   [muhl-t*uh*-PLIS-i-tee]

Meaning: state of being numerous; a large number or variety of

Usage 1: There were *multiplicities* of reasons not to take the plunge in this market.

Usage 2: She gave us a *multiplicity* of items to consider when weighing the pros and cons.

Usage 3: His *multiplicity* of plans to improve the house overwhelmed me.

Usage 4: Which, among the *multiplicity* of lame excuses, are you going to pick?

Usage 5: Of the *multiplicity* of the items to think about, which is the most important?

MUTABLE (adj)   [MYOO-t*uh*-b*uh* l]

Meaning: changing in form; fickle; subject to change; changeable

Usage 1: Our plans are *mutable* if we don't win the vote.

Usage 2: Her feelings were *mutable*, depending on the time of day.

Usage 3: The help sessions are *mutable*, based on the areas where help is needed most.

Usage 4: The ever-changing weather made our picnic plans *mutable*.

Usage 5: When did you realize that her behavior was *mutable* and depended on who she was with?

MUTINOUS (adj)   [MYOOT-n-*uh* s]

Meaning: unruly; rebellious; difficult to control

Usage 1: The angry crew members became *mutinous* when they were told about the food shortage.

Usage 2: The situation between the prison guards and the prisoners had become *mutinous*.

Usage 3: I may become *mutinous* if people around here don't start appreciating the work I do.

Usage 4: With that *mutinous* look in her eye, she was capable of anything.

NADIR (n)   [NEY-der]

Meaning: lowest point; a point of greatest despair

Usage 1: She had reached the *nadir* of despair after five months of unsuccessfully seeking a job.

Usage 2: I could not imagine a deeper *nadir* than that to which he had sunk.

Usage 3: In the valley, the *nadir* between two tall mountains, sat a small farmhouse.

Usage 4: When I lied to him for the third time, I realized I had sunk to the *nadir* of dishonesty.

Usage 5: At what point will you realize that you've reached your *nadir*?

NARRATIVE (adj)   [NAR-*uh*-tiv]

Meaning: pertaining to the telling of a story

Usage 1: I always enjoy my uncle's *narrative* when we pick him up at the airport.

Usage 2: It was a *narrative* filled with danger and adventure.

Usage 3: You began with informational writing, but you have devolved into a *narrative*.

Usage 4: If my life was a *narrative*, it would surely be in the disaster genre.

Usage 5: Have you considered telling this in *narrative* form to an audience?

NOVELTY (n) [NOV-*uh* l-tee]
Meaning: something new; newness; the state or quality of being new
Usage 1: Living in Alaska was such a *novelty* at first that we didn't mind the snow.
Usage 2: The *novelty* of the situation clearly wore off, and we found ourselves miserable.
Usage 3: Those tacky statues are clearly *novelty*; they will soon fade from popularity.
Usage 4: Enjoying my time with the in-laws was incredible *novelty*.
Usage 5: Don't you think that toy is simply a *novelty*?

NUBILE (adj) [NOO-bil]
Meaning: ready to be married; sexually alluring
Usage 1: She was a *nubile* young woman, and she was ready to experience the world.
Usage 2: The beach had an abundance of *nubile* young females in skimpy bathing suits.
Usage 3: I told my brother to be careful when his girls became *nubile*.
Usage 4: I don't think I was ever *nubile*; I went straight to matronly.
Usage 5: Her chances of marrying are better because she is young and *nubile*.

NUGATORY (adj) [NOO-g*uh*-tawr-ee]
Meaning: trifling; lacking value of any kind; worthless
Usage 1: They say the effect of the oil spill on ocean life will be *nugatory*, but I don't believe them.
Usage 2: My sympathy for him by that point was *nugatory*; he had worn me out.
Usage 3: Even test results that are *nugatory* can be useful.
Usage 4: Is it a bad thing if your bank account statement says, beside your balance, the word *"nugatory"*?
Usage 5: Do you think his belief in me had been reduced to a *nugatory* one?

NULLIFY (v) [NUHL-*uh*-fahy]
Meaning: to make invalid; declare legally void
Usage 1: It was only a week before they decided to *nullify* marriage.
Usage 2: These test scores *nullify* any criticism of the efforts you made this year.
Usage 3: If we *nullify* the law, we have no idea of what effect that will have.
Usage 4: I can *nullify* my marriage, but I can't seem to nullify my kids.
Usage 5: What can we do to *nullify* her ridiculous positions?

NUPTIAL (adj) [NUHP-sh*uh* l]
Meaning: pertaining to marriage or mating
Usage 1: They will make their *nuptial* announcement at dinner tonight.
Usage 2: Our *nuptial* plans are to get married in the church and to have reception by the beach.
Usage 3: My grandmother was relieved to learn that we were now a *nuptial* couple.
Usage 4: Ironically, we were somehow booked in the *nuptial* suite at the hotel.
Usage 5: Have you already decided on your *nuptial* vows for the ceremony?

OAF (n) [ohf]
Meaning: awkward person; a stupid, clumsy person
Usage 1: Her new husband is delightful; her former husband was an *oaf*.

Usage 2: I did not raise you to be an *oaf*; you need to pay attention to what you are doing.

Usage 3: The new recruits ranged from high-performers to struggling young men; there was only one *oaf* in the bunch.

Usage 4: Under that exterior of an *oaf* lies a skilled manipulator.

Usage 5: What an *oaf*; how could he miss a ball that was headed straight for him?

OBESE (adj) [oh-BEES]

Meaning: very fat; corpulent; extremely overweight

Usage 1: Being *obese* can lead to many illnesses, including diabetes.

Usage 2: Because she was *obese*, even walking the short distance to the entrance of the grocery store caused her to be out of breath.

Usage 3: If you keep eating French Fries every day, you will soon find that you are *obese*.

Usage 4: I looked in the mirror; I was no longer pudgy—I was *obese*.

Usage 5: Will he work with those who need help with nutrition and/or are *obese*?

OBLIVION (n) [*uh*-BLIV-ee-*uh* n]

Meaning: obscurity; forgetfulness; the state of being unknown or not remembered

Usage 1: Out in space, one false step can send you into *oblivion*.

Usage 2: After the automobile accident, she drank herself into *oblivion* each night.

Usage 3: Those old movie stars seem to have wandered into *oblivion*.

Usage 4: If you don't leave me alone, you are going to experience *oblivion* up close and personal.

Usage 5: Do you think that, after years of constant celebrity attention, she was hoping to sink into the protection of *oblivion*?

OBSIDIAN (n) [*uh* b-SID-ee-*uh*-n]

Meaning: glass made from volcanic rock

Usage 1: We acquired that piece of *obsidian* in Hawaii when visiting the volcanoes.

Usage 2: The statue on the shelf, with its unusual coloring, is actually made of *obsidian*.

Usage 3: Unlike some rocks, when it is broken, *obsidian* can be extremely sharp.

Usage 4: He called it an expensive diamond; I called it cheap *obsidian*.

Usage 5: What are the differences between *obsidian* and regular glass?

OBSOLETE (adj) [ob-s*uh*-LEET]

Meaning: no longer useful; outdated; antiquated; no longer in general use

Usage 1: With the change in construction techniques, our plans for the factory are now *obsolete*.

Usage 2: The new Supreme Court decision is so extraordinary that many cases on the subject of intellectual property will now be *obsolete*.

Usage 3: I have tons of blank CDs, but with flash drives those CDs are now *obsolete*.

Usage 4: It is frustrating that my brand new computer will be *obsolete* within two years.

Usage 5: Do you think DVDs will soon be *obsolete* as streaming technologies become increasingly popular?

OMINOUS (adj) [OM-*uh*-n*uh* s]

Meaning: threatening; full of bad omens; foreboding

Usage 1: The wind-whipped branches and dark sky looked *ominous*.

Usage 2: The current economic climate appears to be an *ominous* one for home buyers.

Usage 3: When I broke her new clock, expression on her face looked *ominous*.

Usage 4: The music in the haunted house sounded *ominous* and added to the atmosphere of creepiness.

Usage 5: Don't you find it *ominous* that she keeps telling us we will be okay?

OMNIPRESENT (adj)   [om-n*uh*-PREZ-*uh* nt]

Meaning: universally present; ubiquitous; present everywhere

Usage 1: Evidence of her skill and beauty were *omnipresent*.

Usage 2: If the signs of global warming were not once considered *omnipresent*, they are now.

Usage 3: The indications of the need for aid and assistance in the country were *omnipresent*.

Usage 4: Jenny arrived with her *omnipresent* good humor; it got on my nerves.

Usage 5: Security at the Olympics in Russia was *omnipresent* and distracting.

OMNIVOROUS (adj)   [om-NIV-er-*uh* s]

Meaning: eating both plant and animal food; devouring everything; eating all kinds of food; taking in everything

Usage 1: I always thought, based on their size that all dinosaurs were *omnivorous*, but many were actually herbivorous.

Usage 2: The aliens in your videogame are surprisingly *omnivorous*: able to eat anything that moves and many things that don't move.

Usage 3: The *omnivorous* nature of these volatile markets means that anyone's savings can be eaten up in a matter of minutes.

Usage 4: Our goats are clearly *omnivorous*; yesterday they ate my geraniums, and the plastic pot in which the geraniums came.

Usage 5: How essential was it that humans be *omnivorous* in order to survive as a species?

ONOMATOPOEIA (n)   [on-*uh*-mat-*uh*-PEE-*uh*]

Meaning: words formed in imitation of natural sounds; words that imitate the sound to which they refer (like crash, boom, meow, etc.)

Usage 1: I welcomed the *onomatopoeia* of the city: the crash of garbage can lids, the bang of angrily-shut front doors, and the screech of police and ambulance sirens.

Usage 2: It was the *onomatopoeia* in the children's poem that made it such fun to read aloud.

Usage 3: My favorite form of figurative language when writing a narrative is *onomatopoeia*.

Usage 4: I am not interested in your *onomatopoeia*: your snorts of anger, your growls of displeasure, or your insane barking.

Usage 5: What sonorous words; have you ever experienced such vivid *onomatopoeia*?

ORDAIN (v)   [awr-DEYN]

Meaning: decree or command; grant holy orders; predestine; to order, command, or appoint (often in a religious sense)

Usage 1: Our church leaders will *ordain* the new preacher on Sunday.

Usage 2: The Pope's decision to *ordain* new cardinals from a variety of countries is an exciting one.

Usage 3: I could not *ordain* that our organization use the funds in this manner.

Usage 4: I decided to *ordain* and establish a "hot tub hour" for myself each day.

Usage 5: How can the legislature *ordain* such a foolish piece of legislation?

ORIENT (v)   [AWR-ee-ent]

Meaning: adjust; place in a definite position; become comfortable with one's surroundings

Usage 1: Whenever I get a new city I *orient* myself using my smartphone.

Usage 2: The most effective way to use a map is to *orient* it, based on your surroundings.

Usage 3: The tours to *orient* new students the layout of the college were extremely helpful.

Usage 4: I will have to *orient* myself to having no more screaming and annoying children in the house.

Usage 5: Did you need to *orient* yourself, or do you know where you are?

OUTSPOKEN (adj)   [OUT-SPOH-k*uh* n]

Meaning: candid; blunt; unreserved in speech

Usage 1: She was *outspoken* about her opinion on the new policy at work.

Usage 2: I admired him most for his *outspoken* ways; you always knew where you stood with him.

Usage 3: Our city leaders need to be *outspoken* about the increase in gun violence in the city.

Usage 4: More than once, I have been fired for being *outspoken*.

Usage 5: Is it better to be *outspoken* or reserved?

PACIFIST (n)   [PAS-*uh*-fist]

Meaning: antimilitarist; one who seeks to make peace and is opposed to use of military force

Usage 1: My grandfather was a *pacifist* during World War II.

Usage 2: It was clear the new leader of the country was a *pacifist*, and that was a relief.

Usage 3: It is his religion that requires him to be a *pacifist*.

Usage 4: I was forever playing the *pacifist* in my family among my argumentative brothers and sisters.

Usage 5: Did it take courage to be a *pacifist* when so many felt that going to war was their patriotic duty?

PACIFY (v)   [PAS-*uh*-fahy]

Meaning: soothe; subdue; to calm down

Usage 1: A half a bottle of formula should *pacify* the baby.

Usage 2: I tried to *pacify* the children during the storm by giving them popsicles and telling a story.

Usage 3: In an effort to *pacify* the feuding families, we allowed each of them uninterrupted time during the group discussion.

Usage 4: I refuse to give in simply to *pacify* my family.

Usage 5: Did the attempts to *pacify* Hitler lead to World War II?

PALATABLE (adj)   [PAL-*uh*-t*uh*-b*uh* l]

Meaning: agreeable; pleasing to the taste; pleasant-tasting; acceptable

Usage 1: This gourmet magazine is full of highly-*palatable*, low-carb recipes.

Usage 2: If it is *palatable* to you, we can swim first and then start the barbecue.

Usage 3: The situation was less than *palatable*; there were four of us and only one bed.

Usage 4: I could no longer taste what was *palatable* or not, I'd burned my tongue a half-hour earlier.

Usage 5: Were the entrées at the new restaurant *palatable*?

PALLID (adj)   [PAL-id]

Meaning: wan; unhealthy; pale or faded; uninteresting

Usage 1: While visiting my 90-year-old aunt, I could not take my eyes off of her *pallid*, gnarled hands.

Usage 2: His face went *pallid* when he realized that he'd been caught in a lie.

Usage 3: The mountainside had turned from deep evergreen to *pallid* beige after so many trees had been clear- cut.

Usage 4: Your dancing tonight was unusually lifeless and *pallid*; what happened?

Usage 5: She may be sick; does her face look *pallid* to you?

PALTRY (adj)   [PAWL-tree]

Meaning: insignificant; petty; trifling; ridiculously small (as in an amount); worthless

Usage 1: Given all that I had done for them, I felt it was a *paltry* request.

Usage 2: I would never argue over such a *paltry* amount.

Usage 3: After my temper tantrum, witnessed by everybody in the company, I felt *paltry* and ridiculous.

Usage 4: I warned my children and my husband that my birthday present needed to be something that was neither *paltry* nor pathetic.

Usage 5: Don't his concerns seem *paltry* compared to our bigger issues?

PANACEA (n)   [pan-*uh*-SEE-*uh*]

Meaning: cure-all; a remedy for all ailments or diseases

Usage 1: My great aunt seems to think Extra Virgin olive oil is a *panacea* for anything that itches.

Usage 2: Amendments to the legislation are no *panacea*; the legislation is still heavily flawed.

Usage 3: I'm afraid I cannot offer you a single *panacea* for all your money problems; you will need to come up with a variety of solutions.

Usage 4: The only *panacea* you have for those zeroes in the gradebook is doing your homework.

Usage 5: Is there a *panacea* for utter and complete stupidity?

PANDEMIC (adj)   [pan-DEM-ik]

Meaning: affecting a majority of people; widespread (especially of an illness)

Usage 1: The disease that started in a small village was quickly growing into a *pandemic*.

Usage 2: If we don't take measures now, we will be facing a *pandemic*.

Usage 3: The YouTube video caused a *pandemic* of enthusiasm for Irish dancing.

Usage 4: Was it wrong to wish for a devastating *pandemic* to end my misery and take lots of people with me?

Usage 5: Has the disease reached *pandemic* proportions?

PANDEMONIUM (n)   [pan-d*uh*-MOH-nee-*uh* m]

Meaning: wild tumult; wild chaos or disorder

Usage 1: The city was in *pandemonium* after its home team won the World Series.

Usage 2: After he'd been six weeks on his own, his house was a *pandemonium* of strewn papers, fast food containers, and unemptied garbage cans.

Usage 3: That fraternity house is constantly in *pandemonium*, and they are going to shut it down.

Usage 4: I cannot bear the *pandemonium* of holiday shopping.

Usage 5: Why must their celebrations always be marked by *pandemonium*?

PARTIALITY (n)   [pahr-shee-AL-i-tee]

Meaning: inclination; bias; state or character of being partial

Usage 1: My great aunt's cooking evidenced her *partiality* for garlic; it pervaded everything she cooked.

Usage 2: She could feel her mother's *partiality* for her older sister and it caused her great sadness.

Usage 3: We found the *partiality* of the judge for the attorney of our opponents to be troubling.

Usage 4: My *partiality* for designer shoes is causing great damage to my bank account.

Usage 5: Do you have a *partiality* for green vegetables or for salad?

PATHOS (n)   [PEY-thos]

Meaning: the quality of literature to produce compassion or sympathy

Usage 1: The playwright's new production was filled with drama and *pathos*.

Usage 2: It was the *pathos* in the story that got to me most; I cried my eyes out.

Usage 3: The *pathos* of the situation was now complete: the young victim had died on the operating table.

Usage 4: As usual, the babysitter's excuse for being late was filled with drama and *pathos*.

Usage 5: Did you find it a strange mixture of slapstick comedy and *pathos*?

PATRONIZE (v)   [PEY-tr*uh*-nahyz]

Meaning: support; act superior toward; be a customer of; behave condescendingly towards

Usage 1: Please don't *patronize* me; I know exactly what I'm doing.

Usage 2: She might *patronize* the opera but she has no taste in music, whatsoever.

Usage 3: There is no need to *patronize* my shop if you're going to be rude to the other customers.

Usage 4: She doesn't hesitate to *patronize* me on the topic of education, even though I am a teacher, and she is not.

Usage 5: Do you *patronize* that bar frequently?

PENANCE (n)   [PEN-*uh* ns]

Meaning: self-imposed punishment for sin; confession of a sin

Usage 1: The priest asked him to do *penance* for his embezzlement of funds from the church.

Usage 2: Her community service was an act of *penance*.

Usage 3: The graduating students felt that some sort of *penance* was required after a weekend of debauchery.

Usage 4: Surely I am doing *penance* for sins from an earlier life.

Usage 5: What *penance* did she do for treating her grandfather so horribly?

PERIMETER (n)   [p*uh*-RIM-i-ter]

Meaning: outer boundary; the outermost limits; the border or boundary

Usage 1: We walked the *perimeter* of the prison grounds to ensure there were no breaks in the fence.

Usage 2: If you take the *perimeter* around the city, you'll avoid most of the downtown traffic.

Usage 3: At the *perimeter* of the town, you'll find housing that is less expensive.

Usage 4: After patrolling the *perimeter* of the yard, I decided to let my children camp in the back.

Usage 5: Is the *perimeter* secure?

PERIPHERY (n)   [p*uh*-RIF-*uh*-ree]

Meaning: edge, especially of a round surface; at the edges of something

Usage 1: My eyesight seems to be experiencing difficulty around the *periphery*.

Usage 2: It was not the center of the spider bite that had me concerned; it was the streaks under my skin around the *periphery*.

Usage 3: There was a great deal of violence in the center of the city, although the *periphery* seemed calmer.

Usage 4: At the *periphery* of my vision I saw the approaching tiger, and I got myself out of the way very quickly.

Usage 5: I see the flowers at the center of the mural, but what is at the *periphery*?

PERJURY (n)   [PUR-j*uh*-ree]

Meaning: false testimony while under oath; the act of lying on the witness stand or while under oath

Usage 1: I knew the moment he had lied on the stand and thereby committed *perjury*.

Usage 2: Perjury is a separate crime for which you can be separately punished.

Usage 3: I cannot defend you if you choose to commit *perjury* on the stand.

Usage 4: If I was asked to say, under oath, that I loved my job, I would be committing *perjury*.

Usage 5: Were the charges of *perjury* in addition to the manslaughter charges?

PERPETUATE (v)   [per-PECH-oo-eyt]

Meaning: make something last; to make perpetual or everlasting

Usage 1: We would like to *perpetuate* the notion that the more one reads, the better one gets at reading.

Usage 2: They want to *perpetuate* his care in your facility as long as they have the money to pay for it.

Usage 3: It is important to *perpetuate* the growth of our forests to provide for future generations.

Usage 4: I didn't want anyone to *perpetuate* the myth that I was a pleasant person.

Usage 5: How did someone *perpetuate* a rumor that was so false?

PERTURB (v)   [per-TURB]

Meaning: disturb greatly; to agitate or throw into disorder

Usage 1: Please don't let me *perturb* you, but I wanted to keep you your mail.

Usage 2: After I got the baby quiet, I asked that they not *perturb* her.

Usage 3: It would *perturb* me greatly if she did not invite me to lunch after I helped her all afternoon.

Usage 4: It takes almost nothing to *perturb* me; even a doorbell can cause me to foam at the mouth.

Usage 5: Will I *perturb* you if I come in here and read quietly?

PESTLE (n)   [PES-*uh* l]

Meaning: a tool, usually made of wood or stone, used for grinding items in a bowl (called a mortar)

Usage 1: I like to grind my herbs fresh with a mortar and *pestle*.

Usage 2: We couldn't find his pill crusher so we used a mortar and *pestle*.

Usage 3: You don't need the mortar; we can simply use the *pestle* to smash the coriander seeds against a hard surface.

Usage 4: We have the mortar; have you seen the *pestle*?

Usage 5: We weren't going to be grinding anything with that *pestle*; it had a crack the whole way through it.

PHYLUM (n)   [FAHY-l*uh* m]

Meaning: a major scientific classification of organisms

Usage 1: A *phylum* in a biological hierarchy ranks below a kingdom but above a class.

Usage 2: The members of a *phylum* are typically distinguishable as members of their own group when compared to other groups.

Usage 3: I was confident the terrifically uncouth man who presented himself as Uncle Joe wasn't a member of our *phylum*, let alone our family.

Usage 4: My last date fell within the *phylum* of jerk; class of arrogant jerk; and order of obnoxious, arrogant jerk.

Usage 5: Do you understand the difference in classification among a *phylum*, a class, an order, and a family?

PIQUE (n)   [peek]

Meaning: in a state of anger, irritation, or resentment

Usage 1: After arguing with her for an hour I ended up in such a *pique* that I could not sleep.

Usage 2: I was in a *pique* after my brother told me I had received nothing under the will.

Usage 3: It is no good being in a *pique* about it; getting angry won't change a thing.

Usage 4: I don't mind being in a good *pique* every now and then; it gets the anger juices flowing.

Usage 5: Was he in the *pique* when he received his termination letter?

PIVOTAL (adj)   [PIV-*uh*-tl]

Meaning: crucial; vital; pertaining to a pivot (on which items turn); of key significance

Usage 1: It was a *pivotal* moment in my career.

Usage 2: One *pivotal* issue is whether everyone in the group will participate.

Usage 3: They were at a *pivotal* point in the discussions with the car manufacturers.

Usage 4: A *pivotal* issue for me these days is whether my car will start in the morning.

Usage 5: Does she think the *pivotal* talking point will occur before or after the company president arrives?

PLUCK (n)   [pluhk]

Meaning: fortitude or courage in the face of adversity

Usage 1: I admired her *pluck*; she didn't let losing the race get her down.

Usage 2: I wish I had his *pluck*; he's a fighter!

Usage 3: It was her *pluck* that brought her to the attention of the judges.

Usage 4: It takes a little *pluck* to get through each day.

Usage 5: When was last time *pluck* got you through a difficult situation?

POLARIZE (v)   [POH-l*uh*-rahyz]

Meaning: split into opposite extremes or camps; to divide sharply into opposing factions or into extremes

Usage 1: It was clear his intent was to *polarize* the two groups who are on our side.

Usage 2: If you *polarize* the magnets, you can eventually get them to spin around each other.

Usage 3: I don't think we can afford to *polarize* our efforts to protect the environment without one or the other effort suffering.

Usage 4: It is my practice each morning to *polarize* my six children into two less-powerful camps.

Usage 5: Do you understand that to *polarize* our concerns reduces the individual impact of each?

POLEMICAL (adj)   [p*uh*-LEM-i-k*uh*l]

Meaning: controversial;argumentative

Usage 1: The afternoon in the committee was spent in a *polemical* debate over basic voting procedures.

Usage 2: I did not mean to be unreasonably *polemical* in this discussion, but I feel strongly about this topic.

Usage 3: The subject of the animated feature proved to be surprisingly *polemical*.

Usage 4: Why must my correction of you and your sister always end up in a *polemical* argument in which someone gets hurt?

Usage 5: His attacks wear me out; why is he so persistently *polemical*?

POLITY (n)   [POL-i-tee]

Meaning: form of government of nation or state; an organized system of government or community

Usage 1: In its infancy, American *polity* was well-grounded in principles from European governments.

Usage 2: It is important to consider the *polity* that will arise before we give support to either warring faction.

Usage 3: The *polity* of a county can sometimes be as complicated as the polity of a country.

Usage 4: The *polity* of our little town seems to be centered around corruption and scandal.

Usage 5: What *polity* will result after this insurgency dies down?

PORTENT (n)   [PAWR-tent]

Meaning: omen; forewarning; an indication that something is about to happen; a sign of something bad to come

Usage 1: I tried to ignore the grave *portent* when a raven flew into our apartment.

Usage 2: It was a mysterious *portent*; I couldn't decide if it was good or bad.

Usage 3: I should have recognized the ill *portent*: the cat and dog were no longer getting along.

Usage 4: My cousin had the insane idea that an earthquake on her wedding day was a *portent* of bad things to come.

Usage 5: Do you think there were any *portents* observed by the passengers of *the Titanic*?

PRACTICABLE (adj)   [PRAK-ti-k*uh*-b*uh* l]

Meaning: Feasible; capable of being accomplished; doable

Usage 1: I think the plans, though expensive, are *practicable*.

Usage 2: The new solution is clearly *practicable*, and we must implement it at once.

Usage 3: You claim that saving money is impossible, but I believe it is both *practicable* and necessary.

Usage 4: I am weary of only doing what is *practicable*; today I will accomplish the impossible.

Usage 5: Was there any *practicable* way to resolve the pollution and save the fish at the same time?

This page is intentionally left blank

Chapter **8**

Practical – Rivulet

This chapter covers the following words, each with its part of speech, pronunciation, and descriptive meaning.

Usage of the word is also illustrated in three to five sample sentences.

practical	psychosis	recrimination
pragmatist	pugnacious	recuperate
precipice	purse	redress
preclude	pylon	refrain
predator	quaint	rejoinder
pre-empt	quarry	relevant
preen	query	relic
procurement	queue	remnant
profusion	rampart	renegade
prognosis	rancor	repulsion
propagate	rationalization	resentment
propulsive	ravage	resignation
proscenium	ravel	resolve
prosody	rebuff	retrench
prosperity	rebus	rigid
protrude	recipient	rivulet
prowess	reconnaissance	

PRACTICAL (adj)   [PRAK-ti-k*uh* l]

Meaning: based on experience; useful; pertaining to items based on practice; items adapted for actual use

Usage 1: Do you have any *practical* experience in pig farming?

Usage 2: As a *practical* matter, this will never work.

Usage 3: Is it important to acquire *practical* experience during a summer internship?

Usage 4: If I were *practical*, I never would've agreed to the job in the first place.

Usage 5: Are there any *practical* applications to your research?

PRAGMATIST (n)   [PRAG-m*uh*-tist]

Meaning: practical person; a person focused on the success or failure of a project

Usage 1: My father was always a *pragmatist*; he just wanted to get the job done.

Usage 2: As the only *pragmatist* on this team, I refuse to care about the precedent we are setting.

Usage 3: You have to be a *pragmatist* for this venture, or you will never get it done.

Usage 4: I'm a *pragmatist* when it comes to mowing my lawn; as long as the mower cuts, I don't care how beautiful the grass looks.

Usage 5: How can you be such a *pragmatist* when it is the future of our children that is at issue?

PRECIPICE (n)   [PRES-*uh*-pis]

Meaning: dangerous position; a steeply vertical cliff; a perilous situation

Usage 1: During the hike, we need to be careful at the *precipice* overlooking the gorge.

Usage 2: She looked down from the top of the *precipice* and laughed.

Usage 3: This purchase takes our fledgling company to the *precipice*, in terms of financing.

Usage 4: I had reached a *precipice* in my career, and the danger was very clear to me.

Usage 5: How close did you get to the edge of that *precipice*?

PRECLUDE (v)   [pri-KLOOD]

Meaning: make impossible; eliminate; prevent; foreclose the possibility of

Usage 1: If we plan carefully now, we can *preclude* problems that might arise later.

Usage 2: If his grades do not get better soon, he will *preclude* any chance of attending college.

Usage 3: The rising gas prices will *preclude* any trip I want to make by car this summer.

Usage 4: Is there a way to *preclude* my family members from erasing shows I record on the DVR?

Usage 5: Will his prison record *preclude* him from getting a job in security or on the police force?

PREDATOR (n)   [PRED-*uh*-ter]

Meaning: creature that seizes and devours another animal; an organism (including humans) that sustain themselves by preying on others

Usage 1: I enclosed the injured deer in a stall in our barn to ensure it would not fall victim to a *predator*.

Usage 2: We must ensure that we do not interfere with the *predator*/prey relationship in this wild environment.

Usage 3: My tiny kitten was already acting like a *predator* towards the chipmunks in our yard.

Usage 4: I would certainly rather be a *predator* than the prey.

Usage 5: What *predator* could have caused this kind of damage to a body?

PREEMPT (v)   [pree-EMPT]

Meaning: head off; forestall by acting first; supplant; take the place of because you acted before others

Usage 1: Please don't *pre-empt* my discussion of the Holocaust next term by reading that Holocaust story with your students this term.

Usage 2: We need to *pre-empt* high employee absenteeism during this stressful time by demonstrating how important it is for everyone to be here for the project

Usage 3: The issue was *preempted* in the news media by a new conflict in northern Africa.

Usage 4: Depressingly, discussions of money problems often *pre-empt* our discussions of going on vacation.

Usage 5: Did our political leaders make any attempt to *pre-empt* the recession before it occurred?

PREEN (v)   [preen]

Meaning: make oneself tidy in appearance; feel self-satisfaction; to trim of unwanted feathers (as in a bird); to dress smartly or neatly; to take pride in oneself

Usage 1: We watched the red–breasted cardinals *preen* themselves on the back deck.

Usage 2: I need to give her an hour to *preen* herself before we go to dinner.

Usage 3: I know he will *preen* when he receives the reward for best film documentary.

Usage 4: I can't be bothered to *preen*, or, for that matter, even comb my hair.

Usage 5: Did you see him *preen* when the female construction workers whistled at him?

PROCUREMENT (n)   [proh-KYOO R-m*uh* nt]

Meaning: obtaining; acquisition; securing of

Usage 1: Their *procurement* of the necessary supplies was delayed by the hurricane.

Usage 2: If a new *procurement* of funding does not occur, production will need to come to a stop.

Usage 3: After the *procurement* of an agreement to discuss peace, the nations also agreed to a cease-fire.

Usage 4: Why is my *procurement* of a decent seat at the movie theater always so difficult?

Usage 5: Without the *procurement* of new funding, will we be able to continue the program?

PROFUSION (n)   [pr*uh*-FYOO-zh*uh* n]

Meaning: overabundance; lavish expenditure; excess; a great amount of

Usage 1: There was a *profusion* of flowers at the front desk, and I assumed they belonged to me.

Usage 2: The Aurora Borealis was gorgeous: a *profusion* of light and magnetic energy.

Usage 3: There was a *profusion* of copycats when the Cabbage Patch doll became so successful.

Usage 4: I hate to even look at the *profusion* of unpaid bills on my desk.

Usage 5: Was there a *profusion* of fans at the back door, waiting to catch a glimpse of the band?

PROGNOSIS (n)   [prog-NOH-sis]

Meaning: forecasted course of a disease; prediction for the progression of a disease or illness

Usage 1: We were overjoyed that his *prognosis*, after treatment, was excellent.

Usage 2: It was devastating to hear that her *prognosis* was grim.

Usage 3: Without a *prognosis*, it is difficult to plan for what is up ahead.

Usage 4: The *prognosis* for his chronic laziness is to live a life that is unfulfilled.

Usage 5: What, do you think, is the *prognosis* for our country's increasing gun violence?

PROPAGATE (v)   [PROP-*uh*-geyt]

Meaning: multiply; to cause to increase in number; to spread

Usage 1: We had warned her that if she shared that photograph of herself on her cell phone, others would propagate it to everyone in the school.

Usage 2: This summer I plan to *propagate* my African violets; would you like one of the new plants?

Usage 3: If we don't spray now, the weeds will *propagate* and choke the rose bushes.

Usage 4: I felt a desire to *propagate* the rumor that he was quitting and moving to the North Pole.

Usage 5: Do you think we were able to *propagate* good will during the peace talks?

PROPULSIVE (adj)   [pr*uh*-PUHL-siv]

Meaning: driving forward; the process of moving forward

Usage 1: The *propulsive* force of the gunshot threw him backwards.

Usage 2: Do not underestimate the *propulsive* ability of the little scooter's engine.

Usage 3: The *propulsive* force of a tightly-strung trampoline, turn sideways, is rather extraordinary.

Usage 4: I've been trying to have a *propulsive* effect on his ambition to succeed, but I'm afraid I've stalled out.

Usage 5: Did the type of string used have an impact on the *propulsive* capability of the crossbow?

PROSCENIUM (n)   [proh-SEE-nee-*uh* m]

Meaning: of stage in front of curtain; the arch separating the stage from the audience

Usage 1: The comedian delivered monologue in the *proscenium*.

Usage 2: While they were dragging a prop along the *proscenium*, it fell into the orchestra pit and injured a musician.

Usage 3: From the *proscenium* you can catch glimpses of the faces of the audience.

Usage 4: While the singers positioned themselves in the *proscenium*, we scurried behind the curtain to set up for the next scene.

Usage 5: Will his speech be delivered from the *proscenium* or from further back in the stage?

PROSODY (n)   [PROS-*uh*-dee]

Meaning: the art of versification; the science and art of poetry

Usage 1: The *prosody* of Emily Dickinson, many claim, is unmatched by modern poets.

Usage 2: Although his word choice was excellent, his *prosody* was lacking.

Usage 3: To become a proficient poet, one cannot ignore the importance of *prosody*.

Usage 4: Sometimes it helps to reduce the pain of an experience to *prosody*; writing poetry becomes a coping technique.

Usage 5: How does the *prosody* of Charles Marlowe compare to that of Shakespeare?

PROSPERITY (n)   [pro-SPER-i-tee]

Meaning: good fortune; financial success; physical well-being; the condition of thriving or being successful

Usage 1: The *prosperity* of the nation could be affected by this economic down turn.

Usage 2: Her *prosperity* only came after many years of slaving over that restaurant.

Usage 3: I was relieved to see his *prosperity*; I had been told that he had fallen on hard times.

Usage 4: They say that living a life filled with *prosperity* is the best revenge against one's enemies.

Usage 5: With such *prosperity*, do we also gain wisdom?

PROTRUDE (v)   [proh-TROOD]

Meaning: stick out; to project forward

Usage 1: During the magic act none of your body parts can *protrude* beyond the curtain.

Usage 2: When you are decorating the cake, be sure not to allow one layer to *protrude* above the other.

Usage 3: The gargoyles will *protrude* from each gutter of the building.

Usage 4: Somehow his nose persistently had the desire to *protrude* into my business.

Usage 5: Won't his head still *protrude* when we close the box?

PROWESS (n)   [PROU-is]
Meaning: extraordinary ability; exceptional skill
Usage 1: He handled the javelin with such *prowess*; we knew he would win the gold medal.
Usage 2: Her *prowess* in running marathons was the result of many years of hard work.
Usage 3: I wished I could match his *prowess* for clear and persuasive debate.
Usage 4: Her *prowess* at making cappuccino endeared her to me the moment I met her.
Usage 5: Have you ever seen such *prowess* at archery in one so young?

PSYCHOSIS (n)   [sahy-KOH-sis]
Meaning: severe mental disorder
Usage 1: It was hard to tell how much his *psychosis* affected his interactions with his family.
Usage 2: She fell victim to *psychosis* after being on the front lines for five years.
Usage 3: Does he take medicine to address the symptoms of his *psychosis*?
Usage 4: It took only six months of teaching kindergarten before I developed signs of *psychosis*.
Usage 5: What are the manifestations of his *psychosis*?

PUGNACIOUS (adj)   [puhg-NEY-sh*uh* s]
Meaning: combative; disposed to fight; inclined to fight
Usage 1: My little brother's *pugnacious* habits earned him more than a few black-eyes.
Usage 2: I don't understand why she is so *pugnacious*; she used to get along with everyone.
Usage 3: There is no need to be *pugnacious*; surely we can solve this in a civilized manner.
Usage 4: If you insist on being *pugnacious,* I insist on beating the stuffing out of you.
Usage 5: Wasn't it difficult to watch the politicians be so *pugnacious* in the television debate?

PURSE (v)   [purs]
Meaning: contract into wrinkles; to pucker
Usage 1: Do not *purse* your lips; it makes you look older.
Usage 2: He did not take the hint when he saw me *purse* my lips.
Usage 3: Draw together the sides of the parchment paper and *purse* them to secure the filet of fish.
Usage 4: If I *purse* my lips, you know you are in deep trouble.
Usage 5: Did you see how much more angry they look when they *purse* their lips?

PYLON (n)   [PAHY-lon]
Meaning: marking post to guide aviators; a post or tower to guide airplane pilots as they land; a tower carrying electrical or other lines
Usage 1: As I looked out the airplane windows, I noticed the well-lit *pylons* leading to the airport.
Usage 2: We will place a *pylon* at each corner of the tiny island so that it will be visible to those flying overhead.
Usage 3: It is important that you look for each *pylon* and any electrical lines connected to it.
Usage 4: Her room was in such mayhem that I needed more than one *pylon* to help me navigate it.
Usage 5: Isn't there a light out on that first *pylon*?

QUAINT (adj)   [kweynt]

Meaning: odd; old-fashioned; picturesque; attractive because old-fashioned; peculiar

Usage 1: What a *quaint* photograph of you and your family!

Usage 2: I think a spinning wheel would be a *quaint* addition to the decor around the fireplace.

Usage 3: He definitely has a *quaint* view of the world.

Usage 4: My ex-husband's new wife said I was *quaint*; I almost knocked her teeth out.

Usage 5: Does it seem rather *quaint* that he felt the need to ask her parents before he asked her?

QUARRY (n)   [KWAWR-ee]

Meaning: victim; object of a hunt; something hunted or pursued

Usage 1: I always feel sorry for the unsuspecting *quarry* of animal predators.

Usage 2: I cannot watch that snake eat its *quarry*.

Usage 3: The posse's *quarry* hid in the barn belonging to the sheriff.

Usage 4: His *quarry* was, of course, me.

Usage 5: How long did that cheetah stalk its *quarry*?

QUERY (n)   [KWEER-ee]

Meaning: inquiry; questioning; a doubt

Usage 1: Does anyone have a *query* before we start?

Usage 2: The line of *query* we are pursuing is whether there are more efficient ways to fight large-scale forest fires.

Usage 3: We are proceeding on a *query* posed by our middle school audience about whether living plants experience pain.

Usage 4: My first *query* in a college class was to ask the location of the bathroom.

Usage 5: Do you intend to pose another brilliant *query*?

QUEUE (n)   [kyoo]

Meaning: an ordering or line of something (especially people)

Usage 1: The British are known for how politely they stand in *queue*.

Usage 2: There was a *queue* for the newest iPhone that wound around the building and out into the parking lot.

Usage 3: She should never have broken into the *queue*; she started a riot!

Usage 4: I've added those romantic movies to the viewing *queue*.

Usage 5: Are you standing in *queue*?

RAMPART (n)   [RAM-pahrt]

Meaning: a wide bank of earth built to protect a fort or a city; a broad mound of earth, usually part of a fortification

Usage 1: The garrison soldiers kept watch from the *rampart* above.

Usage 2: The plan, if an invasion was attempted, was to drop hot oil from the *rampart* onto the invading army below.

Usage 3: As I stood on the *rampart*, I felt a thousand years old, as if I had been there when the fort was first built.

Usage 4: If my relatives act on their threat to stay with us, my family and I will shoot arrows at them from a newly-constructed *rampart*.

Usage 5: Is that *rampart* made of earth or stone?

RANCOR (n)   [RANG-ker]

Meaning: bitterness; hatred; ill will; malice

Usage 1: I understand your *rancor* at her deserting you, but it does you no good.

Usage 2: They had never seen such *rancor*; surely she should have gotten over it by now.

Usage 3: Strangely, he felt no *rancor* at being left out of the will.

Usage 4: The *rancor* between our two families came to a head during the tug of war.

Usage 5: Do you bear any *rancor* towards those who imprisoned you unjustly?

RATIONALIZATION (n)   [rash-*uh*-nl-*uh*-ZEY-sh*uh* n]

Meaning: to explain or decide upon by appealing to reason

Usage 1: Her self-serving *rationalization* was not based in reality.

Usage 2: According to his *rationalization* of the policy, the advantages it offered to the many outweighed the problems it posed for the few.

Usage 3: We need test questions, as well as a *rationalization* for each question.

Usage 4: What *rationalization* did you give for stealing money from your two sons' trust account?

Usage 5: Is he attempting a *rationalization* for his bad behavior?

RAVAGE (v)   [RAV-ij]

Meaning: to ruin and destroy; to plunder; to despoil; to cause extensive damage to

Usage 1: One of the worst parts of war is that some see it as an opportunity to *ravage* areas controlled by their opponents.

Usage 2: We refuse to stand idly by while invading armies *ravage* our town.

Usage 3: Don't *ravage* your sister's closet, or I'll give her permission to ravage yours.

Usage 4: The passage of time can *ravage* a face by adding laugh lines, wrinkles, and sagging skin.

Usage 5: What kind of person devises a plan to *ravage* the homes of those who are already destitute?

RAVEL (v)   [RAV-*uh* l]

Meaning: fall apart into tangles; to entangle; to intertwine; to disentangle

Usage 1: The strange thing is that to *ravel* can mean to disentangle or to entangle!

Usage 2: Did you *ravel* those four strands of wool to form a single, stronger strand?

Usage 3: I cannot *ravel* my crochet thread this time; it has become too deeply entangled.

Usage 4: To try to *ravel* the various family relationships in our small town is an incredibly difficult task.

Usage 5: How do you *ravel* all the hoses when they become so entangled?

REBUFF (v)   [ri-BUHF]

Meaning: snub; beat back; to reject or refuse; to prevent the advance of

Usage 1: How many times must I *rebuff* his offers for a ride home?

Usage 2: I did not want to *rebuff* his offer of a drink, but we were colleagues and I thought it'd be unwise.

Usage 3: Don't let his scowl or nasty comments *rebuff* you; he's harmless.

Usage 4: Please don't *rebuff* his proposal of marriage until the rest of us are out of the room.

Usage 5: How can you *rebuff* another offer of help?

REBUS (n) [REE-b*uh* s]

Meaning: tangle; knot; a puzzle often using pictures

Usage 1: As she sat in the airport, I noticed she was working a *rebus*.

Usage 2: My knitting yarn was transformed into *rebus*, and in the center was my new kitten.

Usage 3: Her hair was a *rebus* of tangles that no one would be able to untie.

Usage 4: My life had become a *rebus*, but there were no pictures to help.

Usage 5: What steps did you take to solve the *rebus*?

RECIPIENT (n) [ri-SIP-ee-*uh* nt]

Meaning: receiver; one who receives something

Usage 1: Dr. King was the *recipient* of the Nobel Peace Prize in 1964.

Usage 2: She is the *recipient* of a multitude of awards for her charitable work.

Usage 3: I cannot tell who the *recipient* of this letter is; the name and address are illegible.

Usage 4: I had no idea I was the *recipient* of his estate under his new will.

Usage 5: Were you the *recipient* of that nasty comment from the audience?

RECONNAISSANCE (n) [ri-KON-*uh*-su*h* ns]

Meaning: survey of enemy by soldiers; reconnoitering; a general examination of an area, especially for military tactical purposes

Usage 1: We were asked to perform a *reconnaissance* and determine whether there were vulnerabilities in our opponents' supply lines.

Usage 2: If the *reconnaissance* failed, they would be entering enemy territory blind.

Usage 3: Using planes for *reconnaissance* made sense, but the pilots could not catch everything.

Usage 4: Two hours into our visit to the theme park, I sent my husband and my eldest on a *reconnaissance* mission to determine the whereabouts of the remaining children.

Usage 5: When should we order another *reconnaissance* to determine troop movements?

RECRIMINATION (n) [ri-krim-*uh*-NEY-sh*uh* n]

Meaning: countercharges; a charge made against an accuser

Usage 1: The angry employee left in a maelstrom of angry *recrimination*.

Usage 2: As long as the discussions are dominated by *recrimination* and resentment, we will never make progress.

Usage 3: The feud was fueled by an endless cycle of charges and *recrimination*.

Usage 4: Our marriage counselor said that in all her years of practice, she'd never seen such capacity for *recrimination*.

Usage 5: Haven't you engaged in *recrimination* merely as a distraction?

RECUPERATE (v) [ri-KOO-p*uh*-reyt]

Meaning: recover; to regain health or strength, especially after an illness

Usage 1: After breaking both legs, he will need a few months to *recuperate*.

Usage 2: I could not wait to *recuperate* from my stomach ailments.

Usage 3: He did not want to *recuperate* because he was enjoying all of the attention he was receiving.

Usage 4: I didn't feel as if I would ever *recuperate* after having bronchitis for so long.

Usage 5: Did he *recuperate* after he almost lost his life climbing Mt. Everest?

REDRESS (n)   [ree-DRES]

Meaning: remedy; compensation for a wrong or an injury

Usage 1: The *redress* for her grievances at City Hall was never forthcoming.

Usage 2: We can attempt a *redress* in the next billing cycle.

Usage 3: He was the only person at fault, so he owed everyone a *redress*.

Usage 4: The *redress* wasn't going well; everyone was dissatisfied with the amount offered.

Usage 5: Are there any plans for a *redress* for damage caused by the runaway train?

REFRAIN (v)   [ri-FREYN]

Meaning: abstain from; resist; holding back from doing; forbearing

Usage 1: I need to *refrain* from eating fried foods; they give me terrible heartburn.

Usage 2: Could you *refrain* from using your cell phone while I am trying to serve you?

Usage 3: He needed to *refrain* from giving instructions while his son was pitching; that was the coach's job.

Usage 4: It took all my restraint to *refrain* from telling her off, then and there.

Usage 5: Could you please *refrain* from talking during the movie?

REJOINDER (n)   [ri-JOIN-der]

Meaning: an answer or reply; response

Usage 1: His *rejoinder* was short and not-so-sweet: no.

Usage 2: I didn't think the ridiculous offer required a *rejoinder*.

Usage 3: I don't know what his *rejoinder* would have been; I had already hung up the phone.

Usage 4: My *rejoinder* to his rude comment would be inappropriate for polite society.

Usage 5: Did she give you a *rejoinder* when you asked her to dance?

RELEVANT (adj)   [REL-*uh-vuh* nt]

Meaning: pertinent; referring to the case in hand; pertaining to the subject at hand

Usage 1: What is your *relevant* job experience?

Usage 2: The professor persistently devolved into discussions that were not *relevant* to the subject of the class.

Usage 3: I tried to make each lesson *relevant* to the skills they needed in life.

Usage 4: I thought it was completely *relevant* that he had never once told me he loved me.

Usage 5: Is that really *relevant* to the issue at hand?

RELIC (n)   [REL-ik]

Meaning: memento; something surviving from the past; a remnant

Usage 1: He was a *relic* of a time when men were chivalrous and held doors for women.

Usage 2: When they unearthed the ancient *relic* from Mesopotamia, I flew out to see it.

Usage 3: The land-line telephone has become a *relic* of the past, with almost all but the elderly abandoning theirs.

Usage 4: I was the *relic* of an age when men pretended they were in power, but it was the women who really were.

Usage 5: What was the significance of the marks on the casket in which that *relic* was placed?

REMNANT (n)   [REM-n*uh* nt]

Meaning: remainder; a remaining part; a fragment or scrap left over

Usage 1: We spent the last *remnant* of the day wallowing beside the pool.

Usage 2: It was a *remnant* from our past: a dried flower from the first corsage I ever gave her.

Usage 3: Could that meteorite be a *remnant* of some passing comet?

Usage 4: By giving me this *remnant*, you imply that I want to remember; I don't want to remember.

Usage 5: Was that a *remnant* from your misbegotten youth?

RENEGADE (n)   [REN-i-geyd]

Meaning: deserter; traitor; one who deserts something; dissenter

Usage 1: The last thing I expected was for him to turn into a *renegade*.

Usage 2: I did not want to continue to fight, but I also didn't consider myself a *renegade*.

Usage 3: The new corporate president was a *renegade* within three months, taking many company secrets with him when he went.

Usage 4: If my family continues to drive me crazy, I will soon become a much–happier *renegade*.

Usage 5: Which one of the soldiers became a *renegade*?

REPULSION (n)   [ri-PUHL-sh*uh* n]

Meaning: act of driving back; the feeling of being repelled; experiencing repugnance

Usage 1: The *repulsion* I felt for him was almost palatable.

Usage 2: His *repulsion* from the rocks by outgoing waves was ultimately what saved him.

Usage 3: She had never felt such *repulsion* for another human being in her entire life.

Usage 4: I needed to work through my *repulsion* towards gardening and housework.

Usage 5: Can you explain the *repulsion* he bears for fancy sportscars?

RESENTMENT (n)   [ri-ZENT-m*uh* nt]

Meaning: indignation; bitterness; anger or ill-feeling as a result of some injury or insult

Usage 1: His *resentment* of the entire situation is real.

Usage 2: I don't want to create any *resentment* among my fellow employees when I receive the award.

Usage 3: After a year of putting up with all her meanness, my *resentment* was real.

Usage 4: His bitter *resentment* over my decision to take the new job in Idaho never left him.

Usage 5: What caused his *resentment* against you in the first place?

RESIGNATION (n)   [rez-ig-NEY-sh*uh* n]

Meaning: patient submissiveness; unresisting acceptance of a situation; communication that one is quitting a job

Usage 1: It was with *resignation* my father submitted to my sister's overbearing attentions.

Usage 2: I'd had enough; I put my *resignation* on her desk, and I left the building.

Usage 3: The oppressors expected eventual *resignation* from their prisoners, but they never got it.

Usage 4: I had hoped my *resignation* would be greeted with regret, not glee.

Usage 5: Does your *resignation* to your situation mean you have stopped fighting it?

RESOLVE (v)   [ri-ZOLV]

Meaning: to settle; to earnestly decide; to solve

Usage 1: Could we *resolve* this issue before our families arrive?

Usage 2: I hadn't a clue how to *resolve* the problem.

Usage 3: I *resolve* to spend more time working on my Spanish this summer.

Usage 4: If we can't *resolve* this issue, how can we move forward?

Usage 5: Did you *resolve* not to tell her about your hidden past?

RETRENCH (v)   [ri-TRENCH]

Meaning: to economize; to return to the trenches for protection; to reconsider; to cut down

Usage 1: After the aerial attack, it was clear the troops desperately needed to *retrench*.

Usage 2: Careful investors will use this opportunity to *retrench* from more risky investments.

Usage 3: The team was exhausted; it was time to *retrench*.

Usage 4: To *retrench*, at this point, seemed "too little, too late."

Usage 5: She's gone bankrupt; how many times did I beg her to *retrench*?

RIGID (adj)   [RIJ-id]

Meaning: stiff and unyielding; strict; hard and unbending; firmly fixed or set

Usage 1: Her father's rules were *rigid*, and she did not dare break them.

Usage 2: She held her back *rigid* as she walked through the taunting crowd.

Usage 3: They held the thin tree trunk *rigid* as they put the brace for it in place.

Usage 4: My standards for their behavior were *rigid*, but I was confident they could meet them.

Usage 5: Don't you need to hold her leg *rigid* when you put it in the splint?

RIVULET (n)   [RIV-*yuh*-lit]

Meaning: a small river or stream; a creek or a brook

Usage 1: The *rivulet* at the campground was the perfect location for finding salamanders.

Usage 2: With the recent storms, that *rivulet* has become more of a raging river.

Usage 3: The *rivulet* surface was covered in darting dragonflies and buzzing insects of every kind.

Usage 4: We wiggled our toes in the silt at the bottom of the *rivulet*.

Usage 5: Has there always been a *rivulet* running behind the house?

This page is intentionally left blank

Chapter **9**

Robust – Terminate

This chapter covers the following words, each with its part of speech, pronunciation, and descriptive meaning.

Usage of the word is also illustrated in three to five sample sentences.

robust	shoddy	stricture
rotundity	singular	strident
rusticate	skirmish	sublime
saline	sliver	subliminal
salutary	somber	succor
sanctuary	somnolent	sunder
sarcasm	sonorous	superimpose
satellite	sparse	supplicate
scoff	spat	supposititious
scuffle	splice	surly
sectarian	spoonerism	sustenance
sedentary	sportive	syllogism
seep	squalid	symmetry
seethe	squat	taper
sere	stifle	tawdry
sever	stilted	terminate
sham	stock	

ROBUST (adj)   [roh-BUHST]

Meaning: vigorous; rich; hardy; strong and healthy

Usage 1: He was a *robust* young man: tall and strong.

Usage 2: Her appetite was strangely *robust* for one so tiny.

Usage 3: The recovery of the economy has been *robust* during the third quarter.

Usage 4: The zucchini plants are looking *robust* after all that rain on Wednesday.

Usage 5: Do you think the protest after the decision of the court yesterday will be *robust*?

ROTUNDITY (n)   [roh-TUHN-di-tee]

Meaning: roundness; sonorousness of speech; plumpness; fullness of speech

Usage 1: His *rotundity* made him appear uncomfortable and a little bit comical.

Usage 2: Notwithstanding all the pressures to be thin, her *rotundity* actually looked good on her.

Usage 3: Even though he was a small man, the *rotundity* of his speaking voice commanded attention.

Usage 4: My *rotundity* came in handy with the students because I could at least intimidate them a little.

Usage 5: Did her musical voice have the same *rotundity* as her speaking voice?

RUSTICATE (v)   [RUHS-ti-keyt]

Meaning: to send a student away from an educational institute as a punishment; to send a person into the countryside or to make someone more like a country person; banish from a university as punishment

Usage 1: Her parents, worried about her big-city ideas, sought to *rusticate* her by sending her to live with an aunt in the country.

Usage 2: I will admit that my friends tried to *rusticate* my speech by teaching me many of their quaint sayings.

Usage 3: It wasn't hard to *rusticate* him; he was a country boy in a city boy's body.

Usage 4: We finally get him to Oxford College in England on a scholarship, and the school tells us they were forced to *rusticate* him for selling drugs.

Usage 5: How would your accent change if your colleagues tried to *rusticate* it?

SALINE (adj)   [SEY-leen]

Meaning: salty; pertaining to salt

Usage 1: I left the *saline* solution for my contacts in my cabinet at home.

Usage 2: A *saline* solution is often used for initially clearing the wound of debris.

Usage 3: The pickle brine needs to be sufficiently *saline* to cause a chemical change in the cucumbers.

Usage 4: I like my margarita salty, but this one is virtually *saline*.

Usage 5: How many parts salt and how many parts water is this *saline* solution?

SALUTARY (adj)   [SAL-y*uh*-ter-ee]

Meaning: tending to improve; beneficial; wholesome; something that improves health and wellbeing

Usage 1: The effects of the spa waters were *salutary* for most of the visitors.

Usage 2: It is incontrovertible that regular exercise has a *salutary* impact on the cardiovascular system.

Usage 3: Using the ointment brought *salutary* relief to my aching muscles.

Usage 4: Seeing my nephew safe after the car accident had a *salutary* effect on my rapidly–beating heart.

Usage 5: Think about it: will eating that cream doughnut be *salutary* for your digestive system?

SANCTUARY (n)   [SANGK-choo-er-ee]

Meaning: refuge; shrine; a holy place; a place of protection and shelter

Usage 1: They delivered several beautiful flower arrangements to the *sanctuary* for use during the service.

Usage 2: The pew at the front of the *sanctuary* and on the left is split along the bench.

Usage 3: The stray dog clearly needed *sanctuary* from the raging storm.

Usage 4: They offered me *sanctuary* from my annoying and selfish family.

Usage 5: Should we offer them *sanctuary* if the angry mob pursues them?

SARCASM (n)   [SAHR-kaz-*uh* m]

Meaning: scornful remarks; stinging rebuke; sneering or cutting remark, often ironic

Usage 1: I could no longer bear his *sarcasm*; I left the room.

Usage 2: Using *sarcasm* in an eighth grade classroom is empowering.

Usage 3: Don't use *sarcasm* with your employer unless you are prepared to be unemployed.

Usage 4: I knew I was tired when my responses all amounted to *sarcasm*.

Usage 5: Were you trying to be helpful or was that just *sarcasm*?

SATELLITE (n)   [SAT-l-ahyt]

Meaning: small body revolving around a larger one; an object revolving around another; a sub branch; something subservient

Usage 1: The Earth has only a single *satellite*: the moon.

Usage 2: This campus operates as a *satellite* to the main campus in Atlanta.

Usage 3: East Germany became a *satellite* of Russia after World War II.

Usage 4: She operated like an obsequious, pathetic *satellite* around the group of cheerleaders.

Usage 5: Are they tracking a newly-discovered *satellite* of Jupiter?

SCOFF (v)   [skawf]

Meaning: mock; ridicule; fail to take seriously

Usage 1: Please don't *scoff* at her attempts to speak English; she is just learning.

Usage 2: I could not *scoff* at her family's misfortune.

Usage 3: He seems to *scoff* at every attempt to help him, but he really does need help.

Usage 4: It's easy to *scoff* at someone else when you are not the one in the hot seat.

Usage 5: Was that her attempt to *scoff* at the situation?

SCUFFLE (v)   [SKUHF-*uh* l]

Meaning: struggle confusedly; move on in a confused hurry; to struggle in confusion; shuffle

Usage 1: Don't *scuffle* your shoes like that, you will mar them.

Usage 2: The crowd began to *scuffle* when they heard the gunshots, which resulted in many injuries.

Usage 3: Through training, you will learn how to handle a situation calmly, rather than to *scuffle* about in confusion.

Usage 4: If you want to *scuffle* about, go visit your grandmother.

Usage 5: Why do you always *scuffle* when the two of you get together?

SECTARIAN (adj)   [sek-TAIR-ee-*uh* n]

Meaning: relating to a religious faction or subgroup; narrow-minded; pertaining to a sect or a division of some sort; not looking at the big picture

Usage 1: The *sectarian* violence in the city is increasing as more groups get involved in the war.

Usage 2: Many of the concerns were *sectarian*, affecting some groups but not others.

Usage 3: Her views on this matter were *sectarian* and did not take into consideration the feelings of all of the subgroups.

Usage 4: They couldn't be called *sectarian* concerns in my household, because each sect was made up of only one person.

Usage 5: What is the progress of the *sectarian* negotiations at the economic forum?

SEDENTARY (adj) [SED-n-ter-ee]

Meaning: requiring sitting; pertaining to the act of sitting

Usage 1: His knees are bad, so he definitely needs a *sedentary* job.

Usage 2: This is a *sedentary* task; you need to stop wandering around.

Usage 3: I had been *sedentary* for so long, my legs no longer operated properly.

Usage 4: People say he is *sedentary* by nature; I say he is incredibly lazy.

Usage 5: Did you consider the *sedentary* nature of the job before considering the position?

SEEP (v) [seep]

Meaning: ooze; trickle; leak out slowly

Usage 1: If the wound is not bandaged correctly, blood will *seep* through to her pants.

Usage 2: We watched the oil *seep* out of the pipe and into the fragile lake.

Usage 3: When you overfill the container, liquid may *seep* out as you put a lid on it.

Usage 4: If the barrels of syrup have begun to *seep*, we have a real problem on our hands.

Usage 5: Is that a cherry cola which is starting to *seep* out of the vents in your locker?

SEETHE (v) [seeth]

Meaning: be disturbed; boil to surge or foam (as if boiling); to be in a state of agitation

Usage 1: I think that soup on the stove has begun to *seethe*.

Usage 2: The fierce winds caused even the water in our pool to *seethe* and roil.

Usage 3: You would *seethe* with anger, too, if your loved one was killed while doing something so incredibly foolish.

Usage 4: If you don't want me to *seethe* with anger and irritation, clean those dishes out of the sink immediately.

Usage 5: Did you see how the heat of the campfire made the pot of stew *seethe* and boil over?

SERE (adj) [seer]

Meaning: parched; dried up; withered

Usage 1: After running fifteen miles, we were *sere* and weary.

Usage 2: The garden had clearly been abandoned; the *sere* plants had not been watered in weeks.

Usage 3: The wrinkles on his *sere* face told us he would be a source of great wisdom.

Usage 4: After twenty days in the desert, I could no longer bear looking at the *sere* and lifeless landscape.

Usage 5: How did the skin on my face and hands become so *sere*?

SEVER (v) [SEV-er]

Meaning: separate; to cut in two

Usage 1: It is important, during surgery, not to *sever* the artery.

Usage 2: Of course I would *sever* my finger the very first time I used the band saw.

Usage 3: The world leaders did not want to *sever* ties with the rogue leaders, but they were running out of options.

Usage 4: I had no choice but to *sever* my relationship with both him and his family.

Usage 5: Did you *sever* that rope or simply untie it?

SHAM (v) [sham]

Meaning: pretend; to make a false showing; to imitate

Usage 1: The family must *sham* their closeness; in reality, they hate each other.

Usage 2: Those thieves may try to *sham* you out of your wallet; be careful!

Usage 3: To *sham* an innocent victim, like an elderly woman, is especially heinous.

Usage 4: I regret my decisions to *sham* sickness when I didn't want to go to work; eventually I was fired.

Usage 5: How do you *sham* sincerity so completely?

SHODDY (adj) [SHOD-ee]

Meaning: sham; not genuine; inferior; poorly executed

Usage 1: The workmanship on our new home was decidedly *shoddy*, and we planned to complain to the builder.

Usage 2: His handling of the tense political situation was *shoddy* and left all the parties angry at each other.

Usage 3: Do not underestimate their anger if your analysis is *shoddy*.

Usage 4: Your design of the vessel was *shoddy*, and that's why it sank.

Usage 5: Is this *shoddy* work on the project a lack of expertise or of care?

SINGULAR (adj) [SING-gy*uh*-ler]

Meaning: unique; extraordinary; odd

Usage 1: Her response to his proposal of marriage was *singular*: "I think I do" was all she said.

Usage 2: We have a *singular* opportunity to increase the amount of industry in our community.

Usage 3: It was a *singular* creation, filled with twisted metal and fake peacock feathers.

Usage 4: My aunt had the *singular* ability to tick me off in a matter of seconds.

Usage 5: Isn't a meteor show of this magnitude a *singular* event?

SKIRMISH (n) [SKUR-mish]

Meaning: minor fight; small battle

Usage 1: The riot and ensuing violence began as a *skirmish* over unfair wages.

Usage 2: When the *skirmish* was over, they hugged each other, and all was well.

Usage 3: I don't have the strength for even a *skirmish* with you right now.

Usage 4: I thought it was a fight that would end in divorce, but it proved to be a *skirmish*.

Usage 5: With which salesman will you *skirmish* today?

SLIVER (n) [SLIV-er]

Meaning: very thin piece, usually of wood; thin pieces or slices of something

Usage 1: The *sliver* of wood that was embedded in my finger hurt terribly.

Usage 2: You must watch for flying *slivers* of wood while he is using that carving tool.

Usage 3: You can give Bonny a *sliver* of meat and no more than that.

Usage 4: If you cut your chicken into *slivers*, the dip is easier for people to eat.

Usage 5: Are those *slivers* of wood going to become part of the design?

SOMBER (adj)   [SOM-ber]

Meaning: gloomy; dark; drab; sad and depressing

Usage 1: The funeral was a *somber* affair, and it was important to dress appropriately.

Usage 2: He is in one of his *somber* moods, so you need to leave him alone.

Usage 3: Contemplating the increase in air pollution in our state is a *somber* thought.

Usage 4: I tried to feign being *somber,* but I was relieved they were leaving.

Usage 5: Don't you find the end of fall and the onset of the cold winter a *somber* transition?

SOMNOLENT (adj)   [SOM-n*uh-luh* nt]

Meaning: half asleep; sleepy

Usage 1: After staying up into the wee hours of the morning writing, the next morning I was *somnolent.*

Usage 2: Her droning voice engendered a *somnolent* stupor from which I could not rouse myself.

Usage 3: The *somnolent* effect of that classical music makes it dangerous for me to listen to it while driving the car.

Usage 4: A full day at the amusement park left the children quiet and *somnolent* for the ride home.

Usage 5: Are you *somnolent* this evening because you spent the day moving?

SONOROUS (adj)   [s*uh*-NAWR-*uh* s]

Meaning: resonant; full of sound; loud and deep

Usage 1: His *sonorous* wheezing was comforting; it told me he was deeply asleep.

Usage 2: Memories of his *sonorous* voice and his powerful words stayed with me for years.

Usage 3: The whale song was lively and *sonorous*; I loved listening to it.

Usage 4: The *sonorous* call of the foghorn told me that we'd gotten too close to the rocky shore.

Usage 5: Was that *sonorous* sound you practicing your trombone?

SPARSE (adj)   [spahrs]

Meaning: not thick; thinly scattered; thinly distributed

Usage 1: The vegetation in the desert was *sparse,* with little to offer the animals that lived there.

Usage 2: After harvesting, the fields are *sparse,* but a few vegetables are scattered here and there.

Usage 3: The evidence at the crime scene was *sparse* because the building had been deserted for years.

Usage 4: His comments on my research paper were *sparse,* but each one was meaningful.

Usage 5: Are sources of food much *sparser* here during the winter?

SPAT (n)   [spat]

Meaning: squabble; minor dispute; small argument

Usage 1: The *spat* between them was more serious than I imagined; they didn't talk again the entire day.

Usage 2: In order to avoid a *spat* with her mother, she simply didn't tell her.

Usage 3: I don't have time for another *spat* over the type of coffee we use in the break room.

Usage 4: I refused to intervene in the latest *spat* between my husband and his car.

Usage 5: Are you in serious disagreement or is it only a minor *spat*?

SPLICE (n/v)   [splahys]

Meaning: fasten together; unite; to join together with adhesive

Usage 1: I had to *splice* the film in five places, it was so severely damaged. (n)

Usage 2: They will now *splice* the cable with special equipment that seamlessly joins it together. (v)

Usage 3: The *splice* in the electrical cord looks as if it is holding. (n)

Usage 4: We will need to *splice* the two pieces of rope because neither is long enough to do the job. (v)

Usage 5: Can't we simply *splice* the two garden hoses together? (v)

SPOONERISM (n)   [SPOO-n*uh*-riz-*uh* m]

Meaning: accidental transposition of sounds in successive words; slip of the tongue (or a tip of the slongue)

Usage 1: The toddler called her favorite candy "belly jeans," a *spoonerism* for jelly beans.

Usage 2: The name of a character on television can form an interesting *spoonerism*, such as "Sart Bimpson" for "Bart Simpson."

Usage 3: I didn't have time to laugh at her latest *spoonerism*; we were about to miss our flight.

Usage 4: Her brother had her convinced that the actual name of the play was *Jomeo and Ruliet*, a *spoonerism* for Romeo and Juliet.

Usage 5: Isn't a famous *spoonerism* a reference to the "Duke and Duchess of Windsor" as the "Duck and Doochess of Windsor"?

SPORTIVE (adj)   [SPAWR-tiv]

Meaning: playful; done in sport or for fun, rather than seriously

Usage 1: The parrot isn't being aggressive, only *sportive*.

Usage 2: Your *sportive* attempts to laugh it off underlie a seriousness that you don't want others to see.

Usage 3: Please don't be *sportive* when you are engaged in the real competition.

Usage 4: His *sportive* attempt to engage her was sadly unsuccessful.

Usage 5: Was he being serious or was he merely being *sportive*?

SQUALID (adj)   [SKWOL-id]

Meaning: very dirty; filthy; foul because of neglect

Usage 1: There was no way I was going to leave the orphan in such *squalid* conditions.

Usage 2: Because she had been ill for so long, the house was *squalid* and unsanitary.

Usage 3: Last year two of the dormitories at camp were so *squalid*, they were unusable.

Usage 4: His obsessive hoarding had resulted in living conditions that could only be described as *squalid*.

Usage 5: Was the pig enclosure as *squalid* as it appeared?

SQUAT (adj)   [skwot]

Meaning: stocky; short and thick; low and broad

Usage 1: The *squat* little house was larger inside than it appeared on the outside.

Usage 2: The new nanny was pleasant, a *squat* woman who was as wide as she was tall.

Usage 3: The ancient computers sat *squat* against a wall of the warehouse and had no more computing power than a modern calculator.

Usage 4: The leprechaun was a *squat* little man dressed all in green; I thought he looked ridiculous.

Usage 5: Is your beach house the *squat* one in the middle, with the two mansion-like ones on either side?

STIFLE (v)   [STAHY-*fuh* l]

Meaning: suppress; extinguish; inhibit; to quell or crush

Usage 1: Even though his mother was the speaker, he had to *stifle* a yawn towards the end of the speech.

Usage 2: It is important to *stifle* any laughter you might have at any single exhibit; this is a serious exhibition.

Usage 3: I always need to *stifle* a snort when she wears her new hat.

Usage 4: I did not want to *stifle* her creativity, but I was not going to allow her to add potato chips to her oatmeal cookie dough.

Usage 5: Doesn't a "no tolerance" policy *stifle* a school administration's ability to consider all the factors in a given situation?

STILTED (adj) [STIL-tid]

Meaning: bombastic; inflated; overly dignified or formal (as if on stilts)

Usage 1: The conversation between us was *stilted* because she was trying to show off her knowledge to those around us.

Usage 2: Be careful not to sound *stilted* during the television interview; it will annoy the audience.

Usage 3: It was such a *stilted* performance, that I was embarrassed for her.

Usage 4: My brother-in-law's interactions with me are always *stilted*; my sister says I make him feel insecure.

Usage 5: Did the actress come off as genuine and sincere or *stilted*?

STOCK (adj) [stok]

Meaning: typical; standard; kept in regular supply; always kept on hand in the supply

Usage 1: That is his *stock* answer when he's angry: "I don't know and I don't care."

Usage 2: Even his *stock* humor is funny, but tonight he pulled out the hidden-away-in-the-cellar jokes.

Usage 3: That video of the Pope is clearly *stock* footage; he looks much younger than he does now.

Usage 4: These are *stock* photos of my family; I don't take current ones anymore.

Usage 5: Do we have our *stock* participants who join us every year in addition to our new ones?

STRICTURE (n) [STRIK-cher]

Meaning: critical comments; severe and adverse criticism; a restriction

Usage 1: Her constant *stricture*, while monitoring the hallway, caused many students to skirt around her.

Usage 2: I don't like the *stricture* any more than you do, but I am not going to argue about it.

Usage 3: What is the latest *stricture* from the powers on high?

Usage 4: A suggestion here would be helpful; a *stricture* would not.

Usage 5: Must we abide by his latest *stricture* about the font we use and its size?

STRIDENT (adj) [STRAHYD-nt]

Meaning: loud and harsh; insistent; shrill and irritating; grating

Usage 1: His *strident* opening remarks got the meeting off to a rocky start.

Usage 2: I have no idea why she is being so *strident* in this matter; there must be something else going on.

Usage 3: The reports from the investigating committee were *strident* in their criticism of the handling of this matter.

Usage 4: If you take that *strident* tone with me, you will find yourself staying home from the party.

Usage 5: Is the debate in community over the issue of expenditures a *strident* one?

SUBLIME (adj) [suh-BLAHYM]

Meaning: exalted or noble and uplifting; lofty; supreme or outstanding

Usage 1: Her caramel, triple-chocolate brownies were *sublime*.

Usage 2: Getting to travel first class internationally was utterly *sublime*.

Usage 3: Her musical talent had gone from exceptional to *sublime*.

Usage 4: I stood there holding my new grandson, lost in the *sublime* experience.

Usage 5: Didn't you find his performance on screen *sublime*?

SUBLIMINAL (adj)   [suhb-LIM-*uh*-nl]

Meaning: below the threshold; below what one consciously recognizes

Usage 1: During the 70s, movie companies were thought to include *subliminal* messages in their films that convinced you to purchase popcorn, soda, and candy.

Usage 2: Her *subliminal* response is always to say "no," and we have to get her past that.

Usage 3: The power of his art is certainly not obvious, because you can't tell what the painting represents; instead, it is *subliminal*.

Usage 4: The tension at our family meeting was *subliminal*, but almost everyone realized it was there.

Usage 5: What was the *subliminal* meaning of his angry outburst?

SUCCOR (v)   [SUHK-er]

Meaning: aid; assist; to comfort or provide relief

Usage 1: Her friends did not fail to *succor* her when her mother died.

Usage 2: The preacher and his wife will *succor* the ailing parishioner.

Usage 3: Even a stranger might *succor* those in need.

Usage 4: My family refuses to *succor* me, so I must help myself.

Usage 5: Was it difficult to *succor* your colleague when her house burned down?

SUNDER (v)   [SUHN-der]

Meaning: separate; to split apart

Usage 1: His sponsor told him that in order to achieve sobriety, he needed to *sunder* his "drinking buddy" friendships.

Usage 2: War can *sunder* some relationships and can strengthen others.

Usage 3: For the sake of the grandchildren, I did not want to *sunder* my connection with my ex-daughter-in- law.

Usage 4: If they aren't nicer to me, I might *sunder* my ties with my children after they leave my house.

Usage 5: What caused their working relationship to *sunder*?

SUPERIMPOSE (v)   [soo-per-im-POHZ]

Meaning: place over something else; exchange: add to

Usage 1: If you *superimpose* this photograph over the other, you can see the progress of the construction.

Usage 2: When you hover your cursor over each of the columns, the column headings *superimpose* the text in the column.

Usage 3: When you *superimpose* your will over the will of others, anger and resentment often arises.

Usage 4: We can use last year's science fair trifold board and simply *superimpose* the stuff from this year.

Usage 5: Does it appear that the new style of building houses will *superimpose* the more traditional methods?

SUPPLICATE (v)   [SUHP-li-keyt]

Meaning: petition humbly; pray to grant a favor; ask or pray for

Usage 1: It seemed appropriate, in that moment, to *supplicate* to our individual gods.

Usage 2: I must *supplicate* your assistance in this matter.

Usage 3: The songwriters claim they frequently *supplicate* the assistance of their Muses.

Usage 4: It galls me to have to *supplicate* their financial support in this matter.

Usage 5: Can you remember the words you are supposed to use when you *supplicate* the help of the ancestors?

SUPPOSITITIOUS (adj)   [s*uh*-poz-i-TISH-*uh* s]

Meaning: assumed; counterfeit; hypothetical; not genuine; posing a hypothesis

Usage 1: It was a *supposititious* rendering of events, based on the evidence found at the crime scene.

Usage 2: Is *supposititious* detailing of his successes proved to be entirely untrue.

Usage 3: The papers proving her identity were *supposititious*, at best.

Usage 4: I was an expert at *supposititious* analysis; I knew when they were lying to me.

Usage 5: What was your *supposititious* location when you were obligated to be at my birthday party?

SURLY (adj)   [SUR-lee]

Meaning: rude; cross; bad-tempered or rude; unfriendly; hostile

Usage 1: Every morning he wakes up *surly*, but after a strong cup of coffee he is fine.

Usage 2: Under her *surly* demeanor lies a hysterically funny person.

Usage 3: There is no need to be *surly* to me; I am only trying to help.

Usage 4: I have had enough of your *surly* responses; get in the car, now.

Usage 5: Was I *surly* to you this morning when you served me breakfast?

SUSTENANCE (n)   [SUHS-t*uh*-n*uh* ns]

Meaning: means of support, food, nourishment; something that sustains life

Usage 1: Our first concern was *sustenance* for such a large crowd of refugees.

Usage 2: It was easy to despair, but we drew *sustenance* from the willingness of so many people to help.

Usage 3: The warm, gentle rain offered *sustenance* to the withered plants.

Usage 4: I would love to say I provided my children with *sustenance*, but it was actually the other way around.

Usage 5: Will this effort at *sustenance* for so many people who are in need prove to be enough?

SYLLOGISM (n)   [SIL-*uh*-jiz-*uh* m]

Meaning: logical formula consisting of a major premise, a minor premise and a conclusion; deceptive or specious argument; a piece of deductive reasoning or inference

Usage 1: His *syllogism* was erroneous, and, therefore, he came to the wrong conclusion.

Usage 2: I enjoyed working through his "If A, then B," *syllogism*, but I got an entirely different result.

Usage 3: He had reduced the world to a *syllogism*, but the world doesn't always work that way.

Usage 4: When I moved beyond *syllogism* to reality, I realized there were additional ways to draw inferences.

Usage 5: Where did you end up in the world as subscribed by the *syllogism*?

SYMMETRY (n)   [SIM-i-tree]

Meaning: arrangement of parts so that balance is obtained; congruity; the state of being same on both sides; in proportion

Usage 1: One of my favorite aspects of crocheting a doily is the exquisite *symmetry* of the doily pattern.

Usage 2: The *symmetry* of the summer and winter seasons at this latitude make it an attractive place to live.

Usage 3: We will need a *symmetry* of efforts between the two countries in order to achieve our goals.

Usage 4: They say beauty lies in *symmetry*, but what if my face is nowhere near symmetrical?

Usage 5: Isn't the natural *symmetry* of this plant leaf appealing?

TAPER (n)   [TEY-per]

Meaning: a candle; something having a gradual decrease in size or strength

Usage 1: With the electricity off until tomorrow we will need more than one *taper* scattered around the house.

Usage 2: The funnel ended in a *taper* that neatly fit the opening of the salt shaker.

Usage 3: Do you have a *taper* in case your flashlight batteries die?

Usage 4: My anger at the situation formed a *taper* and decreased with the passing moments.

Usage 5: Doesn't each *taper* on the candelabra signify something different?

TAWDRY (adj)   [TAW-dree]

Meaning: cheap and gaudy; low; mean; showy

Usage 1: Her brightly- flowered dress looked *tawdry* at the funeral.

Usage 2: Their affair was a *tawdry* one, with neither of their spouses knowing anything about it.

Usage 3: I liked the earrings I'd selected for her, but I worried they looked *tawdry*.

Usage 4: Must all the clothes at the discount store look *tawdry*?

Usage 5: Don't you think her bulbous rings on every finger look *tawdry*?

TERMINATE (v)   [TUR-m*uh*-neyt]

Meaning: to bring to an end; to be dismissed from a job

Usage 1: We will need to *terminate* his contract immediately.

Usage 2: Does this road *terminate* in a dead end?

Usage 3: What would happen if we *terminate* all our efforts to secure peace between the two countries?

Usage 4: I think I may need to *terminate* some of my unbalanced friendships.

Usage 5: When does the trial period of his employment *terminate*?

This page is intentionally left blank

Chapter **10**

Theocracy – Zany

This chapter covers the following words, each with its part of speech, pronunciation, and descriptive meaning.

Usage of the word is also illustrated in three to five sample sentences.

theocracy	unerringly	vindicate
timbre	uniformity	viscid
tonic	uninhibited	visionary
totter	unique	vivisection
tout	unruly	vulnerable
toxic	unsightly	waif
transient	untenable	wallow
transition	vacuous	weather
travail	valedictory	whit
trenchant	valid	wrangle
tribulation	vaunted	wrench
troth	venerable	wrest
trough	venture	wry
truism	verve	yen
turbid	vex	yoke
uncouth	vie	zany
underlying	vigilance	

THEOCRACY (n)   [thee-OK-r*uh*-see]

Meaning: government run by priests; a government in which God is deemed the supreme civil ruler

Usage 1: Given the number of churches in the town, you would think we were a *theocracy*.

Usage 2: With the separation of church and state, we've never experienced a *theocracy*.

Usage 3: We are a government of flawed people, not a *theocracy*.

Usage 4: It's true we went to church each week, but I never claimed my household was a *theocracy*.

Usage 5: Has there ever been a *theocracy* that ruled for a significant period of time?

TIMBRE (n)   [TAM-ber]

Meaning: quality of a musical tone produced by a musical instrument; musicality of a tone of sound

Usage 1: From the *timbre* of his speaking voice, we knew his singing voice was remarkable.

Usage 2: From its very first notes, the *timbre* of the cello delighted us.

Usage 3: We basked in the warm *timbre* of his demeanor.

Usage 4: They can always tell how much they are in trouble by the *timbre* of my screams.

Usage 5: Does the *timbre* of the piano sound off to you?

TONIC (n)   [TON-ik]

Meaning: invigorating medicine; curative liquid; something that heals or strengthens

Usage 1: My great aunt swears by the spoonful of a *tonic* that she takes every day.

Usage 2: Her soft piano- playing was a *tonic* to my troubled mind.

Usage 3: There is no *tonic* that will cure laziness.

Usage 4: Peace and quiet would be the perfect *tonic* for me on Mother's Day.

Usage 5: Did you know this *tonic* contains alcohol?

TOTTER (v)   [TOT-er]

Meaning: move unsteadily; to sway or rock as if about to fall

Usage 1: Don't let the coffee mug *totter* on the edge of the banister like that.

Usage 2: It was fun to watch my baby sister *totter* on the high heels I was wearing to the prom.

Usage 3: If you make that fragile vase *totter* like that, it will surely break and fall.

Usage 4: The earthquake, though mild, caused my tiny crystal figurines to *totter* on their shelves.

Usage 5: Are those stacked crates supposed to *totter* like that?

TOUT (v)   [tout]

Meaning: to publicize; to praise excessively; to promote; to praise extravagantly

Usage 1: I don't know why they always *tout* the successes of the school's football teams over any of its other teams.

Usage 2: Do not hesitate to *tout* the successes of our laboratories whenever you have the chance.

Usage 3: Shouldn't we *tout* the fact that the new restaurant is an huge moneymaker?

Usage 4: If I hear her *tout* the brilliance of her grandchildren even one more time, I'm going to go insane.

Usage 5: Does he have to *tout* his success in the stock market every time we get together?

TOXIC (adj)   [TOK-sik]

Meaning: poisonous; filled with toxins or poison

Usage 1: The chemicals in the pool are not *toxic* to most people.

Usage 2: We must ensure that the levels of medicine in her system do not become *toxic*.

Usage 3: It was a *toxic* mix of alcohol and drugs that killed him.

Usage 4: I had eaten too much cookie dough; the levels of sugar in my bloodstream were probably *toxic*.

Usage 5: Did you notice the warning labels on the drums that indicated the contents were *toxic*?

TRANSIENT (adj)   [TRAN-sh*uh* nt]

Meaning: momentary; temporary; lasting for a small amount of time; existing briefly

Usage 1: The effects of the illness were *transient*, and she recuperated fully.

Usage 2: As a worker, he was *transient*; he came and went all the time.

Usage 3: My feelings on the matter were *transient*; one minute I felt one way, and in the next minute I felt different.

Usage 4: I had a *transient* plan to renovate the house, but I got over it.

Usage 5: Isn't the ability to view the planet and star together in the same quadrant a *transient* one?

TRANSITION (n)   [tran-ZISH-*uh* n]

Meaning: going from one state of action to another; passage from one state or stage to another

Usage 1: In the *transition* to the new school, I lost half of my supplies.

Usage 2: It was a time of *transition* for all of us.

Usage 3: The plan for the *transition* of power in the newly-merged company was controversial.

Usage 4: I do not expect to have any trouble in my *transition* to an empty nest.

Usage 5: Was her *transition* into retirement successful?

TRAVAIL (n)   [tr*uh*-VEYL]

Meaning: painful labor; laborious work; suffering or anguish

Usage 1: The *travail* of last year was washed away by this year's successes.

Usage 2: He never spoke about the *travail* of his military service, but I could see the painful memories in his eyes.

Usage 3: It was easy to see during her appeal to the public that she was crumbling under the *travail* of the situation.

Usage 4: After the *travail* of landscaping the back yard, I couldn't bear to think about what we needed to do in the front yard.

Usage 5: Did he tell you, too, about the *travail* of moving from California to Georgia, and all the mishaps along the way?

TRENCHANT (adj)   [TREN-ch*uh* nt]

Meaning: keen; cutting or incisive; vigorous or energetic

Usage 1: Her persistent, *trenchant* comments kept the work of the committee on track.

Usage 2: His response to the accusations of fraud was unyielding and *trenchant*.

Usage 3: Her humor was not for everyone; it was biting and *trenchant*.

Usage 4: I didn't think of my remark as a *trenchant*, but merely as a polite observation.

Usage 5: How can you expect anything other than a *trenchant* response when you make fun of me like that?

TRIBULATION (n)   [trib-y*uh*-LEY-sh*uh* n]

Meaning: suffering; severe trouble or distress

Usage 1: Life, for her, had become a trial and *tribulation*.

Usage 2: I'm sorry for your *tribulation*; please let me know what I can do.

Usage 3: We must do what we can to relieve his *tribulation* because he has always been there for us.

Usage 4: If you don't follow my instructions, I will be happy to introduce you to *tribulation*.

Usage 5: What *tribulation* would drive her to take her own life?

TROTH (n)   [trawth]

Meaning: of good faith especially in betrothal; promise of fidelity or loyalty

Usage 1: He gave me his *troth* when he made his proposal of marriage.

Usage 2: The soldiers offered their *troth* to the battlefield- appointed captain.

Usage 3: I offered my *troth* to the sorority and promised to uphold its tenants.

Usage 4: Even when he made *troth*, it sounded like he was lying.

Usage 5: Didn't he offer the words in *troth* to the families who lost their loved ones?

TROUGH (n)   [trawf]

Meaning: container for feeding farm animals; lowest point (of a wave, business cycle, etc.); a container used for feeding or watering animals; the lowest point of a cycle

Usage 1: Each *trough* was filled with sweet-smelling hay that welcomed the horses into the barn.

Usage 2: We are definitely experiencing a *trough* in sales, which will affect our factory orders.

Usage 3: His new job was to clean out each *trough* and fill it with either food or water.

Usage 4: I wasn't worried about staying on the surfboard in the *trough* of the wave, but the crest was going to be a problem.

Usage 5: Do you think we are in the *trough* or the crest of the cycle?

TRUISM (n)   [TROO-iz-*uh* m]

Meaning: self-evident truth; an obvious truth

Usage 1: Based on my experience at work, it is a *truism* that "the squeaky wheel gets the grease."

Usage 2: If you ask the tree cutter if the tree should come down, of course he will tell you it does; recall the *truism*, "Never ask a barber if you need a haircut."

Usage 3: The news media's favorite *truism* is, of course, "the pen is mightier than the sword."

Usage 4: My children screamed when I used the *truism* about there being more than one way to skin a cat; they feared Furball had eaten her last meal.

Usage 5: Don't you think a boomerang is the perfect symbol for the *truism*, "What goes around, comes around."?

TURBID (adj)   [TUR-bid]

Meaning: muddy; having the sediment disturbed; obscured because of stirred up sediment

Usage 1: As they searched for the airplane in the *turbid* water, it was clear they might never find it.

Usage 2: Peering into the *turbid* waters, I could not determine if it was an alligator that had brushed up against me.

Usage 3: Every time you move, the water becomes *turbid*, and we can no longer see the fish.

Usage 4: Although I was initially excited, my emotions over the move to Alaska became increasingly *turbid*.

Usage 5: Were the winds of the tornado *turbid* and filled with debris?

UNCOUTH (adj)   [uhn-KOOTH]

Meaning: outlandish; clumsy; boorish; lacking in manners; awkward

Usage 1: His manners were *uncouth*, but he was a sweet young man, at heart.

Usage 2: There was no remedy for her *uncouth* behavior; it was too ingrained from her troubled upbringing.

Usage 3: With some practice, we could at least soften his *uncouth* ways.

Usage 4: Friends who are sophisticated can be annoying, and those who are *uncouth* can be endearing.

Usage 5: Did she say he was *uncouth* simply because he slurped his soup?

UNDERLYING (adj)   [UHN-der-lahy-ing]

Meaning: fundamental; lying below; basic; lying underneath

Usage 1: There was an *underlying* problem: I had no transportation.

Usage 2: The *underlying* message was that their lives were not deemed as important as ours.

Usage 3: My *underlying* concern is that we lack the resources to complete this project.

Usage 4: None of us addressed the *underlying* issue that we were in over our heads.

Usage 5: Doesn't the *underlying* question remain: who is in charge?

UNERRINGLY (adj)   [uhn-*uh*-RING-lee]

Meaning: infallibly; in a manner not involving error or going astray

Usage 1: My teacher is *unerringly* correct, and I find that annoying.

Usage 2: He *unerringly* hit his target every time.

Usage 3: So far my navigation software seems to get me to my destination *unerringly*.

Usage 4: Her goal was to hit her targets *unerringly*, but she fell short of that mark.

Usage 5: Did the guidebook *unerringly* steer you to the best tourist attractions?

UNIFORMITY (n)   [yoo-n*uh*-FAWR-mi-tee]

Meaning: monotony; quality of being uniform; homogeneous

Usage 1: Such *uniformity* among the laws is highly desirable.

Usage 2: The *uniformity* of our procedures, day in and day out, was about to kill me.

Usage 3: The *uniformity* of your thinking comes as no surprise; you two are just alike.

Usage 4: Life is too short to do anything for the sake of convenience or *uniformity*.

Usage 5: Is a *uniformity* of policies your ultimate goal?

UNINHIBITED (adj)   [uhn-in-HIB-i-tid]

Meaning: unrepressed; not restrained by social conventions

Usage 1: It was a pleasure to see her *uninhibited* manners.

Usage 2: Her often-*uninhibited* comments frequently got her into trouble in our small town.

Usage 3: When he played the violin, he was joyful and *uninhibited*.

Usage 4: I wish I were more *uninhibited*, but I keep hearing my mother's voice.

Usage 5: Have you noticed we tend to be *uninhibited* when we are very young and when we are very old, but not in between?

UNIQUE (adj)   [yoo-NEEK]

Meaning: without an equal; single in kind; one of a kind

Usage 1: It was a *unique* opportunity to do some good in this world.

Usage 2: Her approach to solving time-sensitive problems is *unique*: she simply ignores the deadline.

Usage 3: He has a *unique* accent because he has lived in over ten countries.

Usage 4: My determination to fly around the world in a bathtub might be seen as *unique*.

Usage 5: How *unique* are these security codes?

UNRULY (adj**)**   [uhn-ROO-lee]

Meaning: disobedient; lawless; ungovernable

Usage 1: Her little brother and sister are so *unruly,* that I refuse to babysit them for any price.

Usage 2: The bad elements in the town had become *unruly* and had driven out law-abiding citizens.

Usage3: They say he's not *unruly*; he's just "spirited."

Usage 4: When the kids are *unruly,* I shoot them with water guns.

Usage 5: Don't you think her hair is a tangle of *unruly* curls?

UNSIGHTLY (adj**)**   [uhn-SAHYT-lee]

Meaning: ugly; unpleasant to look at

Usage 1: Her room was an *unsightly* mess, with clothes, books, and toys strewn everywhere.

Usage 2: It was an *unsightly,* untreated wound, so I gave it first priority.

Usage 3: I cannot believe some people view those elegant, energy-producing windmills as *unsightly.*

Usage 4: We desperately needed to trim the hedge out front; it had gone from overgrown to *unsightly.*

Usage 5: How did this bathroom become an *unsightly* mess so soon after I cleaned it?

UNTENABLE (adj**)**   [uhn-TEN-*uh*-b*uh* l]

Meaning: indefensible; not able to be maintained; not able to be defended; uninhabitable

Usage 1: Your position on this issue is *untenable*; how can you defend it?

Usage 2: I can't believe they are making the *untenable* argument that a short term gain is more important than considering the long term effects.

Usage 3: Her rude behavior to our parents was *untenable,* and I was not going to tolerate it any longer.

Usage 4: Is it *untenable* if I take a vacation, and I don't invite my kids?

Usage 5: Wasn't the situation she had gotten herself into *untenable*?

VACUOUS (adj**)**   [VAK-yoo-*uh* s]

Meaning: empty; inane; like a vacuum; stupid

Usage 1: We cannot allow their sacrifices on behalf of freedom to be treated as *vacuous* or meaningless.

Usage 2: His *vacuous* smile told me we had nothing in common.

Usage 3: His poetry lacked depth and meaning; much of it was simply *vacuous.*

Usage 4: His supermodel girlfriend was not as shallow or as *vacuous* as I thought she'd be.

Usage 5: Does her *vacuous* lifestyle appeal to you?

VALEDICTORY (adj**)**   [val-i-DIK-t*uh*-ree]

Meaning: pertaining to farewell; leave-taking; pertaining to bidding goodbye

Usage 1: Her *valedictory* speech at graduation was both touching and inspiring.

Usage 2: In a *valedictory* letter, he thanked the company for grooming him for success.

Usage 3: Her *valedictory* shout from the balcony of the cruise ship was a reminder to feed the dogs.

Usage 4: When you run away from home, make sure you leave a *valedictory* note.

Usage 5: Do his comments sound *valedictory* to you?

VALID (adj**)**   [VAL-id]

Meaning: logically convincing; sound; legally acceptable; having legal force; well-founded

Usage 1: My driver's license is no longer *valid*; I need to renew it.

Usage 2: His argument was not *valid* because the facts do not support it.

Usage 3: I'm not sure our findings in our science experiment are *valid* because we did not sufficiently control the variables.

Usage 4: I told him if he gave me three *valid* arguments on the benefits of being exposed to nature, I would take him camping.

Usage 5: Is a law *valid* if it applies retroactively?

VAUNTED (adj)   [VAWN-tid]

Meaning: highly publicized; boasted; something praised excessively

Usage 1: It was a *vaunted* display of art, but I found it to be mediocre.

Usage 2: The restaurant was *vaunted* as much for its wait staff as for its excellent food.

Usage 3: Their *vaunted* philanthropic acts were revealed to be mere publicity; they never really happened.

Usage 4: I humbly told them it was my *vaunted* beauty that intimated others.

Usage 5: Are his *vaunted* accomplishments documented anywhere?

VENERABLE (adj)   [VEN-er-*uh*-b*uh* l]

Meaning: deserving high respect; worthy of reverence or respect

Usage 1: He was a *venerable* leader during the Vietnam and Afghanistan wars.

Usage 2: She was the *venerable* writer of well-constructed mysteries.

Usage 3: I know you treat your time with your grandchildren as *venerable,* and you will let nothing interfere with it.

Usage 4: She'd been a *venerable* leader of her church for many years.

Usage 5: Was it fun to listen to *venerable* classic songs on those albums you found?

VENTURE (v)   [VEN-cher]

Meaning: dare; take a risk; to invest money into

Usage 1: I would *venture* to say that you are not thrilled with this new plan.

Usage 2: To *venture* into the restaurant business was risky, and I wasn't sure my bank account was ready for it.

Usage 3: The new puppy could only *venture* as far as her leash would allow her.

Usage 4: If I ever *venture* into a new job, I'll make sure I'm paid a whole lot more than I am now.

Usage 5: Will you *venture* into a new type of capital fundraising this time?

VERVE (n)   [vurv]

Meaning: enthusiasm; liveliness; animation; vivaciousness

Usage 1: His *verve* and energy during our initial meeting made me confident that he was the right person for the job.

Usage 2: The advertisements for these new pills say they give you the *verve* you once had when you were twenty years old.

Usage 3: It wasn't his *verve,* as much as his intelligence that won us over.

Usage 4: I wish I had the *verve* that I once had to run marathons and swim laps.

Usage 5: Why does he lack *verve* today; is he sick?

VEX (v)   [veks]

Meaning: annoy; distress; irritate; frustrate

Usage 1: I hate to *vex* him when he is trying to finish his work.

Usage 2: It seems almost anything will *vex* her these days; she's become such a grouch.

Usage 3: Will it *vex* you if I borrow the car this morning?

Usage 4: It would *vex* me to know that I could have helped you, but you didn't ask.

Usage 5: Doesn't it *vex* the teachers when you interrupt their instruction?

VIE (v)   [vahy]

Meaning: contend; compete; contest; struggle for

Usage 1: Will you *vie* for first prize in the boxing contest?

Usage 2: If I have to *vie* for your attention all night, I'd rather not go to the party.

Usage 3: Teams of each nation will *vie* for a position on the final roster.

Usage 4: I can not *vie* for his position at the poker table; I'm not that good yet.

Usage 5: Will everyone *vie* for the title of "most elegant" tonight at the ball?

VIGILANCE (n)   [VIJ-*uh*-l*uh* ns]

Meaning: watchfulness; state of being vigilant

Usage 1: The police *vigilance*, after my dad had received death threats, was welcome.

Usage 2: She kept close *vigilance* over the tiniest of the newborn puppies.

Usage 3: We appreciated the health organization's *vigilance* over the health of its community.

Usage 4: It's my unerring *vigilance* that will prevent you from sneaking out tonight.

Usage 5: What could be more important than *vigilance* over the health and safety of our children?

VINDICATE (v)   [VIN-di-keyt]

Meaning: clear from blame; exonerate; justify or support; to clear from accusation or suspicion; to defend against successfully

Usage 1: The lawyers say they are confident this trial will *vindicate* their client.

Usage 2: He will need to *vindicate* his claim that the waste produced by the factory is harmless when expelled into the river.

Usage 3: We cannot *vindicate* those who engaged in cruel acts simply because they are now old and infirm.

Usage 4: To *vindicate* myself from a charge of being a bad neighbor, I finally mowed my lawn.

Usage 5: Does he really hope to *vindicate* the heinous acts he has committed?

VISCID (adj)   [VIS-id]

Meaning: adhesive; gluey; covered by a sticky substance

Usage 1: The back of the leaves were so *viscid* that I had to peel them off my fingers.

Usage 2: The alien saliva was some sort of *viscid* fluid that stung when it came into contact with human flesh.

Usage 3: The smell of the lilies was so overpowering, it was almost *viscid*, sticking to the hairs inside my nose.

Usage 4: If she doesn't shut up soon, I will find something *viscid* to seal her lips.

Usage 5: Is the slime we are using for the slime-ball battle *viscid* so that it will stick to hair and skin?

VISIONARY (n/adj)   [VIZH-*uh*-ner-ee]

Meaning: produced by imagination; fanciful; mystical; having keen foresight; idealistic

Usage 1: Many consider Steve Jobs of Apple, Inc. to have been a *visionary*. (n)

Usage 2: It is astonishing how often science fiction stories prove to be *visionary*. (adj)

Usage 3: This *visionary* approach to treating diabetes is gaining acceptance across the country. (adj)

Usage 4: I have no desire to be a *visionary*; I struggle enough with reality. (n)

Usage 5: Do you think it is a *visionary* view of the world in twenty years' time? (adj)

VIVISECTION (n) [viv-*uh*-SEK-sh*uh* n]

Meaning: act of dissecting living animals; the act of cutting into or dissecting a body

Usage 1: I needed to help the students with their *vivisection* of the frogs today.

Usage 2: Through *vivisection* we have learned much about how the internal organs of animals work.

Usage 3: A true understanding of those body parts comes, not from color plates, but from a controlled *vivisection*.

Usage 4: It was my first *vivisection*, and I fainted on the spot.

Usage 5: Will all of your teachers be present today for the *vivisection* of the cow's eye?

VULNERABLE (adj) [VUHL-ner-*uh*-b*uh* l]

Meaning: capable of being hurt; open to attack

Usage 1: Without information from the reconnaissance pilots, the soldiers were *vulnerable* to a siege at any moment.

Usage 2: Don't leave your left side *vulnerable*; protect it with your elbows.

Usage 3: Without security software to protect your computer, you will leave your personal information vulnerable to attack.

Usage 4: I had to be careful when walking my little dog in the park because she was *vulnerable* to attack by the crows that sat on the treetops.

Usage 5: Was she *vulnerable* and shy at that age?

WAIF (n) [weyf]

Meaning: homeless child or animal; a poor child or animal on the streets; a stray item

Usage 1: The child was no more than a *waif* on the streets of a big city.

Usage 2: She appeared as pale and as thin as a *waif*.

Usage 3: It isn't the adult homeless person I find so troubling; it is the young *waif*.

Usage 4: I vowed never to turn down a *waif*, be it child or animal.

Usage 5: Did you see that *waif* and his dog?

WALLOW (v) [WOL-oh]

Meaning: roll in; indulge in; become helpless

Usage 1: I love to watch the pigs *wallow* in the mud; it makes them so happy.

Usage 2: The puppies have a blast when they are allowed to *wallow* in the raked leaves.

Usage 3: I don't want to *wallow* in misery, but everything is going wrong right now.

Usage 4: One day I hope to *wallow* in luxury, but I'm currently wallowing in debt.

Usage 5: Is that mysterious car going to *wallow* through the town like that?

WEATHER (v) [WE*TH* –er]

Meaning: endure the effects of weather or other forces; to expose to weather or bear up under weather conditions

Usage 1: That wood will *weather* and fade a little more each year.

Usage 2: If we can *weather* this storm, we should come out just fine.

Usage 3: Will the restaurant be able to *weather* another tough winter with fewer customers?

Usage 4: It was clear that my face was unable to *weather* successfully twenty years of winters in Alaska.

Usage 5: Will that country *weather* the many insurgencies this year, or will the government fold?

WHIT (n)   [hwit]

Meaning: smallest speck; tiniest particle

Usage 1: I didn't care a single *whit* whether she came to the party or not.

Usage 2: If I smell even a *whit* of smoke, you will have to put out your cigarette.

Usage 3: Even after she gave me the medicine, I didn't feel one *whit* better.

Usage 4: When I saw my old boyfriend at reunion, I realized he hadn't changed a single *whit*.

Usage 5: Do you give a *whit* if she stays for dinner?

WRANGLE (v)   [RANG-*guh* l]

Meaning: quarrel; obtain through arguing; herd cattle; tackle; argue over

Usage 1: They will need to *wrangle* the cattle in order to take them to market.

Usage 2: To *wrangle* cattle is an almost-forgotten art.

Usage 3: I don't want to *wrangle* with you over this issue; you can have your way.

Usage 4: Although we *wrangle* over the price, I always buy my meat from her.

Usage 5: Have you ever tried to *wrangle* a crocodile?

WRENCH (v)   [rench]

Meaning: pull; strain; twist; to pull away, usually by twisting; to injure by overstraining

Usage 1: The hungry dog tried to *wrench* the sandwich right out of my hand.

Usage 2: Before she could hurt herself, I needed to *wrench* the scissors away from her.

Usage 3: My heart never fails to *wrench* at the sight of animals stranded during a natural disaster.

Usage 4: If you don't give me that phone, I will *wrench* it out of your hands.

Usage 5: Did the machine pull him so hard that it made him *wrench* his shoulder?

WREST (v)   [rest]

Meaning: to pull away; to take by violence; to jerk away from or otherwise take away by force

Usage 1: I saw my little sister rudely *wrest* the doll away from her best friend.

Usage 2: The policeman needs to *wrest* the gun out of the robber's hand as soon as possible.

Usage 3: Every time I would pick up a toy, someone would *wrest* it out of my hands.

Usage 4: I was the only one allowed to *wrest* cash out of my children'shands.

Usage 5: Were you able to *wrest* control away from the majority shareholder?

WRY (adj)   [rahy]

Meaning: with a humorous twist; distorted; contrary; perverse

Usage 1: With a *wry* smile, she admitted that I was correct.

Usage 2: His laughter was *wry* and twisted, like mine.

Usage 3: A *wry* look in her eyes told me that she was being sarcastic.

Usage 4: It was his *wry* sense of humor that drew me to him in the first place.

Usage 5: Can you tell when he is being *wry* and ironic?

YEN (n)   [yen]

Meaning: longing; urge; strong desire; hankering or craving for; currency of Japan

Usage 1: My sister claimed a *yen* for lima beans throughout her pregnancy.

Usage 2: I have a *yen* for fried green tomatoes today.

Usage 3: How much *yen* do you have in your purse for when we reach Tokyo?

Usage 4: He seemed to have a *yen* to tell me every sin he'd ever committed.

Usage 5: What was the exchange rate between the dollar and the *yen* yesterday?

YOKE (v)   [yohk]

Meaning: join together; unite; to attach an animal to a plow or other farm implement; to link or unite

Usage 1: You need to *yoke* the oxen first thing this morning before you go to school.

Usage 2: I hated to *yoke* the horses so early, but we needed to arrive at the market by five.

Usage 3: There was no need to *yoke* the wagon because we would not be using it.

Usage 4: I suppose it isn't legal to *yoke* your children to a merry-go-round so they can grind corn into cornmeal.

Usage 5: Will we need to *yoke* the oxen for the farm show tomorrow?

ZANY (adj)   [ZEY-nee]

Meaning: crazy; comic; clownish; whimsical

Usage 1: My niece's *zany* comments always cracked me up.

Usage 2: His *zany* manners brought a light heartedness to the situation.

Usage 3: I don't often get the opportunity to be *zany*, but this is one of those occasions.

Usage 4: We had a wild and *zany* time at the amusement park.

Usage 5: Even though you are generally reserved, are you also sometimes *zany*?

This page is intentionally left blank

Word List 2

This page is intentionally left blank

Chapter **11**

Abbreviate - Behemoth

This chapter covers the following words, each with its part of speech, pronunciation, and descriptive meaning.

Usage of the word is also illustrated in three to five sample sentences.

abbreviate	anemia	audit
accelerate	anguish	authoritarian
adamant	annals	avarice
addiction	annul	aviary
adept	anthology	balmy
affidavit	anvil	bedizen
agog	application	befuddle
alias	apropos	behemoth
alimentary	archipelago	
alimony	ardor	
alliteration	aria	
allude	array	
allure	arrest	
amazon	artful	
ambulatory	artifacts	
amity	artisan	
amoral	assent	
amulet	assert	
analogy	assumption	
ancestry	astral	
anecdote	asylum	

ABBREVIATE (v)   [*uh*-BREE-vee-eyt]

Meaning: to reduce in length

Usage 1: Although he knew he was running over his allotted time, Peter wasn't sure how he could *abbreviate* his speech.

Usage 2: Comparing Old English to Modern English, it seems sometimes as if there are no set rules on how to *abbreviate.*

Usage 3: Even though she had known it was a possibility, the doctor's girlfriend was frustrated when he had to *abbreviate* their date because he was called in to work.

Usage 4: Because his professor had said the report could be no longer than 10 pages, Joe looked for ways to *abbreviate* his first draft.

Usage 5: If you take medicine, get plenty of rest, and properly hydrate, you may be able to *abbreviate* the length of the common cold.

ACCELERATE (v)   [ak-SEL-*uh*-reyt]

Meaning: to increase in speed, growth, or development

Usage 1: Because his cancer was no longer in remission, the doctors decided to *accelerate* Tom's treatment.

Usage 2: The company had had a much better year than expected, so the board decided to *accelerate* expansion plans.

Usage 3: If you want to *accelerate* learning and increase retention, first you must motivate the students.

Usage 4: In order to *accelerate* her weight loss, Ruth began her new diet with a three-day fast.

Usage 5: Sam became sure that he was being followed when the car behind him began to ominously *accelerate.*

ADAMANT (adj)   [AD-*uh*-m*uh* nt]

Meaning: immovable or inflexible in opinion or position

Usage 1: John said that he was flexible as to the date, but Mary was *adamant* that the marriage had to take place on the 15th of May.

Usage 2: Despite the accusations of the detective, Richard was *adamant* that he was innocent.

Usage 3: Diane implored her toddler to eat, but the little girl continued to refuse, defiant and *adamant* until the end.

Usage 4: If you are so *adamant* that you are right, maybe I am wrong.

ADDICTION (n)   [*uh*-DIK-sh*uh* n]

Meaning: an unhealthy compulsion or dependence

Usage 1: Ed often found himself unable to pay his bills, because of his gambling *addiction.*

Usage 2: Many people say that belief in a Higher Power is the key to overcoming an *addiction.*

Usage 3: Long overdue, Sam finally faced his *addiction* to cocaine by agreeing to enter rehab.

Usage 4: The growing amount of time that he spent online made Fred realize that he had an *addiction* to the Internet.

Usage 5: As if under the spell of some insidious *addiction,* Abelard became obsessed with Heloise.

ADEPT (adj)   [*uh*-dept]

Meaning: expert or skillful

Usage 1: Through many hours of practice, Trevor eventually became *adept* at shooting free throws.

Usage 2: Because she didn't have any of her own, Sally felt that she was not very *adept* at dealing with unruly children.

Usage 3: If a man will become *adept* at preparing his own meals, he will find that he has greatly added to what he has to offer his future wife.

Usage 4: I am not very *adept* at fixing things because I have neither the time nor the inclination to learn.

Usage 5: It was essential to her job performance, so Ann became *adept* at using spreadsheet programs.

AFFIDAVIT (n) [af-i-DEY-vit]

Meaning: a written oath made before an authority

Usage 1: John swore an *affidavit* before the magistrate that he had witnessed Richard break into the house.

Usage 2: Rather than make multiple trips to court and incur debilitating legal fees, Ellen gave her *affidavit* that she relinquished all claim to the property.

Usage 3: Because the earlier *affidavit* was so thorough, the lawyer found no reason to call rebuttal witnesses.

AGOG (adj) [*uh*-GOG]

Meaning: highly excited, curious, or anticipatory

Usage 1: The crowd was *agog* when they saw the outfit that the singer was wearing.

Usage 2: Don't just stand there *agog* with your mouth open – do something!

Usage 3: The children's faces were *agog* with wonder when they saw how many presents were underneath the Christmas tree.

Usage 4: Leslie's face was *agog* with joy and tears rolled down,unbidden,when she saw the engagement ring.

Usage 5: For just a moment, the sportscasters were *agog* and speechless when they witnessed the miracle shot from half-court.

ALIAS (n) [EY-lee-*uh* s]

Meaning: an assumed name

Usage 1: The outlaw's real name was William H. Bonney, but his *alias* was "Billy the Kid".

Usage 2: So as to escape his fan's notice, the rock star checked into the hotel under an *alias*.

Usage 3: Although they are very similar in meaning, "nom de plume" and "*alias*" have very different connotations.

Usage 4: Because of national security, it is virtually impossible to travel using an *alias*.

ALIMENTARY (adj) [al-*uh*-MEN-t*uh*-ree]

Meaning: providing nourishment or sustenance concerned with food

Usage 1: When traveling the Oregon Trail, pioneers often found it very difficult to find *alimentary* provisions.

Usage 2: Foods like bread, cheese, milk, butter, pasta, and flour are considered to be *alimentary* staples, and should therefore be in every home.

Usage 3: Although they may taste good, many junk foods contain few nutrients, and therefore, are not very alimentary.

ALIMONY (n) [AL-*uh*-moh-nee]

Meaning: payment by a husband to his divorced wife (or vice versa)

Usage 1: Unfortunately for people who are seeking bankruptcy protection, *alimony* is not a forgivable obligation.

Usage 2: To make sure that he was always in his ex-wife's good graces, John always sent his *alimony* check promptly on the first of the month.

Usage 3: Because she hadn't yet found adequate employment since her divorce, Joan was grateful for the order of *alimony*, because without it, she would not have been able to support herself.

Usage 4: After deductions for child support, *alimony*, insurance, and retirement, Harry thought his pay check looked positively meager.

Usage 5: Charlie, always known for his thrift, was in no hurry to marry his girlfriend, because that would put an end to the substantial *alimony* payment that she received.

ALLITERATION (n)   [*uh*-lit-*uh*-REY-sh*uh* n]

Meaning: repetition of beginning sound in poetry

Usage 1: When used properly, *alliteration* can add an interesting or whimsical tone to a poem.

Usage 2: Many Marvel superheroes show Stan Lee's penchant for *alliteration* – Peter Parker, Bruce Banner, Reed Richards, and Scott Summers, for example.

Usage 3: One of the most famous examples of the use of *alliteration* in poetry is The Siege of Belgrade, which begins with "An Austrian array, awfully arrayed", and ends with "Zealously, zanies, zealously zeals best."

Usage 4: Many people confuse *alliteration* and onomatopoeia, but the former is the repetition of sounds, while the latter is the imitation of sounds.

Usage 5: Alliteration, similes, personification, onomatopoeia, and metaphors are all examples of literary devices that are used in writing poetry.

ALLUDE (v)   [*uh*-LOOD]

Meaning: to hint at

Usage 1: The song "White Rabbit" manages to *allude* to drugs, while sounding like it is a reference to the children's tale.

Usage 2: Many vitamin supplements are prohibited by law from claiming outright any specific health benefits, but they will *allude* to them without hesitation.

Usage 3: Without stating it directly, the prosecuting attorney was able to *allude* to the defendant's prior criminal record.

ALLURE (v)   [*uh*-LOO R]

Meaning: to attract, charm, or tempt

Usage 1: Often, a sensual perfume is how a woman will *allure* a man she is interested in.

Usage 2: Although the waitress at the cocktail bar did her best to *allure* him, Richard thought it best if he went home to his wife.

Usage 3: The beauty and peace in Hawaii can *allure* even the most jaded of travelers.

AMAZON (n)   [AM-*uh*-zon]

Meaning: a strong, aggressive woman

Usage 1: Because of her forthright nature, many people thought that Joan was at best an *amazon*, and at worst, a harpy.

Usage 2: Like many mothers, Regina is a combination of superwoman, *amazon*, nurse, teacher, chauffeur, and drill sergeant.

Usage 3: With the strength of an *amazon* and the grace of a gazelle, the Olympic gymnast performed a very difficult routine.

Usage 4: Peggy didn't like being called an *amazon*, simply because she liked to be the one doing the asking, when it came to dating.

Usage 5: Some women dislike being referred to as an *amazon*, but it is a better term than battle-ax or harridan.

AMBULATORY (adj)   [AM-by*uh*-l*uh*-tawr-ee]

Meaning: able to walk

Usage 1: After such a horrific crash, the first responders were surprised that the victim was *ambulatory*.

Usage 2: It took great effort, but Albert was *ambulatory* within three months after his accident.

Usage 3: John's grandma had difficulty being *ambulatory*, because she had let her weight go and she never exercised.

Usage 4: Physical therapists have the philosophy that if you are *ambulatory*, you are not going to spend your day sitting or lying down.

AMITY (n)   [AM-i-tee]

Meaning: a peaceful, harmonious relationship

Usage 1: To ensure *amity* between the neighbors, residents took turns hosting get-togethers.

Usage 2: As long as you're willing to apologize and admit when you are wrong, you can live in *amity* with your spouse.

Usage 3: It is a good idea to practice *amity* and teamwork with your coworkers, because it will help everyone's careers.

Usage 4: Learn to forgive, because in the end, *amity* is greatly preferable to hostility.

Usage 5: In the interest of *amity* within the family, Rachel gave up her claim to her mother's wedding ring, even though it had been promised to her.

AMORAL (adj)   [ey-MAWR-*uh* l]

Meaning: libertine; neither moral nor immoral

Usage 1: Within the last few years, many television programs have featured flawed, *amoral* antiheroes, such as Tony Soprano, Don Draper, Walter White, and Dexter Morgan.

Usage 2: In many science fiction movies, technology can be portrayed as evil, but technology is inherently amoral – neither good nor bad.

Usage 3: In many people's eyes, being *amoral* is just as loathsome as being immoral, because they feel that if you're not good, then you're definitely bad.

Usage 4: In our public lives, most of us want to be viewed as very moral people, however in reality, in our private lives, many of us are quite *amoral* for the sake of convenience.

Usage 5: "The end justifies the means" is an example of an *amoral* statement.

AMULET (n)   [AM-y*uh*-lit]

Meaning: a charm or talisman worn for protection

Usage 1: A four-leaf clover cannot be considered an *amulet*, because it is supposed to bring good luck, rather than offer protection.

Usage 2: In Turkey, some citizens wear the Nazar *amulet* to ward off the evil eye.

Usage 3: For his daughter's birthday, Jack bought her a new *amulet* for her charm bracelet.

Usage 4: Contrary to what some people might think, a Catholic medallion is not a sort of *amulet*, because it serves as a reminder of some aspect of Christian doctrine, rather than as a superstitious or pagan protection.

Usage 5: In fantasy literature, a quest for a magical item, such as an enchanted *amulet* or a charmed sword, is a common theme.

ANALOGY (n)   [*uh*-NAL-*uh*-jee]

Meaning: a comparison based on the similarity of two different things

Usage 1: You didn't have to take me quite so literally, it was an *analogy*!

Usage 2: To help her young daughter understand better, Barbara made an *analogy* between her daughter's behavior and the Boy Who Cried Wolf.

Usage 3: In mathematics, it can be very useful to use an *analogy* between similar or equal shapes, so the students can understand the concept better.

ANCESTRY (n)   [AN-ses-tree]

Meaning: family descent, especially if distinguished or honorable

Usage 1: The snobbish social climber claimed that she could trace her *ancestry* back to the Mayflower.

Usage 2: Because I never knew my grandparents, I would be interested to learn about my *ancestry*.

Usage 3: In many European countries, a person's *ancestry* can be of even greater importance than their current station in life.

Usage 4: If we are proud of our *ancestry*, we live our lives in a way where we will never disappoint those who came before us.

Usage 5: While researching her *ancestry*, Susan found out to her chagrin that her great-great-grandparents entered this country illegally.

ANECDOTE (n)   [AN-ik-doht]

Meaning: a short, funny, or interesting retelling

Usage 1: Unfortunately, Don didn't realize that a family reunion wasn't the best place to tell his *anecdote* about the time when he had accidentally visited a nudist colony.

Usage 2: The best part about being a traveling salesman is you always have another amusing *anecdote* about your travels that you can tell.

Usage 3: At his Friar's Roast, Joe's friends kept the crowd roaring by telling one joke or *anecdote* after the other.

Usage 4: On a first date, it's always a good idea to have an *anecdote* or two on hand to keep your date interested.

Usage 5: To capture the attention of his history class, the professor told a gory *anecdote* about Henry VIII.

ANEMIA (n)   [*uh*-NEE-mee-*uh*]

Meaning: a medical condition involving a shortage of red blood cells and characterized by pallor and weakness

Usage 1: Because of his lifelong *anemia*, even the slightest exertion gave Niles the pallor of the grave.

Usage 2: Allison suffered from *anemia* after childbirth, and was usually too weak to properly look after her children.

Usage 3: The combination of the shock, the high altitude, and his own constitutional *anemia* was too much for Harold, and he promptly passed out.

ANGUISH (n)   [ANG-gwish]

Meaning: extreme distress or suffering

Usage 1: The *anguish* Mary felt at her lover's leaving was only matched by her fear that he might return.

Usage 2: When the Navy corpsman ran out of morphine, he could only helplessly watch the *anguish* suffered by his wounded comrades.

Usage 3: Because he was a good man, Truman felt moral *anguish* over his decision, but that pain was overridden by his pragmatism.

Usage 4: Boxer Jim Braddock was full of shame and *anguish* when he was unable to support his family during the Great Depression.

ANNALS (n)   [AN-lz]

Meaning: historical records

Usage 1: The first round of the match will go down as one of the greatest in the *annals* of boxing.

Usage 2: While researching the topic, Ellen had to comb through over 100 years of the city's *annals*.

Usage 3: When the *annals* of your life are written, what do you want it to say – that you were a leader or a follower?

Usage 4: While reviewing the *annals*, it was found that an important passage had been mistranslated.

ANNUL (v) [*uh*-NUHL]

Meaning: to cancel or void

Usage 1: Before he could marry his second wife, John had to have the priest *annul* his first marriage.

Usage 2: Because the statute was unconstitutional, the legislators had no choice but to *annul* the law.

Usage 3: When it was learned that one of the cabinet members has accepted a bribe, the other members moved to *annul* the vote.

Usage 4: If your marriage was never consummated, you may have grounds to ask the church official to *annul* it.

ANTHOLOGY (n) [an-THOL-*uh*-jee]

Meaning: compilation; book of literary selections, most often by various authors

Usage 1: An *anthology* covering a certain genre is an excellent way to discover new authors.

Usage 2: Because its episodes told "standalone" stories, rather than those contained in an ongoing arc, "The Twilight Zone" is considered to be an *anthology* series.

Usage 3: Despite his many longer works, Steven King has often stated that he is a short story writer, which explains why he puts out a new *anthology* every few years.

Usage 4: Currently, the disco album "Saturday Night Fever" by the Bee Gees and other artists is the best- selling *anthology* album of all time, with almost 19 million units sold.

ANVIL (n) [AN-vil]

Meaning: iron block used in hammering out metals

Usage 1: Despite her excellent grades, Jane's unstable home life was like an *anvil* weighing her down.

Usage 2: In many of the old Warner Bros. Road Runner cartoons, an *anvil* was often used as yet another way to make Wile E. Coyote suffer a painful disaster.

Usage 3: In Greek mythology, Hephaestus is often shown at his forge, working with his hammer, tongs, and *anvil* to make the thunderbolts that Zeus would hurl.

Usage 4: Caught between the hammer of life in the *anvil* of reality, we are forged into the people we were meant to be.

Usage 5: Taking an alcoholic to a bar is like using an *anvil* as a life preserver.

APPLICATION (n) [ap-li-KEY-sh*uh* n]

Meaning: a request for a specific type of assistance, or the putting of something to a specific type of use

Usage 1: Hoping silently for approval, Stanley crossed his fingers when he turned in his loan *application*.

Usage 2: Jordan forgot to put her phone number on the job *application*, so the manager wasn't able to call her back.

Usage 3: To help her in her job, the secretary downloaded a computer *application* that would recognize voice dictation.

Usage 4: To have good morals is not enough, because it is the *application* of those morals in everyday life that shows the true measure of the man.

APROPOS (adv)   [ap-r*uh*-POH]

Meaning: fitting the situation

Usage 1: Apropos of nothing, John began discussing his latest surgery during the dinner party.

Usage 2: Larry met with his supervisor for his annual review, and, *apropos*, he asked for a raise.

Usage 3: Mark was visiting the doctor for his yearly checkup; *apropos*, he mentioned the new vitamin supplements he was taking.

ARCHIPELAGO (n)   [ahr-k*uh*-PEL-*uh*-goh]

Meaning: a group or chain of islands

Usage 1: For his vacation, Richard went on an extensive luxury boat tour of the *archipelago*.

Usage 2: The *archipelago* was formed when a violent volcanic eruption tore apart the mainland.

Usage 3: Because there were so very many islands in the *archipelago*, Charlie decided to describe them as a group, rather than individually.

Usage 4: The new students were largely ignored at the party, making them feel like an *archipelago* of lost souls.

ARDOR (n)   [AHR-der]

Meaning: a fervent, intense feeling or enthusiasm

Usage 1: Because he was so smitten with Joan, Roger found it difficult to conceal his *ardor*.

Usage 2: Swept away by his *ardor*, Philip impetuously proposed to his girlfriend of only one month.

Usage 3: I find it hard to express my *ardor* in my own words, so that's why I bought you this greeting card.

Usage 4: The flame of *ardor* burns brighter but shorter than the lasting warmth of true love.

ARIA (n)   [AHR-ee-*uh*]

Meaning: an elaborate song, sung solo, but with accompaniment, typically in an opera

Usage 1: The mezzo-soprano's final *aria* concluded to thunderous applause.

Usage 2: Although she had heard it many times before, "Che Gelida Manina" from La Boheme remained my mother's favorite *aria*.

Usage 3: When the final, heartbreaking *aria* was sung, there wasn't a dry eye in the house.

Usage 4: In the Middle Ages, castrati were able to reach notes on an *aria* that were beyond that of regular adult men.

Usage 5: She hated to say so, but the only part of the opera that Rosalind enjoyed was the *aria*.

ARRAY (n)   [*uh*-REY]

Meaning: a large group or assortment

Usage 1: During the fashion show, the clothes were laid out in a dizzying *array* of styles and colors.

Usage 2: To be a creative cook, it is necessary to have access to an *array* of spices and herbs.

Usage 3: Karen had a hard time deciding on her college schedule, because of the *array* of classes that were available.

Usage 4: Among the *array* of restaurants found in this town, you can always be sure there are some fast food joints.

ARREST (v)   [*uh*-rest]

Meaning: to stop, slow down, or seize by legal authority

Usage 1: Because they had caught it in time, the doctors were able to *arrest* the growth of the tumor.

Usage 2: Too many distractions and too much instability can *arrest* a child's progress in school.

Usage 3: If you want to *arrest* the downward spiral of your life, get up off of your "but's" and do something about it.

Usage 4: David had failed to show up for his hearing, so the judge issued a warrant for his *arrest*.

Usage 5: Mike was lucky that the police officer did not *arrest* him, and instead, let him off with a warning.

ARTFUL (adj)   [ahrt-*fuh* l]

Meaning: characterized by skill, cunning, or craftiness

Usage 1: The suspect was evasive, even *artful*, with his misleading answers to the policeman's questions.

Usage 2: For the duration of the hunt, the *artful* fox was able to elude both the riders and their hounds.

Usage 3: Montresor's *artful* deceit led to the downfall of Fortunato.

Usage 4: Trevor was very impressed with his wife's *artful* ability to make a delicious meal out of what they had on hand when surprise guests dropped by.

Usage 5: Sometimes, to get ahead at work, you must think on your feet and be *artful* when tackling a project.

ARTIFACTS (n)   [AHR-t*uh*-fakts]

Meaning: any man-made objects, but especially those from earlier historical periods

Usage 1: The shopkeeper was both an expert in and a dealer of *artifacts* and antiquities.

Usage 2: Lucy spent the summer on an archaeological dig, searching for *artifacts*.

Usage 3: In order to discourage the desecration of historical sites, many museums will not purchase *artifacts*, and will instead rely on donations and loans.

Usage 4: Burks was mortified when the girls at the party referred to his retro clothing as moldy old *artifacts*.

ARTISAN (n)   [AHR-t*uh*-z*uh* n]

Meaning: a worker that makes high-quality goods in relatively small amounts, usually handmade

Usage 1: Many people travel to Amish country to purchase *artisan* goods from the local craftsmen.

Usage 2: There is something about *artisan* jellies and preserves that mass-marketed imitators just can't reproduce.

Usage 3: When I saw the handmade, *artisan* rocking chair, I felt that the quality was good enough to justify the higher price.

Usage 4: Elizabeth didn't just think of herself as a housewife; she felt that she was an *artisan* when it came to taking care of her family.

ASSENT (v)   [*uh*-SENT]

Meaning: to agree or concur

Usage 1: With no other options, the company president knew that he had to *assent* to a merger.

Usage 2: If I can get you the price and color that you want, will you *assent* to the purchase of this car today?

Usage 3: To *assent* to someone acting dishonestly in your name or on your behalf is just as odious as if you were the perpetrator.

Usage 4: For all practical purposes, to *assent* to evil is to become evil.

Usage 5: Joan told Roger that if he could wait until she graduated college, she would *assent* to his proposal.

ASSERT (v)   [*uh*-SURT]

Meaning: to state or claim strongly or confidently

Usage 1: Despite the evidence to the contrary, Alan kept trying to *assert* his innocence.

Usage 2: If a doctor is willing to *assert* the benefits of a specific supplement, that doctor's word carries more weight than that of the average layman.

Usage 3: My daughter kept trying to *assert* her side of the story, but the fact was, she had broken the rules.

Usage 4: Perhaps overconfidently, the champion began to *assert* how easily he would handle the challenger, and that is why he lost his belt.

Usage 5: If you are going to stand there and *assert* what you are capable of, I am not going to burst your bubble.

ASSUMPTION (n)   [*uh*-SUHMP-sh*uh* n]

Meaning: a supposition or conjecture that is taken for granted

Usage 1: Walter had been friends with Jesse for years, so it was a safe *assumption* that he knew where Walter might be hiding.

Usage 2: Based on an *assumption* of innocence until proven otherwise, the jury had no choice but to acquit the defendant.

Usage 3: When you make an *assumption* before you have all the facts, you set yourself up for a calamitous fall.

ASTRAL (adj)   [AS-tr*uh* l]

Meaning: relating to the stars

Usage 1: Many followers of new-wave psychology believe that *astral* projection can be proven by anecdotal evidence.

Usage 2: Inspired by the panoramic celestial view, the poet wrote about the *astral* blanket above him.

Usage 3: The meteor shower provided the multitude of gawkers below with an exhilarating show of *astral* fireworks.

Usage 4: We are made of *astral* stuff, and all of creation is connected.

Usage 5: Until faster-than-light speed is perfected, true *astral* travel remains impractical.

ASYLUM (n)   [*uh*-SAHY-l*uh* m]

Meaning: a protected refuge or institution for anyone needing special or extraordinary care or assistance

Usage 1: Before the advent of reform and modern psychology, a mental *asylum* was a horrific place to be.

Usage 2: Reaching the steps of the cathedral just before her pursuers, Esmeralda burst in, screaming for *asylum*.

Usage 3: Although he could never return to his homeland, the former dictator was granted *asylum* in a neighboring country.

Usage 4: Even if they enter this country illegally, refugees may be granted political *asylum* in this country, under certain conditions.

Usage 5: Bonnie's bedroom was her only safe haven, her only *asylum* from the noise and the discord in her home.

AUDIT (n)   [AW-dit]

Meaning: official examination of records, especially those that are financial in nature

Usage 1: Because his tax return raised some very serious questions, Philip was scheduled for an *audit* by the government.

Usage 2: The investigator was concerned because there were many discrepancies that showed up during the company's annual *audit*.

Usage 3: Every so often, a person who wishes to be moral should conduct a thorough *audit* of both their actions and motivations.

Usage 4: To determine if the home was adequately efficient, the home improvement salesperson conducted a free energy *audit* of his client's house.

Usage 5: Before he applied for the loan, Richard performed a credit *audit* on himself to see if there were any issues he needed to resolve.

AUTHORITARIAN (adj)   [*uh*-thawr-i-TAIR-ee-*uh* n]

Meaning: requiring total submission and obedience

Usage 1: The populace groaned under the repressive and *authoritarian* regime, but they were too cowed to act.

Usage 2: Donald bristled at his supervisor's *authoritarian* tone, because he was not used to such close management.

Usage 3: Many outsiders wonder why the Army's Chain of Command has to be *authoritarian* in nature, but that is the basis of military discipline.

Usage 4: When they were younger, the kids hated their father's *authoritarian* parenting style, but now that they were older, they realized he had only been preparing them for adulthood.

AVARICE (n)   [AV-er-is]

Meaning: insatiable desire to acquire and hoard wealth

Usage 1: The story of King Midas is a cautionary tale about the dangers of unchecked *avarice*.

Usage 2: In an example of unbelievable *avarice*, Hetty Greene tried to set her son's broken leg herself, and consequently, the leg had to be amputated.

Usage 3: Partially due to incompetence and partially due to their *avarice*, the brothers frittered away what was once their father's company.

Usage 4: Some people call my pursuit of wealth a sign of *avarice*, but I know that it is just my determination to escape my meager beginnings.

AVIARY (n)   [EY-vee-er-ee]

Meaning: a large enclosure for birds

Usage 1: Because she was a novice birder, Louise enjoyed going to the local *aviary*, where she could see some of the species up close.

Usage 2: When the storm damaged the roof of the *aviary*, a pair of bald eagles was able to escape from the enclosure.

Usage 3: Sam hated working at the *aviary*, because cleaning the bottom of a giant bird cage every day was not his idea of career development.

Usage 4: Any time of day, the songs of dozens of bird species could be heard throughout the *aviary*.

BALMY (adj)   [BAH-mee]

Meaning: soothing and mild

Usage 1: Relaxing because of the *balmy* breeze and drowsing because of the late-summer heat, the night watchman never saw the intruder slip past him.

Usage 2: When she remembered the *balmy* Caribbean weather and the languid island tempo, Ellen could not wait to book a return trip.

Usage 3: If you enjoy cool, *balmy* mornings and warm, sunny days, then South Florida is your ideal destination.

BEDIZEN (v)   [bi-DAHY-*zuh* n]

Meaning: dress with vulgar finery

Usage 1: Because it was Halloween, Lewis seized the opportunity to *bedizen* himself ornately, in preparation for the costume party.

Usage 2: Sally decided to *bedizen* her Shi Tzu with a custom-made multicolored studded collar.

Usage 3: Centuries ago, the French aristocracy would *bedizen* themselves in foppish clothing, shoes, and hats that would look absurd today.

BEFUDDLE (v)   [bi-FUHD-l]

Meaning: to confuse thoroughly

Usage 1: The quick-talking salesman continued his doublespeak in an attempt to *befuddle* me.

Usage 2: I simply do not understand calculus, and the more I try to study it, the more I *befuddle* myself.

Usage 3: This is very complicated, and I will explain it very slowly so I do not *befuddle* you.

Usage 4: John could not make any sense of the movie's plot, and whenever one of his friends tried to explain it to him, all that did was *befuddle* him all the more.

BEHEMOTH (n)   [bih-HEE-m*uh* th]

Meaning: an animal of huge or monstrous size

Usage 1: Randy tried his best to stay on the back of the *behemoth*, but no one had ever been able to ride the bull for the full 8 seconds.

Usage 2: With one well-placed shot, Robin brought the *behemoth* down, ending the massive lion's reign of terror.

Usage 3: Ahab hurled the harpoon with all of his might, but the *behemoth* called Mocha Dick ignored this insignificant pinprick.

Usage 4: The two bull guerrillas battled for supremacy, each *behemoth* pounding the other with thunderous blows.

Chapter **12**

Bereavement – Convene

This chapter covers the following words, each with its part of speech, pronunciation, and descriptive meaning.

Usage of the word is also illustrated in three to five sample sentences.

bereavement	carnage	comport
bestial	carping	concise
bevy	catastrophe	concurrent
bland	catcall	conscript
blunder	cathartic	consecrate
bombardment	cede	consign
bombast	celestial	contingent
boon	centigrade	convene
bovine	centrifugal	
boycott	cerebral	
braggart	chalice	
browbeat	check	
bullion	cite	
bureaucracy	civil	
buxom	cog	
callous	cohere	
camaraderie	cohesion	
canon	coin	
caption	colossus	
cardinal	compatible	
carillon	compile	

BEREAVEMENT (n)   [bi-REEV-m*uh* nt]

Meaning: the state of being deprived of something valuable or beloved

Usage 1: The widow wore a veil and dressed in black during her period of *bereavement*.

Usage 2: Psychologists believe that being fired from your job or getting a divorce creates the same sort of feelings as any other type of *bereavement*.

Usage 3: After Pres. Kennedy was assassinated, the entire country was in a state of *bereavement*.

BESTIAL (adj)   [BES-ch*uh* l]

Meaning: beast like or inhuman

Usage 1: Because he had been separated from the rest of mankind for so long, Robinson began to revert to *bestial*, uncivilized behavior.

Usage 2: Young Tyson fought with the *bestial* ferocity of an uncaged jungle animal.

Usage 3: Many readers can subconsciously identify with Mr. Hyde, because he represents man's more *bestial*, uninhibited nature.

Usage 4: His anger was so primal and so *bestial* that it was almost elevated to something pure by its unadulterated vehemence.

BEVY (n)   [BEV-ee]

Meaning: a large assembly or company

Usage 1: A boisterous *bevy* of ballerinas barreled into Bob.

Usage 2: When Johnson made the game-winning touchdown catch, he was afterwards inundated by a *bevy* of endorsement offers.

Usage 3: You can bet that he has a whole *bevy* of excuses why he was unable to finish his work.

Usage 4: Although he was still young, Randy had already managed to break a *bevy* of hearts along the way.

BLAND (adj)   [bland]

Meaning: boring, tasteless, extremely and even overly mild, dull and uninteresting

Usage 1: I'm a person who loves to cook, and when my food turns out *bland*, I feel the meal has been a failure.

Usage 2: Paul fancied himself a lively and interesting person, so when his date told him that she found him to be insipid and *bland*, he was shocked.

Usage 3: The food had been cooked too long, and the result was a *bland*, soggy mess.

Usage 4: I expected the salsa to be a fiery explosion in my mouth, so imagine my surprise when it was thin, watery, and *bland*.

BLUNDER (n)/(v)   [BLUHN-der]

Meaning: a careless, stupid mistake, or, to make such a mistake

Usage 1: The release of the new product without having it first tested by a focus group was a colossal *blunder* that cost the company millions. (n)

Usage 2: Benjamin couldn't believe that he had made such a boneheaded *blunder* during his first date with Ellen. (n)

Usage 3: Always remember that one man's *blunder* is another man's funny story. (v)

Usage 4: Jack is such a legendary klutz that I wouldn't be at all surprised if he managed to *blunder* his way into his own funeral. (v)

BOMBARDMENT (n)   [bom-BAHRD-m*uh* nt]

Meaning: an attack with missiles, artillery, or bombs

Usage 1: Just when the soldiers thought the artillery attack was over, the *bombardment* began again in earnest.

Usage 2: During the endless *bombardment*, the missiles seem to have been launched from all sides.

Usage 3: The hailstones were falling so fast and so furiously, it was like a *bombardment* of miniature ice-bombs launched from the clouds.

Usage 4: The comedian's blistering responses to the heckler detonated upon impact, a verbal *bombardment* of put downs and insults that quashed any possibility of reprisal.

BOMBAST (n)   [BOM-bast]

Meaning: unnecessarily pretentious speech

Usage 1: During his filibuster, the empty words of the politician's *bombast* echoed off the rafters of Congress.

Usage 2: It usually doesn't bother me too much when my boss continually tries to pat himself on the back, because I've learned to tune out his *bombast*.

Usage 3: As usual, the boxing promoter spewed out his *bombast* in a rapid-fire pattern, performing verbal gymnastics for the dubious pleasure of all in attendance.

Usage 4: Most of his elderly constituents had heard the mayor's *bombast* and his rhetoric before, so when he began to pontificate, they began to doze.

BOON (n)   [boon]

Meaning: a benefit or a requested favor

Usage1: When Seamus stumbled upon the bag of money, he could scarcely believe that Fortune had granted him such a *boon*.

Usage 2: The alderman was feeling magnanimous, so he granted the *boon* requested by his sycophant.

Usage 3: Because he was a coward at heart, Robert considered it a *boon* that he had been deemed unfit for military service.

Usage 4: Nelson regarded his wealth as both a *boon* and a curse, because while it brought him any number of material possessions, it also meant that he was denied true love.

BOVINE (adj)   [BOH-vahyn]

Meaning: reminiscent of an ox or cow, slow-witted, dull

Usage 1: He moved ponderously, with exaggerated *bovine* movements, and the graceless ballet continued until he disappeared around the corner.

Usage 2: Jacob always thought there was something vaguely *bovine* about his aunt, and when he saw her chewing gum, the resemblance was uncanny.

Usage 3: Lenny didn't seem to be fully aware of what he had done, for he just stood there with a slack-jawed, *bovine* expression on his face; he didn't even have the good sense to try to run.

Usage 4: Because he went to an agricultural college, my grandfather took courses in *bovine* husbandry, even though he had no intention of ever becoming a farmer or rancher.

BOYCOTT (v)   [BOI-kot]

Meaning: to refrain from buying or using

Usage 1: Because the actions of the bus driver were so unacceptable, the citizens of the area began to *boycott* the bus company, vowing to return only when changes were made.

Usage 2: Although politics are not supposed to be part of the Olympics, nearly every competition is marred by some nation choosing to *boycott* the Games over some imagined slight.

Usage 3: As a method of peaceful protest, choosing to *boycott* a company is a very effective strategy, because it puts considerable economic pressure on the offending Corporation.

BRAGGART (n)   [BRAG-ert]

Meaning: a person who brags or boasts a lot

Usage 1: The *braggart* was so overbearing, those who were within earshot were surprised that he didn't try to take credit for delivering himself when he was a born.

Usage 2: The *braggart* suffered a deflated ego when no one pressed him for more details about his latest tall tale.

Usage 3: Everyone in their little circle of friends agreed that the local *braggart* needed to be taken down a few pegs.

Usage 4: It is an unfortunate contradiction that if you do not actively promote yourself, you are considered to be lacking in confidence, but if you do promote yourself, you can easily be labeled a *braggart*.

BROWBEAT (v)   [BROU-beet]

Meaning: to intimidate or bully by words and stern looks

Usage 1: The interrogating detectives continued to try to *browbeat* the suspect, but he remained unflappable.

Usage 2: Try as she might to *browbeat* the accused on the witness stand, the District Attorney's courtroom antics lost her any sympathy she may have had with the jury.

Usage 3: Thomas was a terrible employer, because he would try to bully, coerce, threaten, or just plain *browbeat* his subordinates into carrying out his often-confusing directives.

Usage 4: My mother ruled our home with just an eyebrow, because with one withering look she could *browbeat* us into compliance.

BULLION (n)   [BOO L-y*uh* n]

Meaning: silver and gold, when it is discussed by its quantity in mass, not in value, especially when it is in the form of bars or ingots

Usage 1: Looking to diversify his holdings, Warren decided to invest in gold *bullion*.

Usage 2: When the salvage experts found gold and silver *bullion* at the site of the shipwreck, they knew that they had made a historic find.

Usage 3: Many collectors find that it is easier and more practical to purchase silver *bullion* in the form of ingots, rather than in bars or bricks.

BUREAUCRACY (n)   [byoo-ROK-r*uh*-see]

Meaning: inefficient administrative system (typically governmental) overly burdened by needless routine, complications, and paper work, or, large group of officials/administrators, especially if that administrative power is excessively concentrated

Usage 1: Many minor government clerks become too convinced of their own importance and soon learn to abuse their power, thereby worsening the snarl of *bureaucracy*.

Usage 2: As bad as the red tape and associated delays are in this country, our petty *bureaucracy* is nowhere near as bad as that of some other nations.

Usage 3: Because there is no escaping *bureaucracy*, I had to fill out forms in triplicate and pay the appropriate fee in the form of a postal money order.

Usage 4: Sometimes, I believe that the government invented *bureaucracy* just as a way of keeping us all confused.

BUXOM (adj)   [BUHK-s*uh* m]

Meaning: possessing large bosoms

Usage 1: As soon as she un-wrapped the dress he had bought her, John realized he had purchased the wrong size, because it was far too small for his *buxom* wife.

Usage 2: One of the biggest challenges of being a *buxom* woman was fending off unwanted advances from men who were too forward.

Usage 3: When he was caught staring overlong at the attractive *buxom* woman, Charles blushed beet-red in embarrassment.

CALLOUS (adj)   [KAL-*uh* s]

Meaning: unsympathetic or indifferent

Usage 1: Parker was infamous for his *callous* disregard for the safety of others, and his racing style reflected that.

Usage 2: While some people chided Wilson for his *callous* attitude, he viewed himself as merely pragmatic.

Usage 3: Rommel was as coolly calculating and efficient as he was spartan and *callous*.

Usage 4: The defendant's *callous* statements about the victim were met with severe disapproval from the jury.

CAMARADERIE (n)   [kah-m*uh*-RAH-d*uh*-ree]

Meaning: good-fellowship

Usage 1: Connor enjoyed going to the pub, because he was able to enjoy the *camaraderie* of fellow football fans.

Usage 2: During his stay at the hostel, Tanner struck up an easy *camaraderie* with a group of students from the Ukraine.

Usage 3: During World War II, many Americans and Brits became fast friends, due to the warm *camaraderie* shared by all soldiers, regardless of nationality.

Usage 4: Because he was such a bon vivant, Donald could often be sustained by the *camaraderie* of his fellow carousers.

CANON (n)   [KAN-*uh* n]

Meaning: a fundamental standard or general rule

Usage 1: The revealing outfits that she wore violated the *canon* of good taste and modesty.

Usage 2: Within the *canon* of acceptable male behavior are guidelines on how to be courteous to the opposite sex.

Usage 3: The *canon* of good sportsmanship dictates that you play within the established rules.

CAPTION (n)   [KAP-sh*uh* n]

Meaning: a title or explanation for an illustration, or explanatory text superimposed upon a film

Usage 1: It was a good thing that the volume of the television was turned up, because Ruth was too nearsighted to read the *caption*.

Usage 2: Although the comic strip picture was funny, it was the *caption* underneath that made John laugh out loud.

Usage 3: Sheila did not recognize the painting that was shown in her art book, but the *caption* helped her identify it.

CARDINAL (adj)   [KAHR-dn-l]

Meaning: of chief importance

Usage 1: The boxer was knocked out because he ignored the *cardinal* rule of boxing – to protect himself at all times.

Usage 2: The *cardinal* safety precaution that one should always take when handling a firearm is to treat every gun as if it is loaded.

Usage 3: When he lied to her, he broke the *cardinal* law in their relationship.

Usage 4: During his ordeal aboard the life raft, the *cardinal* thought that guided his every action was "survival".

Usage 5: As any gambler can tell you, the *cardinal* principle that you should follow when gambling is to never bet more than you can afford to lose.

CARILLON (n)   [KAR-*uh*-lon]

Meaning: set of stationary bells or plates used as a musical instrument

Usage 1: Every morning, the priest arose to the sound of the *carillon*.

Usage 2: The musician struck the panels of the *carillon* rhythmically, keeping in time with the rest of the orchestra.

Usage 3: The tinkling tones produced by a *carillon* make it an instrument that is ideal for holiday programs.

CARNAGE (n)   [KAHR-nij]

Meaning: the destruction of a large number of human lives

Usage 1: After the skirmish, the commander looked around the battlefield at all the needless *carnage*.

Usage 2: The scene of the horrific accident could only be described as one of *carnage*.

Usage 3: The terror and *carnage* of the Hutu-Tutsi Conflict was nearly unparalleled in human history.

Usage 4: Hurricane Katrina resulted in destruction and *carnage* on a scale that is almost unimaginable.

CARPING (adj)   [KAHR-ping]

Meaning: characterized by the fussy finding of fault

Usage 1: Roger became quite annoyed at his wife's *carping* criticism.

Usage 2: It seemed as if his mother-in-law's *carping* comments were nonstop.

Usage 3: The constant *carping* protestations, coupled with the overly anxious hypochondria, made it very difficult to take seriously anything that Pam had to say.

CATASTROPHE (n)   [k*uh*-TAS-tr*uh*-fee]

Meaning: a disaster or fiasco

Usage 1: In times of *catastrophe*, both the best and the worst of human nature come out.

Usage 2: Their first date was a *catastrophe*, but because they could laugh about it, they decided to see each other again.

Usage 3: Because Ellen wasn't a very good cook, her first dinner party turned into a *catastrophe* of epic proportions.

Usage 4: The stock market crash created a *catastrophe* for investors worldwide.

Usage 5: Looking back on his misfortune, sometimes Jonathan believed that his life was little more than one catastrophe after another.

CATCALL (n)   [KAT-kawl]

Meaning: a shrill or raucous shout of disapproval

Usage 1: When the comedian froze up on stage, he heard first one *catcall*, then another, and then the floodgates of derision opened wide.

Usage 2: Ignoring the rude *catcall*, the actors soldiered on like true professionals and made it through the scene.

Usage 3: The sound of that first *catcall* reverberated through the tiny theater.

Usage 4: The beleaguered politician managed to continue past the vulgar *catcall* from the heckler, but he was unable to dodge the tomato that was thrown next.

CATHARTIC (adj) [k*uh*-THAHR-tik]

Meaning: causing the release of pent-up emotions

Usage 1: For many veterans, the movie "Saving Private Ryan" was a *cathartic* experience.

Usage 2: Finally being able to tell her mother-in-law off was a kind of *cathartic* explosion for Susan.

Usage 3: A good crying jag can be simultaneously *cathartic* and healthy, both emotionally and physically.

Usage 4: When she first attended the opera, it was a shattering, *cathartic* night in her life.

CEDE (v) [seed]

Meaning: to formally yield or surrender

Usage 1: Faced with such a concerted alliance of nobleman, King John had no choice but to *cede* a portion of his power.

Usage 2: Under the terms of the treaty, France had to *cede* a large territory to the United States.

Usage 3: After the merger, the smaller company had to *cede* control of daily operations.

Usage 4: Foreseeing his upcoming impeachment, the congressman agreed to *cede* his seat to his replacement.

CELESTIAL (adj) [s*uh*-LES-ch*uh* l]

Meaning: having to do with the sky, the stars, or heaven

Usage 1: Lying on his back in his sleeping bag, looking up at the *celestial* canopy above him, Jacob was convinced that he was in the presence of the Divine.

Usage 2: The more he studied the *celestial* bodies in the heavens, the more Professor Jenkins began to understand the earth.

Usage 3: Thus far, the Earth's moon is the only *celestial* body to which mankind has traveled.

CENTIGRADE (adj) [SEN-ti-greyd]

Meaning: a scale and a unit of measure for temperature

Usage 1: One of the key characteristics of the *centigrade* system is the fact that the freezing point and the boiling point of water are separated by 100°.

Usage 2: Although the *centigrade* system is the predominant means of measuring temperature throughout most of the world, it has not yet caught on here in the United States.

Usage 3: As the temperature dropped below zero degrees *centigrade*, ice began to form on the surface of the pond.

Usage 4: The summer temperature was a balmy 25 degrees *centigrade*, and the children were making the most of it.

Usage 5: An early version of the *centigrade* temperature system was first introduced in 1742.

CENTRIFUGAL (adj) [sen-TRIF-y*uh*-g*uh* l]

Meaning: radiating from the center

Usage 1: Tommy spun around and around, until the *centrifugal* force made him dizzy.

Usage 2: It is through the use of applied *centrifugal* physics that those who throw the shot put or the discus are able to succeed.

Usage 3: The *centrifugal* pump is able to separate the red blood cells from the plasma.

CEREBRAL (adj) [s*uh*-REE-br*uh* l]

Meaning: pertaining to the intellect

Usage 1: Barney was not a fan of sports, and instead preferred more *cerebral* pursuits, like chess.

Usage 2: Professor William's calculus class was extremely advanced, and strained the *cerebral* capacity of even the most industrious of students.

Usage 3: The doctors were worried because the infection had spread to the patient's *cerebral* fluid, and was now threatening to spread to the brain.

CHALICE (n)   [CHAL-is]

Meaning: goblet, an ornate drinking cup, especially if used for Mass

Usage 1: The priest raised the *chalice* to his lips and drank the sacramental wine.

Usage 2: The *chalice* was golden and encrusted with precious jewels.

Usage 3: Because of its shape, in the Wiccan religion, a *chalice* is symbolic of the feminine mystique.

Usage 4: Many Christians believe that a *chalice* was used at the Last Supper, and consequently, legend has presented several different vessels as the one true cup.

CHECK (v)   [chek]

Meaning: curb or restrain

Usage 1: The United States Constitution was set up in such a way that one branch could *check* the power of another branch.

Usage 2: Simply by increasing the police presence in high crime neighborhoods, law enforcement can do much to *check* criminal activity in the area.

Usage 3: The military set up roadblocks to *check* suspected terrorist or insurgent activity in the region.

Usage 4: Unfortunately, the recent recession did much to *check* the progress that had been gained by small businesses over the past decade.

Usage 5: With an early diagnosis, the doctors were able to *check* the progression of the disease.

CITE (v)   [sahyt]

Meaning: to quote a source as an authority

Usage 1: If you are going to *cite* a source to support your argument, you should always make sure that the citation is accurate.

Usage 2: I did not know how to *cite* the author of the quotation, because I did not know the original source.

Usage 3: There was a huge academic scandal when the graduate student tried to *cite* obscure sources that were, in fact, nonexistent.

CIVIL (adj)   [SIV-*uh* l]

Meaning: adequate in politeness

Usage 1: After the divorce, Peter and Meredith made a concerted effort to be *civil* to each other for the sake of the children.

Usage 2: Blinded by his resentment over the way he had been mistreated, Patrick found it difficult to be *civil* to his former in-laws.

Usage 3: The judge admonished the defendant that if he did not want to be held in contempt, he had better learn to keep a *civil* tongue in his head.

Usage 4: Even when you dislike someone intensely, sometimes the mature thing to do is practice *civil* detachment.

Usage 5: No one would ever mistake the candidates for friends, but when they were in public, they were able to hold *civil* discussions.

COG (n)   [kog]

Meaning: a fitted gear tooth that corresponds with a gear wheel, or a very minor person in a large corporation

Usage 1: From his unique vantage point, Michael was to see the operation of every *cog* in the giant corporate machine called Big Business.

Usage 2: A broken *cog* was all that it took to bring the mighty mechanized cavalry unit to a grinding halt.

Usage 3: Without artifice or evasion, Jason had always known that he was little more than a tiny, but essential, *cog* in his company's hierarchy.

Usage 4: Due to a logistical logjam, the *cog* was on back order, dead-lining the equipment and placing the entire project in jeopardy.

COHERE (v)   [koh-HEER]

Meaning: to be connected logically or naturally

Usage 1: The disparate elements of her story did not *cohere* in any semblance of sense.

Usage 2: Without supporting documentation, this explanation to the official did not *cohere* in a manner that helped his case.

Usage 3: I would hope that the story I just told you could *cohere* in a way that could adequately convey my intentions.

COHESION (n)   [koh-HEE-zh*uh* n]

Meaning: a tendency to keep together

Usage 1: In the summer heat, the adhesive began to melt, and the *cohesion* of the entire project was jeopardized.

Usage 2: For the company to be successful, the partners needed to have a synergistic *cohesion* created by a common goal.

Usage 3: It is a sad but true fact that if you cannot have *cohesion* within your marriage, you can just as easily have separation.

COIN (v)   [koin]

Meaning: to fabricate, make, or create

Usage 1: Most English linguists agree, no playwright in history could *coin* a phrase like Shakespeare.

Usage 2: When coach Pat Riley said that his Lakers team was going to "threepeat", he decided to *coin* the term.

Usage 3: Edison's method of invention was to *coin* an idea and then have others work on its development.

COLOSSUS (n)   [k*uh*-LOS-*uh* s]

Meaning: anything huge or powerful

Usage 1: Wilt Chamberlain was an athletic *colossus* never before seen in the sport of basketball.

Usage 2: As an engineering feat, the Titanic lived up to its name and was a *colossus* of a ship.

Usage 3: Despite their recent struggles on the baseball diamond, the Yankees remain a *colossus* in sports merchandising.

COMPATIBLE (adj)   [k*uh* m-PAT-*uh*-b*uh* l]

Meaning: capable of existing together in harmony

Usage 1: One of the hardest challenges in college life is finding a *compatible* roommate.

Usage 2: John and Mary managed to stay married for so long because they had such *compatible* interests.

Usage 3: Working in a bar is not a *compatible* environment for a recovering alcoholic.

Usage 4: Unfortunately, Greg found that his phone charger was not *compatible* with the electrical outlets in Europe.

COMPILE (v)   [k*uh* m-PAHYL]

Meaning: to assemble or gather together

Usage 1: When he made a mix tape for his girlfriend, Gary had to *compile* songs from his favorite albums.

Usage 2: In accordance with his supervisor's orders, Fred began to *compile* data from the last quarter.

Usage 3: After finishing the novel, the students began to *compile* reasons and motivations for the character's actions.

COMPORT (v)   [k*uh* m-PAWRT]

Meaning: to bear one's self

Usage 1: Even in the face of such disheartening news, Reginald was able to *comport* himself as a gentleman.

Usage 2: Because this was a function that was sponsored by the school, the students were still expected to *comport* themselves within the rules of the campus.

Usage 3: The debate was quite spirited, and at times, even combative, but the candidates were able to *comport* themselves with dignity and courtesy.

Usage 4: After a few drinks, Steven could no longer *comport* himself accordingly, so he was asked to leave.

CONCISE (adj)   [k*uh* n-SAHYS]

Meaning: brief yet comprehensive

Usage 1: The news program's version of the day's events was *concise*, yet accurate.

Usage 2: During the debate, the president gave a *concise* account of his plan for the next six months.

Usage 3: When he recommended the sergeant for the medal, the infantry captain wrote a *concise* report about the specific relevant operation.

Usage 4: Because of limited space, journalists learn to write in a *concise* and straightforward manner.

Usage 5: The victim was in a state of shock, and told a story that was neither *concise* nor coherent.

CONCURRENT (adj)   [k*uh* n-KUR-*uh* nt]

Meaning: happening at the same time

Usage 1: Luckily for the defendants, the judge decided to hand out *concurrent* sentences.

Usage 2: Helen was able to lose so much weight because her adoption of a new diet and a new exercise program were *concurrent*.

Usage 3: To maximize their chances of success, the coalition forces staged *concurrent* attacks on land and through the air.

Usage 4: The doctors decided that the most effective treatment would be a *concurrent* program of aggressive chemotherapy and radiation.

CONSCRIPT (n)   [KON-skript]

Meaning: a person forced into labor or military service

Usage 1: The idea that a citizen needs to serve as a *conscript* because he "owes" something to his country is an ancient idea going back to the time of Hammurabi.

Usage 2: Many a peasant in China was forced into life as a *conscript* to help build the Great Wall of China.

Usage 3: By perfecting the modern concept of using a *conscript* as a soldier, Napoleon was able to field an army that sometimes outnumbered the opposition by a ratio of 10 to 1.

Usage 4: For some lower socioeconomic classes, life as a military *conscript* can actually be preferable to civilian life when there are no other viable employments or educational prospects.

CONSECRATE (v)   [KON-si-kreyt]

Meaning: to make sacred or worthy of veneration

Usage 1: In his famous Gettysburg Address, Lincoln poetically stated that the living could not *consecrate* the battlefield more than the honored dead already had.

Usage 2: Before a church is built, the priest will usually *consecrate* the land as a way of blessing the project.

Usage 3: Contrary to popular belief, to *consecrate* an item does not make it worthy of worship, only of honor.

Usage 4: Many people believe that an interdenominational committee of religious leaders should *consecrate* the site of the 9/11 Memorial.

CONSIGN (v)   [k*uh* n-SAHYN]

Meaning: to entrust, to set apart, to officially deliver

Usage 1: If one more person in this office comes to me with an emergency assignment, I will immediately consign that project to my trashcan!

Usage 2: Kerry thought about volunteering to help the company during the annual inventory, but he did not want upper management to *consign* him to the task on a regular basis.

Usage 3: The captain knew that if he did not do everything within his power to help these refugees, then the guerrilla army would *consign* them to a life of slavery and torture.

CONTINGENT (adj)   [k*uh* n-TIN-j*uh* nt]

Meaning: conditional, or without a known cause, unforeseen

Usage 1: It is impossible to plan for every possible *contingent* outcome.

Usage 2: After searching for months, Jessica had finally found her dream home, *contingent* upon the bank's approval.

Usage 3: Even though the weather for the next few days was not certain, we made *contingent* plans to meet.

Usage 4: Like many people of her generation, Ruth set aside a bit of "mad money", which she often used for *contingent* expenses.

CONVENE (v)   [k*uh* n-VEEN]

Meaning: to come together

Usage 1: The special committee voted to *convene* to discuss the proposed legislation.

Usage 2: Whenever a Pope dies, a committee of cardinals must *convene* to elect the next one.

Usage 3: During the hostile takeover attempt, the Chairman of the Board wanted to *convene* a meeting of the partners.

Usage 4: To air their grievances about the new campus policies, the students decided to *convene* at the Activity Center.

This page is intentionally left blank

Chapter **13**

Convention – Dwindle

This chapter covers the following words, each with its part of speech, pronunciation, and descriptive meaning.

Usage of the word is also illustrated in three to five sample sentences.

convention	demur	docile
conversant	denounce	doggerel
converse	dermatologist	dormer
convert	desecrate	dote
convex	determinate	dowdy
corollary	devise	droll
correlation	dilapidated	duration
corrode	diligence	dwindle
covert	dilute	
cow	disband	
cringe	disclaim	
cupidity	disclose	
curator	disinclination	
cynical	dislodge	
dappled	dispel	
deadpan	dispirited	
decipher	disquietude	
degradation	dissent	
deign	distinction	
delusive	distraught	
demise	divine	

CONVENTION (n)   [k*uh* n-VEN-sh*uh* n]

Meaning: established social or moral custom

Usage 1: Early feminists would frequently flout the *convention* of the day by wearing trousers instead of dresses.

Usage 2: It may go against *convention*, but speed dating is becoming increasingly popular among busy professionals.

Usage 3: The congressman was not one to stand for a *convention* of formality, and began to relax many of the social dictates of his office.

Usage 4: Because we are of different generations, I sometimes feel that my daughter pushes the borderlines of *convention* with what she chooses to wear, but she just tells me I'm being old-fashioned.

CONVERSANT (adj)   [k*uh* n-VUR-s*uh* nt]

Meaning: familiar with

Usage 1: Although I am no expert, I am *conversant* on the subject of 3-D printing.

Usage 2: Surprisingly, many priests are very *conversant* on the topic of marital relations.

Usage 3: Even though she has no children, Elizabeth believes herself to be fairly *conversant* about parenting.

Usage 4: It is almost laughable to see people who pretend to be *conversant* on a subject, when in reality, they haven't a clue.

CONVERSE (n)   [KON-vurs]

Meaning: a talk between two or more people

Usage 1: When profits were down for the second quarter in a row, it was time for a *converse* between the partners.

Usage 2: Because he was concerned about his grades, Victor set down for a *converse* with his teacher.

Usage 3: The military has a chain of command because it is not efficient in combat situations to stop for a *converse* every time you don't agree with your orders.

CONVERT (n)   [KON-vurt]

Meaning: one who has a adopted a different religion or opinion

Usage 1: There is no person who is as zealous or as earnest as a recent *convert*.

Usage 2: Although I was raised a Democrat, as an adult I became a *convert* to the Grand Old Party.

Usage 3: In order to get married in her husband's church, Sally took instruction as a *convert* to the Catholic faith.

Usage 4: Contrary to his earlier position, the President was a *convert* to the idea of global warming.

Usage 5: Kenneth was a new *convert* to this philosophy, but he remained skeptical.

CONVEX (adj)   [kon-VEKS]

Meaning: curving outward

Usage 1: The large *convex* mirrors in the funhouse grossly distorted the reflections of anyone who entered.

Usage 2: The damage to the *convex* lens made the telescope inoperable.

Usage 3: The *convex* shape of the "eyebrow" window was in keeping with the architectural style of the rest of the house.

Usage 4: Although it had been able to contain the explosion, the bomb canister was now deformed with a number of *convex* bulges.

COROLLARY (n) [KAWR-*uh*-ler-ee]

Meaning: a natural consequence or obvious conclusion

Usage 1: When inflation and unemployment goes up, the *corollary* is often a stagnated economy.

Usage 2: He was frequently late and lax in his performance, so the impending *corollary* of his dismissal was obvious to all.

Usage 3: After a high school career that included social sacrifices and long nights spent studying, the *corollary* was a full scholarship to a very prestigious university.

Usage 4: If you spent your youth rushing around always thinking about tomorrow, the *corollary* will be seniority spent thinking about yesterday.

CORRELATION (n) [kawr-*uh*-LEY-sh*uh* n]

Meaning: mutual relationship or similarity

Usage 1: Social science has shown that there is a *correlation* between poverty and a lack of education.

Usage 2: The research team worked to show a definitive *correlation* between childhood obesity and adult-onset diabetes.

Usage 3: Many 21st-century parents were surprised to learn that there is a *correlation* between attention deficit disorder and excessive television watching.

Usage 4: Despite all the evidence to the contrary, many cigarette companies still refuse to admit that there is a proven *correlation* between cigarette smoking and lung cancer.

Usage 5: If there is a *correlation* between cell phone usage and brain cancer, it has yet to be proven.

CORRODE (v) [k*uh*-ROHD]

Meaning: destroy by chemical action

Usage 1: The exterior of the car began to *corrode* due to the salty coastline environment.

Usage 2: If a battery is left too long in a device, it will begin to leak and *corrode* the interior of the battery compartment.

Usage 3: Because it is acidic in nature, tomato sauce can *corrode* certain types of cookware.

Usage 4: The drinking of too many carbonated soft drinks will eventually *corrode* the enamel on your teeth.

COVERT (adj) [KOH-vert]

Meaning: secret or hidden

Usage 1: The mission to hunt down the terrorist leader was one of the most successful *covert* missions in recent military history.

Usage 2: After a successful career as a *covert* operative, the agent was finally allowed to retire.

Usage 3: The specially-commissioned task force organized a *covert* operation to capture the drug kingpin.

Usage 4: When he was caught leaking insider secrets, the executive was convicted of *covert* corporate espionage.

COW (v) [kou]

Meaning: to frighten with threats or actual violence

Usage 1: The fear of violent reprisal can *cow* even the bravest of activists.

Usage 2: Even with direct threats, the extremist groups found that they could not *cow* Dr. King.

Usage 3: Even in the face of the violence, the hurled epithets, and the abusive threats, Gandhi refused to flinch, *cow*, or kowtow to the British.

CRINGE (v)   [krinj]

Meaning: to shrink back as if in fear

Usage 1: Call me a pansy if you must, but I *cringe* at the sight of a needle when I am at my doctor's office.

Usage 2: The sudden appearance of the monster on the movie screen caused Susan to *cringe* and let out an embarrassed little shriek.

Usage 3: Peter was so cheap he would actually *cringe* at the sight of the dinner check.

Usage 4: The poor dog had been beaten so often that now, he would automatically *cringe* at the sight of his master.

CUPIDITY (n)   [kyoo-PID-i-tee]

Meaning: excessive greed or desire to possess something

Usage 1: According to myth, it was King Midas's *cupidity* that caused eventually his downfall.

Usage 2: Even with all their riches, many celebrities eventually lose their fortunes because of their own cupidity.

Usage 3: The 1980s were characterized by excessive consumption, *cupidity*, and the adage, "Greed is Good".

Usage 4: Although it is on the opposite end of the spectrum, miserly frugality is just as bad as obsessive *cupidity*.

CURATOR (n)   [kyoo-REY-ter]

Meaning: the person who selects and is in charge of content, especially for a museum or a website

Usage 1: Although her late husband's art collection was quite extensive, the donations still had to be approved by the *curator* of the museum.

Usage 2: Philip took his job as *curator* very seriously, and therefore, made sure that each exhibit was thoroughly authenticated and documented before it was placed on display.

Usage 3: Some of the facts quoted by the blogger were inaccurate, so they were removed by the *curator* of the website.

Usage 4: After weeks of negotiating, the *curator* was able to secure the loan of a Renaissance painting that could serve as the showpiece for the summer season.

CYNICAL (adj)   [SIN-i-k*uh* l]

Meaning: skeptical of human motives

Usage 1: Thomas had been wrongly imprisoned for years, so it came as no surprise that he became hardened and *cynical*.

Usage 2: Because of his *cynical* nature, Edgar found it very difficult to build any lasting personal relationships.

Usage 3: Much of today's television programming is very *cynical* in tone, professing almost no belief in the inherent goodness of human nature.

Usage 4: It may be *cynical* of me, but I have often found it very difficult to trust in the altruism of others.

DAPPLED (adj)   [DAP-*uh* ld]

Meaning: mottled, possessing spots that are of a different color from the background

Usage 1: The sunlight shone through the trees, and the shadows created *dappled* patterns on the ground.

Usage 2: Out of all his horses, the *dappled* mare was his favorite.

Usage 3: The *dappled* coat of a jaguar actually serves as a sort of camouflage that helps it stalk prey.

Usage 4: The *dappled* pattern of the carpet in my living room hides stains better than the solid-color carpet in my study.

DEADPAN (adj)   [DED-pan]

Meaning: displaying no emotion

Usage 1: Without ever betraying his facetiousness, Harry told the anecdote in a *deadpan* manner that was totally convincing.

Usage 2: A *deadpan* expression can be very useful when playing poker, because it will keep your opponents unsure about the cards that you are holding.

Usage 3: The comedian's *deadpan* method of delivery was a large part of his appeal.

Usage 4: Most physicians have mastered a *deadpan* facial expression that many people take to be sympathetic.

DECIPHER (v)   [dih-SAHY-fer]

Meaning: interpret secret code

Usage 1: Working around the clock, the crack team of analysts was able to *decipher* the enemy code.

Usage 2: Because her predecessor had been so lax with entries, it took several weeks before Diane was able to decipher the company's account books.

Usage 3: The scientific community was all abuzz when it was announced that researchers would be able to decipher the Rosetta stone.

Usage 4: To successfully *decipher* a code, the pattern of substitution must first be discovered.

DEGRADATION (n)   [deg-r*uh*-DEY-sh*uh* n]

Meaning: the act of humiliating another or the state of being humiliated

Usage 1: When the incontrovertible evidence of his guilt was made public, Victor's *degradation* was complete.

Usage 2: Susan refrained from making fun of her obese classmate because she refused to participate in the *degradation* of another.

Usage 3: Dropping out of high school, becoming addicted to drugs, and running away from home all set the stage for her *degradation* at the hands of others.

Usage 4: Far from feeling exploited or the victim of a form of *degradation*, Amanda felt empowered as a liberated female.

DEIGN (v)   [deyn]

Meaning: to condescend

Usage 1: The executive was so haughty that it was a shock whenever he would *deign* to speak to one of his subordinates.

Usage 2: Despite the fact that the interview had been scheduled for weeks, the reporter was not sure that the notoriously-reclusive author would *deign* to answer any questions.

Usage 3: If you come down off of your high horse and *deign* to interact with the people who work for you, you just might find that they have some pretty good ideas.

DELUSIVE (adj)   [dih-LOO-siv]

Meaning: tending to deceive or mislead

Usage 1: Eventually, Sandra became disenchanted with her husband's *delusive* actions and sought a divorce.

Usage 2: His *delusive* behavior was met with justifiable suspicion, so his security clearance was denied.

Usage 3: The tobacco companies were guilty of disseminating *delusive* information, so the jury added substantial punitive damages.

Usage 4: The defendant was warned repeatedly that *delusive* answers could result in a charge of perjury.

DEMISE (n)   [dih-MAHYZ]

Meaning: death or termination of existence

Usage 1: The apathy on the part of the corporate officers was perhaps the biggest factor in the *demise* of the once-healthy business.

Usage 2: An unhealthy, sedentary lifestyle, combined with a genetic predisposition for disease, hastened his early *demise*.

Usage 3: The development and proliferation of new technology will inevitably lead to the *demise* of older systems.

Usage 4: Video-on-demand has some experts already proclaiming the *demise* of television viewing as we know it.

DEMUR (v)   [di-MUR]

Meaning: to make an objection, especially on the grounds of scruples

Usage 1: If you want me to make a decision right away, I'm afraid I must *demur*, because I need more time to think.

Usage 2: Because of what she knew about his past, Hannah was forced to *demur* when John was nominated.

Usage 3: Benjamin did not believe in increased gun control, so he was obliged to *demur* when the petition was circulated.

Usage 4: Paul wholeheartedly supported the new candidate, so he felt no need to *demur* when he was asked if he would lead the fundraising efforts.

DENOUNCE (v)   [di-NOUNS]

Meaning: to publicly condemn

Usage 1: The mayoral candidate seized the opportunity during the debate to publicly *denounce* his opponent's record.

Usage 2: Rather than support the controversial statements of their CEO, the company instead voted to denounce both his words and his policies.

Usage 3: For political reasons, the President chose to *denounce* the chosen stance of the special interest group, even though he privately agreed with many of their statements.

DERMATOLOGIST (n)   [dur-m*uh*-TOL-*uh*-jist]

Meaning: a doctor who studies diseases of the skin

Usage 1: Christopher was worried about the size and shape of the mole on his shoulder, so he made an appointment to see the *dermatologist*.

Usage 2: Any *dermatologist* will tell you that it is best to wear a strong sun-block and limit your exposure to direct sunlight.

Usage 3: In addition to studying the skin, a *dermatologist* will also specialize in diseases and conditions of the hair and nails.

DESECRATE (v)   [DES-i-kreyt]

Meaning: to violate the sanctity of

Usage 1: His grave was unmarked so potential vandals would not have an opportunity to *desecrate* the headstone.

Usage 2: The deputy could not imagine that anyone could be so morally bankrupt as to *desecrate* a war memorial.

Usage 3: It is enough that we were able to defeat their armies, we do not need to *desecrate* their holy sites as well.

DETERMINATE (adj)   [di-TUR-m*uh*-nit]

Meaning: having definite limits

Usage 1: It is in the best interest of the American public if campaign fundraising adheres to *determinate* limits.

Usage 2: The prisoners were warned not to go beyond the *determinate* boundaries when they were working on the road crew.

Usage 3: By having preset, *determinate* time limits on their speeches, the candidates were able to stay on point during the debate.

Usage 4: Because she had a *determinate* budget within which to work, the housewife often found herself relying on her creativity to make ends meet.

DEVISE (v)   [dih-vahyz]

Meaning: to imagine or to form a plan

Usage 1: Some people think that Edison was able to *devise* the modern light bulb instantly, when in reality, it was the result of years of hard work and trial and error.

Usage 2: Improv theater is often the most entertaining form of comedy, because the performers have to *devise* their skits on the spur of the moment.

Usage 3: It took meticulous planning, but the operative was finally able to *devise* a scheme to circumvent the enemy's security measures.

Usage 4: With weeks to prepare, the coach was able to *devise* a defensive package capable of stopping the offensive onslaught of the other team.

Usage 5: Houdini's claim to fame was his ability to *devise* an escape plan for any restraint that any challenger could come up with.

DILAPIDATED (adj)   [di-LAP-i-dey-tid]

Meaning: fallen into disrepair

Usage 1: At the old homestead, the fields were fallow and the main house was *dilapidated* and weather-beaten.

Usage 2: Because the abandoned apartment complex was so *dilapidated,* no one noticed when the squatters took up residence.

Usage 3: With no husband or children around to help her with the upkeep, the widow's home soon became dilapidated.

Usage 4: Despite its earlier glory days, the old hotel was *dilapidated* and shabby, perfectly reflecting the lives of its residents.

Usage 5: The remote hunting cabin was *dilapidated* and barely livable, because Nature had long since taken over.

DILIGENCE (n)   [DIL-i-j*uh* ns]

Meaning: steady, persistent effort

Usage 1: Due to the *diligence* of the investigating police officer, the district attorney was able to build a strong case.

Usage 2: While performing her due *diligence*, the County Clerk found evidence that the title of the land had never been properly transferred.

Usage 3: Thanks to the tireless *diligence* of the researchers, an alternative treatment to that particular viral strain was found.

Usage 4: To be a success in any field requires *diligence*, competence, perseverance, and a modicum of luck.

DILUTE (v)   [dahy-LOOT]

Meaning: to reduce in strength

Usage 1: The solution was too caustic, so the scientist attempted to *dilute* it by adding more water.

Usage 2: When the ice melted, it began to *dilute* the flavor of the punch.

Usage 3: Impure components can *dilute* the potency of a medicine, and cause it to be much less effective.

Usage 4: Mary turned on the ceiling fan to *dilute* the strong burnt smell coming from the kitchen.

Usage 5: Undue familiarity with superior officers can *dilute* their authority.

DISBAND (v)   [dis-BAND]

Meaning: to break up

Usage 1: Most people remember where they were when the Beatles announced their intention to *disband*.

Usage 2: Despite their fantastic success and their multiple championships, the owner decided to *disband* the team as a cost-cutting measure.

Usage 3: Because our professional goals and ideals seem to be at odds, we decided to *disband* our partnership so we could sell the business.

Usage 4: Many bands allow their members to pursue separate projects, without having to *disband* the group permanently.

DISCLAIM (v)   [dis-KLEYM]

Meaning: to deny, reject, or renounce

Usage 1: Although I have attended the churches of other denominations, I *disclaim* any interest in converting.

Usage 2: Because his actions were done without the authority or knowledge of his superiors, the agency had no choice but to *disclaim* any involvement.

Usage 3: It is not unusual for a politician to *disclaim* any past associates when their actions become controversial.

Usage 4: When the team owner was caught making controversial statements, the league voted to *disclaim* any involvement and censure any further speech.

DISCLOSE (v)   [dih-SKLOHZ]

Meaning: to reveal or make known

Usage 1: Faced with the legal consequences, Joseph had no choice but to *disclose* the depth of his involvement.

Usage 2: Josephine kept silent, because the secret was not hers to *disclose*.

Usage 3: It is a violation of my professional ethics to *disclose* the identity of my client.

Usage 4: By federal law, any candidate for public office must publicly *disclose* their income.

Usage 5: Under the concept of freedom of religion, a priest is not obligated to *disclose* any information that he hears in the confessional.

DISINCLINATION (n)   [dis-in-kl*uh*-NEY-sh*uh* n]

Meaning: unwillingness or reluctance

Usage 1: Because of an earlier negative experience, the food company had a *disinclination* to rehire the advertising firm.

Usage 2: Her husband had a pattern of infidelity, so Betty had a *disinclination* to listen to his apologies and excuses.

Usage 3: I hope you can understand my *disinclination* to work with someone who has such an extensive criminal record.

Usage 4: When he fell behind on his loan payments, the bank expressed their *disinclination* to extend his line of credit.

Usage 5: For months, the business had been operating at a loss, so the board unanimously voted their disinclination to award yearly bonuses.

DISLODGE (v)   [dis-LOJ]

Meaning: to forcibly remove

Usage 1: Even though he followed the method that he had been taught in training, the soldier was unable to dislodge the jammed round from his weapon.

Usage 2: Finally, the police resorted to high-pressure water hoses in an attempt to *dislodge* the protesters from their position.

Usage 3: Frustrated, Jeremy crawled underneath his truck to try to *dislodge* the chain that had become wrapped around the axle.

Usage 4: Jordan shook the remote from side to side, and then she banged it against the table, but it was no use – she could not *dislodge* the battery.

Usage 5: Mrs. Adams had to contact the sheriff so she could *dislodge* the unwanted squatters from her property.

DISPEL (v)   [dih-SPEL]

Meaning: to disperse or cause to vanish

Usage 1: After the merger, a meeting was held with the shareholders, to *dispel* any fears they might have.

Usage 2: The Mayor decided to proactively *dispel* any myths and suppositions by giving an immediate press conference.

Usage 3: Although the boxer had won the fight, the close decision helped to *dispel* any belief that he was unbeatable.

Usage 4: I am happy to be working here, and I would like to *dispel* any notion that anyone has that I might be looking for another job.

DISPIRITED (adj)   [di-SPIR-i-tid]

Meaning: dejected or discouraged

Usage 1: After yet another defeat, the team left the arena *dispirited* and downtrodden.

Usage 2: Do not become *dispirited* if you are ever fired from a job, because you can use that as an opportunity to find a better one.

Usage 3: For months after his divorce, John woke up every morning feeling *dispirited*, abandoned, and unworthy.

Usage 4: Because he was unable to support his family, Charlie became depressed and *dispirited*.

DISQUIETUDE (n)   [dis-KWAHY-i-tood]

Meaning: a state of uneasiness

Usage 1: Do not let my calm demeanor fool you, because the *disquietude* here is almost palatable.

Usage 2: When the new mistress of the house was introduced, the entire household staff was overcome with a feeling of *disquietude*.

Usage 3: On election night, the candidate and his Chief of Staff battled with their own sense of *disquietude*, until the returns started coming in.

Usage 4: If you can be alone and triumph over your own personal perception of *disquietude*, then you should have no problem quelling a crowd.

DISSENT (v)   [dih-SENT]

Meaning: to disagree with the majority

Usage 1: Because I believe that the defendant is innocent, I must *dissent* with a vote of guilty.

Usage 2: Because he had decided to *dissent* with a vote of impeachment, the congressman was censured by his party for a month.

Usage 3: The school board member opted to *dissent* with a vote of dismissal, arguing that the teacher could be suspended temporarily, instead.

Usage 4: Mrs. Johnson chose to *dissent* with the neighborhood organization, because she felt that they needed to research and discuss the subject further.

DISTINCTION (n)   [dih-STINGK-sh*uh*n]

Meaning: distinguishing quality or characteristic

Usage 1: The Buffalo Bills have the dubious *distinction* of being the only professional football team to lose four Super Bowls in a row.

Usage 2: Audie Murphy holds the *distinction* of being the most-decorated soldier in American history.

Usage 3: There is no way that you can downplay the *distinction* that Barack Obama has earned by being the first African-American to hold the office of President.

Usage 4: Although it may be a *distinction* to be the only member of my family who has gone to college, I could not have done it without the help of others.

DISTRAUGHT (adj)   [dih-STRAWT]

Meaning: extremely agitated or unbalanced

Usage 1: When she lost her daughter at the mall, Ellen became *distraught* with worry.

Usage 2: Despite the assurances of upper management, many of the employees became *distraught* at the possibility of being laid off due to the merger.

Usage 3: Phillip's arrest had cost him his scholarship, and he became positively *distraught* at the thought of having to tell his parents.

Usage 4: When Jane's husband died, she was *distraught* with grief, and almost became overwhelmed with sadness.

DIVINE (v)   [dih-VAHYN]

Meaning: to perceive intuitively, to portend

Usage 1: Fortunes are made and lost each year in Las Vegas as sports prognosticators try to *divine* what will happen during the upcoming football season.

Usage 2: The fortune-teller claimed to be able to *divine* a person's future just by reading their palms.

Usage 3: War is so fraught with uncertainty that even the most insightful person cannot easily *divine* what is going to happen next.

DOCILE (adj)   [DOS-*uh* l]

Meaning: easily managed

Usage 1: Riley had no hesitation to let her children ride the *docile* horse.

Usage 2: She mistook my *docile* behavior for weakness, but she soon learned the error of her ways.

Usage 3: There was something about her *docile* demeanor and kind countenance that gave her an allure unmatched by most women.

Usage 4: In her dotage, the widow became known as a *docile* and unassuming soul.

Usage 5: Certain breeds of dogs make excellent pets because of their intelligence and *docile* behavior.

DOGGEREL (n)   [DAW-ger-*uh* l]

Meaning: verse that is crude, comic, or burlesque in nature

Usage 1: The King enjoyed the inventive *doggerel* sang by the minstrel.

Usage 2: As the emcee, he would come out, sing a few lines of *doggerel*, tell a few jokes, and then introduce the next act.

Usage 3: The ribald nature of his *doggerel* made the men chuckle and caused the women to blush.

DORMER (n)   [DAWR-mer]

Meaning: a window or structure projecting from a sloping roof

Usage 1: Stepping back to admire his handiwork, Jimmy realized that he had forgotten to paint the *dormer* on the second floor.

Usage 2: Due to weather damage, the *dormer* required extensive carpentry repair.

Usage 3: The *dormer* windows were headed by metal awnings that kept the sun out of the interior of the room.

DOTE (v)   [doht]

Meaning: to demonstrate excessive love or fondness, or, to suffer a noticeable decline in mental faculties

Usage 1: Whenever she would visit from boarding school, Curtis would *dote* on his oldest daughter, showering her with attention and tokens of his affection.

Usage 2: Even though he was a full grown man, Russell's mother tended to *dote* upon him, even going so far as to tuck him in at night.

Usage 3: Bob's family began to worry about him when he started to *dote*, because once, he even mistook the maid for his mother.

DOWDY (adj)   [DOU-dee]

Meaning: shabby and old-fashioned

Usage 1: With her faded and shapeless dress, Hortense appeared like a *dowdy* relic from a bygone era.

Usage 2: The singer appeared to be almost comically *dowdy*, but her voice was angelic.

Usage 3: Eleanor's *dowdy* appearance belied her underlying exuberance.

Usage 4: She was *dowdy*, mousy, and utterly nondescript, and in three years, she would not be remembered by anyone.

DROLL (adj)   [drohl]

Meaning: whimsically amusing

Usage 1: Rather than being known for telling jokes, the comedian was adept at making *droll* observations about society.

Usage 2: If you take his comments with a grain of salt, you might find his statements to be quite *droll*, and you might find yourself smiling in spite of your earlier outrage.

Usage 3: John's *droll* attempts to be funny seemed to be lost on his boss, who appeared to have misplaced his sense of humor.

Usage 4: I enjoy humor that is *droll* or absurdist in nature, rather than slapstick or physical comedy.

DURATION (n)   [dyoo-REY-sh*uh* n]

Meaning: length of time that something exists or lasts

Usage 1: Because she had missed her curfew, Monica was grounded for the *duration* of the summer.

Usage 2: To stay out of jail, Edward had to stay out of all legal trouble for the *duration* of his probation.

Usage 3: For the *duration* of the fiscal year, all expenditures over $100 have to be approved in advance by management.

Usage 4: In an attempt to preserve their slim lead, the football team only ran rushing plays for the *duration* of the fourth quarter.

Usage 5: After the argument, John and Mary didn't speak to each other again for the *duration* of the evening.

DWINDLE (v)   [DWIN-dl]

Meaning: to waste away

Usage 1: Rachel saw her savings *dwindle* away when she tried unsuccessfully to start her own business.

Usage 2: When he was laid off at such an advanced age, Richard saw both his fortunes and his prospects *dwindle*.

Usage 3: it was positively alarming to see how fast Sam's inheritance started to *dwindle* once he reached his maturity.

Usage 4: As the night wore on and the losses started to mount, the poker player's stack of chips rapidly began to *dwindle*.

Chapter 14

Earthy – Galvanize

This chapter covers the following words, each with its part of speech, pronunciation, and descriptive meaning.

Usage of the word is also illustrated in three to five sample sentences.

earthy	exhilarating	fodder
eclipse	exhort	foreshadow
elucidate	exhume	forgo
emanate	exodus	formality
emancipate	exorbitant	fracas
embark	expertise	frolicsome
embezzlement	extant	fusion
engage	exude	galvanize
entrance	facile	
epicure	fallow	
epigram	fancier	
equine	fanciful	
errant	fervent	
escapade	fiat	
espionage	figurine	
eulogistic	filibuster	
evoke	finale	
exacting	fissure	
exceptionable	flit	
excise	flounder	
exemplify	fluke	

EARTHY (adj)   [UR-thee]

Meaning: unrefined or without affectation

Usage 1: Abraham Lincoln was known for his *earthy*, often ribald, sense of humor.

Usage 2: The simple, *earthy* charm of Amish furniture has led to its increasing popularity with collectors.

Usage 3: No matter where he was in her house, Samuel could smell the warm *earthy* aromas emanating from his grandmother's kitchen.

Usage 4: Jack had an *earthy* charm that people were drawn to immediately.

ECLIPSE (v)   [ih-KLIPS]

Meaning: to surpass or make less important

Usage 1: In her heart of hearts, Jennifer secretly knew that her protege's accomplishments would *eclipse* her own one day

Usage 2: Many sports experts think that no one will ever be able to match Nolan Ryan's pitching records, let alone *eclipse* them.

Usage 3: Susan's self-confidence was so fragile that she felt that this one mistake would *eclipse* the rest of her achievements.

ELUCIDATE (v)   [ih-LOO-si-deyt]

Meaning: to explain or make clear

Usage 1: In case you do not understand what I mean, allow me to *elucidate*.

Usage 2: When the students continued to stare at her with blank expressions, the teacher realized that she needed to *elucidate* on the subject.

Usage 3: Sometimes, the largest part of an attorney's job is to *elucidate* the intricacies of the law to clients.

EMANATE (v)   [EM-*uh*-neyt]

Meaning: to come forth or originate from

Usage 1: As soon as it was turned on, unfamiliar glowing energies began to *emanate* from the mysterious machine.

Usage 2: The explorers pried open the crypt, and immediately, a foul odor began to *emanate* from somewhere inside.

Usage 3: Despite his wife's reassurances, nagging suspicions started to *emanate* from the darkest recesses of Charlie's mind.

EMANCIPATE (v)   [ih-MAN-s*uh*-peyt]

Meaning: to liberate

Usage 1: Many southern plantation owners made the decision to *emancipate* their slaves even before the end of the Civil War.

Usage 2: You can never fire me-- you can only *emancipate* me from this dead-end job.

Usage 3: Jerry entered rehab because he hoped it would *emancipate* him from the heavy chains of addiction.

EMBARK (v)   [em-BAHRK]

Meaning: to begin a journey or an enterprise

Usage 1: After he retired, Paul began to plan for the time when he might *embark* upon his next adventure.

Usage 2: Florida seemed like the logical choice of location from whence we might *embark* on our vacation cruise.

Usage 3: Before you *embark* on starting your own business, it is necessary to have both a detailed business plan and an adequate source of capital.

EMBEZZLEMENT (n) [em-BEZ-*uh* l m*uh* nt]

Meaning: the fraudulent use of another's money or property

Usage 1: When his *embezzlement* was discovered, the executive was summarily discharged.

Usage 2: Because he had been convicted of *embezzlement*, John found it difficult to find a job in management.

Usage 3: In her position as Chief Financial Officer, Rebecca had commanded a huge salary, and this made her *embezzlement* all the more shocking.

ENGAGE (v) [en-GEYJ]

Meaning: to attract, bind, or secure

Usage 1: Suzette had dozens of suitors, but not one of them managed to *engage* any real interest on her part.

Usage 2: Since they were alone in the elevator, Thomas seized the opportunity to *engage* his employer in conversation.

Usage 3: If you want to avoid an argument, please don't *engage* Howard in any sort of political discussion.

Usage 4: Thomas forgot to *engage* the parking brake, and that is what eventually led to the accident.

ENTRANCE (v) [EN-tr*uh* ns]

Meaning: to put under a spell

Usage 1: With his dark flashing eyes and his European accent, Alejandro never failed to *entrance* a significant portion of the female audience.

Usage 2: The television's overall size and unique clarity of picture served to *entrance* any visitor to the electronics department.

Usage 3: Linda closed her eyes and let the music *entrance* her soul and soothe her troubled mind.

Usage 4: Historical legend tells of how Rasputin could mysteriously *entrance* virtually any woman to whom he spoke.

EPICURE (n) [EP-i-ky*oo* r]

Meaning: connoisseur of fine food and drink

Usage 1: As an *epicure*, I make it a point to sample local cuisine whenever I am traveling.

Usage 2: No *epicure* worth his or her salt would ever eat at a fast-food restaurant.

Usage 3: Donald was an accomplished *epicure*, but only when it came to French food and wine.

EPIGRAM (n) [EP-i-gram]

Meaning: a short, witty remark or poem

Usage 1: Mark Twain would fire off a withering *epigram* at his critics with the slightest of provocations.

Usage 2: John's *epigram* went too far, crossing the border from satirical into hurtful.

Usage 3: Milton's presence at cocktail parties was all the rage, because when he was in his cups he would entertain the rest of the guests with one *epigram* and anecdote after another.

EQUINE (adj) [EE-kwahyn]

Meaning: resembling or having to do with a horse

Usage 1: George had an odd, *equine* face, with elongated cheekbones and prominent front teeth.

Usage 2: After years of working at the ranch, Buck considered himself to be an expert in all things *equine*.

Usage 3: The air in the barn was a sickly-sweet melange of both *equine* and bovine odors.

ERRANT (adj)   [ER-*uh* nt]

Meaning: straying from the normal course

Usage 1: Far from condemning him, John welcomed his *errant* son with open arms.

Usage 2: The quarterback's *errant* throw sailed out of bounds, far out of the reach of the receiver.

Usage 3: Ground control initiated the auto-destruct sequence of the *errant* rocket, before it could pose a threat to any residential neighborhoods.

Usage 4: The help center was a valuable resource that helped *errant* youths regain their footing.

ESCAPADE (n)   [ES-k*uh*-peyd]

Meaning: a wild adventure or prank

Usage 1: Charlene's last summer before her senior year was one fabulous *escapade* after another.

Usage 2: To forestall any disappointment, Richard had meticulously planned his vacation *escapade*.

Usage 3: After Rachel's latest reckless *escapade*, her parents were at their wits' ends as to how they could control her behavior.

Usage 4: This latest trip was more than just an *escapade* because Gordon would finally be meeting his long-lost father.

ESPIONAGE (n)   [ES-pee-*uh*-nahzh]

Meaning: the practice of spying, especially when conducted by a government or corporate entity

Usage 1: During the 1960s, the nations on oppositional sides of the Cold War engaged in almost-nonstop *espionage* against one another.

Usage 2: Corporate *espionage* explains why so many similar products exist on the market.

Usage 3: Strangely, the measurable value of international *espionage* is both overrated and underrated.

Usage 4: Although the service of *espionage* may use some unsavory tactics, those tactics are usually justifiable in the name of national security.

EULOGISTIC (adj)   [yoo-l*uh*-JIS-tik]

Meaning: to be praiseful and appreciative

Usage 1: To John, receiving the award was rather anticlimactic, because it seemed *eulogistic*, rather than merit-based.

Usage 2: When Bob and Mary celebrated their 60th wedding anniversary, they received dozens of *eulogistic* cards in the mail.

Usage 3: Too many interviews of political candidates turn into *eulogistic* "puff pieces", rather than real news articles.

EVOKE (v)   [ih-VOHK]

Meaning: to call up or elicit

Usage 1: The demagogue deliberately used fiery language to *evoke* a strong emotional response from the crowd.

Usage 2: Larry hoped that the atmosphere of the restaurant he had chosen would *evoke* a romantic response from his girlfriend.

Usage 3: Few songs can *evoke* such a passionate and patriotic response as the national anthem.

Usage 4: If you want charitable contributions to increase, you must first *evoke* feelings of both sympathy and empathy among the potential donors.

Usage 5: Somehow, I always seem to *evoke* a hostile mood from my ex-wife.

EXACTING (adj) [ig-ZAK-ting]

Meaning: demanding close attention and adherence to standards

Usage 1: Chemistry is an extremely *exacting* science, because one mismeasurement can cause an experiment to fail.

Usage 2: Jennifer had an extremely difficult time adjusting to her new boss's *exacting* nature.

Usage 3: Steven had an *exacting* academic schedule that left little time for a social life.

Usage 4: The cadets practiced an *exacting* drill movement in preparation for the graduation ceremony.

EXCEPTIONABLE (adj) [ik-SEP-sh*uh*-n*uh*-b*uh* l]

Meaning: liable to objection

Usage 1: The studio heads did not support the director's *exceptionable* decision to recast the lead roles.

Usage 2: Truman's decision to use the atomic bomb was viewed as *exceptionable* by many, but necessary by most.

Usage 3: When he was found to be keeping *exceptionable* company, the pastor was asked to resign.

Usage 4: The alderman's *exceptionable* announcement was met with hoots of derision from the crowd.

EXCISE (v) [EK-sahyz]

Meaning: to cut out or off

Usage 1: It took hours for the surgeons to *excise* the tumor, but in the end, the surgery was a success.

Usage 2: Bill often wondered how his ex-wife had been able to *excise* him from his children's lives so completely.

Usage 3: Sometimes an editor must *excise* whole passages from books for the sake of clarity.

EXEMPLIFY (v) [ig-ZEM-pl*uh*-fahy]

Meaning: to serve as an example of

Usage 1: The brave men and women who serve in our Armed Forces *exemplify* all that is best about our country.

Usage 2: Because Anne had risen so far above her humble beginnings, the sponsors thought she could *exemplify* the power of hard work and a good education.

Usage 3: Unnecessary delays, cost overruns, and a general lack of accountability all serve to *exemplify* some of the major problems commonly found within a bloated bureaucracy.

EXHILARATING (adj) [ig-ZIL-*uh*-reyt-ing]

Meaning: making one feel elated or thrilled

Usage 1: The panoramic view from atop the precipice was *exhilarating*.

Usage 2: Many members of the Polar Bear Club say that the initial cold shock is *exhilarating*.

Usage 3: Bannister felt his fatigue vanishing and his stride quickening when he heard the *exhilarating* cheer from the assembled throng.

EXHORT (v) [ig-ZAWRT]

Meaning: to strongly urge or advise

Usage 1: The politician gave speeches in an attempt to *exhort* his constituents to support his newest legislative proposal.

Usage 2: After considering all options, I must *exhort* you not to pursue this course of action any further.

Usage 3: Despite the score, the cheerleaders continued to *exhort* the crowd into cheering for their hapless team.

Usage 4: Late-night infomercials usually feature a fast-talking huckster of a spokesperson whose only role is to try to *exhort* gullible viewers into making an impulsive purchase.

EXHUME (v)   [ig-ZYOOM]

Meaning: to disinter or bring to light

Usage 1: Faced with this new evidence, the judge gave the order to *exhume* the victim's body.

Usage 2: After poring over decades of financial records, the investigator was able to *exhume* a number of improprieties.

Usage 3: Just weeks after the initial discovery, archaeologists were able to *exhume* a number of historically-significant artifacts.

EXODUS (n)   [EK-s*uh*-d*uh* s]

Meaning: a departure or withdrawal, typically by a large group

Usage 1: The city's high crime rate led to a mass *exodus* by thousands of its residents.

Usage 2: During the summer free agency period, it is not unusual to see an *exodus* of players leaving their teams in search of more lucrative contracts.

Usage 3: The end-of-summer *exodus* that happened every year as tourists returned to their homes left the vacation town as deserted as a graveyard.

EXORBITANT (adj)   [ig-ZAWR-bi-t*uh* nt]

Meaning: excessive beyond propriety, custom, or reason

Usage 1: Many moviegoers balk at paying the theater's *exorbitant* prices for refreshments.

Usage 2: The interest rate charged by payday loan companies is often *exorbitant*, and unwary borrowers can be easily victimized by predatory lenders.

Usage 3: If you feel that gas prices are too high in the Midwest, you should see the *exorbitant* prices charged on either coast!

EXPERTISE (n)   [ek-sper-TEEZ]

Meaning: specialized knowledge

Usage 1: Because he had never served in the military, the president relied on the *expertise* of his advisers.

Usage 2: I appreciate you coming to me with this, but I really have no *expertise* in this area.

Usage 3: After the initial consultation, the attorney realized that the case was outside his area of *expertise*, so he recommended another lawyer.

EXTANT (adj)   [EK-st*uh* nt]

Meaning: still in existence

Usage 1: There are only a handful of authentic examples of William Shakespeare's signature *extant* today.

Usage 2: If you visit Normandy beach, you will still find *extant* German fortifications from World War II.

Usage 3: Because of the encroachment of modern civilization, it is virtually impossible to find any *extant* indigenous tribes that remain unspoiled.

Usage 4: Originally, all copies of the film were ordered to be destroyed, but decades later, a few *extant* copies were discovered.

EXUDE (v)   [ig-ZOOD]

Meaning: to project or radiate

Usage 1: Many voters tended to gravitate towards Kennedy, because he seemed to *exude* charisma, confidence, and the promise of prosperity.

Usage 2: After a fifth consecutive losing season, even the once-optimistic coach began to *exude* defeatism and negativity.

Usage 3: Whenever he had a meeting with his clients, Joseph would *exude* complete professionalism and competence.

FACILE (adj)   [FAS-il]

Meaning: proceeding or working with ease, or simple to perform

Usage 1: Lucero liked doing crossword puzzles because he felt that they kept his mind in nimble and *facile* shape.

Usage 2: The crowd watched, astonished, as the juggler moved the balls faster and faster between his *facile* fingers.

Usage 3: After a series of adjustments by the engineer, the control lever was soon operating in a *facile* manner again.

FALLOW (adj)   [FAL-oh]

Meaning: uncultivated, inactive, or not in use

Usage 1: It is an egregious sin for a farmer to let his fields go *fallow*.

Usage 2: The *fallow* bank accounts were soon overdrawn and closed due to a lack of deposits.

Usage 3: A *fallow* mind is the result when an individual stops reading, discovering, and learning.

FANCIER (n)   [FAN-see-er]

Meaning: a person with an interest or enthusiasm in something

Usage 1: John had always been a *fancier* of fine Italian sports cars, but he had never been able to afford one.

Usage 2: Joan was a *fancier* of television cooking shows, and her own skills improved as a result.

Usage 3: Her impeccable coiffure and elegant clothing demonstrated that she was a *fancier* of the finer things in life.

FANCIFUL (adj)   [FAN-si-*fuh*l]

Meaning: unreal, or guided by whimsy rather than reason

Usage 1: Joshua's *fanciful* daydreams often had a deleterious effect upon his school work.

Usage 2: Mary had her daughter's room decorated with a fairytale motif, replete with *fanciful* designs and storybook characters.

Usage 3: Children believe in the Boogeyman, the Easter Bunny, the Man in the Moon, and any number of fanciful creatures.

FERVENT (adj)   [FUR-v*uh*nt]

Meaning: having a great intensity of feeling

Usage 1: Because he himself had never been able to, it was Jesse's *fervent* wish that his children would receive a college education.

Usage 2: Julia was completely flabbergasted at Edward's sudden, *fervent* expressions of affection.

Usage 3: Unless tempered by reason, *fervent* devotion to any cause can easily become a misguided obsession.

FIAT (n)   [FEE-aht]

Meaning: an official command or decree

Usage 1: The king issued a *fiat* forbidding any commenter from hunting deer on royal grounds.

Usage 2: The governmental *fiat* set forth strict guidelines as to which fruits may pass through customs.

Usage 3: The very essence of individual morality dictates that moral behavior must occur even in the absence of a *fiat* prescribed by the ruling class.

FIGURINE (n)   [fig-y*uh*-REEN]

Meaning: a small ornamental statuette

Usage 1: As a child, Suzette was always fascinated by the lifelike *figurine* of a ballerina that was in her mother's curio cabinet.

Usage 2: In some cultures, it is considered taboo to make a *figurine* in the image of a human being.

Usage 3: Whenever his model could not be present, Michelangelo would use a *figurine* for reference.

FILIBUSTER (v)   [FIL-*uh*-buhs-ter]

Meaning: to attempt to block legislation by obstructive practices, usually by making overly-long speeches

Usage 1: When he saw that his proposed bill wasn't going to pass, the Majority Whip decided to *filibuster* until the proper support could be gained.

Usage 2: Political parties *filibuster* as a time-honored and effective strategy to advance their own agendas.

Usage 3: When it came time to *filibuster*, the oratorial stamina of the congressman from Ohio was legendary.

FINALE (n)   [fi-NAL-ee]

Meaning: the final part of any performance

Usage 1: The grand *finale* of the fireworks demonstration was spectacular.

Usage 2: When my date became ill, we had to leave before the *finale* of the concert.

Usage 3: For his *finale* of the evening, the magician required two volunteers from the audience to help him with one last illusion.

FISSURE (n)   [FISH-er]

Meaning: a narrow crevice or crack made by cracking or splitting, most typically in rock or earth

Usage 1: Millions of years ago, the Grand Canyon was only a small *fissure* caused by the river's running water.

Usage 2: Seismologists were keenly concerned about the sulfuric smoke rising from the *fissure*.

Usage 3: At the epicenter of the earthquake, entire homes vanished into the *fissure* that had suddenly opened.

Usage 4: Petty jealousies and backbiting created a *fissure* between the owners of the once-solid company.

FLIT (v)   [flit]

Meaning: to pass swiftly by

Usage 1: The days seemed to *flit* by, and before we knew it, summer vacation was over.

Usage 2: The hummingbird would *flit* from plant to plant, drinking nectar from each flower.

Usage 3: Whenever Julie was nervous, she was unable to concentrate, and so she would *flit* from task to task.

FLOUNDER (v)   [FLOUN-der]

Meaning: to struggle clumsily

Usage 1: I would rather do it myself than to see someone else *flounder* about uselessly.

Usage 2: Because he had never learned proper study habits, it was no surprise that Tom began to *flounder* once he enrolled in college.

Usage 3: When the wildebeest wandered too far into the muck, it became trapped and began to *flounder* hopelessly.

FLUKE (n)   [flook]

Meaning: a stroke of luck, or an accidental success

Usage 1: In golf, sometimes your best shot is nothing more than a *fluke*.

Usage 2: Contrary to what many sports writers believed, Douglas's success was not a *fluke*, because he had diligently trained for the fight.

Usage 3: It was only a *fluke* that the guard left the gate unlocked, but the prisoners quickly capitalized upon their good fortune.

FODDER (n)   [FOD-er]

Meaning: coarse food or raw material

Usage 1: During the blight, Jack often struggled to find *fodder* for his farm animals.

Usage 2: When they lost their officers, the soldiers of the second platoon panicked, and were soon naught but fodder for the enemy's cannons.

Usage 3: If you are not aggressive once the opening bell sounds, you'll be *fodder* for the other, more aggressive traders.

FORESHADOW (v)   [fawr-SHAD-oh]

Meaning: to indicate beforehand

Usage 1: Often, the music in a movie will *foreshadow* what is about to happen next.

Usage 2: Indiscriminate use of a credit card can be an indicator of poor financial habits, and may *foreshadow* account default or even bankruptcy.

Usage 3: Many people believe that the behavior of animals can *foreshadow* impending changes in the weather.

FORGO (v)   [fawr-GOH]

Meaning: to give up or do without

Usage 1: In the interest of neighborly peace, Franklin decided to *forgo* his claim to the easement.

Usage 2: In an effort to end the war once and for all, the United States chose to *forgo* harsher penalties against the Japanese.

Usage 3: If we can move forward, I will *forgo* this one point, and hopefully, we can reach an agreement.

FORMALITY (n)   [fawr-MAL-i-tee]

Meaning: an action or a ceremony performed simply for the sake of procedure

Usage 1: The hiring manager assured Jacob that he had been awarded the job, and that the background check was a mere *formality*.

Usage 2: In many traditional families, it is no mere *formality* for potential suitors to ask permission of a girl's parents before calling upon her socially.

Usage 3: When George Washington was President, he instituted the *formality* where bows were exchanged with visitors, rather than handshakes.

FRACAS (n)   [FREY-k*uh* s]

Meaning: a noisy fight or disturbance

Usage 1: Sean was always more than happy to join in any barroom *fracas* that might happen on a given night.

Usage 2: In the aftermath of the *fracas*, four people were arrested and three others were hospitalized.

Usage 3: Whenever my rowdy neighbors host a party, it always ends in a ferocious *fracas* that has to be broken up by the police.

FROLICSOME (adj)   [FROL-ik-s*uh* m]

Meaning: lively, gay, or playful

Usage 1: As a child growing up on a farm, Glenn could spend hours watching the *frolicsome* animals lead and play.

Usage 2: After being cooped up in the house all day, the children began to get more and more boisterous and frolicsome in their play.

Usage 3: To remain young at heart, you should never let your age rob you of the *frolicsome* spirit of your youth.

FUSION (n)   [FYOO-zh*uh* n]

Meaning: an intermingled or blended joining

Usage 1: The new restaurant downtown was an odd *fusion* of Mexican and Japanese cuisines.

Usage 2: When teammates can achieve cooperative *fusion*, the whole becomes greater than the sum of the individual parts.

Usage 3: The musical style of many of today's artists is a *fusion* of rock, pop, hip-hop, and funk.

GALVANIZE (v)   [GAL-v*uh*-nahyz]

Meaning: to shock or startle into activity

Usage 1: The sudden sounding of the klaxon could *galvanize* the sailors into immediate action.

Usage 2: Usually the firemen sat around the station performing routine tasks, until an alarm would *galvanize* them into frenzied activity.

Usage 3: After his traumatic experience, nothing could *galvanize* Jack into looking for a job.

Chapter **15**

Gambit – Innovation

This chapter covers the following words, each with its part of speech, pronunciation, and descriptive meaning.

Usage of the word is also illustrated in three to five sample sentences.

gambit	hoodwink	inconsistency
gamely	hovel	incredulous
gargantuan	humility	industrious
gaudy	illicit	inevitable
generate	illusory	ingrate
gingerly	imbibe	inimitable
glaze	immaculate	innate
glib	immolate	innovation
gloss	impartial	
glutton	impenitent	
gnarled	imperial	
grotto	impetuous	
guy	implement	
haggle	impotent	
haphazard	inalienable	
harbor	inarticulate	
headlong	incantation	
heterodox	inception	
heyday	incidence	
hoax	inclusive	
homage	incompatible	

GAMBIT (n)   [GAM-bit]

Meaning: a movement or action meant to gain a more advantageous position

Usage 1: When his *gambit* for more control failed, Jason had no choice but to leave the company.

Usage 2: Fortune favors the bold, so a *gambit* that catches your adversary unawares is sometimes well worth the risk.

Usage 3: Using his life's savings to open a new business was both the most terrifying and the most rewarding *gambit* that Dave had ever attempted.

GAMELY (adv)   [GEYM-lee]

Meaning: pluckily, with spirit

Usage 1: When her manuscript was rejected yet again, Susan *gamely* submitted it to another publisher.

Usage 2: Even in the face of crushingly unfavorable odds, the brave soldiers of the 75th Brigade *gamely* soldiered on.

Usage 3: The outmatched boxer rose from the canvas after the knockdown and *gamely* continued to fight.

GARGANTUAN (adj)   [gahr-GAN-choo-*uh* n]

Meaning: enormous, having great mass

Usage 1: Just like any other tourist, Peggy walked the streets of Manhattan and craned her neck upwards to marvel at the *gargantuan* skyscrapers.

Usage 2: The *gargantuan* aircraft carrier effectively functioned as a small city, with its own power system, infrastructure, and even a sort of economy.

Usage 3: The breathtaking panoramic view of the *gargantuan* Grand Canyon has to be seen firsthand to be accurately understood.

GAUDY (adj)   [GAW-dee]

Meaning: garishly showy, sometimes to a tasteless degree

Usage 1: Headlining performers in Las Vegas are often known for their elaborate set designs and *gaudy* costumes.

Usage 2: The *gaudy* diamond on Mrs. Vanderburg's reign was nearly the size of a robin's egg.

Usage 3: During Carnival, street dancers will festoon their bodies with *gaudy* attire and garish makeup.

GENERATE (v)   [JEN-*uh*-reyt]

Meaning: to create or produce

Usage 1: The new advertising campaign was judged to be a failure, because it did not *generate* any increase in business.

Usage 2: Because the recent weather failed to offer sufficient sunlight, the solar panels could not *generate* any appreciable amount of electrical power.

Usage 3: Sometimes members of the paparazzi will deliberately provoke a celebrity in an attempt to *generate* a news story.

GINGERLY (adj)   [JIN-jer-lee]

Meaning: extremely cautious or careful

Usage 1: Trying to salvage what he could, Dmitri *gingerly* picked through the pile of rubble that once was his home.

Usage 2: The wound was healing but still tender, so Charles had to *gingerly* hobble from place to place instead of walking normally.

Usage 3: Trying not to upset the witness, the attorney *gingerly* asked a series of questions concerning her recollections about the night in question.

Usage 4: I would prefer that you just spoke plainly to me, rather than *gingerly* sidestepping the real issue.

GLAZE (v) [gleyz]

Meaning: thinly cover with a smooth or shiny surface

Usage 1: When he chose to *glaze* the countertop, Chester had a good idea of what the finished project would look like.

Usage 2: Try as he might, Ed could not *glaze* over the truth and lie his way out of trouble this time.

Usage 3: Regina knew that she wanted to *glaze* her patio tiles in a new patina, but she wasn't sure what her next project would be.

GLIB (adj) [glib]

Meaning: easily fluent and capable, especially with speech, and often without thought or sincerity

Usage 1: No matter what question was put to him, Steve always seemed to have a *glib* answer readily at hand.

Usage 2: Laura had an easy-going manner and a *glib* way of speaking, so people often had doubts about her seriousness.

Usage 3: If you are going to give such flippant, *glib* responses, I see no point in continuing this conversation.

GLOSS (v) [glos]

Meaning: to deceptively or artificially create or possess an attractive appearance

Usage 1: As much as she wanted to *gloss* over the truth, Teresa knew inside that it was time to come clean.

Usage 2: Many politicians routinely engage in political doublespeak and try to *gloss* over the facts in order to mislead the public.

Usage 3: Because he so desperately needed the job, Ross tried to *gloss* over the irregularities in his work history.

GLUTTON (n) [GLUHT-n]

Meaning: a person with a large desire or capacity for something, especially eating or drinking

Usage 1: Sally must be a *glutton* for punishment, because she keeps making up with her inattentive and unfaithful boyfriend.

Usage 2: Every time I go to an all-you-can-eat buffet, I leave feeling like a bloated *glutton*.

Usage 3: Some people called Victor a *glutton* because of his voracious appetite, but he just shrugged and said he loved food.

Usage 4: Betty eats like a 400-pound *glutton*, but she never seems to gain any weight.

GNARLED (adj) [nahrld]

Meaning: bent and twisted, weather-beaten

Usage 1: In the dead of night, the forest's *gnarled* trees cast nightmarish shadows.

Usage 2: While walking down the street, Julius was accosted by a *gnarled* old panhandler who was looking for a handout.

Usage 3: Her arthritic hands were swollen and *gnarled*, and she was in constant pain because of them.

GROTTO (n) [GROT-oh]

Meaning: a small cave or cave-like structure

Usage 1: The *grotto* was dark, isolated, and utterly still, and it was easy to imagine it teeming with primordial life.

Usage 2: On the walls and ceiling of the *grotto* were dusky smudges of candle and lamp smoke, serving as visual reminders of past exploration.

Usage 3: There was only one way into and out of the *grotto*, and now that entrance had been blocked by the rockslide.

GUY (n)   [gahy]

Meaning: an informal term for a boy or man

Usage 1: Philip was the type of *guy* who would do anything to help out his friends.

Usage 2: Joaquin was universally known as a good *guy*, and everyone in the neighborhood liked him.

Usage 3: Because he usually played the bad *guy* when he was cast in a movie, Michael was often not even considered for other roles.

HAGGLE (v)   [HAG-*uh*l]

Meaning: to negotiate over price in a persistent manner

Usage 1: Abraham certainly knew how to *haggle* with the used car salesman, and often received a substantial discount from the original asking price.

Usage 2: Because he was in such a rush, Connor had no time to *haggle* with the merchant, and as a result, significantly overpaid for his purchase.

Usage 3: Experienced negotiators know that after you have arrived at a price, you can continue to *haggle* for considerations on delivery, options, and extra services.

HAPHAZARD (adj)   [hap-HAZ-erd]

Meaning: in a disorganized manner

Usage 1: Everything in Jordan's closet was simply tossed in a *haphazard* fashion.

Usage 2: Most home improvement experts suggest that you try to handle projects one at a time, rather than trying to tackle too much all at once in a *haphazard* rush.

Usage 3: Benjamin's desk appeared to be extremely *haphazard*, but if pressed, he could tell you the precise location of any file.

HARBOR (v)   [HAHR-ber]

Meaning: to shelter, maintain, or hide; to give refuge to

Usage 1: Even after the public debate was over, the incumbent continued to *harbor* dismissive, negative opinions about his challenger.

Usage 2: When Josef agreed to *harbor* refugees, he had no idea how much his life was about to change.

Usage 3: If you *harbor* any ill will against me, I would like to take this opportunity to clear the air and make peace with you.

HEADLONG (adj)   [HED-lawng]

Meaning: lacking in restraint, hasty

Usage 1: Disregarding his own safety, the soldier made a *headlong* rush toward the enemy bunker.

Usage 2: Bernard confounded the experts with his blind, *headlong* rise to success.

Usage 3: Caesar made one last *headlong* charge at his attackers before he finally succumbed to his wounds.

HETERODOX (adj)   [HET-er-*uh*-doks]

Meaning: having or holding opinions that are contrary to accepted doctrine

Usage 1: The pastor spent many hours with his young protege discussing the latter's *heterodox* philosophy.

Usage 2: The biggest problem that the baby boomers had with the hippies was the younger generation's *heterodox* ideology, which in some ways was anathema to traditional American values.

Usage 3: When the newly-promoted manager revealed his *heterodox* plan for the company, the Executive Board was understandably dubious.

HEYDAY (n)   [HEY-dey]

Meaning: period of greatest success

Usage 1: In his *heyday*, Muhammed Ali was the most famous athlete on the planet.

Usage 2: When the reporter failed to recognize who he was, the actor realized that his *heyday* had long since passed.

Usage 3: Due to the Internet, the music industry has declined dramatically since its *heyday*.

HOAX (n)   [hohks]

Meaning: an action or thing intended to deceive or defraud

Usage 1: The widely-circulated story chronicling the musician's death was yet another Internet *hoax*.

Usage 2: It was astonishing to see how many people blindly fell for the con man's *hoax*.

Usage 3: Although it has been definitively proven to be a *hoax*, many people still maintain a belief in the Loch Ness monster.

Usage 4: Jonathan is not likely to fall for a garden-variety *hoax* because he is a very levelheaded person.

HOMAGE (n)   [HOM-ij]

Meaning: an acknowledgment of respect or reverence

Usage 1: The band's latest album was *homage* to the venues that welcomed their earliest performances.

Usage 2: The new movie paid *homage* to the slapstick comedies of the 1930s and 40s.

Usage 3: In a moving speech, the actress offered *homage* to the women of color who had paved the way.

HOODWINK (v)   [HOO D-wingk]

Meaning: to take in or fool by deceptive means

Usage 1: Robin completely reveled in his cunning, and missed no opportunity to *hoodwink* the authorities.

Usage 2: Many elderly individuals are overly trusting, and are prime targets for unethical conmen looking to *hoodwink* them and defraud them of their savings.

Usage 3: You might *hoodwink* me once, but after that, I will be on guard for your shenanigans.

HOVEL (n)   [HUHV-*uh* l]

Meaning: a filthy or wretched dwelling

Usage 1: After months of being homeless, even the most decrepit *hovel* is a welcome improvement.

Usage 2: The widow and her children lived in crowded squalor in a one-room *hovel*.

Usage 3: You may call this place a *hovel*, but I call it home.

Usage 4: When they first moved in, the house was little more than a *hovel*, but after weeks of hard work, it was slowly being transformed into a charming little cottage.

HUMILITY (n)   [hyoo-MIL-i-tee]

Meaning: humbleness of spirit

Usage 1: Gregory was not known for his *humility*, and in fact, often alienated people with his arrogance.

Usage 2: Devotion, *humility*, and a willingness to serve are necessary traits for those individuals considering entering the priesthood.

Usage 3: Mason accepted the award with grace, profound gratitude, and a large measure of *humility*.

ILLICIT (adj)   [ih-LIS-it]

Meaning: not permitted for legal, ethical, or moral reasons

Usage 1: During the Prohibition Era, many people would stop by a hidden speakeasy to enjoy an *illicit* drink or two.

Usage 2: Everyone in the office knew that the sales manager was carrying on an *illicit* affair with one of the secretaries.

Usage 3: Carmen loved her brother, even though she could not condone his *illicit* activities.

Usage 4: The flood of *illicit* drugs into this country is as dangerous as any invasion by a hostile foreign power.

ILLUSORY (adj)   [ih-LOO-*suh*-ree]

Meaning: misleading or unreal

Usage 1: The happy perfection of their marriage was *illusory*, because they had already filed for divorce.

Usage 2: Any job satisfaction you experience can usually be described as fleeting and *illusory*.

Usage 3: When success and happiness is defined by others, the joy felt is *illusory*.

IMBIBE (v)   [im-BAHYB]

Meaning: to drink, especially alcoholic beverages; or, to soak up or absorb

Usage 1: Because Bill didn't *imbibe*, he only drank water or soft drinks at parties.

Usage 2: John was an accomplished drinker, and he never missed an opportunity to copiously *imbibe* more cocktails.

Usage 3: During the long train ride, Jerry sat back and let his soul *imbibe* the view of the countryside passing by.

IMMACULATE (adj)   [ih-MAK-y*uh*-lit]

Meaning: free from stain, blemish, or flaw

Usage 1: It was a special day, so the family's finest bone china and polished silverware were arranged artfully on top of and *immaculate* white linen tablecloth.

Usage 2: All eyes were upon the bride and her *immaculate* wedding gown as she glided ethereally down the aisle.

Usage 3: Richard worked tirelessly every weekend to keep his lawn as *immaculate* and well-tended as possible.

Usage 4: The background check revealed that Angela's references were impeccable, her work history was impressive, and her credit rating was *immaculate*.

IMMOLATE (v)   [IM-*uh*-leyt]

Meaning: to destroy by fire; or, to offer up as a sacrificial victim, usually by fire

Usage 1: George knew that with one strike of a match, he could *immolate* his rival's business.

Usage 2: Everyone thought that it was quite ironic that faulty electrical wiring could cause a short that could *immolate* the area's largest swimming pool company.

Usage 3: Once again being overly dramatic, Jennifer stated that she was a modern-day martyr who was ready to *immolate* herself upon the altar of her convictions.

IMPARTIAL (adj) [im-PAHR-sh*uh* l]

Meaning: without favoritism, fair

Usage 1: A jury has to be absolutely *impartial*, relying upon the evidence presented within the framework of the law.

Usage 2: It is always a good parenting idea to remain *impartial* when your children get into an argument.

Usage 3: Nowadays, many companies require that employee-employer disputes be handled by an independent and *impartial* third-party arbiter.

Usage 4: The judge recused himself when he realized that he could not be *impartial* in this particular case.

IMPENITENT (adj) [im-PEN-i-t*uh* nt]

Meaning: showing no remorse for one's crimes or sins

Usage 1: The death row prisoner remained defiant and *impenitent* until the end.

Usage 2: Because reflection and contemplation were not part of his psyche, it was not surprising that Carlos was still *impenitent* after all these years.

Usage 3: It is far better to acknowledge the harm we have done and ask for forgiveness than it is to stay oblivious and *impenitent*.

IMPERIAL (adj) [im-PEER-ee-*uh* l]

Meaning: with a commanding or regal quality or manner; or, having to do with an empire

Usage 1: Seated behind his immense mahogany desk, the Chairman of the Board had a haughty, almost imperial air about him.

Usage 2: Although England still has a monarchy, it is now governed by democracy, rather than by *imperial* rule.

Usage 3: Throughout history, *imperial* powers have been abused by despots just as often as they have been used righteously by benevolent monarchs.

IMPETUOUS (adj) [im-PECH-oo-*uh* s]

Meaning: impulsive, characterized by rash or emotional action

Usage 1: In those few defining moments, the *impetuous* teenager made a decision that affected the rest of his life.

Usage 2: Furious at his boss, Patrick made the *impetuous* choice to resign on the spot.

Usage 3: Giddy with emotion and caught up in the moment, Gloria accepted Edgar's *impetuous* proposal.

Usage 4: When you are married with children, have a mortgage, a job, and important obligations, it becomes difficult to make *impetuous*, spur-of-the-moment life choices.

IMPLEMENT (v) [IM-pl*uh*-ment]

Meaning: to put into effect

Usage 1: If we are going to *implement* this new program, first we have to have a detailed plan of action.

Usage 2: Edward wanted to *implement* a new training schedule, but first he needed to know everyone's availability.

Usage 3: The general manager of the store was fired when he failed to *implement* the policy changes that have been ordered.

IMPOTENT (adj) [IM-p*uh*-t*uh* nt]

Meaning: utterly powerless or ineffective

Usage 1: Because he could do nothing at the moment, David could only seethe in *impotent* rage when he thought about his current situation.

Usage 2: His words are empty and meaningless, full of whining protestations and *impotent* threats.

Usage 3: When he was laid off, Jason felt as unmanned and *impotent* as an eunuch.

Usage 4: Without his army to back him, the dictator was reduced to little more than an *impotent* and angry demagogue.

INALIENABLE (adj)   [in-EYL-y*uh*-n*uh*-b*uh* l]

Meaning: not able to be taken away or transferred to another

Usage 1: Human beings are born with certain *inalienable* rights that are not granted by governments.

Usage 2: Although Americans have the privilege and the duty to vote, it is not one of their *inalienable* rights.

Usage 3: Some basic *inalienable* rights can be temporarily curtailed when a person is incarcerated.

INARTICULATE (adj)   [in-ahr-TIK-y*uh*-lit]

Meaning: unable to communicate or be communicated clearly or coherently

Usage 1: All of Bobby's responses were terse, monosyllabic, and borderline *inarticulate*.

Usage 2: Because his jaw was wired shut, William could only vocalize in a series of *inarticulate* grunts.

Usage 3: It's not that I am *inarticulate*; it's that these feelings are hard to put into words.

Usage 4: Just because someone is functionally *inarticulate*, it doesn't mean that they do not have the lot to say.

INCANTATION (n)   [in-kan-TEY-sh*uh* n]

Meaning: a magical charm that is spoken, chanted, or sung

Usage 1: More out of superstitious habit than actual belief, the old woman would recite a blessing *incantation* whenever she received bad news.

Usage 2: The magical ritual required lighted candles, strange herbs, and an arcane *incantation* that was chanted by all of the coven members.

Usage 3: Anthony kissed his religious medal and said a prayer to his higher power that seemed to be more incantation than supplication.

INCEPTION (n)   [in-SEP-sh*uh* n]

Meaning: a start or beginning

Usage 1: Since the *inception* of tougher drunk driving laws, fatalities have decreased significantly.

Usage 2: At *inception*, the program went through a period of adjustment and growing pains, but the process is considerably smoother now.

Usage 3: With the *inception* of a new and more frequent inspection schedule, the company demonstrated its commitment to safety.

Usage 4: Daniel felt a twinge of sadness whenever he finished writing a novel, just as he was exhilarated at the *inception* of a new story.

INCIDENCE (n)   [IN-si-d*uh* ns]

Meaning: a particular event, or a rate of occurrence

Usage 1: This particular *incidence* is the exception that proves the rule.

Usage 2: Local authorities are becoming concerned about the increasing *incidence* of texting while driving.

Usage 3: Primarily due to advances in medicine, the *incidence* of birth defects has declined across the globe.

INCLUSIVE (adj)   [in-KLOO-siv]

Meaning: containing or including everything concerned, all-encompassing

Usage 1: Perhaps the best thing about *inclusive* vacation packages is the fact that there are no unexpected charges or fees.

Usage 2: If the mineral rights are *inclusive* with the rest of the property, then the price is more than fair.

Usage 3: Although it is acceptable to have private clubs for adults, youth organizations should be entirely *inclusive*.

Usage 4: Helen chose that particular insurance carrier because the coverage was *inclusive* when it came to pre-existing conditions.

INCOMPATIBLE (adj)   [in-k*uh* m-PAT-*uh*-b*uh* l]

Meaning: contrary to harmony, unable to coexist

Usage 1: To his dismay, Bernard learned that the charger he had purchased was *incompatible* with his cell phone.

Usage 2: Dishonesty, infidelity, and selfishness are *incompatible* with a happy and healthy relationship.

Usage 3: Their personalities were extremely *incompatible*, and many of their friends thought it a wonder that they had been able to stay together this long.

INCONSISTENCY (n)   [in-k*uh* n-SIS-t*uh* n-see]

Meaning: lack of uniformity or steadiness; contradiction

Usage 1: The detective listened to the tape of the conversation again and again, hoping to find an *inconsistency* in the suspect's story.

Usage 2: The patrons of the restaurant were frustrated by the *inconsistency* of service.

Usage 3: There was an *inconsistency* between the two prescriptions, and the medicine in the second batch was neither as strong nor as effective as that of the first batch.

Usage 4: There is no need to report an *inconsistency*, because the deviation is within acceptable parameters.

INCREDULOUS (adj)   [in-KREJ-*uh*-l*uh* s]

Meaning: showing disbelief

Usage 1: When Rodney finished speaking, the investigating officer was openly *incredulous* of his story.

Usage 2: The *incredulous* expression never left my wife's face as I tried to explain why I was getting home so late.

Usage 3: Many people are justifiably *incredulous* about the legitimacy of the home run record.

Usage 4: After she had finished grading the examinations, the teacher was *incredulous* at Jeffrey's score, and therefore suspicious that he had done so well without cheating.

INDUSTRIOUS (adj)   [in-DUHS-tree-*uh* s]

Meaning: hard-working

Usage 1: In America, there is no reason that an *industrious* person cannot go far in life.

Usage 2: By the *industrious* and judicious use of her study time, Jordan was able to earn a scholarship to an Ivy League college.

Usage 3: Paolo was an *industrious* worker, and he had soon saved enough money to open his own shop.

Usage 4: Nature dictates that many animals must be *industrious* enough to gather enough food during the summer to last them all winter.

INEVITABLE (adj)   [in-EV-i-t*uh*-b*uh* l]

Meaning: bound to happen, unable to be avoided

Usage 1: After the downpour from the heavy summer storm came the *inevitable* humidity.

Usage 2: Many people purchase food staples in bulk as a bulwark against *inevitable* price increases.

Usage 3: The members of the survivalist group were sure that a governmental collapse and subsequent revolt was *inevitable*.

Usage 4: Death is *inevitable*, so why waste the finite amount of time that you have by worrying?

INGRATE (n)   [IN-greyt]

Meaning: an ungrateful person

Usage 1: Because he was such an *ingrate*, Charles never showed gratitude or appreciation for what he had been given.

Usage 2: I do not want to seem like an *ingrate*, but what you are offering comes with too many strings attached.

Usage 3: Susan was a self-absorbed *ingrate* who never for a moment considered the sacrifices that her parents had made.

INIMITABLE (adj)   [ih-NIM-i-t*uh*-b*uh* l]

Meaning: incapable of being copied

Usage 1: The boxer's intensive workout regimen is so extreme that it is *inimitable* by the average person.

Usage 2: Try as I might, I was rapidly learning to my dismay that my mother's cooking was *inimitable*.

Usage 3: The actor's Scottish burr and masculine swagger was laughably *inimitable* by his successors in the role.

INNATE (adj)   [ih-NEYT]

Meaning: present or originating at birth

Usage 1: Albert almost never used a map, because he had an *innate* and almost uncanny sense of direction.

Usage 2: Many philosophers express a belief in the *innate* goodness of mankind.

Usage 3: Cats have an *innate* sense of balance that helps them invariably land on their feet.

Usage 4: The detective prided himself in his *innate* ability to accurately judge a person's truthfulness.

INNOVATION (n)   [in-*uh*-VEY-sh*uh* n]

Meaning: the introduction of something new

Usage 1: It is rumored that the next wave of *innovation* in the cell phone industry will include a three- dimensional display

Usage 2: The biggest *innovation* in the current generation of gaming consoles is the fusion of different entertainment platforms.

Usage 3: Even though millions of dollars are spent in research and development, not every *innovation* catches on with the general public.

Chapter **16**

Inopportune – Monotheism

This chapter covers the following words, each with its part of speech, pronunciation, and descriptive meaning.

Usage of the word is also illustrated in three to five sample sentences.

inopportune	listless	misdemeanor
inscrutable	lofty	missile
insidious	loll	mock
introvert	ludicrous	molt
intrude	lumber	momentous
invocation	lunar	momentum
invulnerable	lurid	monochromatic
iota	luscious	monotheism
irony	maculated	
irremediable	magisterial	
jollity	malady	
jostle	malcontent	
jovial	malevolent	
jubilation	malicious	
kinetic	mammal	
kismet	mangy	
laceration	marked	
lament	meek	
licentious	melancholy	
limbo	mercenary	
liquidate	migrant	

INOPPORTUNE (adj)   [in-op-er-TYOON]

Meaning: untimely or inconvenient

Usage 1: Charlie chose a very *inopportune* moment to try to speak to his supervisor, and so his concerns were never heard.

Usage 2: Suzette quickly realized that she had arrived at an *inopportune* time, so she cheerfully told her friend that she would come by for a visit another day.

Usage 3: Never known for his discernment, Gilbert chose that *inopportune* moment to begin drinking.

INSCRUTABLE (adj)   [in-SKROO-t*uh*-b*uh* l]

Meaning: not easily understood

Usage 1: Jim's father was a very private person, and his feelings were often *inscrutable* even to those closest to him.

Usage 2: Charlie's wife wished that he would be more forthcoming with his emotions instead of being so quiet and *inscrutable* all of the time.

Usage 3: Many people think that tax laws are needlessly complicated and purposefully *inscrutable* to the point of being nearly indecipherable by the average person.

Usage 4: The *inscrutable* shopkeeper had his secrets, but so did I, and it was going to be a while before we trusted each other.

INSIDIOUS (adj)   [in-SID-ee-*uh* s]

Meaning: seemingly innocent and harmless, but in actuality destructive or harmful

Usage 1: At first, the symptoms were mild, but the *insidious* disease rapidly grew progressively worse.

Usage 2: The effects of poor morale within a company can be both apparent and *insidious*.

Usage 3: He used his position to exert an *insidious* influence upon the Prime Minister, and the populace suffered because of it.

INTROVERT (n)   [IN-tr*uh*-vurt]

Meaning: a person who retreats mentally or whose thoughts are primarily concerned about their own interests and emotions

Usage 1: As an *introvert*, James did not particularly like attending large parties.

Usage 2: I would rather be a virtual *introvert* with few real friends than an overly-gregarious social butterfly.

Usage 3: The ability to stream music and movies to our homes brings out the *introvert* in all of us.

Usage 4: Even though she was an *introvert* by disposition, Charlene still found time to do a considerable amount of volunteer work.

INTRUDE (v)   [in-TROOD]

Meaning: to bring in without permission or welcome

Usage 1: Stephanie did not want to *intrude* upon her sister's privacy, but her curiosity got the best of her.

Usage 2: Franklin always took great care that the stresses of his job did not *intrude* into his home life.

Usage 3: Carl felt a lonely pang of jealousy when he saw his neighbors having a backyard party, but he stayed away because he did not wish to *intrude*.

INVOCATION (n)   [in-v*uh*-KEY-sh*uh* n]

Meaning: a petition or entreaty for aid or guidance, usually from a deity or higher power

Usage 1: At the beginning of every service, the pastor would recite an *invocation* asking God to bless the entire congregation.

Usage 2: The group leader would usually close the meeting by asking all participants to join in an *invocation* requesting wisdom and guidance for all.

Usage 3: It is not uncommon for the priest's *invocation* to ask for peace throughout the world.

INVULNERABLE (adj)   [in-VUHL-ner-*uh*-b*uh* l]

Meaning: unable to be harmed or injured

Usage 1: One of the characteristics of the young is the fact that they consider themselves to be *invulnerable*, which makes it all the more tragic when they find out that they are not.

Usage 2: The armor plating on many of the newer military vehicles makes them virtually *invulnerable* to small arms fire.

Usage 3: The bonds of their marriage were so strong that John and Mary were effectively *invulnerable* to the perils that befell so many other couples.

Usage 4: There is no such thing as a corporation that is grown so large as to be *invulnerable* to changing market conditions.

IOTA (n)   [ahy-OH-t*uh*]

Meaning: a very small amount

Usage 1: Jacob's boss was completely fed up and did not care one *iota* about his excuses or explanations.

Usage 2: In the end, none of the supplements that Ruth took made an *iota* of difference in her health.

Usage 3: It is very discouraging that all of my efforts do not seem to merit a single *iota* of praise or appreciation.

IRONY (n)   [AHY-r*uh*-nee]

Meaning: an outcome that is different or even opposite of what might have been expected

Usage 1: The *irony* is this: John was devastated when his wife left him, even though he didn't love her anymore.

Usage 2: Life can be very dull and dreary indeed if one does not find joy in the *irony* and humor of everyday existence.

Usage 3: There is *irony* in the fact that a man who does not pay his child support can go to jail, which would subsequently make him unable to pay his child support.

IRREMEDIABLE (adj)   [ir-i-MEE-dee-*uh*-b*uh* l]

Meaning: beyond repair or remedy

Usage 1: The gulf between the two opposing sides was too vast, and in the end, their differences were *irremediable*.

Usage 2: The broken treaty created disputes that were *irremediable*, and the two countries broke off all diplomatic relations.

Usage 3: If one has patience, a willingness to listen, and a predisposition toward compromise, there are very few disagreements that are *irremediable*.

JOLLITY (n)   [JOL-i-tee]

Meaning: a merry mood or activity

Usage 1: The annual Christmas party was an occasion for *jollity*, feasting, drinking, and the handing out of holiday bonuses.

Usage 2: Behind the laughter and *jollity* of many comedians, there is a darker side that often hides real pain.

Usage 3: The clown that Anita had hired brought a raucous blend of hilarity and *jollity* to her daughter's birthday party.

JOSTLE (v)   [JOS-*uh* l]

Meaning: to show or push roughly, or to exist in close proximity with

Usage 1: Caitlin knew that if her family had a bigger house then the ten of them would not have to constantly jostle for individual space.

Usage 2: The rude gang members thought that it was the height of hilarity to roughly *jostle* any passengers who boarded the subway car.

Usage 3: When the passengers rushed out of the elevator, I had to step aside so they wouldn't *jostle* me and make me spill my coffee.

Usage 4: Our family is so large that we all have to *jostle* for position if we want to be included in the annual photo.

JOVIAL (adj)   [JOH-vee-*uh* l]

Meaning: characterized by a robust humor

Usage 1: Curtis was a *jovial* fellow and never had a bad word to say about anyone.

Usage 2: Bob had a *jovial* relationship with his coworkers, and that is why everyone was sad to see him retire.

Usage 3: Johnnie loved the boisterous, *jovial* atmosphere of the sports bar, and it soon became his regular hangout.

Usage 4: The annual softball game was the perfect opportunity to engage in a little *jovial* competition.

JUBILATION (n)   [joo-b*uh*-LEY-sh*uh* n]

Meaning: an extremely joyful feeling or expression, or a festive celebration

Usage 1: When she received her acceptance letter, Shelby could barely contain her *jubilation*.

Usage 2: There is no feeling that compares to the *jubilation* one feels at the birth of a child.

Usage 3: Andrea's coming-out party was the reason for the next *jubilation*, and people were already lining up their dates.

KINETIC (adj)   [ki-NET-ik]

Meaning: pertaining to or caused by motion or movement

Usage 1: Sometimes it seems as if young children are little more than indefatigable balls of *kinetic* energy.

Usage 2: The cushioned insole absorbed the stresses and *kinetic* forces generated by walking.

Usage 3: The driving rhythm of the music kept perfect time with the *kinetic* dance that was being performed.

KISMET (n)   [KIZ-mit]

Meaning: fate or destiny

Usage 1: When they ran into each other for the third time in less than a week, they had to laughingly agree that it was *kismet*.

Usage 2: From the first day that I saw you, I knew that it was *kismet* that one day, we would be married.

Usage 3: Regina was too busy texting to pay attention, but *kismet* stepped in and prevented her from being struck by the bus.

LACERATION (n)   [las-*uh*-REY-sh*uh* n]

Meaning: a jagged wound; gash

Usage 1: Although both injuries needed attention, the doctor worked on the puncture wound in his patient's side before he worked on the *laceration* on his back.

Usage 2: The skateboard accident resulted in numerous abrasions, a broken tooth, and a *laceration* that ran the length of his forearm.

Usage 3: Before it could be bandaged, the *laceration* needed to be cleaned and then stitched up

Usage 4: The strip-mining operation looked like an ugly *laceration* on the land.

LAMENT (v)   [l*uh*-MENT]

Meaning: to express sorrow

Usage 1: The peasants had ample cause to *lament*, because they were being forced to leave their homes.

Usage 2: Lament in private, for the world has little sympathy for the problems of its denizens.

Usage 3: In some cultures, it is considered bad form to *lament* to excess.

LICENTIOUS (adj)   [lahy-SEN-sh*uh* s]

Meaning: morally unrestrained

Usage 1: The entire congregation was shocked when they learned of the pastor's *licentious* behavior.

Usage 2: Although he was now a well-respected member of his community, in his youth, Thomas lived a *licentious* and dissolute lifestyle.

Usage 3: Without moral support, it is far too easy for even the most well-meaning individual to fall prey to licentious diversions.

LIMBO (n)   [LIM-boh]

Meaning: a place of oblivion or confinement to which people and things are relegated when cast aside

Usage 1: Until news of the merger's approval or denial, the fates of hundreds of employees remained in *limbo*.

Usage 2: The stress of being kept in *limbo* about the results of is medical test was taking its toll on Charlie.

Usage 3: Francis could not finalize her plans until she was released from the *limbo* of not knowing which colleges had accepted her.

LIQUIDATE (v)   [LIK-wi-deyt]

Meaning: to reduce all holdings and investments to cash; to get rid of

Usage 1: To pay off the company's creditors, the owners had to *liquidate* most of their overseas holdings.

Usage 2: John decided to *liquidate* his life insurance policy and instead, open his own business.

Usage 3: Even though she desperately needed money, Yvette decided not to *liquidate* her retirement account because of the substantial tax penalties she would incur.

LISTLESS (adj)   [LIST-lis]

Meaning: without energy or spirit

Usage 1: She slept for hours because of the medication, and even when she was awake, she felt confused and *listless*.

Usage 2: Johnny's parents were concerned, because after graduation, he spent months in a *listless*, drug-fueled haze.

Usage 3: Following her divorce, Barbaro was *listless* and unfocused, and it was affecting every facet of her life.

LOFTY (adj)   [LAWF-tee]

Meaning: of imposing height, elevated in station; arrogant or haughty

Usage 1: From a young age, Thomas learned that *lofty* ambitions often lead to superior results.

Usage 2: Parker could see the whole midtown area from his *lofty* penthouse window.

Usage 3: Mary's *lofty* ideals often seemed unrealistic when contrasted with the grim reality of the rest of her life.

Usage 4: John had a *lofty*, if overdeveloped, sense of self-importance, and it usually rubbed people the wrong way.

LOLL (v)   [lol]

Meaning: to lounge about in an indolent manner

Usage 1: Jack did little more than *loll* on his couch and play video games the entire summer.

Usage 2: On his photo safari, Bill watched a sleepy hippopotamus *loll* in the mud surrounding the watering hole.

Usage 3: On my next vacation, the most active thing that I am going to do is *loll* about on the beach.

LUDICROUS (adj)   [LOO-di-kr*uh* s]

Meaning: ridiculous to the point of deserving derision

Usage 1: The idea that I should work for such pitiful wages is patently *ludicrous*.

Usage 2: The panel was divided, because although some members thought the plan had merit, others thought the idea was *ludicrous*.

Usage 3: Some people enjoy filing *ludicrous* lawsuit after lawsuit, often at the slightest of provocation.

LUMBER (v)   [LUHM-ber]

Meaning: to move heavily or clumsily

Usage 1: In the morning, the first thing Dorothy would do is *lumber* down the hallway to put on a pot of coffee.

Usage 2: Clumsy because of his size, Bruce appeared to *lumber* along with awkward, almost precarious, steps.

Usage 3: When properly motivated, Dennis would heave his bulk off of the couch and *lumber* forward with a rapidity that belied his earlier inactivity.

LUNAR (adj)   [LOO-ner]

Meaning: pertaining to the moon

Usage 1: Much of the general public wonders why there hasn't been another *lunar* expedition.

Usage 2: Until the astronauts actually stepped out of the module, scientists were not entirely sure about the condition of the *lunar* surface.

Usage 3: No matter how many times she witnessed it, Helen was always fascinated and enthralled by the *lunar* eclipse.

Usage 4: The soft *lunar* light lent a ghostly, otherworldly appearance to the garden.

LURID (adj)   [L*OO* R-id]

Meaning: intensely sensational, gruesome, or shocking

Usage 1: The supermarket tabloids are known for their outlandish stories and *lurid* photographs.

Usage 2: The *lurid* images were replayed again and again on nearly every network.

Usage 3: The politician's career was derailed when recordings of inappropriate *lurid* conversations were made public.

Usage 4: The star's autobiography made many allusions to her steamy, *lurid* past.

LUSCIOUS (adj)   [LUHSH-*uh* s]

Meaning: highly appealing to the senses, perhaps even exceedingly so

Usage 1: The best part of the homemade coffeecake was a double measure of *luscious*, in -season blueberries.

Usage 2: Little Jimmy gorged himself on the *luscious* strawberries until rivulets of juice ran down his chin.

Usage 3: Suzette had a *luscious* figure, one that men had a taste for.

Usage 4: Even though it ruined her diet, Samantha could not resist ordering a *luscious* piece of the restaurant's famous pie.

MACULATED (adj)   [MAK-y*uh*-leyt-id]

Meaning: spotted, stained, or defiled

Usage 1: The walls of the run-down apartment were *maculated* with mildew, and the carpet was worn by constant traffic.

Usage 2: It was clear that the vandals cared for nothing when they left the altar *maculated* with all manner of filth.

Usage 3: The fleabag motel offered no amenities whatsoever, unless you counted the bedspread that was *maculated* with odd-smelling stains.

MAGISTERIAL (adj)   [maj-*uh*-STEER-ee-*uh* l]

Meaning: pertaining to an authority, of importance

Usage 1: The issuing of marriage licenses fell well within the scope of his *magisterial* duties.

Usage 2: The councilwoman was removed from office when she was charged with abusing her *magisterial* authority.

Usage 3: The Mayor claimed *magisterial* privilege when he attempted to park in spaces reserved for disabled drivers.

Usage 4: When he was wearing his robe, the judge was the very epitome of both sartorial perfection and *magisterial* authority.

MALADY (n)   [MAL-*uh*-dee]

Meaning: a disease or disordered condition, especially one that is chronic

Usage 1: Historians debate to this day about the mysterious *malady* that killed Mozart.

Usage 2: Steven languished in bed for weeks suffering from the *malady* that had plagued him all of his life.

Usage 3: Elizabeth was eternally grateful to the medical team that had successfully diagnosed and treated her chronic *malady*.

MALCONTENT (n)   [mal-k*uh* n-TENT]

Meaning: a person who is chronically dissatisfied

Usage 1: The police chief was more than happy to throw the vociferous *malcontent* into the city jail.

Usage 2: Sometimes I think that you are a professional *malcontent*, because nothing ever seems to make you happy.

Usage 3: The *malcontent* made his dissatisfaction publicly known with regular updates on his popular blog.

MALEVOLENT (adj)   [m*uh*-LEV-*uh*-l*uh* nt]

Meaning: evil, harmful, or malicious

Usage 1: The medium's skin crawled as she sensed the presence of a *malevolent* entity.

Usage 2: Nathan's parents were terribly concerned about his *malevolent* behavior toward other children.

Usage 3: Peter soon found out that her brilliant smile and pleasant demeanor hid a far darker, much more *malevolent* psyche.

Usage 4: His wolfish grin faded, and was replaced by a *malevolent* smile that sent icy chills down her spine.

MALICIOUS (adj)   [m*uh*-LISH-*uh* s]

Meaning: characterized as hateful or spiteful

Usage 1: His *malicious* behavior could no longer be tolerated, so he was asked to leave the premises immediately.

Usage 2: Not only did he break into her house, but he did so with the *malicious* intent to do her harm.

Usage 3: When he opened the e-mail, he unwittingly made his computer vulnerable to a *malicious* virus.

MAMMAL (n)   [MAM-*uh* l]

Meaning: hairy, warm-blooded vertebrate that gives birth to live offspring and which suckles its young

Usage 1: Even though it lays eggs, the platypus is still considered a *mammal*.

Usage 2: Some people are surprised to learn that a dolphin is classified as a *mammal*, and not a fish.

Usage 3: The blue whale is the largest *mammal* on earth, while the hog-nosed bat is the smallest.

MANGY (adj)   [MEYN-jee]

Meaning: squalid, shabby, or contemptible

Usage 1: The *mangy*, ramshackle hovel always seemed to be just on the verge of caving in around them.

Usage 2: The drifter had a *mangy*, unkempt appearance, and the sheriff hastened him out of town.

Usage 3: Caleb kept a *mangy* old mongrel chained up in his backyard, and the dog was so vicious that no one dared to intrude.

Usage 4: The horse was *mangy* and malnourished, and animal control deemed it needed to be put down.

MARKED (adj)   [mahrkt]

Meaning: extremely noticeable; or, existing as a target for vengeance

Usage 1: After a few weeks of therapy, Sonia could see a *marked* difference in her daughter's behavior.

Usage 2: At the conclusion of the trial, Mark feared that he would live out the rest of his life as a *marked* man.

Usage 3: The newspaper article highlighted a *marked* improvement in the traffic flow now that the overpass was completed.

MEEK (adj)   [meek]

Meaning: patient and long-suffering

Usage 1: Sabrina was so quiet and *meek* that many people did not remember her at her high school reunion.

Usage 2: When they decided to buy a horse for their daughter, John and Mary hoped to find one with a *meek* and docile temperament.

Usage 3: Blessed are those who are not *meek*, because the squeaky wheel gets the grease.

MELANCHOLY (adj)   [MEL-*uh* n-kol-ee]

Meaning: characterized by a gloomy, ill-humored mood

Usage 1: With his *melancholy*, hangdog expression, Gilbert never was much of a hit with the ladies.

Usage 2: At the party, people soon stopped talking to George, because his *melancholy* attitude was spoiling their fun.

Usage 3: Steven's jubilation was cut short when he looked around and saw the *melancholy* faces of his friends.

MERCENARY (adj)   [MUR-s*uh*-ner-ee]

Meaning: working solely for personal or monetary gain

Usage 1: The *mercenary* practices of many personal injury lawyers seem almost unethical.

Usage 2: The free agent shooting guard can be regarded as a *mercenary* athlete, because he sells his skills to the highest bidder, without regard to loyalty or the prospect of a championship.

Usage 3: Susan's *mercenary* attitude began to wear a bit thin, and her avarice was definitely off-putting.

MIGRANT (adj)   [MAHY-gr*uh* nt]

Meaning: moving from place to place

Usage 1: Every season, farms throughout America count on *migrant* laborers as a valuable resource.

Usage 2 : Terri lived a *migrant* life, because she found herself never wanting to settle in one place too long.

Usage 3: On the tiny island, tourist season always coincided with the arrival of the *migrant*shorebirds.

MISDEMEANOR (n)   [mis-di-MEE-ner]

Meaning: a minor criminal offense

Usage 1: Carlos had a good attorney who was able to get the charge reduced to a *misdemeanor*.

Usage 2: These days, even a minor *misdemeanor* can be a problematic bar to employment.

Usage 3: This was the fifth time that Butch had been convicted of a *misdemeanor*, further evidencing his life as a career petty criminal.

Usage 4: Because he had a *misdemeanor* on his record, Joseph was denied a security clearance.

MISSILE (n)   [MIS-*uh* l]

Meaning: an object, typically a weapon that is thrown, hurled, or shot

Usage 1: In the latter part of the 20th century, defense systems were developed that were designed to shoot down or incapacitate any type of launched intercontinental *missile*.

Usage 2: The launch doors opened, and the *missile* took flight, carrying its devastating payload to the enemy.

Usage 3: The *missile* from his sling flew straight and true, and the mighty giant fell to the ground, dead.

Usage 4: The archers shot their bows at will, and missile after fiery *missile* rained down from the skies.

Usage 5: The linebacker launched his body at the quarterback like a *missile* in flight.

MOCK (v)   [mok]

Meaning: to attack with contempt, to imitate

Usage 1: When his deception was discovered, hecklers would loudly *mock* the mayor at every opportunity.

Usage 2: Rowdy students would *mock* the school teacher whenever her back was turned.

Usage 3: Amazingly, the gorilla could effectively *mock* the hand and finger movements of the sign language translator.

MOLT (v)   [mohlt]

Meaning: to shed hair, feathers, or skin

Usage 1: When a bird first begins to *molt*, for a brief period, they take on an extremely ungainly appearance.

Usage 2: When a snake outgrows its skin, it will *molt* by rubbing up against rough surfaces.

Usage 3: A chicken will stop laying eggs while its chicks *molt*, and will not resume until their feathers have regrown.

Usage 4: After hermit crabs *molt*, they will then consume their former exoskeletons.

Usage 5: Most mammals *molt* in response to the amount of melatonin in their system, which in turn is governed by sunlight variations.

MOMENTOUS (adj)   [moh-MEN-t*uh* s]

Meaning: of great importance

Usage 1: Reporters and photographers from around the state were present to record this *momentous* occasion.

Usage 2: Juanita would later say that the day she swore in as a citizen was the most *momentous* day of her entire life.

Usage 3: A bride's wedding day is supposed to be the most *momentous* experience of her young life, so it is a good idea to hire the best photographer money can buy.

MOMENTUM (n)   [moh-MEN-t*uh* m]

Meaning: the force caused by movement

Usage 1: John's *momentum* carried him into and over the barrier.

Usage 2: The discus thrower spun around and around, gaining *momentum* with each revolution.

Usage 3: The wide receiver leapt high into the air to catch the football, but his *momentum* caused him to come down out of bounds.

Usage 4: Lilly applied the brakes in plenty of time, but the car's *momentum* still propelled it forward into the other vehicle.

MONOCHROMATIC (adj)   [mon-*uh*-kroh-MAT-ik]

Meaning: having only one color

Usage 1: Painting a room in a *monochromatic* shade can actually make the space appear larger.

Usage 2: His only eccentric affectation was dressing in a different *monochromatic* color from head to foot everyday.

Usage 3: The company's *monochromatic* fleet of cars was part of the reason that it was universally -recognized anywhere in the United States.

MONOTHEISM (n)   [MON-*uh*-thee-iz-*uh* m]

Meaning: a belief in only one God

Usage 1: Catholicism, Judaism, and Islam are examples of religions that practice *monotheism*.

Usage 2: In ancient times, *monotheism* was not widely practiced because most societies believed in multiple deities.

Usage 3: Christianity is more properly defined as trinitarian *monotheism*, because Christians follow the doctrine of God in three persons.

Chapter **17**

Mores - Predicament

This chapter covers the following words, each with its part of speech, pronunciation, and descriptive meaning.

Usage of the word is also illustrated in three to five sample sentences.

mores	outstrip	phenomena
mote	ovation	piecemeal
munificent	pantomime	pigment
murkiness	parameter	pillage
naivete	paraphrase	
natty	parlance	pithy
nauseate	parley	ponderous
notable	parody	prattle
novice	partial	predicament
nuance	passive	
nurture	pathetic	
obscure	patriarch	
obstinate	patrician	
odium	peerless	
omnipotent	perdition	
opalescent	perforate	
opaque	perigee	
optician	pernicious	
orator	perpetual	
ordeal	pertinent	
ornithologist	petty	

MORES (n)   [MAWR-eyz]

Meaning: social conventions or moral standards

Usage 1: In most cities, public nudity is contrary to acceptable social *mores*.

Usage 2: The traditional *mores* of the Amish dictate that they shun modern technology and conveniences.

Usage 3: Weary of restrictive legislation here in America, Daniel longed to experience the relaxed social *mores* of Europe.

Usage 4: Societal *mores* are not set in stone, and can change from place to place and over time.

MOTE (n)   [moht]

Meaning: a small speck, usually of dust

Usage 1: There is an old biblical saying about not criticizing a *mote* in someone else's eye until you have taken care of the beam in yours.

Usage 2: The light shining through the window highlighted every *mote* of dust floating in the air.

Usage 3: Jennifer vigorously scrubbed the entire bathroom, until every surface was gleaming and not a *mote* of dust or grime could be found.

MUNIFICENT (adj)   [myoo-NIF-*uh-suh* nt]

Meaning: characterized by extremely liberal generosity

Usage 1: Jessica made the trip because she wanted to personally express her gratitude to her *munificent* benefactor.

Usage 2: The foundation's *munificent* donation was enough to keep the crisis center open for another three years.

Usage 3: Even with all of his accomplishments and rewards in business, it was his *munificent* endeavors that gave Andrew Carnegie his sense of purpose.

MURKINESS (n)   [MUR-kee nis]

Meaning: vagueness, obscurity, or gloominess

Usage 1: The first officer stood at the conn and peered intently into *murkiness*, but the iceberg still took him by surprise.

Usage 2: Due to the *murkiness* of the water, the antelope never saw the crocodile's stealthy approach.

Usage 3: The future is shrouded in *murkiness*, and is therefore impossible to predict.

Usage 4: The *murkiness* outside of his plane window was as thick as pea soup, totally obscuring his view of the city lights below.

NAIVETE (n)   [nah-eev-TEY]

Meaning: the quality of being unsophisticated or ignorant of the ways of the world

Usage 1: Because of her inherent sweetness and her innocent *naivete*, Joan's friends thought that she could never make it in the big city.

Usage 2: In a young girl, *naivete* is endearing, but in a young woman, it is irresistible.

Usage 3: John was often the butt of many jokes because of his affability and *naivete*.

Usage 4: It is always a sad moment in a person's life when *naivete* and optimism give way to distrust and pessimism.

NATTY (adj)   [NAT-ee]

Meaning: neatly or smartly dressed

Usage 1: Red was quite a *natty* figure as he swaggered down the street in his brand-new zoot suit.

Usage 2: My grandparents got married at the turn of the 20th century, and while my grandfather looked *natty* in his new pair of overalls, my grandmother was radiant in a plain cotton dress.

Usage 3: John was known for being a *natty* dresser, because he never went anywhere unless he was outfitted in full sartorial splendor.

Usage 4: Thomas was red-faced with rage and embarrassment when the waiter spilled a drink on his *natty* new jacket.

NAUSEATE (v)   [NAW-zee-eyt]

Meaning: to disgust or violently sicken

Usage 1: The sight of starving children overseas would *nauseate* Eleanor, yet she was never moved enough to actually take action.

Usage 2: After everything that she had put him through, just the mention of his ex-wife was sometimes enough to *nauseate* Philip.

Usage 3: The extreme roller coaster moves so rapidly and contains so many loops, twists, and hills that it can even *nauseate* seasoned enthusiasts.

NOTABLE (adj)   [NOH-t*uh*-b*uh* l]

Meaning: prominent or important, worthy of notice

Usage 1: The latest World Cup match was especially *notable* because of the extremely unlikely high final score.

Usage 2: In her life, Yvette had met a number of *notable* people, but none was as exceptional as the World War II veteran she met while volunteering at the retirement home.

Usage 3: The works of Shakespeare are *notable* not only for the tales they tell, but also for their imaginative and inventive use of language.

NOVICE (n)   [NOV-is]

Meaning: a beginner, someone new to their circumstances

Usage 1: As a nun who was still a *novice*, Sister Agnes was expected to spend her limited free time in private meditation and prayer.

Usage 2: Even as a *novice* playwright, William attracted the enthusiastic interest of critics throughout the city.

Usage 3: Early on, while he was still a *novice* skateboarder, Tony would intently watch the tricks and stunts performed by the others around him.

NUANCE (n)   [NOO-ahns]

Meaning: a subtle difference, typically in color, meaning, or expression

Usage 1: After 20 years of marriage, Horace could recognize every *nuance* in his wife's catalog of expressions.

Usage 2: Raphael was a master of expressing emotion by using every *nuance* of color and shading possible.

Usage 3: A barely-perceptible *nuance* in the suspect's inflection alerted the detective that all was not as it seemed.

Usage 4: By playfully engaging the *nuance* between each word and their different shades of meaning, a poet can create a powerful word sculpture.

NURTURE (v)   [NUR-cher]

Meaning: to nourish, educate, or foster

Usage 1: It is every parent's highest duty to *nurture* the very best aspects of the child's personality.

Usage 2: Charlotte painstakingly attempted to *nurture* the seedling's growth, but in the end she realized that gardening just wasn't her forte.

Usage 3: Whenever possible, the editor attempted to *nurture* talents of the young writers who were among these charges.

OBSCURE (adj)   [*uh* b-SKY*OO* R]

Meaning: not clear or plain to the understanding; indistinct to the senses

Usage 1: Jonathan wasn't sure what to expect, because the motives of his boss were often nonsensical at their worst and *obscure* at their best.

Usage 2: The precise meaning of the enemy soldiers' shouts was *obscure*, but their intent was evident.

Usage 3: Kenny was perturbed because his girlfriend was upset with him for some *obscure* reason, and she refused to tell him plainly what was wrong.

OBSTINATE (adj)   [OB-st*uh*-nit]

Meaning: inflexibly persistent in one's opinion; not easily yielding

Usage 1: When she set her mind to it, Albert's wife could be as *obstinate* and immovable as stone.

Usage 2: When you are done being quite so *obstinate*, perhaps we can sit down and negotiate in good faith.

Usage 3: Elizabeth had hoped that her husband would try to see her side of things, but he remained *obstinate* and totally impervious to her entreaties.

ODIUM (n)   [OH-dee-*uh* m]

Meaning: intense dislike or even hatred for something that is repugnant; the imposed burden of being the object or target of such hate

Usage 1: Lester had no idea why he was the focus of so much *odium* in town, but he was determined to find out.

Usage 2: Peter could feel the crowd's *odium* even before he heard the cacophony of boos and catcalls.

Usage 3: If there is anything that I have done to earn your *odium*, please give me an opportunity to make it up to you.

OMNIPOTENT (adj)   [om-NIP-*uh*-t*uh* nt]

Meaning: having infinite power

Usage 1: The belief in an *omnipotent* power greater than humanity is a belief held by most civilizations.

Usage 2: When they are very young, most children believe that their parents are *omnipotent*, but when those children get older, they believe their parents are merely impotent.

Usage 3: Even though it might sound like a contradiction, *omnipotent* beings are fundamentally limited in power if they are not also omniscient.

OPALESCENT (adj)   [oh-p*uh*-LES-*uh* nt]

Meaning: possessing a bright, pearly, multicolored shimmer

Usage 1: The midwinter moon shone down upon the valley, bathing the entire region in a cool, *opalescent* light.

Usage 2: When Andre ordered his new car, he paid extra for the custom *opalescent* paint job.

Usage 3: Although it used to be used as a cheap carnival prize, *opalescent* glass is now highly sought after by collectors.

OPAQUE (adj)   [oh-PEYK]

Meaning: not permitting light to pass through; or, hard to understand, stupid

Usage 1: Regina drew the *opaque* drapes, and the room was instantly and completely darkened.

Usage 2: The book was hard to follow, because the plot was *opaque* and the conflicts seemed contrived.

Usage 3: The clouds were almost completely *opaque,* and the miniscule amount of moonlight that shone through did little to illuminate the estate.

OPTICIAN (n)   [op-TISH-*uh* n]

Meaning: a maker of eyeglasses and contact lenses

Usage 1: Typically, an ophthalmologist or optometrist will determine the prescription, and the *optician* will craft the glasses accordingly.

Usage 2: Teresa always liked her annual trip to the *optician* to pick out her new frames and lenses.

Usage 3: When Charlie broke his eyeglasses, he called his local *optician* to schedule a repair appointment.

ORATOR (n)   [awr-*uh*-ter]

Meaning: a person giving a speech, especially if that speech is of great eloquence

Usage 1: Before the Modern Era, listening to a great *orator* was as close to public entertainment as many people ever got.

Usage 2: Every person in attendance listened with rapt attention as the *orator* dramatically railed against the war.

Usage 3: I've often wondered if I could have been a professional *orator,* because I've never been afraid of speaking before a crowd.

ORDEAL (n)   [awr-DEEL]

Meaning: a protracted, horrific experience

Usage 1: When she was rescued and her *ordeal* was finally over, Patricia was able to return home.

Usage 2: After the assault, Helen had to relive the *ordeal* in painstaking detail on the witness stand.

Usage 3: For some teenagers, high school is just an *ordeal* to be endured for four interminable years.

ORNITHOLOGIST (n)   [awr-n*uh*-THOL-*uh*-jist]

Meaning: a zoologist who studies birds

Usage 1: Because reptiles and birds have so much in common, an *ornithologist* will often be a semi-expert about the subject of dinosaurs.

Usage 2: When he couldn't identify the eggs in the nest on his property, Charles decided to consult an *ornithologist.*

Usage 3: The *ornithologist* was thrilled to find a living, breathing, specimen of a species that had long been thought extinct.

OUTSTRIP (v)   [out-STRIP]

Meaning: to exceed, or to pass, as if in a race

Usage 1: He stumbled at the start, but Dennis was soon able to *outstrip* the other racers.

Usage 2: Due to her military service, Elaine graduated college later than her friends, but her experience allowed her to *outstrip* them professionally within just a few years.

Usage 3: The productivity of Sam's company would routinely *outstrip* that of others within the industry.

OVATION (n)   [oh-VEY-sh*uh* n]

Meaning: Public recognition accompanied by protracted applause

Usage 1: When the play finally closed after 10 years of record-setting achievement, the cast took their final bows to a thunderous *ovation.*

Usage 2: N'Djamena waited until the *ovation* had subsided, then she stepped forward to address the crowd.

Usage 3: Normally known for his stoic demeanor, the retiring general was moved to tears when his unit gave him a standing *ovation*.

PANTOMIME (n)   [PAN-t*uh*-mahym]

Meaning: a play without dialogue, where meanings are expressed through music or gestures

Usage 1: The *pantomime* was a popular form of entertainment in ancient Rome and Greece.

Usage 2: Many acting students are surprised to learn that they will receive several lessons in the art of *pantomime*.

Usage 3: Although most *pantomime* is done for a comedic effect, there is often an undertone of tragedy.

PARAMETER (n)   [p*uh*-RAM-i-ter]

Meaning: a distinguishing feature or characteristic

Usage 1: Extreme want is nearly always a *parameter* of extreme poverty.

Usage 2: It is unfortunate that greed seems to be a *parameter* of political office.

Usage 3: Transparency is the one non-negotiable *parameter* of our agreement.

PARAPHRASE (v)   [PAR-*uh*-freyz]

Meaning: to express meaning by using different words

Usage 1: If you will permit me to *paraphrase* the author's words, I will attempt to clarify what he meant.

Usage 2: The candidate asked that the journalists not *paraphrase* his speech, but instead quote him exactly.

Usage 3: The student did not want to write out the entire passage, so he opted to *paraphrase* its meaning.

PARLANCE (n)   [PAHR-l*uh* ns]

Meaning: a particular manner of speaking

Usage 1: Because he was from another country, Fritz often had trouble understanding the local *parlance*.

Usage 2: Many politicians will use the *parlance* of their constituency in an attempt to build rapport.

Usage 3: Each branch of the military has a *parlance* that is unique unto itself, and is therefore not readily understood by the general public.

PARLEY (n)   [PAHR-lee]

Meaning: a talk between leaders of opposing forces in order to make a truce

Usage 1: Ships at war may indicate that they wish to enter *parley* with their enemies by raising a black flag.

Usage 2: After a long *parley*, a temporary truce was agreed upon, so that both sides might have an opportunity to attend to their wounded.

Usage 3: Caesar violated the rules of *parley* when he seized the leaders who had come to negotiate with him.

PARODY (n)   [PAR-*uh*-dee]

Meaning: an imitation that is deliberately exaggerated for the purpose of comedic effect

Usage 1: Although it is a violation of copyright to duplicate a published work, many of those rules are relaxed when the similarities are for the purpose of *parody*.

Usage 2: When an actor repeatedly plays the same type of roles, they invariably become a *parody* of themselves.

Usage 3: Sometimes, the most effective way to criticize a politician is to showcase a *parody* of their most unwise decisions.

PARTIAL (adj)   [PAHR-sh*uh* l]

Meaning: existing only in an incomplete state; or, favoring a thing or an idea

Usage 1: Jerry was disappointed, because even a year after his accident, he had still only made a *partial* recovery.

Usage 2: Susan was rather *partial* to gold jewelry, but her husband always seemed to buy her silver pieces.

Usage 3: Because he had lost his job, Wayne was only able to make a *partial* payment toward his credit card bill.

PASSIVE (adj)   [PAS-iv]

Meaning: accepting of or allowing whatever happens without resistance

Usage 1: Although it may seem like a misnomer, *passive* resistance has proven to be one of the most effective ways to elicit societal changes.

Usage 2: Elizabeth was surprised at her husband's *passive* reaction, because he had always been such a fighter.

Usage 3: Resigned to her fate, Joan simply sat there, *passive*, silent, and bereft of hope.

PATHETIC (adj)   [p*uh*-THET-ik]

Meaning: arousing feelings of pity, compassion, or poignancy

Usage 1: The condition of the house was so *pathetic*, that Susan could not even understand how someone could live there.

Usage 2: Your lies are so *pathetic*, that it is not even necessary to get angry about them!

Usage 3: After serving six years in prison, Richard emerged a *pathetic* shell of his former self.

PATRIARCH (n)   [PEY-tree-ahrk]

Meaning: male head of a family or tribe

Usage 1: As *patriarch* of the family, Harry felt that it was his duty to provide for the futures of all of his progeny.

Usage 2: Before he could ask for her hand in marriage, John had to first seek the blessing of the family *patriarch*.

Usage 3: Historically, if a society was led by *patriarch*, women invariably held lesser status within that society.

PATRICIAN (adj)   [p*uh*-TRISH-*uh* n]

Meaning: of or belonging to the aristocracy

Usage 1: Despite his rather plebian background, Nixon was able to realize his most *patrician* aspirations.

Usage 2: Abraham's workmanlike attitude was in sharp contrast to his *patrician* upbringing.

Usage 3: With her tailored clothing, impeccable coiffure, and condescending manner, there was no doubt that Rose belonged to the *patrician* class.

PEERLESS (adj)   [PEER-lis]

Meaning: beyond comparison, having no equal

Usage 1: It is said that the *peerless* beauty of Helen of Troy launched a thousand ships.

Usage 2: Sherlock Holmes' *peerless* intellect and his masterful powers of observation enabled him to solve so many cases.

Usage 3: For a female scientist of that era, Marie Curie was *peerless* within her gender.

PERDITION (n)   [per-DISH-*uh* n]

Meaning: a state of eternal punishment

Usage 1: The road to *perdition* is often paved with good intentions, which proves that your actions are more important than your words.

Usage 2: Every night, before he went to bed, the preacher would say a special prayer for the souls in *perdition*.

Usage 3: Jack would often say that turning away from alcohol is what ultimately freed him from *perdition*.

PERFORATE (v)   [PUR-f*uh*-reyt]

Meaning: to make a hole in

Usage 1: Armor-piercing bullets can easily *perforate* most protective vests.

Usage 2: The cold, harsh words from his wife would *perforate* John's very soul.

Usage 3: The kindergarten class enjoyed using the hole punch to *perforate* the craft paper.

PERIGEE (n)   [PER-i-jee]

Meaning: the point in the orbit of a heavenly body, most commonly the moon, at which it is closest to the Earth

Usage 1: High tides usually occur during the moon's *perigee*, as do the greatest variations between the high and low tide.

Usage 2: The moon's *perigee* and apogee are not usually discernible with the naked eye, unless photographs are taken and compared.

Usage 3: A "supermoon" is a good example of a *perigee* of the Earth-Moon-Sun system.

PERNICIOUS (adj)   [per-NISH-*uh* s]

Meaning: having a harmful effect, usually gradually or in a subtle manner

Usage 1: The *pernicious* effects of smoking usually do not manifest themselves for years.

Usage 2: Over time, Charlene's snide comments began to have a *pernicious* effect upon their relationship.

Usage 3: Unbeknownst to the newlywed couple, a colony of termites had begun to inflict *pernicious* damage upon their dream home.

PERPETUAL (adj)   [per-PECH-oo-*uh* l]

Meaning: never changing, endless and uninterrupted

Usage 1: Many scientists have had their reputations destroyed by their futile search for the seemingly- impossible secret of *perpetual* motion.

Usage 2: Sociologists believe that if a *perpetual* energy source could be found, many of the world's conflicts would likewise be eliminated.

Usage 3: As a child, Charles Dickens was extremely affected by his family's *perpetual* money problems.

PERTINENT (adj)   [PUR-tn-*uh* nt]

Meaning: relevant to the task at hand

Usage 1: Viewers were encouraged to call the police station to share any *pertinent* information about the case.

Usage 2: Lisa thought that it was odd that her boss insisted on asking her personal questions that were not *pertinent* to her job.

Usage 3: We could talk about this for hours, but unfortunately, it is not *pertinent* to the task at hand.

PETTY (adj)   [PET-ee]

Meaning: trivial or unimportant

Usage 1: The supervisor was annoyed at being bothered with such *petty* details.

Usage 2: After 25 years of marriage, Richard had become accustomed to his wife's incessant complaining about the most *petty* of grievances.

Usage 3: Sometimes, even the most overlooked and *petty* problems can become major issues, if left unattended.

PHENOMENA (n)   [fi-NOM-*uh*-n*uh*]

Meaning: observable facts or occurrences

Usage 1: Darwin formed his theory of evolution after years of witnessing *phenomena* that could not be otherwise explained.

Usage 2: The scientific method is used to prove the theories that we have about the *phenomena* that occur around us.

Usage 3: Although they may seem like disparate events, all of these *phenomena* are in fact linked.

PIECEMEAL (adj)   [PEES-meel]

Meaning: characterized by unsystematic partial measures

Usage 1: I acquired my collection in a *piecemeal* fashion, but over the years, my inventory became quite impressive.

Usage 2: There are certain tasks that simply cannot be done in a cavalier or *piecemeal* way, because they require a more systematic process.

Usage 3: The sculpture was hideous, and each component looked as if it had been tacked on in a *piecemeal*, haphazard way.

PIGMENT (n)   [PIG-m*uh* nt]

Meaning: a substance that gives color to something else

Usage 1: By continually adding *pigment*, the tanner was finally able to produce fine leather of the desired dark shade.

Usage 2: Many artists prefer to make their own paints by gradually adding the *pigment* to the base liquid until they have their personally-selected colors.

Usage 3: Human skin color is determined by a *pigment* called melanin.

PILLAGE (v)   [PIL-ij]

Meaning: to rob using violence, particularly during wartime

Usage 1: During the Civil War, General Sherman would often allow his soldiers to *pillage* confederate towns before ordering his men to set fire to the buildings.

Usage 2: A hostile corporate takeover usually results in an attempt to *pillage* the acquired company's assets before selling it piecemeal to the highest bidders.

Usage 3: It is commonplace for conquering soldiers to *pillage* villages for booty and souvenirs.

PITHY (adj)   [PITH-ee]

Meaning: effectively conveying meaning in just a few words

Usage 1: Rather than launch into a long and verbose tirade, the writer responded to his critics with a few *pithy* bon mots.

Usage 2: Mark Twain was known for his pointed and *pithy* jabs at the bourgeoisie.

Usage 3: Ernest Hemingway's novels were written in a fast-paced, *pithy* style that eschewed unnecessary exposition.

PONDEROUS (adj)   [PON-der-*uh* s]

Meaning: clumsy, slow, or awkward, typically because of great weight

Usage 1: Unbeknownst to anyone, John carried a *ponderous* burden on his back, and the strain of that weight pained him greatly.

Usage 2: During the Civil War, artillery regiments usually moved with a *ponderous* slowness, making them ineffective during quick skirmishes.

Usage 3: Although his books are considered to be classics, many of Hugo's books are written in a bloated, *ponderous* style that tries the patience of modern readers.

PRATTLE (v)   [PRAT-l]

Meaning: to talk in a foolish or inconsequential way

Usage 1: John was far too busy to sit still and listen to his mother *prattle* on about the misdeeds of the neighbors.

Usage 2: Usually, the mayor would offer nothing new, and would instead *prattle* on endlessly with a speech full of rhetoric and clichés.

Usage 3: Are you simply going to *prattle* all day, or are you going to get to the point?

PREDICAMENT (n)   [pri-DIK-*uh*-m*uh* nt]

Meaning: a tricky, embarrassing, or unpleasant situation

Usage 1: Thomas had no idea how he had gotten himself into such a *predicament*, but he was determined to rise above it.

Usage 2: The *predicament* we find ourselves in is going to require a good deal of thought, if we hope to rise above it.

Usage 3: The soldier found himself in quite a *predicament* when he was taken prisoner by the rebel forces.

Chapter **18**

Premise – Rig

This chapter covers the following words, each with its part of speech, pronunciation, and descriptive meaning.

Usage of the word is also illustrated in three to five sample sentences.

premise	pundit	replete
presentiment	qualms	repress
preternatural	quench	reprise
prey	quip	reputable
primp	quizzical	reputed
privy	ramble	resonant
Progeny	rant	retiring
promiscuous	rave	retrospective
prone	ravine	rift
prophetic	raze	rig
proselytize	rebate	
prostrate	rectify	
protocol	recurrent	
provender	redundant	
provisional	regal	
proximity	relinquish	
pulchritude	remunerative	
pulsate	rendezvous	
pummel	repeal	
punctilious	repine	

PREMISE (n)   [PREM-is]

Meaning: basis for an argument

Usage 1: If original *premise* is in error, then your conclusion will be just as faulty.

Usage 2: Starting from the *premise* that the husband was the most likely suspect, the detectives built their case.

Usage 3: Many people had been looking forward to the new science fiction series, but the *premise* was just a bland and unoriginal retread.

PRESENTIMENT (n)   [pri-ZEN-t*uh*-m*uh* nt]

Meaning: a feeling about the future, especially one of disaster or foreboding

Usage 1: Laura had a *presentiment* of disaster, so she never boarded the plane.

Usage 2: After any major disaster, there will invariably be a group of people who fraudulently claim that they had felt a *presentiment* days or even weeks earlier.

Usage 3: Physicians say that a heart attack is often preceded by a *presentiment* of impending doom.

PRETERNATURAL (adj)   [pree-ter-NACH-er-*uh* l]

Meaning: beyond what is natural or normal

Usage 1: He had survived so long as a mercenary because of his seemingly *preternatural* sense of danger.

Usage 2: Helen seemed possessed of a *preternatural* ability to know when her children were in trouble.

Usage 3: In comic books, superheroes often have *preternatural* skills that they use for the good of all mankind.

PREY (n)   [prey]

Meaning: an animal hunted for food; or, a person who is a victim

Usage 1: Most carnivorous creatures tend to stalk their *prey* at night.

Usage 2: Most predators rely on the element of surprise to capture their smaller, more elusive *prey*.

Usage 3: A highly advanced sense of smell is a shark's biggest tool by which they can discover potential *prey*.

PRIMP (v)   [primp]

Meaning: to groom carefully, typically by making minor adjustments

Usage 1: Sometimes, Marianne would *primp* and preen for over an hour in preparation for a date.

Usage 2: Every time Rachel passes a mirror, she pauses to *primp* her hair and makeup.

Usage 3: Theodore was inordinately proud of his handlebar mustache, and would *primp* it several times a day.

PRIVY (adj)   [PRIV-ee]

Meaning: possessing knowledge of a secret

Usage 1: As an Officer of the Court, Krista was often *privy* to the trials and tribulations of her neighbors.

Usage 2: Because little pitchers have big mouths, Sharon, a first-grade teacher, was usually *privy* to embarrassing information about her students' parents.

Usage 3: Police officers are invariably *privy* to the most sordid secrets of a city's citizens.

PROGENY (n)   [PROJ-*uh*-nee]

Meaning: the descendants or children of a plant, animal, or person

Usage 1: The mother opossum swam across the creek with her tiny *progeny* latched onto her back.

Usage 2: On his deathbed, Oliver was comforted by the presence of his *progeny*.

Usage 3: Biblical patriarchs often did not personally know each of the hundreds of individuals that were their *progeny*.

PROMISCUOUS (adj)   [pr*uh*-MIS-kyoo-*uh* s]

Meaning: involving indiscriminate mixing or association, especially when referring to sexual relations

Usage 1: Promiscuous behavior can lead to an unwanted reputation that is hard to escape.

Usage 2: To his dismay, Edward realized too late that a *promiscuous* woman does not necessarily change her behavior simply because she has gotten married.

Usage 3: Helen was rather *promiscuous* in her wild youth, but she was much more responsible as an adult.

PRONE (adj)   [prohn]

Meaning: liable to do or experience something

Usage 1: People who really knew Albert understood that he was *prone* to unpredictable manic outbursts.

Usage 2: Older newspapers and magazines are *prone* to yellowing, and should be stored carefully.

Usage 3: Because of their macho, testosterone-fueled lifestyle, many athletes are especially *prone* to domestic violence.

PROPHETIC (adj)   [pr*uh*-FET-ik]

Meaning: accurately describing what will happen in the future

Usage 1: When his verses are read with a liberal interpretation, many of Nostradamus' writings seem eerily prophetic.

Usage 2: His skill at choosing stocks was almost *prophetic*, and he was able to amass a sizable fortune in a short time.

Usage 3: It is surprising how so many *prophetic* science-fiction authors predict a future that is apocalyptic rather than utopian.

PROSELYTIZE (v)   [PROS-*uh*-li-tahyz]

Meaning: to attempt to convert a person from one religion or belief to another, or, to promote one's ideas or beliefs

Usage 1: When he was "born again", the first thing James did was go out and try to *proselytize* all of his friends and family members.

Usage 2: The priest hoped that the new youth ministry could *proselytize* many of the teenagers at the high school.

Usage 3: The purpose of evangelical music is twofold – to celebrate and praise God, and to *proselytize* the unsaved masses.

PROSTRATE (v)   [PROS-treyt]

Meaning: to stretch out fully upon the ground, face downward

Usage 1: After the death of a loved one, many people will *prostrate* themselves in grief.

Usage 2: It is unseemly to *prostrate* yourself before unworthy leaders.

Usage 3: When the village elder refused to *prostrate* himself before the warlord, he was summarily executed before he could inspire others to rebellion.

PROTOCOL (n)   [PROH-t*uh*-kawl]

Meaning: rules and regulations, especially those dealing with diplomatic formality

Usage 1: *Protocol* demanded that the general be treated as a head of state, although in actuality, he was little more than the usurping leader of a coup.

Usage 2: Fortunately, the possibility of just such an emergency had been foreseen, and an appropriate *protocol* had been devised.

Usage 3: For most situations, the *protocol* of diplomatic immunity is followed when dealing with foreign officials on American soil.

PROVENDER (n)   [PROV-*uh* n-der]

Meaning: food or provisions, especially for livestock or domestic animals

Usage 1: Every week, the farmer made the trek into town to purchase *provender* for his animals.

Usage 2: The harsh winter made for scarce *provender*, and the cattle were rail-thin by the time spring arrived.

Usage 3: Pitching hay was hard, sweaty work, but it was very fulfilling to see the barn filled with *provender* for the animals.

PROVISIONAL (adj)   [pr*uh*-VIZH-*uh*-nl]

Meaning: temporarily existing for the present

Usage 1: After the war was over, the occupying force set up a *provisional* government until elections could be held.

Usage 2: Thomas understood that his promotion to department head was merely *provisional* until a more suitable permanent solution could be found.

Usage 3: Because his tenure as *provisional* head coach had been so successful, Rick was officially offered the position the following season.

PROXIMITY (n)   [prok-SIM-i-tee]

Meaning: nearness in space or relationship

Usage 1: It is an extremely bad idea to place a container of gasoline in close *proximity* to a heat source.

Usage 2: Because of the forced *proximity* of the elevator, Philip could smell the perfume that Angelina wore, and it had a dizzying effect upon him.

Usage 3: It seems as if every time my brother and I share any sort of *proximity*, an argument is bound to ensue.

PULCHRITUDE (n)   [PUHL-kri-tood]

Meaning: physical beauty

Usage 1: Contrary to popular belief, a man's appreciation of feminine *pulchritude* does not typically diminish with age.

Usage 2: John counted himself lucky that a woman of such *pulchritude* had consented to be his wife.

Usage 3: Every era has a different woman who serves as the ideal of *pulchritude*.

PULSATE (v) [PUHL-seyt]

Meaning: to produce a strong, regular throbbing sensation or sound

Usage 1: At the concert, the system was rigged so that the main lights would *pulsate* in time with the music.

Usage 2: Whenever Cindy would suffer a migraine, it seemed as if her nerves would actually painfully *pulsate* behind her eyes.

Usage 3: Before every competition, Michael's blood would race through his veins, his heart would *pulsate* in his chest, and the adrenaline would begin to flow.

PUMMEL (v)   [PUHM-*uh* l]

Meaning: to strike or hit repeatedly, typically with the fists

Usage 1: In her grief, Scarlett fell to her knees and began to *pummel* the ground hysterically.

Usage 2: For 12 years, Edward's teachers have tried to *pummel* information into his head, seemingly to no avail.

Usage 3: When the boxer began to mercilessly *pummel* his defenseless opponent, the referee stepped in and stopped the fight.

PUNCTILIOUS (adj)   [puhngk-TIL-ee-*uh* s]

Meaning: showing great attention to detail, especially in terms of correct behavior

Usage 1: Jane prided herself on being a *punctilious* hostess who catered to her guests every need.

Usage 2: Because we were old friends, I saw no need to stand on *punctilious* ceremony when the Mayor visited my home.

Usage 3: The Chief of Protocol was *punctilious* when it came to providing for the comfort of visiting dignitaries.

PUNDIT (n)   [PUHN-dit]

Meaning: an expert in a particular subject, especially one who is called upon to give a public opinion

Usage 1: Viewers were both surprised and secretly bemused when the financial *pundit* was forced into bankruptcy.

Usage 2: Due to the inflammatory nature of his previous comments, the television *pundit* was forced to issue a public apology.

Usage 3: It should be remembered that the job of a *pundit* is often to intentionally make controversial statements, simply to elicit passionate responses from the audience.

QUALMS (n)   [kwahms]

Meaning: uneasy feelings of worry or doubt, usually about one's own conduct

Usage 1: With her justifiable reputation as a legal shark, Joan had no *qualms* about using the victim's past against him.

Usage 2: I had too many *qualms* about possible favoritism to continue as coach of my son's baseball team.

Usage 3: Usually, if a person is experiencing moral *qualms*, it is because they already know that their actions are wrong.

QUENCH (v)   [kwench]

Meaning: to satisfy one's desire (typically thirst); or, to extinguish a fire

Usage 1: Distance could not *quench* the fire of his desire, and indeed, only served to fan the flames.

Usage 2: Diabetics often have a thirst that they are unable to *quench*, no matter how much they drink.

Usage 3: The firefighters desperately tried to *quench* the conflagration before it spread to the adjoining buildings.

QUIP (n)   [kwip]

Meaning: a witty remark

Usage 1: The emcee always had a devastating *quip* at the ready, in order to deal with any drunken hecklers.

Usage 2: Mark was well-known in his circle of friends for his ability to deliver a razor-sharp *quip* in any circumstance.

Usage 3: As a talk show host, David always hoped for a memorable *quip* from his famous guests.

QUIZZICAL (adj)   [KWIZ-i-k*uh* l]

Meaning: indicating amusement or mild puzzlement

Usage 1: Despite the seriousness of the charges, the defendant wore an arrogant, almost *quizzical* expression throughout the trial.

Usage 2: Betty had a *quizzical* look on her face when her seven-year-old daughter tried to explain the "facts of life" to her four-year-old brother.

Usage 3: Looking back, perhaps I shouldn't have made that *quizzical* chuckle when my wife asked what I was getting her for our anniversary.

RAMBLE (v) [RAM-b*uh* l]

Meaning: to walk for pleasure, usually without a destination in mind; or, to talk at length in a confused manner

Usage 1: On many a Saturday morning, we would wake up early and *ramble* about the neighborhood, discovering what adventures life had in store.

Usage 2: Whenever he was in his cups, Jonathan had a tendency to *ramble* on about the most esoteric subjects.

Usage 3: One of the great pleasures in life is the freedom to *ramble* where one will, without a goal or destination in mind.

RANT (v) [rant]

Meaning: to shout or speak at length passionately or angrily

Usage 1: The bombastic radio personality missed no opportunity to *rant* against the policies of the newly- elected president.

Usage 2: Every time they watched a football game together, Jack had to listen to his father *rant* about the decline of the sport.

Usage 3: Suzanne had neither the time nor the inclination to sit there and listen to her boss *rant* at her for her supposed incompetence.

RAVE (n) [reyv]

Meaning: an overly enthusiastic appraisal or recommendation

Usage 1: Much better than a letter of recommendation, Leslie's old employer gave a *rave* that was sure to win her the new job.

Usage 2: Salvador was acutely embarrassed, but secretly pleased, when his teacher praised him in a *rave* to the Dean of Admissions.

Usage 3: Unfortunately, the team captain's *rave* about the newly-acquired free agent made his veteran teammates resentful and jealous.

RAVINE (n) [r*uh*-VEEN]

Meaning: a narrow valley with steep sides

Usage 1: The outlaws rode into the *ravine* at a breakneck speed, hoping to elude the posse.

Usage 2: The herd of cattle meandered into the *ravine* in search of new areas in which to graze.

Usage 3: As the rain continued to fall, Thomas realized with a chill that perhaps he should have made camp in somewhere other than a *ravine* that was prone to flooding.

RAZE (v) [reyz]

Meaning: to completely destroy (as in a building or town)

Usage 1: If there was any resistance from the populace, the Nazi Army would not hesitate to *raze* the town.

Usage 2: Before construction on the new Civic Center could begin, the crews needed to demolish and *raze* the old facilities.

Usage 3: A large crowd was in attendance when the day came to *raze* the historic old theater, and many of them shared fond memories of the past.

REBATE (n)   [REE-beyt]

Meaning: a partial refund to someone who has paid too much

Usage 1: Too many people who are purchasing cars pay more attention to the size of the *rebate,* rather than the overall price of the car.

Usage 2: Eleanor was happily surprised to receive a *rebate* from her electric company after she had installed a smart thermostat.

Usage 3: Gregg decided to take advantage of the *rebate* before it expired at the end of the month.

RECTIFY (v)   [REK-t*uh*-fahy]

Meaning: to settle or make amends

Usage 1: Robert was ready to make every effort to *rectify* the situation with his estranged father.

Usage 2: After so long a time, and after all the bitter words that have been said, the reality may be that there is no way to *rectify* the past.

Usage 3: Gregory bought flowers for his wife and gave her a nice card to try and *rectify* his recent mistakes.

RECURRENT (adj)   [ri-KUR-*uh* nt]

Meaning: occurring repeatedly, often, or regularly

Usage 1: The ability of someone to rise far above their original station in life is a *recurrent* theme in the author's books.

Usage 2: Shelby seemed to have a *recurrent* cough that came back every time the weather changed.

Usage 3: The army was called out in force to beat down the *recurrent* rebellions.

REDUNDANT (adj)   [ri-DUHN-d*uh* nt]

Meaning: unnecessary or no longer needed or useful

Usage 1: One of the worst things about a bureaucracy is the endless pile of *redundant* paperwork.

Usage 2: The private had already been fined and restricted to the barracks, and to demote him was deemed redundant.

Usage 3: With the party's coffers overflowing, attendance at yet another fundraiser seemed *redundant* and a complete waste of time.

REGAL (adj)   [REE-g*uh* l]

Meaning: resembling or fit for a monarch; magnificent, dignified

Usage 1: Whenever she entered her room, everyone in attendance could not help but notice her *regal* bearing and her striking beauty.

Usage 2: The artist was both flattered and humbled by the patronage of such august and *regal* supporters.

Usage 3: The cabin's *regal* appointments and luxurious furniture made Jack appreciate this once-in-a-lifetime trip.

RELINQUISH (v)   [ri-LING-kwish]

Meaning: to voluntarily give something up

Usage 1: For the sake of his love for a mere commoner, the King announced his decision to *relinquish* his throne.

Usage 2: After much consideration, the boxer decided to retire and *relinquish* his title.

Usage 3: In the interest of keeping the family peace, Joshua was willing to *relinquish* any claim he had on his father's estate.

REMUNERATIVE (adj)   [ri-MYOO-ner-*uh*-tiv]

Meaning: yielding suitable profit, rewarding

Usage 1: In his job search, William only focused on those openings that afforded him the most *remunerative* opportunities.

Usage 2: The basketball player moved from team to team, always following the most *remunerative* salary, and in that way, he was akin to a gun-for-hire.

Usage 3: There is more to a career than simply which one is most *remunerative*, because a person must also find personal satisfaction.

RENDEZVOUS (n)   [RAHN-d*uh*-voo]

Meaning: a prearranged meeting, often in secret

Usage 1: The chosen spot of their *rendezvous* was usually some out-of-the-way diner or café.

Usage 2: Charlie hurried out the door so he could keep his *rendezvous* with Helen.

Usage 3: Gen. MacArthur viewed each battle as another *rendezvous* with destiny.

REPEAL (v)   [ri-PEEL]

Meaning: to annul or revoke

Usage 1: When Congress decided to *repeal* Prohibition, liquor flowed freer than ever before.

Usage 2: The Prime Minister's first action was to *repeal* the Labor Act signed by her predecessor.

Usage 3: The proposal failed to garner the necessary support needed to *repeal* the President's Executive Order.

REPINE (v)   [ri-PAHYN]

Meaning: to be discontented, to complain

Usage 1: Whether the news was for good or ill, Paul's mother could always find some reason to *repine*.

Usage 2: All in all, it was a good experience, and I cannot *repine* or regret having gone through it.

Usage 3: If you must *repine*, it is a good idea to be constructive with your criticisms.

REPLETE (adj)   [ri-PLEET]

Meaning: extremely filled or well-stocked with something

Usage 1: The new soap opera was *replete* with adultery, unbelievable storylines, betrayal, and the requisite bevy of beautiful people.

Usage 2: After such a sumptuous meal, I fell asleep on the couch, relaxed and *replete* with food.

Usage 3: Their family get-togethers were always *replete* with warm greetings, shared histories, and a plethora of new drama.

REPRESS (v)   [REE-PRES]

Meaning: to subdue by force

Usage 1: In order to *repress* the rebellion, the soldiers often resorted to brutal methods.

Usage 2: The dictator attempted to *repress* any insurrection by declaring martial law.

Usage 3: In the age of social media, it is virtually impossible to *repress* the free flow of information.

REPRISE (n)   [r*uh*-PREEZ]

Meaning: a repetition, especially of a performance

Usage 1: At the end of the concert, fans were treated to a *reprise* of the band's biggest hits from the past.

Usage 2: When the feature film was announced, there was a hope that the actors from the TV series would be able to give a *reprise* of their roles.

Usage 3: Adam made a comedic *reprise* of the role that made him famous, but the magic was gone.

REPUTABLE (adj)   [REP-y*uh*-t*uh*-b*uh* l]

Meaning: highly regarded

Usage 1: Donald was pleased that his daughter was dating such a *reputable* young man.

Usage 2: Stephanie always did her research beforehand so she could be sure that she was donating to a reputable organization.

Usage 3: Because he trusted the opinion of the *reputable* scout, the coach decided to take a second look at the prospect.

REPUTED (adj)   [ri-PYOO-tid]

Meaning: generally believed about

Usage 1: There was little surprise when the *reputed* gangster was found shot to death.

Usage 2: For years, William had been the *reputed* father of Angela's child, but he had never officially claimed her as his daughter.

Usage 3: One should always be wary of the *reputed*, but unproven, benefits of mass-produced supplements.

RESONANT (adj)   [REZ-*uh*-n*uh* nt]

Meaning: possessing a deep and clear sound

Usage 1: Adam's soul thrilled every time he heard the *resonant* foundering of the canons during the national anthem.

Usage 2: The *resonant* sound of the guitar was in perfect contrast to the delicate piano notes.

Usage 3: The strong, *resonant* timbre of the basso profundo's voice echoed off of the rafters of the music hall.

RETIRING (adj)   [ri-TAHY*UH* R-ing]

Meaning: describing a person who is shy or unassuming

Usage 1: Joshua was a *retiring* person who preferred the company of his books to that of people.

Usage 2: Due to her *retiring* personality, many of her students were surprised to learn that Mrs. Adams once was an actress of some renown.

Usage 3: Some people might call me *retiring* or even introverted, but in actuality, I simply prefer familiar surroundings.

RETROSPECTIVE (adj)   [re-tr*uh*-SPEK-tiv]

Meaning: relating to things that happened in the past

Usage 1: In this introductory course, the professor began with a *retrospective* critique of the author's body of work.

Usage 2: On the 10th anniversary of its premiere date, the television show ran a special *retrospective* episode that chronicled the evolution of the characters.

Usage 3: The art gallery expected quite a crowd to the *retrospective* showing of the artist's complete portfolio.

RIFT (n)   [rift]

Meaning: a break, split or crack in something

Usage 1: During the cursory inspection, the civil engineers noticed a serious *rift* in one of the bridge's support columns.

Usage 2: Matthew's decision to drop out of college caused a serious *rift* between him and his father.

Usage 3: The explorers carefully skirted around the deep *rift* in the glacier.

RIG (v)   [rig]

Meaning: to manipulate, generally in a dishonest manner

Usage 1: Baseball's biggest scandal came when a group of gamblers were able to *rig* the World Series.

Usage 2: After the controversial decision, an inquiry was made to see if someone had been able to *rig* the outcome of the boxing match.

Usage 3: Ballot-stuffing used to be a widely-used technique employed by dishonest candidates who wanted to *rig* an election.

Chapter **19**

Roster – Temporize

This chapter covers the following words, each with its part of speech, pronunciation, and descriptive meaning.

Usage of the word is also illustrated in three to five sample sentences.

roster	sibylline	submissive
rousing	silt	subordinate
ruddy	simper	subversive
saboteur	sinister	sundry
saccharine	slacken	supple
saga	sleeper	surmise
sate	slight	swathe
satire	sloth	tanner
satirical	sluice	taxonomist
scale	slur	temporize
scanty	sophisticated	
scapegoat	spectral	
scavenge	spry	
scintilla	stagnant	
scintillate	stamina	
scruple	statutory	
scurry	stem	
seedy	stem	
serpentine	from	
shambles	stratum	
	subjective	

ROSTER (n)   [ROS-ter]

Meaning: a list of individuals or duty schedules within a group or organization

Usage 1: Soldiers were required to check the duty *roster* often to ensure that they reported to the right areas.

Usage 2: It came as a surprise when the popular outfielder was cut from the *roster*.

Usage 3: When the undrafted rookie made the final *roster*, it was one of the most inspiring sports stories of the year.

ROUSING (adj)   [ROU-zing]

Meaning: done or said with great enthusiasm or excitement, or causing the same

Usage 1: Before every hockey game, the bar joined together for a *rousing* chorus of "O Canada".

Usage 2: There is nothing like a *rousing* series of calisthenics to get the blood pumping in the morning.

Usage 3: A *rousing* cheer from the crowd reinvigorated the exhausted team.

RUDDY (adj)   [RUHD-ee]

Meaning: having a healthy red color, usually pertaining to a person's face

Usage 1: When he stepped in from the biting weather, Arthur's cheeks were *ruddy* from the cold.

Usage 2: Emerging from the shower, Paul's freshly-scrubbed skin was positively glowing and *ruddy* from the heat.

Usage 3: After spending the entire winter sick in bed, Sarah's face had lost its usual *ruddy* color.

SABOTEUR (n)   [sab-*uh*-TUR]

Meaning: a person who destroys or damages property or equipment with the intention of harming or hindering the actions of another

Usage 1: When he was captured, the *saboteur* was tried as a spy, and faced execution by firing squad.

Usage 2: With surgical precision, the *saboteur* placed the explosives along the support structures of the bridge.

Usage 3: Because of the destruction of vital enemy property, and the hindrances that the enemy experienced as a result, the importance of the role of *saboteur* during wartime cannot be overstated.

SACCHARINE (adj)   [SAK-er-in]

Meaning: overly sweet; or, facetiously pleasant or charming

Usage 1: Today, jaded audiences are often indifferent to the *saccharine* sentimentality of television shows from the 1950's.

Usage 2: Peter's love letter went past the borders of sentiment, over the hurdles of mushiness, and into the realm of *saccharine* pablum.

Usage 3: The *saccharine*, almost syrupy flavor of the soft drink was overpowering, and Sharon had to spit it out.

SAGA (n)   [SAH-g*uh*]

Meaning: a long story, typically of a heroic achievement

Usage 1: The *saga* of Beowulf is required reading in many school curriculums.

Usage 2: It required several volumes to tell the complete *saga* of the McCain family.

Usage 3: If you have time, sit down, and I will tell you the whole sordid *saga* of how it all began.

SATE (v)   [seyt]

Meaning: to satisfy, often to excess

Usage 1: When he called for a third helping, it became obvious that regular servings did little to *sate* the appetite of the famous trencherman.

Usage 2: Jeff went on a hedonistic weekend holiday, hoping to *sate* his carnal cravings by engaging in a marathon of unbridled debauchery.

Usage 3: Is this not enough filthy lucre to *sate* your all-encompassing avarice?

SATIRE (n)   [SAT-ahy*uh* r]

Meaning: the use of ridicule, humor, exaggeration, or irony to highlight and expose the stupidity and vices of others, especially within the context of topical issues

Usage 1: Many of the behaviors that we put up with from our elected officials appear patently ridiculous when exposed by the light of *satire*.

Usage 2: The Mayor was not amused by the *satire* that was performed at his expense.

Usage 3: Besides being amusing, *satire* can also serve as a catalyst for change.

SATIRICAL (adj)   [*suh*-TIR-i-k*uh* l]

Meaning: exposing to folly; expressing ridicule

Usage 1: The candidate's campaign was effectively destroyed by the *satirical* caricature of him published by the underground press.

Usage 2: Many of Shakespeare's plays were sly, *satirical* commentaries about the relationship between different classes in society.

Usage 3: The author James Thurber was a master of *satirical* essays that served to hoist many a snobbish blueblood upon their own petard.

SCALE (v)   [skeyl]

Meaning: to climb or rise higher

Usage 1: The Commodore was the first explore to *scale* the northern peak, but his success meant that he would definitely not be the last.

Usage 2: It was impressive that a person of such humble beginnings and modest resources could *scale* the lofty heights of modern academia.

Usage 3: The invading horde charged several times in an attempt to *scale* the ramparts, but each time, they were repelled by the entrenched defenders.

SCANTY (adj)   [SKAN-tee]

Meaning: meager or insufficient

Usage 1: Betty's father forbade her from going out wearing such *scanty* clothing.

Usage 2: The workers were kept in almost abject poverty because of their *scanty* wages.

Usage 3: The wagon train stopped at the Fort to resupply, because there was no way they were going to be able to continue on with such *scanty* provisions.

SCAPEGOAT (n)   [SKEYP-goht]

Meaning: a person or group made to suffer the blame deserved by another

Usage 1: Gary did not realize that he had been made an unwitting *scapegoat* until it was far too late to do anything about it.

Usage 2: There are some people who will never accept blame or responsibility for their own actions as long as they have a convenient *scapegoat*.

Usage 3: I am your partner and your friend, but I will not be the *scapegoat* for your crimes!

SCAVENGE (v)   [SKAV-inj]

Meaning: to hunt for and find a use for waste that has been discarded

Usage 1: If there is one thing that the poverty of my childhood taught me, it is how to *scavenge* for items that I can resell.

Usage 2: The abandoned dog was forced to *scavenge* for food, and this often meant rooting through trash cans.

Usage 3: Some unfortunate souls will *scavenge* through discarded tickets at the racetrack, hoping in vain for a winner.

SCINTILLA (n)   [sin-TIL-*uh*]

Meaning: a tiny trace or amount of something

Usage 1: In John's mind, there was not even a *scintilla* of doubt as to the guilt of the defendant.

Usage 2: Even though she was by nature and experience cautious and distrustful, Elizabeth could not even find the smallest *scintilla* of artifice or evasion in her client's voice.

Usage 3: I had hoped that by being completely open and forthright I could remove every *scintilla* of doubt from your mind.

SCINTILLATE (v)   [SIN-tl-eyt]

Meaning: to flash or shine; or, to throw off sparks

Usage 1: Every rhinestone on her evening gown seemed to catch the light, making her dress *scintillate* blindingly.

Usage 2: Years after her retirement from touring and traveling, Janice seemed to *scintillate* brightly when a reunion performance was scheduled.

Usage 3: The fireworks would *scintillate*, explode, and then cascade down in a fiery shower.

SCRUPLE (v)   [SKROO-p*uh* l]

Meaning: to have qualms about doing something that one believes might be wrong

Usage 1: Even though she was hungry, Ellen would *scruple* to beg or ask for charity.

Usage 2: Vincent would not *scruple* to divulge personal information about his coworkers if he thought that it would advance his career.

Usage 3: Billy Mack was a confirmed lothario, and he would not *scruple* to hit on anything in a skirt.

SCURRY (v)   [SKUR-ee]

Meaning: to move hurriedly with small, quick steps

Usage 1: Elizabeth shrieked and jumped up on a chair when she saw the rat *scurry* across the floor.

Usage 2: In the old, dilapidated apartment, the unfettered roaches would *scurry* from one shadow to the next.

Usage 3: Ed would slink and *scurry* when he moved, and this made him appear akin to some sort of human weasel.

SEEDY (adj)   [SEE-dee]

Meaning: run-down and dilapidated, disreputable

Usage 1: I wasn't exactly comfortable staying at the *seedy* hotel, but it was all that I could afford.

Usage 2: Everyone in the county knew better than to do business with the *seedy* car lot on the east side of town.

Usage 3: The *seedy* neighborhood had an overabundance of liquor stores, check-cashing establishments, and pawn shops manned by cantankerous shysters.

SERPENTINE (adj)   [SUR-p*uh* n-teen]

Meaning: winding or turning one way and another; of or resembling a snake

Usage 1: It was difficult to follow the *serpentine* trail over rocky soil in failing light.

Usage 2: I cannot fathom how anyone is expected to follow your *serpentine* logic and come up with the same preposterous solution.

Usage 3: The bomb expert removed the device's cover and quailed at the sight of the *serpentine* mass of wires underneath.

SHAMBLES (n)   [SHAM-b*uh* ls]

Meaning: a state of total chaos or disorder

Usage 1: When the punk rock band checked out of the hotel, their rooms were left in *shambles*.

Usage 2: It is a unique characteristic of the American teenager that their bedrooms be maintained constantly in *shambles*, without rhyme, reason, or organization.

Usage 3: The general manager's sudden death left the organization in *shambles*, and it took several weeks before everything was reorganized.

SIBYLLINE (adj)   [SIB-*uh*-leen]

Meaning: possessing the characteristics of a prophet

Usage 1: Fisher's uncanny ability to predict his opponent's next move bordered on *sibylline*.

Usage 2: Other people may think that you are some sort of *sibylline* prognosticator, but I just think you are adept at guessing.

Usage 3: Green's success in the stock market was neither serendipitous nor *sibylline*, but no one wanted to believe that simple hard work could have paid off so handsomely.

SILT (n)   [silt]

Meaning: fine sand, earth, or debris that is carried by moving water and deposited as sediment

Usage 1: The prospector meticulously panned through the *silt*, hoping to find gold dust or nuggets.

Usage 2: Their footprints disturbed the *silt* and clouded the water, so they were unable to locate the ring that Jill had lost.

Usage 3: Buried in the *silt* were a number of Spanish doubloons that had rested here since the ship had been sunk hundreds of years ago.

SIMPER (v)   [SIM-per]

Meaning: to gesture or smile in a coy or ingratiating manner, typically affectively

Usage 1: Hoping to forbear any harsher judgment, Angelica began to *simper* facetiously and talk in a subdued, coquettish manner.

Usage 2: Extraordinarily pleased with herself, Ruth began to *simper* at the problems she had purposely caused since her arrival.

Usage 3: It was infuriating to watch Mary *simper* and preen, unconcerned, while others struggled all around her.

SINISTER (adj)   [SIN-*uh*-ster]

Meaning: creating a forbidding or baleful impression

Usage 1: The *sinister* expression on his face sent chills down her spine.

Usage 2: There were dark and *sinister* forces at work within the government, and the Attorney General made it his personal mission to expose them.

Usage 3: There was something *sinister* in his voice, and Amanda steeled herself for whatever was to come next.

SLACKEN (v)   [SLAK-*uh* n]

Meaning: to loosen; or, to slow or become less active

Usage 1: The storm let loose with an impressive fury that was not expected to *slacken* for hours.

Usage 2: Despite his fatigue, Roger knew that he could not afford to *slacken* his pace if he expected to complete the project on time.

Usage 3: The petty officer taught his young sailors to regularly check the moorings, because they had a tendency to *slacken* if they were not tightened periodically.

SLEEPER (n)   [SLEE-per]

Meaning: a person who sleeps; or, someone or something originally unnoticed that later achieves prominence or importance

Usage 1: A single phone call, a few uttered trigger words, and the long-dormant *sleeper* was activated.

Usage 2: For independent filmmakers, it is always encouraging when an unmarketed *sleeper* becomes a box office success.

Usage 3: If life is but a dream, then let the *sleeper* not awake!

SLIGHT (n)   [slahyt]

Meaning: an insult to one's dignity

Usage 1: I do not have the time to continually stroke your ego over every imagined *slight*.

Usage 2: Dorothy was mortified, and she apologized continuously for the unintended *slight*.

Usage 3: This decision was made for business reasons, and was not meant as a *slight*.

SLOTH (n)   [slawth]

Meaning: reluctance to make an effort, the state of being lazy

Usage 1: Paul's mother was exasperated at her son's apathy and *sloth*, and was determined to confront him about it.

Usage 2: Sloth is considered one of the Seven Deadly Sins, and many would say that it is the precursor to many of the remainder.

Usage 3: Just because I clean up after you doesn't mean that I condone your pervasive *sloth*.

SLUICE (n)   [sloos]

Meaning: a sliding gate that controls the flow of water; or the act of showering or rinsing with water

Usage 1: When the *sluice* malfunctioned, the road in front of the school was flooded.

Usage 2: The plumber was unable to immediately fix the jammed *sluice*, so our home would be without water for another day.

Usage 3: At the end of every workday, the drivers were required to give their vehicles a *sluice* to rinse off the accumulated road grime.

SLUR (v)   [slur]

Meaning: to speak indistinctly or unclearly

Usage 1: As the liquor began to take effect, Logan gradually started to *slur* his words.

Usage 2: If a person begins to *slur* his speech, that can be a sign of a medical emergency.

Usage 3: She was uncouth, unkempt, and had an alarming tendency to *slur* each profane word that she uttered.

SOPHISTICATED (adj)   [*suh*-FIS-ti-key-tid]

Meaning: possessing refined or cultured tastes, habits, and characteristics

Usage 1: The sommelier was widely known for his *sophisticated* palate, and he rarely was unable to identify even the most esoteric of vintages.

Usage 2: Born into a life of privilege, Olivia was exposed to more *sophisticated* forms of entertainment, such as ballet and opera.

Usage 3: Curtis liked to pretend that he was worldly and *sophisticated*, but he would always be the dirty little boy who grew up on the wrong side of the tracks.

SPECTRAL (adj)   [SPEK-tr*uh* l]

Meaning: of or like a ghost; disembodied

Usage 1: Over the course of one Christmas Eve, Scrooge was visited by three *spectral* entities.

Usage 2: She was emaciated to the point that she now presented a visage that was nearly *spectral* in appearance.

Usage 3: On Halloween, it is said that *spectral* beings are allowed to once again walk the earth.

SPRY (adj)   [sprahy]

Meaning: agile and energetic, usually referring to an older person

Usage 1: For an octogenarian, Harold was surprisingly *spry*, and enjoyed surprising people with his athleticism.

Usage 2: On cold winter days, Betty would not feel as *spry* as she would during the springtime.

Usage 3: The new medications had Buford feeling as *spry* and gay as a twenty-year-old.

STAGNANT (adj)   [STAG-n*uh* nt]

Meaning: sluggish or showing no activity

Usage 1: The pool of water had been *stagnant* for so long that it was no longer safe to drink.

Usage 2: There was a decided dearth of opportunities because of the *stagnant* economy.

Usage 3: When Amanda realized that her career had become *stagnant*, she looked into changing fields.

STAMINA (n)   [STAM-*uh*-n*uh*]

Meaning: the ability to sustain a prolonged effort

Usage 1: Mary lost the race because she no longer had the *stamina* to keep up with her younger rivals.

Usage 2: Smoking will rob you of your *stamina*, your beauty, and ultimately, your health.

Usage 3: Norman had slept little the night before, and today, his *stamina* was suffering as a result.

STATUTORY (adj)   [STACH-*oo*-tawr-ee]

Meaning: required or permitted by law

Usage 1: The *statutory* age of majority is defined differently in different countries.

Usage 2: The *statutory* number of votes was not reached, so the bill was defeated.

Usage 3: By *statutory* decree, the candidates had to submit five years of tax returns.

STEM (v)   [stem]

Meaning: to restrain or check; or, to occur as a consequence

Usage 1: The medic applied pressure with a clean bandage in a desperate attempt to *stem* the blood flow from the wound.

Usage 2: Frank's suspension from school was not the only consequence to *stem* from his recent defiance.

Usage 3: Naturally, the University wanted to share credit for any discoveries that might *stem* from the latest expedition.

STEM FROM (v)   [stem from]

Meaning: to be caused by

Usage 1: Sometimes, it seems as if all of my troubles in life *stem from* my unstable childhood.

Usage 2: Doctors will tell you that a large number of health issues can *stem from* an improper diet.

Usage 3: The home economics instructor taught her students that many of the frustrations felt by homemakers *stem from* a lack of organization or prioritization of tasks.

STRATUM (n)   [STREY-t*uh* m]

Meaning: an individual layer, typically of the Earth's surface, but also referring to of society

Usage 1: When they failed to strike water, the crew decided to deepen the well another *stratum*.

Usage 2: Each *stratum* of society seems to have its own set of rules, and a newcomer can often feel lost and ostracized.

Usage 3: Every *stratum* of the earth is typified by the type of rocks and minerals that can be found there.

SUBJECTIVE (adj)   [s*uh* b-JEK-tiv]

Meaning: influenced by personal opinions or tastes

Usage 1: Any opinions given are based upon *subjective* experiences and may not reflect what might be typical for all users.

Usage 2: By definition, my memories are *subjective*, and in their totality they define who I am.

Usage 3: The doctor's evaluation was disregarded, because it was determined that her *subjective* opinion would be unfairly biased.

SUBMISSIVE (adj)   [s*uh* b-MIS-iv]

Meaning: meekly conforming to the will of others

Usage 1: Gerald's *submissive* nature around his parents was extremely off-putting to his date.

Usage 2: Make no mistake – there is a world of difference between being accommodating and being *submissive*.

Usage 3: The medication's sedating effect had her in a pliable, almost *submissive* state of mind.

SUBORDINATE (adj)   [s*uh*-BAWR-dn-it]

Meaning: possessing a lesser rank or position

Usage 1: Even though Williams was of a *subordinate* military rank, he took the time to educate the new officer.

Usage 2: Cheryl decided that she would prefer to quit her job, rather than be transferred to a *subordinate* position.

Usage 3: Fitzsimons was acutely embarrassed when he admitted to his obliviousness to the *subordinate* partner.

SUBVERSIVE (adj)   [s*uh* b-VUR-siv]

Meaning: causing an undermining of support, rebellious

Usage 1: Every positive action that the President takes is thwarted by the *subversive*, backroom negotiations of the opposing party.

Usage 2: Over time, the battles became part of a covert war, and each side would engage in clandestine *subversive* actions designed to wreak havoc upon the other side.

Usage 3: Because of her oppositional nature and her *subversive* machinations, the Board decided to buy out Caroline's contract.

SUNDRY (adj) [SUHN-dree]

Meaning: of several kinds

Usage 1: The general store sold construction materials and *sundry* goods that might be needed on the frontier.

Usage 2: He presided over *sundry* projects, and impressed his superiors when he came in on time and under budget on all of them.

Usage 3: The proclamation was made publicly to all and *sundry*, and the word spread quickly among the populace.

SUPPLE (adj) [SUHP-*uh* l]

Meaning: moving and bending easily, flexible

Usage 1: His *supple* body moved with the power and energy of youth.

Usage 2: Billy oiled and worked his baseball glove until the leather was *supple* and fit his hand perfectly.

Usage 3: As one ages, regular exercise is necessary if one wants to stay *supple*, strong, and healthy.

SURMISE (v) [ser-MAHYZ]

Meaning: to deduce or infer

Usage 1: If I had to *surmise* your intentions based upon your actions, I don't think that I would like my own conclusions.

Usage 2: Based upon the evidence, the detectives could only *surmise* that Mark was the most likely suspect.

Usage 3: No one has ever been able to convincingly *surmise* where the treasure was actually buried.

SWATHE (v) [swoth]

Meaning: to wrap in several layers

Usage 1: Sue would *swathe* her infant in multiple layers of clothing and blankets before venturing out into the cold.

Usage 2: Whenever little Billy would hurt himself, his mother would clean the scrape, *swathe* it in bandages, and then give it a kiss to make it all better.

Usage 3: To protect the antiques during shipment, the curator decided to *swathe* the more delicate items in cushioning muslin.

TANNER (n) [TAN-er]

Meaning: a person who turns animal hides into leather

Usage 1: We brought the deer hides to a *tanner*, and two weeks later, we had supple buckskin that could be used for any number of projects.

Usage 2: The *tanner* expertly dyed the leather to a deep burgundy shade that would perfectly complement the room's décor.

Usage 3: Like many other businesses that require the skills of a craftsman, the profession of *tanner* finds few practitioners today.

TAXONOMIST (n)   [tak-SON-*uh*-mist]

Meaning: a person who specializes in the classification of animals

Usage 1: The decaying carcass of the strange animal was difficult to identify and created quite a puzzle for the taxonomist.

Usage 2: For Peter, the best part about being a *taxonomist* was the search for new and fascinating creatures.

Usage 3: The *taxonomist* was thrilled when she witnessed firsthand the colony of animals that had been thought extinct.

TEMPORIZE (v)   [TEM-p*uh*-rahyz]

Meaning: to avoid deciding or committing oneself in order to stall for time

Usage 1: Rather than answering the question directly, the politician began to ramble on about tangents in an attempt to *temporize*.

Usage 2: To avoid being called upon, the unprepared student would normally *temporize* by asking for a bathroom pass.

Usage 3: Helen's tendency to *temporize* made her unpopular with the fund-raising committee.

Chapter **20**

Tendentious – Zephyr

This chapter covers the following words, each with its part of speech, pronunciation, and descriptive meaning.

Usage of the word is also illustrated in three to five sample sentences.

tendentious	unfaltering	wax
tenet	unfeigned	whiff
testy	unfetter	whinny
theoretical	unfettered	wince
thermal	vagary	wizardry
timidity	vantage	woe
torque	veer	yoke
touchy	vent	zephyr
trajectory	verisimilar	
trappings	verity	
trek	vicissitude	
trigger	virtue	
tundra	virus	
tutelage	vise	
tycoon	vital	
tyro	volition	
unearth	voluble	
unearthly	voracious	
unequivocal	wanderlust	
unerringly	wane	
unexceptionable	wangle	

TENDENTIOUS (adj)   [ten-DEN-sh*uh* s]

Meaning: promoting a point of view, especially one that is controversial

Usage 1: The television journalist made a very *tendentious* and inflammatory statement when he claimed that mental disease is a form of moral weakness.

Usage 2: She was of the rather *tendentious* opinion that women should not be allowed to breast-feed in public.

Usage 3: Many politicians shy away from polarizing or *tendentious* issues, resulting in a bland homogeny among the candidates.

TENET (n)   [TEN-it]

Meaning: a precept of belief, most especially of a philosophy or religion

Usage 1: Monotheism is a basic *tenet* of Christianity, Judaism, and Islam.

Usage 2: Despite the circumstances, Cassandra could not bring herself to steal, because it was against the most fundamental *tenet* taught to her when she was a young girl.

Usage 3: If you break this *tenet*, what will keep you from violating the others?

TESTY (adj)   [TES-tee]

Meaning: possessing an irritable or grouchy disposition

Usage 1: Philip was in a *testy* mood, and was not likely to suffer foolish behavior easily.

Usage 2: Whenever Jonathan was under a deadline, he would become *testy* and impatient with his staff.

Usage 3: After a long day of frustrating delays, April found herself getting *testy* with the ticket agent.

THEORETICAL (adj)   [thee-*uh*-RET-i-k*uh* l]

Meaning: concerned with conjecture rather than practical applications

Usage 1: After forming his *theoretical* principle, Theodore was anxious to see it put into practice.

Usage 2: Because *theoretical* philosophy is concerned mainly with metaphysics, there is some doubt as to how useful it is in the real world.

Usage 3: The conjectures of *theoretical* medicine have often led to advancements that were previously unimagined.

THERMAL (adj)   [THUR-m*uh* l]

Meaning: pertaining to heat

Usage 1: The *thermal* reading clearly showed which of the home's areas were allowing the most heat to escape.

Usage 2: It was a bitterly cold day, so Austin slipped on a set of *thermal* underwear beneath his work uniform.

Usage 3: When it is too dark for regular photography, *thermal* imaging can give a remarkably accurate picture of the local topography.

TIMIDITY (n)   [tim-ID-i-tee]

Meaning: lack of courage or confidence

Usage 1: David's reticence and *timidity* were very off-putting, and his fiancée ended their engagement.

Usage 2: When it comes to promoting yourself professionally, *timidity* is not a viable strategy.

Usage 3: Fortune favors the bold, but *timidity* dashes hope for better things.

TORQUE (n)   [tawrk]

Meaning: a twisting force that causes rotation

Usage 1: In such a cramped space, it was difficult to apply enough *torque* to free the frozen nut.

Usage 2: The machinist adjusted the power settings on the generator in order to achieve greater *torque*.

Usage 3: By adding an extension, the mechanic was able to generate sufficient *torque* to seal the clamp properly.

TOUCHY (adj)   [TUHCH-ee]

Meaning: irritable and hypersensitive; or requiring deft handling

Usage 1: It was a *touchy* situation, so the company sent in their most experienced negotiator.

Usage 2: Because so many students had taken advantage of his generosity, the teacher was now very *touchy* about the subject of time extensions.

Usage 3: Bob had lost his job, so right now, money was a *touchy* subject.

TRAJECTORY (n)   [truh-JEK-tuh-ree]

Meaning: the path of the projectile; or, a progression or development resembling the same

Usage 1: The artillery lieutenant was able to quickly calculate the *trajectory* of the next salvo.

Usage 2: His career *trajectory* was much more vertical than had been originally expected.

Usage 3: By tracing the *trajectory* of the incoming rounds, they were able to ascertain the location of the enemy artillery.

TRAPPINGS (n)   [TRAP-ingz]

Meaning: outward features or objects that are associated with a particular role or situation

Usage 1: He had all the *trappings* and accoutrements of a respectable businessman, without having the requisite professional integrity.

Usage 2: Even though she had all of the finest things that make up the *trappings* of success, she still felt like a failure inside.

Usage 3: Sometimes, maintaining the *trappings* of his position required more effort than the duties of the position itself.

TREK (n)   [trek]

Meaning: a long and difficult journey, usually made on foot

Usage 1: The *trek* between Sydney and Brisbane took almost four days.

Usage 2: We were definitely not prepared for an unarmed *trek* through the savanna.

Usage 3: The *trek* was slow going, because they had to hack their way through thick jungle almost every step of the way.

TRIGGER (v)   [TRIG-er]

Meaning: to cause to happen

Usage 1: If the welders were not careful, they could accidentally cut through the gas main and *trigger* an explosion.

Usage 2: Economists are constantly on the lookout for any developments that could *trigger* another recession.

Usage 3: Jeremy was extremely cautious around his mother, because he never could tell what might *trigger* another of her outbursts.

TUNDRA (n)   [TUHN-druh]

Meaning: a large, barren Arctic region in Asia, Europe, and North America

Usage 1: He drove his team of dogs hard across the *tundra*, but he was still doubtful of making the settlement before the storm struck.

Usage 2: As he looked out across the *tundra*, he felt the sharp pang of incomparable melancholia.

Usage 3: Game was scarce in the *tundra*, as evidenced by the exposed rib cages of the pack of hungry wolves.

TUTELAGE (n)   [TOOT-l-ij]

Meaning: guardianship or authority over someone or something; or, training or instruction

Usage 1: Students under the *tutelage* of Professor Warren were taught the skill of critical thinking, not just dry, dusty facts.

Usage 2: I spent my formative years under the strict *tutelage* of impersonal priests and forbidding nuns.

Usage 3: Mary Lou found her skills developing rapidly under the *tutelage* of Coach Bela.

TYCOON (n)   [tahy-KOON]

Meaning: wealthy and powerful leader in industry or business

Usage 1: The real estate *tycoon* proceeded to buy all of the properties on and near the marina.

Usage 2: It was a mistake to make a personal enemy of a newspaper *tycoon* who was devoid of a conscience.

Usage 3: Although he was very successful in his chosen field, he was far from a *tycoon*.

TYRO (n)   [TAHY-roh]

Meaning: a novice or beginner

Usage 1: The new mayor might have been a political *tyro*, but she was also a seasoned businessperson with decades of experience.

Usage 2: Even though Zelda was an excellent cook, she was a complete *tyro* when it came to managing a restaurant.

Usage 3: Because he was an absolute *tyro* as a high school teacher, Johnson found himself viewing the football coach as a kind of mentor.

UNEARTH (v)   [uhn-URTH]

Meaning: to discover or dig up

Usage 1: Almost invariably, the reporter would *unearth* critical collateral information when researching an investigative topic.

Usage 2: It is not uncommon for construction crews to *unearth* unexpected vaults and crypts when preparing a site for development.

Usage 3: At the excavation site, the archaeological crew meticulously worked to *unearth* the ruins of the ancient city without damaging the artifacts.

UNEARTHLY (adj)   [uhn-URTH-lee]

Meaning: mysterious or unnatural, especially in a manner that disturbs

Usage 1: Even though she was a skeptic, Helen felt the undeniable presence of an *unearthly* entity during the séance.

Usage 2: The demonologist was by definition an expert on the occult, and was knowledgeable about all manner of phantasmagorical and *unearthly* creatures.

Usage 3: Minutes before the explosion, there was an *unearthly* silence that eerily pervaded the surrounding woods.

UNEQUIVOCAL (adj)   [uhn-i-KWIV-*uh*-*kuh* l]

Meaning: leaving no doubt or ambiguity

Usage 1: During a staff meeting, the new manager let his employees know that he was the *unequivocal* leader of the company.

Usage 2: This is our *unequivocal* destiny – to grow, prosper, and become masters of our domain.

Usage 3: Susan had endured many things since her marriage, but she was *unequivocal* about the subject of infidelity.

UNERRINGLY (adj)   [uhn-UR-ing lee]

Meaning: without mistake or deviation

Usage 1: No matter where we were, my father could always *unerringly* lead us in the right direction, even without a map.

Usage 2: John *unerringly* picked the right course for his business to take, and he was soon very successful.

Usage 3: Christina had the preternatural ability to *unerringly* pick the wrong man in her romantic life.

UNEXCEPTIONABLE (adj)   [uhn-ik-SEP-sh*uh*-n*uh*-b*uh* l]

Meaning: not open to objection

Usage 1: Because he was a court-appointed volunteer, the work performance of the special advocate was, as a rule, *unexceptionable*.

Usage 2: The opinions of the Pope are considered *unexceptionable* when he is speaking about matters of faith.

Usage 3: The general considered his orders to be *unexceptionable*, and therefore, he expected his subordinates to follow them to the letter.

UNFALTERING (adj)   [uhn-FAWL-ter-ing]

Meaning: not wavering or tiring; steadfast

Usage 1: Even in the face of such insurmountable odds, Jordan had an *unfaltering* optimism and confidence in her own abilities.

Usage 2: In his quest for moral perfection, Luther was the very picture of *unfaltering* and resolute determination.

Usage 3: It is of little use to be *unfaltering* in your ambition if you are haphazard in your vocation.

UNFEIGNED (adj)   [uhn-FEYND]

Meaning: honest and without affectation

Usage 1: When she opened the door and saw the gathering of her friends, Renée could not hide her *unfeigned* surprise.

Usage 2: His *unfeigned* appreciation was evident on his face, and that expression made the expenditure of effort worthwhile.

Usage 3: There was no disguising the *unfeigned* disgust that he felt when he took the first bite of the rancid food.

UNFETTER (v)   [uhn-FET-er]

Meaning: to free from restraint or inhibition

Usage 1: She had reached adulthood, and her parents had no choice but to *unfetter* her from her constraints and treat her as such.

Usage 2: Normally, Benjamin was an easy-going person, but when sufficiently crossed, he could *unfetter* a rage that would shake the heavens.

Usage 3: It is a special occasion, so please *unfetter* your wallet and stop worrying about how much everything is going to cost.

UNFETTERED (adj)   [uhn-FET-erd]

Meaning: rampant and freed from restriction

Usage 1: *Unfettered* ambition can cause both a meteoric rise and a disastrous fall.

Usage 2: It was his *unfettered* hedonism that ultimately led to his ruination.

Usage 3: The flame from her *unfettered* anger ultimately burned everyone she knew, including Regina herself.

VAGARY (n)   [v*uh*-GAIR-ee]

Meaning: an unexpected change, typically in situations or in someone's behavior

Usage 1: When it snowed in August, this was a *vagary* of the weather for which they were totally unprepared.

Usage 2: Her sudden moodiness was a *vagary* that hinted at a more serious problem.

Usage 3: Honestly, I cannot be expected to keep up with every *vagary* that you concoct without warning.

VANTAGE (n)   [VAN-tij]

Meaning: a position or place that grants a good view or advantage

Usage 1: From my point of *vantage*, I could see the changes coming on the horizon, and this gave me ample time to prepare.

Usage 2: It is imperative that once you reach a *vantage*, you use your new insight and information to better those around you.

Usage 3: From his *vantage*, the general knew that his forces had the element of surprise on their side.

VEER (v)   [veer]

Meaning: to change direction quickly or suddenly

Usage 1: Every time we thought we understood what the teacher was talking about, he would *veer* off onto another tangent.

Usage 2: I need you to concentrate on the task at hand, and not *veer* off in another direction.

Usage 3: Jeff had just enough time to *veer* to the left and avoid a disastrous collision.

VENT (v)   [vent]

Meaning: to freely express a strongly-felt emotion

Usage 1: Albert was glad that he had a chance to *vent* his frustrations, but he didn't expect anything to change.

Usage 2: It is better to *vent* any pent up feelings periodically, rather than let them build up even further.

Usage 3: Elizabeth knew that she was only a sounding board, so she let her partner *vent* her concerns without comment.

VERISIMILAR (adj)   [ver-*uh*-SIM-*uh*-ler]

Meaning: having the appearance of truth

Usage 1: The public was clamoring for just one *verisimilar* fact instead of the usual political rhetoric.

Usage 2: On the face of it, she told a very *verisimilar* story, so the detectives were disinclined to investigate further.

Usage 3: The company made what seemed to be a number of *verisimilar* claims about their product, but upon investigation, each of those claims was spurious or misleading.

VERITY (n)   [VER-i-tee]

Meaning: a true principle that is of fundamental importance

Usage 1: The police assured him that he could be released once the *verity* of his story was confirmed.

Usage 2: I am not one who normally casts aspersions, but I strongly doubt the *verity* of what you are telling me.

Usage 3: If you make *verity* your watchword in all things, you will never have to worry about covering up your own lies.

VICISSITUDE (n)   [vi-SIS-i-tood]

Meaning: a change in fortune or circumstances, most especially, one that is unwelcome

Usage 1: I prefer to make my own destiny, instead of relying on the *vicissitude* of Providence.

Usage 2: She had owned her own business, but a *vicissitude* due to a natural disaster ruined her prospects.

Usage 3: Ambition and hard work trump *vicissitude* almost invariably.

VIRTUE (n)   [VUR-choo]

Meaning: conformance to high moral standards

Usage 1: She was admired for her beauty, appreciated for her goodness, and respected for her *virtue*.

Usage 2: Jonathan let them know unequivocally that neither his *virtue* nor his integrity was for sale at any price.

Usage 3: Today, many young people think that the concept of *virtue* is outdated, and they live like the ends really do justify the means.

VIRUS (n)   [VAHY-r*uh* s]

Meaning: a disease that is caused by an ultra microscopic agent that spreads by replication; or, a malicious computer program that behaves the same way

Usage 1: Healthcare workers were advised to wear protective clothing to try and arrest the proliferation of the virus.

Usage 2: The company lost valuable customer information when its computers were disabled by a *virus*.

Usage 3: Luckily, he had caught the mildest version of the *virus*, and was expected to make a full recovery.

VISE (n)   [vahys]

Meaning: a type of tool that holds work tightly incidentally; or, something likened to the same

Usage 1: Once the sheet was secured in the *vise*, Robert began the engraving process.

Usage 2: Her addiction held her as fast as a *vise*, and she found it very difficult to maintain appearances.

Usage 3: Without a *vise*, the machinist was unsure how he could complete the fabrication.

VITAL (adj)   [VAHYT-l]

Meaning: absolutely essential or important

Usage 1: Before they could act, the agency was waiting on some *vital* intelligence that would give them a better idea of the situation.

Usage 2: In business, there are several concepts that are absolutely *vital* to long-term success.

Usage 3: Without artifice, Pauline knew that she was valuable to the company, but she had no clue as to how absolutely *vital* she was to its smooth operation.

VOLITION (n)   [voh-LISH-*uh* n]

Meaning: the power of one's own will

Usage 1: Of her own *volition*, Catherine began to explain the events that had led up to her crimes.

Usage 2: Without nagging or prompting and by her own *volition*, the teenager began to tidy up her bedroom.

Usage 3: It is by my own *volition* that I make this statement, in an effort to clear my name and that of my family.

VOLUBLE (adj)   [VOL-yuh-buh l]

Meaning: speaking incessantly

Usage 1: Matthew's colleague was a nice enough fellow, but he had a tendency to be rather *voluble* when Matthew needed time to think.

Usage 2: She was a pretty and *voluble* young thing, with no shortage of suitors and admirers.

Usage 3: It's hard to be considered *voluble* when the only conversation that you ever have is via text messages.

VORACIOUS (adj)   [vaw-REY-shuh s]

Meaning: having a great or eager desire for something, most especially food

Usage 1: Usually, Robert could be counted on for his *voracious* appetite, but tonight, he was rather peckish.

Usage 2: Shelby was a *voracious* reader, and it was a rare sight whenever she was without yet another book.

Usage 3: During her pregnancy, Mickey became a *voracious* and indiscriminate eater, because she would eat almost anything, as long as there was a lot of it.

WANDERLUST (n)   [WON-der-luhst]

Meaning: a strong desire to travel

Usage 1: Upon graduation, many young people experience *wanderlust* and feel the call of the open road.

Usage 2: It is a rite of passage among some young men to satisfy their *wanderlust* by taking a backpack trip through Europe.

Usage 3: One exceptional youth gave in to his *wanderlust* by riding a motorcycle through the entirety of North America down through South America.

WANE (v)   [weyn]

Meaning: to become progressively weaker, smaller, or less powerful

Usage 1: When he was not reelected, the president saw his powers *wane* during the last part of his term.

Usage 2: At long last, the combat began to *wane*, and the steady flow of casualties started to diminish.

Usage 3: A series of photographs showed the various phases of the moon as it would wax and *wane*.

WANGLE (v)   [WANG-guh l]

Meaning: to gain something by devious or fraudulent means

Usage 1: By pretending to be handicapped, George would often *wangle* a great parking space.

Usage 2: Suzanne told her teacher that she had been busy taking care of her sick grandmother, hoping to *wangle* an extension for the assignment.

Usage 3: Thomas began dropping names and hinting at imagined friendships, hoping to *wangle* an invitation to the party.

WAX (v)   [waks]

Meaning: to increase in strength, intensity, or numbers; or, to speak about enthusiastically

Usage 1: Whenever he was in his cups, my father tended to *wax* poetically about the Good Old Days.

Usage 2: If you want to be there when my fortunes start to *wax*, then you had better stand by me while they are still waning.

Usage 3: Watching the moon *wax* gave Armstrong its strong sense of his tiny place in the grander schemes of the universe.

WHIFF (n)   [hwif]

Meaning: a faint or brief impression, most typically of a smell

Usage 1: Chester poked his head inside the door just to get a *whiff* of his wife's delicious cooking.

Usage 2: Despite searching all evening, Joanne's parents could not even get a *whiff* of her whereabouts.

Usage 3: If you ever get a *whiff* of the spray of a skunk, you will understand what all of the fuss is about.

WHINNY (v)   [HWIN-ee]

Meaning: to make the sound of a horse

Usage 1: Whenever Scarlett would enter the stable, her horse would *whinny* in recognition.

Usage 2: After she crossed the finish line four lengths in front of the other horses, the mare gave a *whinny* of triumph and excitement.

Usage 3: Dale had quite a talent for mimicry, because he could *whinny* like a horse, bleat like a lamb, gecker like a jackal, and even bellow like an alligator.

WINCE (v)   [wins]

Meaning: to shrink back involuntarily because of pain or in anticipation of pain

Usage 1: Most young patients *wince* at the pain of a shot, often before the needle even touches them.

Usage 2: The sudden rush of heat when she opened the door made her *wince* back in alarm.

Usage 3: The harsh sting of the antiseptic made him *wince* and sharply draw in a hissing breath.

WIZARDRY (n)   [WIZ-er-dree]

Meaning: the art of magic; or, exceedingly great skill at an activity

Usage 1: The best part of his technological *wizardry* was the fact that movie-going audiences were never conscious of the fact that they were watching generated special effects.

Usage 2: While the mage was in his tower perfecting his skills at *wizardry*, armies were gathering to the north.

Usage 3: Julian never failed to impress her guests with her *wizardry* in the kitchen.

WOE (n)   [woh]

Meaning: great sorrow or sadness; or, anything that causes great sorrow

Usage 1: When she found herself alone yet again, her *woe* was almost more than she could bear.

Usage 2: It is quite vexing that our chosen spouses and our chosen occupations are so often the greatest source of *woe* in our lives.

Usage 3: When he started looking at his problems as simply challenges that could be overcome, his burden of *woe* was greatly lightened.

YOKE (v)   [yohk]

Meaning: to join together, especially in order to work together

Usage 1: If you agree, then I will *yoke* myself to you in life, and we will work together for the rest of our days.

Usage 2: Susan was a strong creative talent, and her boss did not want to *yoke* with anyone who did not share her genius.

Usage 3: The farmer decided to *yoke* his oxen together and let them share the burden of pulling the plow.

ZEPHYR (n)   [ZEF-er]

Meaning: a soft breeze

Usage 1: The air was completely still, and not even the softest *zephyr* could be felt.

Usage 2: Stepping into the sunlight, Anna felt a warm *zephyr* on her face, and the sensation made her smile broadly.

Usage 3: A sudden *zephyr* blew the paper across the yard before William catch it.

Challenging Word List

This page is intentionally left blank

Chapter **21**

Acclivity – Ballast

This chapter covers the following words, each with its part of speech, pronunciation, and descriptive meaning.

Usage of the word is also illustrated in three to five sample sentences.

acclivity	asteroid	avocation
apprehensive	astigmatism	avuncular
arboretum	astringent	axiom
arcane	asunder	azure
archaic	asymmetric	bacchanalian
archetype	atavism	badinage
archives	atheistic	baleful
argot	atrocity	ballast
arid	attest	
armada	attribute	
arrears	atypical	
arroyo	augment	
articulate	augury	
artifice	aureole	
ascendancy	auspicious	
ascribe	authenticate	
asinine	automaton	
askance	autopsy	
askew	avalanche	
asperity	avenge	
assail	avert	

ACCLIVITY (n)   [*uh*-KLIV-i-tee]

Meaning: sharp upslope of a hill; an upward slope

Usage 1: In the last few miles of the marathon, Derek was forced to face a steep *acclivity*; thereby exhausting all the energy he had left to finish the race.

Usage 2: The *acclivity* of the haphazard badminton court led to many missed shots and falls.

Usage 3: The road ascended over miles by a slight *acclivity*, ending in an overlook of the deep gully and thousands of pine trees.

APPREHENSIVE (adj)   [ap-ri-HEN-siv]

Meaning: fearful; discerning; cautious or wary about something

Usage 1: Toddlers often go through a phase when they are *apprehensive* about all sorts of loud noises.

Usage 2: Tracy was too *apprehensive* to sign up for skydiving lessons, so she opted for swimming classes instead.

Usage 3: All of a sudden he looks *apprehensive*, which is bothersome to me because he looked at ease until she walked into the room.

Usage 4: All of my neighbors are *apprehensive* about the weather, as last month we had a terrible ice storm that caused widespread damage.

ARBORETUM (n)   [ahr-b*uh*-REE-t*uh* m]

Meaning: place where different tree varieties are exhibited; a place where plants are cultivated for display

Usage 1: For family pictures, the town *arboretum* is a beautiful setting complete with rose bushes and blooming plants year-round.

Usage 2: During Rick's training as a horticulturist, he spent many late nights at the *arboretum*, caring for plants.

Usage 3: The university's *arboretum* staff spent all week preparing for the spring gala, in which benefactors were able to receive private dinners in the greenhouse and tours of new exhibits.

Usage 4: The National *Arboretum* contains thousands of varieties of plants and flowers, and is a huge attraction for tourists and locals alike.

ARCANE (adj)   [ahr-KEYN]

Meaning: secret; mysterious; known only to the initiated; understood by only a few

Usage 1: Sororities are known for their *arcane* songs, handshakes, and rituals familiar only to members.

Usage 2: For some *arcane* reason, Jim and Sue decided to renovate the kitchen of their brand-new home.

Usage 3: Some believe Freud's ideas about the subconscious are *arcane*, but others hold fast to his theories.

Usage 4: Ted seemed to have some *arcane* ideas about women in the workplace, as sometimes he said women are meant to serve coffee yet he supports equal pay.

ARCHAIC (adj)   [ahr-KEY-ik]

Meaning: antiquated; of a much earlier period

Usage 1: When her grandmother died, the only family heirloom she wanted to keep was the *archaic* jug that had been in the family for generations.

Usage 2: One of my favorite childhood memories is going with my grandfather to the county fair to watch the parade of *archaic* tractors.

Usage 3: My grandfather, a Quaker since birth, frequently used *archaic* language in conversation.

Usage 4: To modern day society, laws about child labor in the 19th century seem *archaic*, but it still exists in some countries around the globe.

ARCHETYPE (n)   [AHR-ki-tahyp]

Meaning: prototype; primitive pattern; an original pattern after which other things are modeled

Usage 1: Richard loves sports, video games, beer, and women; he is the *archetype* of the typical American male.

Usage 2: Once she moved to Hollywood, she settled into the *archetype* of the starving artist, living out of her car and asking for money from strangers in between commercial auditions.

Usage 3: Sandra wasn't sure which *archetype* she fit into on the dating website - "Girl Next Door," "Trouble," or "Cosmopolitan."

ARCHIVES (n)   [AHR-kahyvs]

Meaning: public records; place where public records are kept; a collection of records

Usage 1: Professor Johnson made several trips to the university library each week to examine the first 100 years of the town *archives*.

Usage 2: Paleontologists often refer to previously-found fossils and other *archives* to draw conclusions about more recent discoveries.

Usage 3: All of these family photos from the 19th century surfaced from my great-aunt's *archives* when we went through her attic.

Usage 4: The National *Archives* are an amazing collection of all sorts of recorded documents and audio files that had some important role in American history.

ARGOT (n)   [AHR-goh]

Meaning: slang particular to a certain group

Usage 1: When they meet up for coffee or drinks, the two public policy majors often resort to political *argot* in their heated discussions.

Usage 2: I have trouble understanding the New Orleans *argot* that inevitably rules the conversation when I'm visiting my roommate's family.

Usage 3: The bulletin that accompanied the play contained a list of over 20 terms from Belfast *argot* so the audience could fully understand the dialogue.

ARID (adj)   [AR-id]

Meaning: dry; barren; dull; unimaginative; lifeless

Usage 1: Even though it was cold at nighttime, we were all parched upon wakening in the morning due to the arid air.

Usage 2: Rather than being interesting or funny, the conversations around the table at the work banquet were quite *arid*.

Usage 3: In *arid* climates it is important to protect against the dry wind, which can cause chapping almost immediately.

Usage 4: It was an *arid* summer, the city was in a drought, and we could only water our lawn every third day.

ARMADA (n)   [ahr-MAH-d*uh*]

Meaning: fleet of warships; a fleet of moving things

Usage 1: In the last leg of the race, an *armada* of sailboats rounded the bend of the lake.

Usage 2: I finally called the police, as the noise level from the *armada* of motorcyclists circling our neighborhood was disturbing my afternoon nap.

Usage 3: When the wealthy family was sued for copyright infringement, they employed an *armada* of lawyers and other associates to argue in favor of their case.

ARREARS (n)   [uh-REERZ]

Meaning: being in debt; an unpaid debt

Usage 1: The Collins family was in deep *arrears* after months of their premature twins being in the ICU and receiving top-notch medical care.

Usage 2: The bookstore finally had to close its doors to the public after years of being in *arrears*.

Usage 3: As a loan officer, Jonathan was baffled as how a family that makes a half-million dollars a year could ever get in *arrears*.

Usage 4: After graduating from college, thousands of young people find themselves in serious *arrears* before they even have a job.

ARROYO (n)   [*uh*-ROI-oh]

Meaning: a deep gully

Usage 1: Peering down into the *arroyo*, he could barely see turtles that he knew were at least a foot in diameter.

Usage 2: The cat, running toward a small mouse, had to stop suddenly when the prey leapt over the edge of an *arroyo*.

Usage 3: In the summer, the *arroyo* was deep and cracked, but following a snowy winter it ran fast with rushing water.

ARTICULATE (adj)   [ahr-TIK-y*uh*-lit]

Meaning: effective; distinct; coherent; capable of speaking easily and clearly

Usage 1: Elementary school teachers must speak *articulately* so students can understand and learn specific letter sounds.

Usage 2: The poet comes across as an *articulate* speaker, but his poems are always awkward.

Usage 3: The politician won over everyone at the benefit, as his *articulate* speech and friendly manner made all of us want him to win.

Usage 4: My feelings following the breakup were overwhelming and confusing; I wasn't sure how to *articulate* them.

ARTIFICE (n)   [AHR-t*uh*-fis]

Meaning: trickery; subtle deception

Usage 1: In order to avoid being captured by the enemy, they used the *artifice* of faking death by starvation.

Usage 2: During the race for student body president, the underdog insinuated that the opposing candidate was using *artifice* to win the election.

Usage 3: McDonald's uses the *artifice* of large images of tasty food on its windows to encourage customers to stop and eat.

ASCENDANCY (n)   [*uh*-SEN-d*uh* n-see]

Meaning: controlling influence; domination or power

Usage 1: As soon as she entered senior year of high school, Mary began enjoying her *ascendancy* over freshman girls and their tendency to admire her.

Usage 2: One of the reasons abused women have such difficulty leaving romantic relationships is that their partners have such intimidating *ascendancy* over them that the women feel helpless.

Usage 3: I remember learning in my science course that the modern-day chicken must have experienced evolutionary *ascendancy*, as they are related to dinosaurs.

Usage 4: After he was elected Pope, Pope John Paul II experienced a speedy *ascendance* to sainthood.

ASCRIBE (v) [*uh*-SKRAHYB]

Meaning: refer; assign; to attribute to a cause

Usage 1: I can *ascribe* my excellent cooking and meal preparation skills to Julia Child, who taught me everything I know.

Usage 2: In her acceptance speech, the award-winning actress *ascribed* her success to her parents and mentors.

Usage 3: I *ascribe* my dog's excellent manners and response to commands to the trainer's diligent hours spent with him.

Usage 4: As a devoted Catholic, Margaret *ascribed* her chaste lifestyle to everything she learned in church.

ASININE (adj) [AS-*uh*-nahyn]

Meaning: utterly stupid or foolish; failing to exercise good judgment

Usage 1: Her husband is a smart man, but often does *asinine* things like stay out late without calling.

Usage 2: The burglar made an *asinine* mistake by forgetting to wear gloves and leaving his cell phone on the counter of the house.

Usage 3: It is completely *asinine* to think that if you delete your browsing history, anyone with some computer knowledge couldn't look up what you've been doing online.

ASKANCE (adj) [*uh*-SKANS]

Meaning: with a sideways or indirect look; with suspicion or disapproval

Usage 1: Mary looked *askance* at her boyfriend as he tried to engage her mother in a conversation about crochet.

Usage 2: The little boy sometimes curses, then looks *askance* at his teachers to see if they are paying attention.

Usage 3: The dog looked *askance* at her owner to see if she was looking, then quickly stole the drumstick right off the counter.

ASKEW (adj) [*uh*-SKYOO]

Meaning: slanted; awry; crooked or tilted to one side

Usage 1: Even though her hat was *askew*, Lila looked beautiful and composed.

Usage 2: The earthquake was relatively mild, though afterward all the framed pictures on the wall were *askew*.

Usage 3: After running through the downpour, his jacket was soaked and his hair was *askew*.

Usage 4: Each time I come back home after a trip to Europe, my internal time clock is *askew* and I feel completely disoriented for several days.

ASPERITY (n) [*uh*-SPER-i-tee]

Meaning: sharpness (of temper); roughness, harshness, or rudeness

Usage 1: Nick took after his father, as he shouted at his wife with such *asperity* that even the neighbors could hear.

Usage 2: It's like walking on eggshells every time I step into English class, as lately the professor has a short temper and yells with *asperity*.

Usage 3: When Tracy ran into her ex-husband at a friend's party, she first tried to act nice but then stated with *asperity* that she hoped "life was working out for him."

ASSAIL (v) [*uh*-SEYL]

Meaning: assault; to attack, particularly with words or thoughts

Usage 1: During the political debate, the two most popular candidates *assailed* each other with such intensity the moderator was obliged to intervene.

Usage 2: Throughout the murder trial, the main suspect was *assailed* with questions from the media each time he tried to leave his house.

Usage 3: Ever since he was diagnosed with skin cancer, intrusive thoughts and fears about dying *assailed* him.

Usage 4: The terrorists *assailed* over 50 people and set off bombs all around the city.

ASTEROID (n)   [AS-t*uh*-roid]

Meaning: small planet; star-shaped; a celestial body that revolves around the sun

Usage 1: One of my favorite things about science class was learning about *asteroids* and an existence of objects outside my own, known world.

Usage 2: Some geologists claim that *asteroids* are responsible for decimating the dinosaur population millions of years ago.

Usage 3: Little George got a telescope for his eighth birthday, and makes nightly searches for *asteroids*.

ASTIGMATISM (n)   [*uh*-STIG-m*uh*-tiz-*uh* m]

Meaning: eye defect that prevents proper focus; a defect causing blurry vision

Usage 1: Due to Sue's worsening *astigmatism*, she is no longer able to drive.

Usage 2: My grandmother has *astigmatism,* which is due to the fact that the eye does not always have a perfectly spherical shape.

Usage 3: Laser vision correction can correct *astigmatism* as well as less-complicated vision problems.

ASTRINGENT (adj)   [*uh*-STRIN-j*uh* nt]

Meaning: binding; causing contraction; sharp or severe

Usage 1: After getting in trouble during the school day, the young child cowered under his father's *astringent* comments.

Usage 2: Teenagers are known for their *astringent* judgments of others, resulting in bullying and outcasts in high school.

Usage 3: Rather than sweet, fruity wines, Raymond liked dry *astringent* wines.

Usage 4: She was often put off by the *astringent* customs of her native country, and yearned for a freer society.

ASUNDER (adv)   [*uh*-SUHN-der]

Meaning: into parts; apart; in separate pieces

Usage 1: After they both lost their high-paying jobs, their marriage was full of conflict and torn *asunder*.

Usage 2: The five-year-old was so angry that he was not allowed to play video games after bedtime that he threw his books and games on the floor and tore his room *asunder*.

Usage 3: The United States' Civil War created division, generated the loss of thousands of lives, and tore the nation *asunder*.

Usage 4: Jodie's parents' divorce tore the entire family *asunder*, even grandparents and uncles.

ASYMMETRIC (adj)   [ey-s*uh*-ME-trik]

Meaning: not identical on both sides of a dividing central line; having no balance

Usage 1: His face is quite *asymmetric* but even though his looks aren't perfect I still think he's handsome.

Usage 2: Jane was wearing an off-kilter, *asymmetric* hat, but even though it was unconventional she somehow managed to pull off the look.

Usage 3: Asymmetric polarization occurs when Republicans and Democrats are not equally liberal or conservative, creating unbalanced opposites.

Usage 4: Asymmetric warfare is war between two sides whose tactics or strategies differ significantly.

ATAVISM (n) [AT-*uh*-viz-*uh* m]

Meaning: resemblance to remote ancestors rather than to parents; deformity returning after passage of two or more generations; the reappearance of a characteristic after absence in several generations

Usage 1: In many high-end restaurants, culinary *atavism* is resurfacing as wild ingredients such as chickweed are being served on the menu.

Usage 2: My mother says I'm resorting to *atavism* when I insist on only eating three meals every day, as my great grandmother did.

Usage 3: Thanks to *atavism*, the modern day three-toed sloth originated from the dinosaurs.

ATHEISTIC (adj) [ey-thee-IS-tik]

Meaning: denying the existence of god; disbelieving the existence of a god

Usage 1: I grew up going to church every Sunday, so the idea of an *atheistic* way of thinking was essentially not an option.

Usage 2: Polls have shown that, over time, Americans are more and more willing to consider an *atheistic*

lifestyle and to vote for an atheist President.

Usage 3: Atheistic groups of people have protested many times in our town while monthly town council meetings begin in prayer.

Usage 4: Even though June grew up as a Protestant Christian and continues to go to Bible study every week, she is married to an *atheistic* man.

ATROCITY (n) [*uh*-TROS-i-tee]

Meaning: brutal deed; appalling behavior

Usage 1: The entire town took years to recover from the *atrocity* of the mayor brutally murdering his wife.

Usage 2: The Republican senator lectures the legislature about raises in taxes, abortion, and other *atrocities* for which the Democrats are responsible.

Usage 3: I am not surprised by any *atrocity* these days, as exposure to the media has left us numb to the brutalities that exist in the world.

ATTEST (v) [*uh*-TEST]

Meaning: testify; bear witness; to affirm to be correct

Usage 1: I can *attest* that Mr. Jones is the best piano teacher around; he taught me to play Beethoven in only a few weeks.

Usage 2: Most women can *attest* that childbirth is the most painful yet also the most gratifying experience of their lives.

Usage 3: As those of you who have seen my garden can *attest*, I do not have a green thumb.

Usage 4: After watching the first round of the tennis championship, we all can *attest* to the fact that she needs to continue practicing her serve.

ATTRIBUTE (v) [A-tr*uh*-byoot]

Meaning: ascribe; explain; to relate to a cause

Usage 1: Meteorologists *attribute* the extreme winter of 2014 to typical cycles in weather patterns.

Usage 2: Susanna *attributed* her popularity to her outgoing personality rather than her long legs and good looks, as some others had mentioned.

Usage 3: I can *attribute* my laidback personality to my father, but my general lack of motivation I got from my dog.

Usage 4: Laney *attributed* the messy kitchen counter to her lazy husband, then later learned that her 6-year-old daughter had cooked her own breakfast.

ATYPICAL (adj)   [ey-TIP-i-k*uh* l]

Meaning: not normal; unusual or abnormal

Usage 1: Winters in North Carolina are typically mild, so it was *atypical* to have four major snowstorms in one season.

Usage 2: Their relationship is *atypical* of any between a younger man and older woman; she caters to his every need while he lounges around the house.

Usage 3: Atypical antipsychotic drugs, such as Seroquel, are now used more often than their predecessors to treat symptoms of psychosis.

Usage 4: Mary showed me her *atypical* flower arrangement - eleven white roses with one bright purple hydrangea.

Usage 5: The family - a couple with three young children - was *atypical* for that part of the city, but ended up fitting right in.

AUGMENT (v)   [awg-MENT]

Meaning: to increase or add to

Usage 1: One day, we will all have computers that will serve to *augment* our memories.

Usage 2: His rock band was *augmented* by a saxophone and euphonium.

Usage 3: They finally decided to *augment* their family with one more child.

AUGURY (n)   [AW-gy*uh*-ree]

Meaning: prophecy; a sign of things to come in the future; an omen

Usage 1: Our local baseball team has lost every game out of the first ten, an *augury* of things to come this season.

Usage 2: While the couple was looking at the house up for sale a huge strike of lightning hit a tree in the yard, which they interpreted to be an *augury* and immediately left.

Usage 3: Troops seemed to believe that the battle victory was a good *augury* for the entire war.

Usage 4: Some people believe that letting a black cat cross your path is an *augury* of bad luck.

AUREOLE (n)   [AWR-ee-ohl]

Meaning: sun's corona; halo; radiant light or halo surrounding the head of a person or animal

Usage 1: Medieval artists are known for painting people with *aureoles* behind their heads.

Usage 2: In a parody of a painting of Herod, the humorous artist included an *aureole* around his head.

Usage 3: After giving birth, the new mother seemed to have a kind of *aureole*, as if she had a glow around her.

Usage 4: In the sky following sunset, the ring of fire was an *aureole* surrounding the cat as it jumped through soundlessly.

AUSPICIOUS (adj)   [aw-SPISH-*uh* s]

Meaning: favoring success; faring well for the future; propitious; indicating that good things are to come

Usage 1: The day after his graduation, Mark received an *auspicious* phone call inviting to interview with one of the top firms in the country.

Usage 2: The *auspicious* story of the prodigal son is one which teaches readers that forgiveness is key.

Usage 3: The state legislature met again today, an *auspicious* sign that negotiations are being made to decrease the income tax rate.

AUTHENTICATE (v)   [aw-THEN-ti-keyt]

Meaning: prove genuine; to establish as correct or genuine

Usage 1: There are numerous companies in America whose main objective is to *authenticate* artwork in order to prevent fraudulent pieces from being sold at auctions.

Usage 2: George's doctor has not yet been able to *authenticate* the specific type of cancer George has, though he hopes to be able to pinpoint it soon.

Usage 3: Because his license could not be *authenticated*, Dr. Jones was no longer allowed to work at his practice anymore.

Usage 4: Because he was unable to *authenticate* the origins of the essay, Dr. Jones elected not to include it in his syllabus materials.

Usage 5: He tried desperately to *authenticate* that his love for Sandy was real, but ultimately she left him for someone else.

AUTOMATON (n)   [aw-TOM-*uh*-ton]

Meaning: mechanism that imitates actions of humans; a self-operating machine or robot

Usage 1: After she lost the election, Sylvia was no longer the *automaton* lecturing about tax reform and abortion.

Usage 2: The movie's plot was about zombie-like *automatons* who defy the typical laws of mating and reproduction.

Usage 3: One of my favorite movies is about an *automaton* that falls in love with a human.

AUTOPSY (n)   [AW-top-see]

Meaning: examination of a dead body; post-mortem; an examination to confirm the cause of death

Usage 1: An *autopsy* is planned for tomorrow to confirm the suspicion that death was the result of an overdose.

Usage 2: An *autopsy* has determined that the woman overdosed on cocaine and prescription drugs when she died in her apartment last week.

Usage 3: Even though everyone knew the horse died of a severe heart problem, an *autopsy* was required to be performed for insurance purposes.

Usage 4: The *autopsy* revealed that the cause of death was a heart attack, rather than a seizure as first suspected.

AVALANCHE (n)   [av-*uh*-lanch]

Meaning: great mass of falling snow and ice; a massive or overwhelming amount

Usage 1: Following her safe return home after being kidnapped for days, Ashley received an *avalanche* of mail on a daily basis.

Usage 2: Near one of the most dangerous parts of the mountain, Rosa witnessed the *avalanche* coming down the mountain and burying people in its wake.

Usage 3: When the convicted murdered stepped outside the courtroom, he was pummeled with an *avalanche* of questions and insults by the media.

AVENGE (v)   [*uh*-venj]

Meaning: take vengeance for something; inflict punishment by inflicting something on the wrong-doer

Usage 1: The first thing I wanted to do when I got home and saw that eggs were thrown at my house was *avenge* the egg-thrower by doing something far worse.

Usage 2: The problem with children is that they are too forgiving; they forget about being wronged too easily and rarely *avenge* those who steal their toys or bite them.

Usage 3: I love the classic stories of abused women who *avenge* their alcoholic husbands by making their lives miserable.

AVERT (v)   [*uh*-VURT]

Meaning: to prevent; to turn away

Usage 1: In order to *avert* an outbreak of the norovirus at the hospital, masks were required for all staff members.

Usage 2: If someone suspects child abuse, it is best to call the authorities immediately to *avert* future incidents of harm to the child.

Usage 3: The conflict could have been *averted* if she had only kept her thoughts to herself.

AVOCATION (n)   [av-*uh*-KEY-sh*uh* n]

Meaning: secondary or minor occupation; a hobby or recreational activity

Usage 1: Even though I'm a banker by day, my main *avocation* is gardening.

Usage 2: Since I've become a mother of very young children, all my *avocations* - running, reading, and playing Bingo - have suffered.

Usage 3: Some people say that the key to enjoying your work and career is to have at least one *avocation* about which you are passionate.

Usage 4: Even though Mr. Smith was a scientist by profession, his *avocation* is rehearsing with his rock band every week and performing gigs around town.

AVUNCULAR (adj)   [*uh*-VUHNG-ky*uh*-ler]

Meaning: like an uncle; kind or benevolent

Usage 1: My pastor is an *avuncular* and gentle man, who is kind to everyone he meets.

Usage 2: Donald Rumsfield is often thought of as an *avuncular* politician, likeable and approachable by the general public.

Usage 3: My teacher is an easygoing, *avuncular* guy who always has a joke but never makes us feel uncomfortable.

AXIOM (n)   [AK-see-*uh* m]

Meaning: self-evident truth, requiring no proof; a universally accepted rule

Usage 1: One of my favorite *axioms* is: "It doesn't matter if you win or lose, but how you play the game."

Usage 2: David annoyed others to no end with his constant use of *axioms* in daily conversation instead of his own words.

Usage 3: She lived by *axioms* taken from others rather than living by her own experiences and wisdom.

Usage 4: "Through a pair of distinct points passes a straight line" is an *axiom* well-known to millions of mathematics students.

AZURE (adj)   [AZH-er]

Meaning: sky blue; light, purplish blue color

Usage 1: Mike loved the Midwest for its swaying cornfields, *azure* skies, and friendly people.

Usage 2: Her eyes were a strange color - not quite cyan, and not quite blue, but two *azure* windows into a pure and loving soul.

Usage 3: The movie star wore an elegant dress made of *azure* chiffon, which was striking but not as overwhelming as the magenta and gold mini dresses of her counterparts.

BACCHANALIAN (adj)   [bak-*uh*-NEY-lee-*uh* n] *Meaning:* drunken; relating to the festival of Bacchus

Usage 1: I left the party just as the atmosphere started to become wild and *bacchanalian*.

Usage 2: When she was in college she enjoyed the *bacchanalian* lifestyle, but she is ready to get married and have children now.

Usage 3: The *bacchanalian* atmosphere of New Orleans during Mardi Gras is one I've never wanted to see, as I enjoy quiet gatherings rather than rowdy crowds.

Usage 4: You would think that a retirement community would have a calm, quiet atmosphere, but it actually has a *bacchanalian* flavor to it, with lots of partying and calls from the police.

BADINAGE (n)   [bad-n-AHZH]

Meaning: teasing conversation; playful banter

Usage 1: As the senator's ratings plummeted, he continued to use self-deprecating *badinage* when giving interviews to the press as a way of making light of the situation.

Usage 2: Steven tried to lighten the mood by engaging in *badinage,* but this only served to make his companions more skeptical of his character.

Usage 3: The play was highly enjoyable and full of *badinage* as characters laughed and made fun of each other.

BALEFUL (adj)   [BEYL-*fuh* l]

Meaning: deadly; having a malign influence; ominous; intending to be harmful

Usage 1: Sue gave her boss a *baleful* look after Sue was told that she was required to work the entire holiday weekend.

Usage 2: During the trial, the mother of the boy killed in the car accident stared at the defendant with a *baleful* glare.

Usage 3: The years of the American civil war cast a *baleful* shadow on the success of the United States to work out differences without resorting to violence.

BALLAST (n)   [BAL-*uh* st]

Meaning: heavy substance used to add stability or weight; something that gives stability and weight

Usage 1: I was afraid of going on the hot air balloon ride, and my nerves weren't relieved even after the pilot explained that the *ballast* provides stability.

Usage 2: The interim president of the hospital provided short-term *ballast* to the corrupt politics that have existed between administration and direct care staff for decades.

Usage 3: My little motor boat always needs someone to sit opposite the engine as *ballast* to prevent it from rolling over.

This page is intentionally left blank

Chapter 22

Bandy – Colloquial

This chapter covers the following words, each with its part of speech, pronunciation, and descriptive meaning.

Usage of the word is also illustrated in three to five sample sentences.

bandy	clairvoyant	cognitive
bane	clamber	cognizance
barb	clamor	cohabit
blurt	clangor	cohorts
bohemian	clarion	coiffure
bouillon	claustrophobia	colander
brunt	clavicle	collaborate
brusque	cleave	collage
buccaneer	cleft	collate
bucolic	clemency	colloquial
buffoonery	cliché	
bulwark	climactic	
bungle	clime	
burlesque	clique	
burly	cloister	
chary	clout	
chase	codicil	
chastened	coeval	
cipher	cogitate	
citadel	cognate	

BANDY (v)   [BAN-dee]

Meaning: discuss lightly or glibly; exchange (words) heatedly; to exchange back and forth

Usage 1: The US Open finals are some of the best tennis matches to watch, and often spectators can see the ball *bandied* for several minutes at a time.

Usage 2: Caroline and Josephine get together monthly to chat and *bandy* gossip.

Usage 3: The twin sisters never seemed to stop *bandying* insults and sarcastic remarks, even when around other people.

BANE (n)   [beyn]

Meaning: curse; cause of injury or ruin

Usage 1: My study group has been more of a *bane* than a boon for my test grades, as we usually just end up talking about everything other than the course material.

Usage 2: Gambling was the *bane* of Jimmy's existence; he loved it so much that it ruined his marriage, job, and finances.

Usage 3: His *bane* was the severe depression which ran in his family, and seemed to affect him as well.

Usage 4: That narrow cliffside trail straight up the mountain is the *bane* of all who hike there.

BARB (n)   [bahrb]

Meaning: sharp projection from fish-hook, etc; a cutting remark

Usage 1: Chile and Argentina traded *barbs* over Pascua-Lama mine, as Chile is in support of blocking work on the mine and Argentina is highly critical.

Usage 2: After years of her older sister's *barbs* about Cassie marrying and having children while in high school, Cassie stopped speaking to her sister all together.

Usage 3: You must be careful when fishing, as the tiny *barbs* on the fish-hooks can catch your fingers and cause injury.

Usage 4: The political candidate threw back some *barbs* at his opponent on his campaign commercials, accusing him of accepting bribes.

BLURT (v)   [blurt]

Meaning: utter impulsively; to utter suddenly

Usage 1: Before he began taking medication for impulsivity, little Benji would *blurt* out answers constantly in class rather than waiting for the teacher to call on him.

Usage 2: Jeffrey *blurted* out at the Thanksgiving table, "But I'm gay, Dad!" which stopped everyone in mid-conversation.

Usage 3: He *blurted* out, "But I love you!" to his date as she turned angrily away from him following an argument.

Usage 4: It was extremely difficult to get through a live recording of the quiz show, as almost once every show a member of the audience would *blurt* out the answer before one of the contestants.

BOHEMIAN (adj)   [boh-HEE-mee-*uh* n]

Meaning: unconventional, particularly in habits, dress, or artistic interests

Usage 1: The Haight-Ashbury district of San Francisco is known for its *bohemian* inhabitants, who wear hippie-style clothing, smoke marijuana, and sleep in parks at night.

Usage 2: He took a *bohemian* approach to teaching, allowing students to choose their own assignments and grade each other's work.

Usage 3: We spent the night in a *bohemian* town, where residents make their own granola and soap and frown at anyone who shops at big-box stores.

BOUILLON (n)   [BOO L-yon]

Meaning: clear beef soup

Usage 1: It's amazing that a soup so delicious can be made from only a few vegetables, herbs, and *bouillon*.

Usage 2: Even though Emma is mostly a vegetarian, she eats soups and stews made with chicken *bouillon*.

Usage 3: When suffering from a cold or stomach virus, one of the best foods to eat is *bouillon*, as it is easy on the stomach and replaces lost electrolytes.

BRUNT (n)   [bruhnt]

Meaning: main impact or shock

Usage 1: The family dog often took the *brunt* of Clive's aggression, as Clive tended to kick the dog whenever he was frustrated.

Usage 2: Our little town always seems to take the *brunt* of the bad weather, and surrounding areas never get as much snow or rain.

Usage 3: The local police seem to take the *brunt* of jokes, as they typically hang out in doughnut shops and never seem to actually solve any crimes.

Usage 4: The basketball star's finger bore the *brunt* of the impact when the ball was thrown at his hand.

Usage 5: State employees bear the *brunt* of political matches, as it is their salaries and benefits that lay on the line.

BRUSQUE (adj)   [bruhsk]

Meaning: blunt; abrupt and curt in speech

Usage 1: Margie ended the conversation with Jim with the *brusque* remark, "I suppose we can agree to disagree," then walked away.

Usage 2: In uncharacteristic fashion, Todd was *brusque* in the meeting rather than appeasing everyone else and allowing conversations to go on for hours.

Usage 3: He has a short-tempered and *brusque* personality.

Usage 4: As soon as he realized his favorite football team was going to lose the championship game, his good-natured personality disappeared and he became *brusque* and irritable.

BUCCANEER (n)   [buhk-*uh*-NEER]

Meaning: a pirate or ruthless adventurer

Usage 1: The little boy enjoyed building forts and pretending he was a *buccaneer*, raiding ships for treasure.

Usage 2: In true *buccaneer* American fashion, Billy sold his home and moved out west, where he believed he could get cheaper land and a better job.

Usage 3: Captain Hook is one of the best *buccaneer* movies around, and its parody of the pirate lifestyle is clever and humorous.

BUCOLIC (adj)   [byoo-KOL-ik]

Meaning: rustic, pastoral, or like the country

Usage 1: Visiting Vermont in the summer is so peaceful, with its *bucolic* farms and charming covered bridges.

Usage 2: Teddy had a difficult time transitioning from urban life in the city to quiet streets and *bucolic* neighborhoods.

Usage 3: The wedding was perfect - it was held on a breezy fall day, by a *bucolic* covered bridge in Vermont.

Usage 4: Just a quick ride over the Golden Gate Bridge takes you to the *bucolic* town of Sausalito, complete with seaside homes and small ice cream shops.

BUFFOONERY (n)   [b*uh*-FOO-n*uh*-ree]

Meaning: clowning; foolishness and silliness, such as ridiculous pranks

Usage 1: I have never seen such *buffoonery* as that which took place in class today when it was covered by a new substitute teacher.

Usage 2: Unfortunately, much of what occurs during fraternity initiations are pranks, excessive drinking, and overall *buffoonery*.

Usage 3: May was so enamored by Bruce, her new husband, that she never blinked an eye at his *buffoonery*.

BULWARK (n)   [B*OO* L-werk]

Meaning: earthwork or other strong defense; person who defends; a defensive fortification

Usage 1: Amy attempted to create a *bulwark* against her opponent by starting rumors and turning the bulk of voters against him.

Usage 2: The developing nation's new government is hoping to be a *bulwark* against future corruption and terrorism.

Usage 3: The conservative government offered state employees a raise in salary and benefits, which they hoped would be a *bulwark* against widespread protest as the Medicaid budget was slashed in half.

BUNGLE (v)   [BUHNG-g*uh* l]

Meaning: mismanage; blunder; to act clumsily

Usage 1: Unfortunately for the US senator, he *bungled* the press conference and left his supporters defensive and embarrassed.

Usage 2: Cierra seriously *bungled* her cheerleading tryouts by falling repeatedly while doing pyramids and straining her hamstring while doing jumps.

Usage 3: I have it on good authority that the typo in the local paper was *bungled* and will be corrected tomorrow.

Usage 4: Recently, prisons have *bungled* many executions in which prisoners have died clearly while in pain.

BURLESQUE (v)   [ber-LESK]

Meaning: give an imitation that ridicules; to imitate mockingly

Usage 1: Jackson was always bringing home items of no value home to his wife and children, as if he were burlesquing his role as a provider.

Usage 2: The entire play *burlesqued* the high school experience, complete with cheerleaders dating football players and partying the night before the SATs.

Usage 3: The 'mockumentary' *burlesqued* the entire industry of dog shows and made those who spend lots of time and energy on them seem like fools.

BURLY (adj)   [BUR-lee]

Meaning: husky; strong and muscular

Usage 1: She always dates *burly* men who are the polar opposite of her small-statured, un-athletic father.

Usage 2: The college football team was composed of *burly* men who never came to class but could bench press twice their weight.

Usage 3: When creating her profile for the online dating website, Sherri had no concerns with stating that she was looking only for an athletic, *burly* match.

Usage 4: His little sports car was pushed off the exit ramp by a *burly* SUV.

CHARY (adj)   [CHAIR-ee]

Meaning: sparing or restrained about giving; very cautious, careful, or wary

Usage 1: I am often *chary* about signing up for activities I know I might not be good at doing.

Usage 2: The little girl has been *chary* about starting Kindergarten for weeks; she asks her parents questions numerous times a day and has been having a few nightmares about school.

Usage 3: I am terribly *chary* about giving out my phone number, as several years ago I was near-stalked by a complete stranger.

CHASE (v)   [cheys]

Meaning: ornament a metal surface by indenting; to cut a groove into an object

Usage 1: In art school, James learned how to *chase* by locking up lead type for letterpress printing.

Usage 2: When newspapers were made on printing presses, it took specialized training to *chase* by accurately placing characters onto the newsprint.

Usage 3: Ever since the digital age, the art of *chase* in news printing has drastically gone underappreciated.

CHASTENED (adj)   [CHEY-s*uh* n]

Meaning: humbled; subdued; rebuked; corrected

Usage 1: The mother *chastened* her little boy for running into the road and forgetting to knock on the bathroom door.

Usage 2: I feel like I deserve to be *chastened*, as I make so many mistakes at work I'm not sure what else would help me improve.

Usage 3: The autobiographer of JFK was sufficiently *chastened* after revealing secrets that had not yet been brought to the public's attention.

Usage 4: The father *chastened* his children by forcing them to stand in a line and recite poems for hours.

CIPHER (n)   [SAHY-fer]

Meaning: secret code; a secret message

Usage 1: Every time Terra and Derek get together, they speak in *cipher* which is very frustrating for anyone around them.

Usage 2: I despise calculus; all those formulas are like *cipher* to me.

Usage 3: Concerned that someone in administration might overhear, the employees spoke guardedly in *cipher* between themselves.

CITADEL (n)   [SIT-*uh*-dl]

Meaning: a strong fortress that sits high above or near a city

Usage 1: The *citadel* in the play about the duchess and dragon was lined by a moat.

Usage 2: A *citadel* served as the basis for the city's army, as it contained hundreds of hiding places and provided a view of many miles.

Usage 3: When I think of dragons, I always imagine a stone *citadel* complete with princess, a moat, and lots of knights on horses.

Usage 4: The little boy loved to play pretend, and imagined he was living in a *citadel* responsible for protecting his fortress.

Usage 5: Living in this neighborhood would be a lot easier if we could turn this house into a *citadel* that provides safety against robbers and vandals.

CLAIRVOYANT (adj)   [klair-VOI-*uh* nt]

Meaning: having foresight; fortune-teller; able to see the future

Usage 1: Rather than basing her conclusion on concrete evidence, Detective Simmons had a *clairvoyant* surge of insight as to who might be the boy's killer.

Usage 2: Millie and Bill know each other so well that they have *clairvoyant* moments when they know what the other is thinking.

Usage 3: Charlotte spends her weekends touring with carnivals and fairs, using her *clairvoyant* crystal ball to convince people her predictions are worth the money.

Usage 4: My mother's *clairvoyant* prediction that my marriage would not last longer than five years was wrong; I have been married to John for twenty.

CLAMBER (v)   [KLAM-ber]

Meaning: climb by crawling; a climb with difficulty

Usage 1: Two-year-olds are mastering the skill of climbing, and it is not abnormal to see them *clamber* up piles of rocks or dirt.

Usage 2: In my nightmare, I am forced to choose between *clambering* up a rocky cliff or be eaten alive by alligators.

Usage 3: As an airplane flew by, the toddlers *clambered* from their seats to the window to watch it fly by.

Usage 4: I love that obstacle show on television in which ordinary people *clamber* up muddy slopes and face other obstacles for one million dollars.

Usage 5: The fast food restaurant business is brilliant for building play structures for children to *clamber* on while their parents relax.

CLAMOR (n)   [KLAM-er]

Meaning: loud noise or chaos

Usage 1: I heard the *clamor* in the living room, and when I went to see what the noise was about I found a squirrel in the center of the room, the dog blocking the doorway.

Usage 2: You would think that a second-grade band concert would just be a *clamor* of sound, but it actually was quite good.

Usage 3: The teenager made a *clamor* of asking for a raise in his allowance, but because he wouldn't agree to more chores, the pay remained the same.

Usage 4: Republics in our state created a *clamor* for drastic changes during the last election, but I have yet to see any true differences.

CLANGOR (n)   [KLANG-er]

Meaning: loud, resounding noise; a loud racket or sharp sound

Usage 1: Working in the bowels of the ship exposed Jim to *clangor* as the engine worked.

Usage 2: I love playing percussion instruments, but the *clangor* can sometimes give me a headache.

Usage 3: Once it was declared that the war was over, the celebratory *clangor* could be heard for miles.

Usage 4: Some days I yearn for the time when the *clangor* of the digital age did not interfere with my daily living.

Usage 5: In order to prevent wildcats from invading the campsite, the hikes created a great *clangor*.

CLARION (adj)   [KLAR-ee-*uh* n]

Meaning: shrill; loud and clear, like the sound of a trumpet

Usage 1: The trumpeter was able to produce a *clarion* sound despite the fact he hadn't played in months.

Usage 2: The candidate's *clarion* message was heard by all; he wanted higher taxes and lower governmental interference in business policies.

Usage 3: The organ's *clarion* tone was known worldwide for its beauty and depth.

CLAUSTROPHOBIA (n)   [klaw-str*uh*-FOH-bee-*uh*]

Meaning: fear of enclosed spaces

Usage 1: I have had *claustrophobia* for as long as I can remember; I cannot bring myself to ride an elevator.

Usage 2: His *claustrophobia* probably originated from his early traumatic experiences of being shut in a closet for hours by his siblings.

Usage 3: As Gilbert gets older, his *claustrophobia* has become so bad that he will not get on an airplane.

Usage 4: I think my cat has *claustrophobia*; she yowls and scratches every time I place her in her carrier.

Usage 5: Claustrophobia often strikes people who are naturally anxious, as it prevents people from gaining control over the situation and makes them feel trapped.

CLAVICLE (n)   [KLAV-i-k*uh* l]

Meaning: collarbone; the bone at the top of the chest between the base of the neck and the shoulder

Usage 1: The equine therapist broke her *clavicle* when she was thrown from a young horse onto the ground, and landed on her chest.

Usage 2: Raymond gave his new bride a delicate silver necklace with a charm that lay on top of her *clavicle*.

Usage 3: I don't know how to swim, but I am comfortable with the water coming up to my *clavicle* when I'm in a pool or the ocean.

Usage 4: The football player took a hard hit to the chest, though thanks to the padding his *clavicle* remained unharmed.

CLEAVE (v)   [kleev]

Meaning: split or sever; cling to; remain faithful to

Usage 1: The black labrador retriever *cleaved* to its owner until its death, sleeping on the bedroom floor and always glad to see him walk through the door.

Usage 2: When Gillian's boyfriend told her he wanted to see other people, she felt as if her heart had been cleaved in half.

Usage 3: There is an infinite number of issues that can *cleave* a political party, taxes being only one of them.

Usage 4: When a man and woman marry, some say they are *cleaved* for the rest of their lives.

CLEFT (adj)   [kleft]

Meaning: divided, split, or halved into two parts

Usage 1: Jay Leno is known for his *cleft* chin, which gives him a friendly and unique appearance.

Usage 2: When the tissues forming the upper lip do not join in the middle correctly, someone is said to have a *cleft* palate.

Usage 3: There are many nonprofit organizations, including Operation Smile, which bring doctors to Third World countries to perform surgery for free on people with *cleft* palates.

CLEMENCY (n)   [KLEM-*uh* n-see]

Meaning: disposition to be lenient; mildness, as of the weather; a merciful act; mildness of temper

Usage 1: He was a forgiving person, and no one was surprised to hear that he gave *clemency* instead of revenge to his daughter's killer.

Usage 2: Unfortunately, the government does not typically act out of *clemency* but of justice.

Usage 3: The *clemency* of the Southern California climate is one reason Ashley and her family decided to stay.

CLICHÉ (n)   [klee-SHEY]

Meaning: phrase dulled in meaning by repetition; an overused expression

Usage 1: It is considered *cliché* in this town to speak of personal vegetable gardens; the new trend is to support local farms.

Usage 2: It might sound *cliché*, but I love you more than I ever thought I could.

Usage 3: The most interesting thing about *clichés* is they continue to appear despite the fact that people seem to feel the need to apologize for them.

Usage 4: I try to avoid *cliché* expressions, but they are so pervasive in the English language it is difficult not to use them.

CLIMACTIC (adj)   [klahy-MAK-tik]

Meaning: relating to the highest point; reaching a decisive moment

Usage 1: Wanda was reaching the most *climactic* point in the novel, and was so engrossed in the book she didn't even flinch when the bell rang.

Usage 2: After weeks of hiking, the group of young men and women were finally in a day's walk of the *climactic* peak of the mountain.

Usage 3: I love dramatic mysteries for their *climactic* endings and suspenseful plots.

Usage 4: The couple's argument reached a *climactic* point, as the entire neighborhood could hear their shouts and insults.

Usage 5: My day was rather anti-*climactic*; while I had anticipated a phone call from the company offering me a job, my phone didn't ring once.

CLIME (n)   [klahym]

Meaning: climate; geographical region or area

Usage 1: I love the mild, temperate *clime* of North Carolina - not too cold in the winter or too hot in the summer.

Usage 2: Because Alexa was heading to the frigid *clime* of northern Maine, she bought boots, extra socks and gloves, and long underwear for the trip.

Usage 3: The *clime* of tropical cruises is sublime, though I also like the adventure and sight-seeing of European cruises.

Usage 4: During the summer, I spent three months in the mild *clime* of southern Sweden.

CLIQUE (n)   [kleek]

Meaning: small, exclusive group

Usage 1: One of the things I hated most about high school was the *cliques*, none of which I ever seemed to be a part.

Usage 2: That church seems friendly at first, but I've heard that it's full of *cliques* and difficult to make friends there.

Usage 3: Nora's *clique* was one that believed themselves prettier and better than all others.

Usage 4: *Cliques* can be helpful if the individuals in them support one another rather than pass judgments.

Usage 5: My cats walk around in the neighborhood in their own little *clique*, never separating from the group to greet neighbors and casting unfriendly glances in other cats' directions.

CLOISTER (n) [KLOI-ster]

Meaning: monastery or convent; secluded place

Usage 1: When she was feeling overwhelmed by life, Lisa made a special trip to the *cloisters* where she could gather her thoughts and spend some time alone.

Usage 2: On Sunday afternoons, I like to go on walks through the *cloister* of woods near my home to prepare myself for the next week.

Usage 3: After a life left open to the scrutiny of the public, he retired to a *cloister* in the mountains where he could go outside without being ambushed by media.

Usage 4: This meeting will consist of hundreds of educational professionals in a *cloister* of a hotel, talking school politics and art lessons.

CLOUT (n) [klout]

Meaning: great influence (especially political or social) over a large group of people

Usage 1: Due to her family's ancestry, the woman was able to exert great *clout* over the politicians as she lobbied for higher pay among teachers.

Usage 2: My co-workers and I lack any *clout* with the administration, and our ideas are often brushed aside.

Usage 3: Latin America lacks the economic *clout* of China, but the region is beginning to emerge as a source of many goods.

Usage 4: It can be difficult to gain admission to exclusive universities for students who lack any type of *clout* with admissions personnel.

CODICIL (n) [KOD-*uh*-s*uh* l]

Meaning: supplement to the body of a will; addition to a will

Usage 1: In her *codicil*, Andie made sure to add the antique car she just acquired.

Usage 2: My mother and I had a conversation last week about any final *codicils* she should add to her will before she dies.

Usage 3: After he was diagnosed with cancer, Jerry reviewed his will to make sure there were no *codicils* he needed to make before his death.

COEVAL (adj) [koh-EE-v*uh* l]

Meaning: living at the same time as; contemporary; living during the same period

Usage 1: If I was *coeval* with Michelangelo, I would do everything in my power to obtain an apprenticeship with him.

Usage 2: It is difficult to imagine what it would be like to be *coeval* with powerful rulers such as Alexander the Great.

Usage 3: If you want to avoid divorce, you must know that disagreements are *coeval* with marriage.

COGITATE (v) [KOJ-i-teyt]

Meaning: think over; to think deeply

Usage 1: Rather than *cogitate* over the math assignment, roger completed the worksheet right away.

Usage 2: Andrea spent so much time *cogitating* over the menu that everyone else's food arrived before she even placed her order.

Usage 3: Our town council has been *cogitating* for years about whether or not to join the mass transit system, and they still haven't made a final decision.

COGNATE (adj)   [KOG-neyt]

Meaning: related linguistically; allied by blood; similar or akin in nature; related closely

Usage 1: Social work is *cognate* to psychology in that both fields are related to the state of human thoughts and emotions.

Usage 2: Even though ice cream and gelato are *cognate*, there is something about gelato that makes me crave it much more than ice cream.

Usage 3: Laura wanted to enter a *cognate* discipline for her studies, such as anthropology or psychology.

COGNITIVE (adj)   [KOG-ni-tiv]

Meaning: having to do with knowing or perceiving; related to the mental processes; related to mental functioning

Usage 1: Cognitively she is above-average, but her achievement skills in school are very low.

Usage 2: When I first wake up in the morning, my *cognitive* processes are delayed and I sometimes have to ask others to repeat themselves before I understand.

Usage 3: In the world of psychology *cognitive* testing refers to the many measures that have been developed that test an individual's mental processes and their ability to understand higher level information.

Usage 4: Research shows that physical exercise can benefit *cognitive* functioning, as it improves overall blood flow to the brain.

COGNIZANCE (n)   [KOG-n*uh-zuh* ns]

Meaning: awareness; conscious knowledge or recognition

Usage 1: She didn't even have the *cognizance* to realize that the window was shattered and the lock on the door was broken.

Usage 2: It often seemed as if he didn't have the *cognizance* to see that his relationship was crumbling before his very eyes.

Usage 3: Once the doctor obtained *cognizance* about the fatal virus that was spreading through the town, she immediately ordered patients to be quarantined.

Usage 4: I did not have the *cognizance* to notice that the people sitting directly in front of me were my parents.

COHABIT (v)   [koh-HAB-it]

Meaning: to coexist or to live together

Usage 1: Angie and Zach *cohabit* in New York City, where it makes sense to split the cost of a loft apartment.

Usage 2: It is amazing how powerful and majestic animals like lions can *cohabit* with small, vulnerable creatures.

Usage 3: The millions of couples in the country who *cohabit* lack basic privileges that married couples have, such as inheritance and visiting privileges as hospitals.

Usage 4: Years ago, it was illegal to *cohabit* with a romantic partner.

COHORTS (n)   [KOH-hawrts]

Meaning: armed band; groups of people; associates

Usage 1: She chose the social work program at that particular university because 20% of the *cohort* is non-American.

Usage 2: Sometimes it is best to train *cohorts* together, as it offers people practice for responding to an event.

Usage 3: This *cohort* of graduates is incredibly talented; we will see great things from them.

Usage 4: The ageing *cohort* of Americans is larger than any other group, including babies.

COIFFURE (n)   [kwah-FYOO R]

Meaning: a hairstyle or hair arrangement

Usage 1: Jenny's new *coiffure* caused lots of murmuring in the crowd, as she had kept her hair in the same style for decades until now.

Usage 2: The puppy was taken to the groomer's and returned home with a *coiffure* full of little pink bows.

Usage 3: The movie star's *coiffure* inspired millions of women's haircuts.

Usage 4: There are specialists who know more about *coiffures* of Broadway stars than most of us know about ourselves.

COLANDER (n)   [KUHL-*uh* n-der]

Meaning: utensil with perforated bottom used for straining; bowl with holes used for straining liquids

Usage 1: I use my *colander* almost daily when washing greens, cooking pasta, or draining beans.

Usage 2: Leroy likes to grab a handful of sand, and then let it fall through his fingers like a *colander* back onto the ground.

Usage 3: Add the greens to a *colander*, rinse well, and give it a few shakes to drain all the water out.

COLLABORATE (v)   [k*uh*-LAB-*uh*-reyt]

Meaning: work together

Usage 1: The best part about group work in graduate school was the chance to *collaborate* with motivated and intelligent students.

Usage 2: In many research studies, scientists *collaborate* together to take on complex experiments.

Usage 3: It would be good for our nation to have more and more organizations *collaborate* about problems such as hunger and lack of medical care.

Usage 4: The two musicians *collaborated* on an album that sold more copies than either artist could have sold on their own.

COLLAGE (n)   [k*uh*-LAHZH]

Meaning: work of art put together from fragments; an artwork made by pasting objects onto a surface

Usage 1: Hannah Hoch is a famous *collage* artist, who drew together parts of magazines, newspapers, and photography to create her works.

Usage 2: My earliest memories of making *collages* are in preschool, when I pasted colored pictures of faces to construction paper.

Usage 3: *Collage* is a great art project for young children, as they do not have to have sophisticated art skills to glue pictures or objects onto paper.

Usage 4: My husband gave me a *collage* of our first five years together, complete with photographs and tickets of movies we had seen together.

COLLATE (v)   [k*uh*-LEYT]

Meaning: examine in order to verify authenticity; arrange in order

Usage 1: Our office's new copier can staple, print on both sides, and *collate* if we are making booklets.

Usage 2: Robin finally had the chance to *collate* all of her children's baby pictures once she had retired.

Usage 3: As a paralegal, Jim was given the task of *collating* the history of Iowa laws governing the sale of self-published books.

COLLOQUIAL (adj)   [k*uh*-LOH-kwee-*uh* l]

Meaning: pertaining to conversational or common speech; relating to speech

Usage 1: He is *colloquially* known as "The Beast," as he can beat anyone at any sport, hands down.

Usage 2: The huge city's building *colloquially* known as "The Pencil" houses a bank and hundreds of law offices.

Usage 3: In research papers, avoid using *colloquial* expressions, as they can come across as before sounding unprofessional.

Chapter **23**

Colloquy – Dulcet

This chapter covers the following words, each with its part of speech, pronunciation, and descriptive meaning.

Usage of the word is also illustrated in three to five sample sentences.

colloquy	detonation	docket
colossal	detrimental	doddering
comatose	diadem	dolt
comely	dialectic	dossier
compilation	diaphanous	dour
complacent	didactic	draconian
complementary	diffusion	dross
conflate	dilettante	drudgery
congruent	diorama	dubious
conscientious	disapprobation	dulcet
consternation	discernible	
contiguous	discombobulated	
creed	discursive	
crestfallen	disgruntle	
dabble	disjunction	
damp	disport	
debunk	disputatious	
derision	dissimulate	
desideratum	distrait	
despicable	diurnal	

COLLOQUY (n)   [KOL-*uh*-kwee]

Meaning: formal, serious, intellectual discussion

Usage 1: In the professor's philosophy class, we had an engaging *colloquy* about the meaning of knowledge.

Usage 2: At the psychology conference, the *colloquy* revolved around the application of operational conditioning in the modern digital age.

Usage 3: Rather than feeling like a relaxed party, the dinner Matt was invited to consisted of dull *colloquies* about mathematical theories and such.

Usage 4: Stella was expecting to enjoy herself, but instead was forced into a *colloquy* about religion and theology on their first date.

Usage 5: The televised debate was a *colloquy* between the three candidates about taxes, fracking, and commercial development.

COLOSSAL (adj)   [k*uh*-LOS-*uh* l]

Meaning: huge; extremely large or of extraordinary size

Usage 1: Marian felt like a *colossal* failure after losing her job, and spent the next several weeks lounging in bed without showering or eating.

Usage 2: The *colossal* sculpture made the spectators seem like tiny dolls.

Usage 3: The Grand Canyon is an example of a *colossal* topographical feature, and can be seen from thousands of miles above the ground.

Usage 4: Lilly's cat was only a kitten when he ran away, and seemed *colossal* when he returned three years later.

Usage 5: The dinner was *colossal*; it consisted of six courses plus drinks.

COMATOSE (adj)   [KOM-*uh*-tohs]

Meaning: in a coma; in a state of extreme sleepiness

Usage 1: Brandon always seems awake during recreational time, but during math class becomes *comatose*.

Usage 2: After weeks of waking up in the middle of the night with newborn twins, the new parents were *comatose*.

Usage 3: After a night of having a stomach virus, there was no possible way the *comatose* college student could go to class.

Usage 4: Our dog Molly was spayed yesterday at the vet, and returned home *comatose* though perked up the next day.

Usage 5: Even one pint of beer or one cocktail leaves me feeling *comatose*; I just can't handle alcohol.

COMELY (adj)   [KUHM-lee]

Meaning: agreeable; pleasing, attractive, and wholesome in appearance

Usage 1: Ever since she lost the weight, everyone is talking about her *comely* figure.

Usage 2: Golden Retrievers are usually *comely* dogs, but the one I saw today was scraggly and underweight.

Usage 3: The prince was a *comely* gentleman, with a full head of hair and a muscular body.

Usage 4: The *comely* canine has won the dog show three years in a row.

COMPILATION (n)   [kom-p*uh*-LEY-sh*uh* n]

Meaning: the process of gathering together

Usage 1: His favorite album was a *compilation* of Bruce Springsteen greatest hits.

Usage 2: That large book is a *compilation* of all the short stories written by O. Henry.

Usage 3: The report is a *compilation* of information gathered over many years from hospitals and doctors around the country.

COMPLACENT (adj) [k*uh* m-PLEY-s*uh* nt]

Meaning: self-satisfied and unconcerned; contented with one's self to a fault

Usage 1: It is easy to become *complacent* in one's job after performing the same duties for twenty years.

Usage 2: Jeffrey was becoming extremely *complacent* in his swimming skills, so much so that he began bragging to his friends that he could beat Michael Phelps in the butterfly.

Usage 3: The little girl was never given consequences, so remained *complacent* as she lived a life that had no limits.

Usage 4: Even though we use antibacterial hand gel all the time, that is no reason to become *complacent* and stop washing our hands.

COMPLEMENTARY (adj) [kom-pl*uh*-MEN-t*uh*-ree]

Meaning: serving to complete something

Usage 1: Abigail and Ashley, twin girls, are *complementary* to each other; Abigail is outgoing and talkative, and Ashley is quiet and thoughtful.

Usage 2: Even though it doesn't sound like it would match, your blue blouse is quite *complementary* to your yellow skirt.

Usage 3: I am a believer of *complementary* and alternative medicine, as I go to my doctor once a year but also visit my acupuncturist regularly.

Usage 4: I believe traditional methods of teaching, such as lecturing, can be *complementary* to newer methods such as digital integration.

CONFLATE (v) [k*uh* n-FLEYT]

Meaning: meld or fuse; to bring together

Usage 1: Tina and Tim have been married for forty years, and by this time their thoughts and behaviors seem to have *conflated* into one.

Usage 2: It's easy to *conflate* the Ku Klux Klan with conservatism, but surprisingly there were many liberals who affiliated with the organization.

Usage 3: His compliments are confusing; he usually *conflates* a genuinely nice comment with something sarcastic.

CONGRUENT (adj) [KONG-groo-*uh* nt]

Meaning: in agreement

Usage 1: Parker was not necessarily *congruent* with his parents when they brought home his baby sister; he was upset that he now had to share the attention.

Usage 2: Congruent angles are simply angles of the same degrees or radians.

Usage 3: While Roberta did not feel *congruent* emotions when her friend was in pain, she could sympathize with her friend's disappointment about her job and relationships.

CONSCIENTIOUS (adj) [kon-shee-EN-sh*uh* s]

Meaning: scrupulous; careful; thorough

Usage 1: She believes it is incredibly important to be *conscientious* about how she dresses; she always matches her shoes with her sweater and her earrings with her necklace.

Usage 2: One of the keys to being a great student is to be *conscientious* about checking answers and taking the time to complete assignments thoroughly.

Usage 3: He was a *conscientious* employee for seventeen years at his company, but was rewarded with a pink slip and two weeks of severance pay.

CONSTERNATION (n)   [kon-ster-NEY-sh*uh* n]

Meaning: anxiety; astonishing dismay or horror

Usage 1: My mother tends to speak in *consternation* toward my father when he comes home late without calling or spends money without consulting her first.

Usage 2: Professor Sullivan spoke in deep *consternation* to her class after it was discovered that several students had cheated on the last exam.

Usage 3: The journalist who misquoted many of the organization's representatives was met with much consternation by the public.

Usage 4: I quickly cleaned up my room and put away my clothes to avoid my mother's *consternation*, as she always expects me to do as she says immediately.

CONTIGUOUS (adj)   [k*uh* n-TIG-yoo-*uh* s]

Meaning: adjacent to; touching upon; sharing an edge or boundary

Usage 1: The newlyweds did not sleep well at night unless some parts of their bodies were *contiguous* to one another.

Usage 2: When redesigning the bathroom, Maureen was insistent that the vanity was *contiguous* to the sink.

Usage 3: The *contiguous* United States includes all 50 states, whereas the continental United States excludes Hawaii and Alaska.

CREED (n)   [kreed]

Meaning: system of religious or ethical belief; statement of religious belief

Usage 1: I am in the process of joining the Presbyterian Church, and feel obligated to learn the *creed* as well.

Usage 2: The Boy Scout *creed* is meant to equip members to make ethical and moral decisions throughout their lives.

Usage 3: You will soon find out that there exists a military *creed* that is not explicitly said in training.

CRESTFALLEN (adj)   [KREST-faw-l*uh* n]

Meaning: dejected, dispirited, and depressed

Usage 1: She was so sure the job interview had gone well, and was *crestfallen* when she got the call telling her she wasn't chosen for the position.

Usage 2: When the little boy was not allowed to watch Sesame Street, he was *crestfallen* and began to cry.

Usage 3: I just love to shop, and when I discovered that the shoes I had my eyes on for weeks were not in my size, I was *crestfallen*.

Usage 4: Daria was *crestfallen* when her boyfriend of six months called her to tell her they needed to talk.

DABBLE (v)   [DAB-*uh* l]

Meaning: work at in a non-serious fashion; to participate in something, but not seriously

Usage 1: Marsha *dabbles* in a variety of activities, but never stays with anything very long.

Usage 2: Harry *dabbles* in cooking and pottery, and has a few favorite recipes and mugs to show for it.

Usage 3: When I was in college, I *dabbled* in student government but ended up dropping my political science major and studying biology.

Usage 4: I speak English and French fluently, and *dabble* in German, Spanish, and a few other languages.

Usage 5: During the workweek Mario was employed by a bank, but on the weekends he *dabbled* in photography.

DAMP (v)   [damp]

Meaning: lessen in intensity; to depress or restrain; to weaken or discourage

Usage 1: The publicist was able to *damp* the media from portraying the company as an evil employer by negotiating bribes.

Usage 2: The toddler was resistant to going to bed despite his mother's attempts to *damp* his energy.

Usage 3: Our radio's speaker is broken, and we must constantly *damp* the sound by placing a towel over it.

DEBUNK (v)   [dih-BUHNGK]

Meaning: expose as false, exaggerated, worthless, etc; ridicule

Usage 1: The researchers spent months attempting to *debunk* the claims the pharmacological company made about the benefits of the antidepressant medication.

Usage 2: Sonya, a massage therapist and acupuncturist, often feels the need to *debunk* the myth that alternative medicine is "all in your head."

Usage 3: By and large scientists have been able to *debunk* the claim that organic foods are always better for you than nonorganic.

Usage 4: Charles's dream job is to travel around the country, *debunking* myths and crushing dreams wherever he goes.

DERISION (n)   [dih-RIZH-*uh* n]

Meaning: jeering laughter or harsh ridicule

Usage 1: The opposing team suffered *derision* from the home team's opponents, but ultimately won the game anyway.

Usage 2: Middle school is a time when children must face the brutality of *derision* and embarrassment.

Usage 3: The *derision* was aimed at the Hollywood actor who had recently admitted to cheating on his wife.

Usage 4: Charlotte was prepared to face *derision* when she walked into class wearing new braces, but instead received a few compliments on her appearance.

DESIDERATUM (n)   [dih-sid-*uh*-REY-t*uh* m]

Meaning: a thing lacking, but desired or needed; something that is desired

Usage 1: The play was overall well-executed, and the only *desideratum* was a shining female lead.

Usage 2: Desideratum such as wealth and fame are often undesired once they are obtained.

Usage 3: The small nation lacked the *desideratum* of motivation and spirit to separate from its mother country, and was destined to be ruled by another forever.

DESPICABLE (adj)   [DES-pi-k*uh*-b*uh* l]

Meaning: contemptible; deserving contempt or scorn; vile

Usage 1: After Todd was arrested for drunken driving, he apologized profusely for his *despicable* words toward his family.

Usage 2: The *despicable* rumors flying around about the President's cabinet were soon put to rest by the President himself.

Usage 3: The senior dance was postponed following the *despicable* actions of the senior class toward freshmen.

Usage 4: *Despicable* acts of terrorism seem to be becoming more common, but it is likely that the media is to blame instead.

Usage 5: The criminal's *despicable* acts earned him the pity of the entire city and a life's sentence in prison.

DETONATION (n)   [det-n-EY-sh*uh* n]

Meaning: a loud explosion, such as by firearms

Usage 1: It seems we hear of *detonations* in the Middle East on a daily basis.

Usage 2: Roger heard the *detonation* from his bedroom, and later found out his neighbor's gas lawnmower had exploded in the garage.

Usage 3: Two days before Christmas, there was a major *detonation* scene when the newest video game was released at the toy store.

Usage 4: Ever since she was a little girl, Rebecca was extremely anxious around July 4th, when the *detonation* of fireworks was inescapable.

DETRIMENTAL (adj)   [de-tr*uh*-MEN-tl]

Meaning: causing injury, damage, or harm

Usage 1: Frank's partying and staying out all night was *detrimental* to his academic studies.

Usage 2: Though Jean liked having some time to herself, even she had to admit that Thomas' travel schedule was *detrimental* to their marriage.

Usage 3: Research shows that any type of substance use can have long-term *detrimental* effects to the brain.

Usage 4: Crowded classrooms, slashed arts programs, and subpar teachers all have *detrimental* effects on students' outcomes.

Usage 5: Unfortunately, I believe the election of a Republic governor will have *detrimental* effects on our state's healthcare system.

DIADEM (n)   [DAHY-*uh*-dem]

Meaning: a crown worn as a sign of royalty

Usage 1: The prince's crown was made of fine silver, and at the center of the *diadem* was a single, flawless emerald.

Usage 2: The painting shows the angel wearing a *diadem* of holly around her head.

Usage 3: The beautiful bride wore a veil in the back of her head and a sparkling *diadem* in front.

Usage 4: One of Jennifer's favorite places to visit is the Tower of London, where she can see all the *diadems* of past royalty.

Usage 5: The little girls often played dress-up, and would wear pink gowns and *diadems* made of rhinestones.

DIALECTIC (n)   [dahy-*uh*-LEK-tik]

Meaning: art of debate; the art of arriving at the truth by the exchange of logical arguments

Usage 1: The master-slave *dialectic* was one that was frequently discussed particularly in 19th century America.

Usage 2: On one side of the *dialectic* is co sleeping from infancy, and on the other is the 'cry it out' method of sleep training.

Usage 3: In philosophy classes we have weekly *dialectics* as the professor raises topics and students debate various points of the issue.

DIAPHANOUS (adj)   [dahy-AF-*uh*-n*uh* s]

Meaning: sheer; transparent or easily seen through

Usage 1: The ballerinas' costumes were made of *diaphanous* material that gracefully swayed to the tune of the music.

Usage 2: The evening was perfect - the temperature was warm but not humid, and the moon bathed the lake in *diaphanous* light.

Usage 3: In order to create a *diaphanous* appearance to the ghost in the school play, the costumers painted a white sheet with metallic paint.

Usage 4: Raymond and Rachel finally divorced after years of having a *diaphanous* barrier between them.

Usage 5: He seems to think that by wearing that *diaphanous* shirt more women will be attracted to him.

DIDACTIC (adj)   [dahy-DAK-tik]

Meaning: instructional or intended to teach or demonstrate

Usage 1: I love reading, but in my down time I will always choose a fiction novel rather than a *didactic* book.

Usage 2: My least favorite part of biology class is the *didactic* portion; I would rather do labs all day.

Usage 3: Emily liked the book overall, though the detailed *didactic* parts about cell development made the text lengthy.

Usage 4: In order to be hired as a college professor, it is essential that you have excellent teaching and *didactic* skills.

Usage 5: Though the acting class was not necessarily meant to be *didactic*, the teacher usually ended up giving a short lecture at the beginning introducing the skills the students were about to practice.

DIFFUSION (n)   [dih-FYOO-zh*uh* n]

Meaning: wordiness; spreading in all directions like a gas; the act of spreading in all directions

Usage 1: After the principal made his announcement, it was easy to hear the *diffusion* of chatter among the school teachers.

Usage 2: Due to the *diffusion* of information across the web, Rhonda simply posted her picture on her blog and waited for the comments.

Usage 3: The prism gave off a *diffusion* of light as the sun shone directly through the window.

DILETTANTE (n)   [DIL-i-tahnt]

Meaning: aimless follower of the arts; amateur; a dabbler in a field of knowledge or a lover of the fine arts

Usage 1: Charles is quite a *dilettante*; he has a job at the law firm but also dabbles in the field of rare books.

Usage 2: Most people don't know that on the weekends I'm a *dilettante* photographer who takes pictures of flowers for fun.

Usage 3: One of the reasons Terri was attracted to Bob was his *dilettante* lifestyle - he played several musical instruments, rode horses, and read biology textbooks in his free time.

DIORAMA (n)   [dahy-*uh*-RAM-*uh*]

Meaning: life-size three-dimensional scene from nature or history; a three-dimensional display of a scene

Usage 1: My friend's father, a rabbi, loved making *dioramas* of Old Testament scenes, complete with figures and trees.

Usage 2: It is a rite of passage that all children must create some sort of *diorama* for a science fair in their lifetimes.

Usage 3: Carl loved *dioramas* because lots of time and focus are put into freezing just one moment in time.

Usage 4: The science museum is known for its extensive collection of *dioramas* depicting everything from the dinosaur age to the life of a cell.

Usage 5: At Christmas time, it is a family tradition to create holiday *dioramas* complete with houses, reindeer, and lights.

DISAPPROBATION (n)   [dis-ap-r*uh*-BEY-sh*uh* n]

Meaning: moral disapproval or condemnation

Usage 1: Having seen the look of *disapprobation* on her parents' faces, Jeanie turned away and silently walked to her room.

Usage 2: The *disapprobation* apparent on the jurists' faces made it clear that the guilty verdict would not take long to be returned.

Usage 3: Though Michelle expressed *disapprobation* at the institute of marriage when she was a teenager, she has been happily married to Tim for seven years and has three children.

Usage 4: Some dogs seem to respond to their owners' looks of *disapprobation*, but cats never seem to care.

Usage 5: At the gallery opening, the looks of *disapprobation* on the faces of attendees told the artist he had gone too far with his nude paintings.

DISCERNIBLE (adj)   [dih-SUR-n*uh*-b*uh* l]

Meaning: distinguishable; perceptible by vision or intellect

Usage 1: After drying, the change of the colors on the canvas was barely *discernible*.

Usage 2: I have lots of great resources, but they aren't in *discernible* order.

Usage 3: The only *discernible* difference between the twins is the small mole on Skye's left shoulder.

Usage 4: Over several years, there became a *discernible* difference in the way Emma and Teddy communicated with each other.

Usage 5: The *discernible* movements on the lake's surface were due to the swimming of the minute fish.

DISCOMBOBULATED (adj)   [dis-k*uh* m-BOB-y*uh*-ley-tid]

Meaning: discomposed; confused or disoriented

Usage 1: When I wake up early in the morning, I am *discombobulated* until I get my coffee.

Usage 2: After he woke up from surgery, the little boy was terribly *discombobulated* and cried for quite awhile before remembering where he was.

Usage 3: The elderly dog often appeared *discombobulated*, walking into doors and staring at her owners as if she didn't know them.

Usage 4: The baseball pitcher became so *discombobulated* that his throws began going to the left and right of the plate.

Usage 5: After awakening from a vivid dream, I feel *discombobulated* and it is difficult for me to separate dream from reality for a few minutes.

DISCURSIVE (adj)   [dih-SKUR-siv]

Meaning: digressing; rambling or talking without a clear point

Usage 1: Jake continued on his *discursive* monologue as the others stood by, rolling their eyes at each other and sighing out loud.

Usage 2: Nora had a *discursive* education, as she spent seven years trying to decide on a major and obtained two different postgraduate degrees.

Usage 3: My English teacher prefers our essays to get right to the point rather than engage in any *discursive*, descriptive dialogue.

Usage 4: I enjoy deep, *discursive* conversations with friends rather than superficial exchanges.

DISGRUNTLE (v)   [dis-GRUHN-tl]

Meaning: to make discontented or cross

Usage 1: Shawn was a *disgruntled* young man who always seemed to find the worst in everything.

Usage 2: The politician did his very best to *disgruntle* his opponent by mentioning the opponent's failed marriage and estranged children.

Usage 3: The CEO left the company without warning, *disgruntling* thousands of employees.

Usage 4: The Bulls fans were *disgruntled* following the championship game and the questionable referee calls.

Usage 5: The female lead in the Broadway show was substituted by the understudy, leaving many ticketholders *disgruntled*.

DISJUNCTION (n) [dis-JUHNGK-sh*uh* n]

Meaning: state of being separated

Usage 1: This *disjunction* between reality and fantasy can easily be reconciled if you try to live in the present.

Usage 2: Though the book was based on a true story, I've heard there is *disjunction* between the character's personality and the personality of the woman on whom the book was based.

Usage 3: Gerald tried to impress his date by talking about the stock market, but there was clear *disjunction* between his statements and the reality of the economy.

DISPORT (v) [dih-SPAWRT]

Meaning: to amuse oneself in a light manner

Usage 1: By the mid afternoon, we must *disport* ourselves by doing stretches and playing games.

Usage 2: The group of women met monthly for dinner, where they could *disport* themselves by eating and reconnecting.

Usage 3: My cats *disport* themselves by playing with a pretend mouse and chasing shadows.

DISPUTATIOUS (adj) [dis-pyoo-TEY-sh*uh* s]

Meaning: argumentative; fond of arguing; inclined to argue or debate

Usage 1: Due to his *disputatious* personality, Cliff's parents suggested to him from an early age that he attend law school.

Usage 2: Her temper was atrocious, so it was no wonder her family disowned her due to her *disputatious* tendencies.

Usage 3: The *disputatious* atmosphere of our board meetings was toned-down because the chairman was out sick.

Usage 4: Tara's little boy was not nearly as *disputatious* as she; he went along with the games the other children suggested without complaint.

Usage 5: Though our graduating class is intelligent, it is made up of many *disputatious* people who easily create an uncomfortable atmosphere.

DISSIMULATE (v) [dih-SIM-y*uh*-leyt]

Meaning: pretend; conceal by feigning; deceive; to disguise under a feigned appearance

Usage 1: Margie often *dissimulated* her shyness by keeping her head held high and speaking in a clear tone.

Usage 2: Little Noah truly believed that he could *dissimulate* by donning his superhero cape and mask.

Usage 3: Though Mr. Culpepper tried to *dissimulate* his years of neglecting to tend the yard, even with new flowers and plants the weeds made everything look unkempt.

DISTRAIT (adj) [dih-STREY]

Meaning: absent-minded, inattentive, or preoccupied

Usage 1: Whenever my sister takes a *distrait* tone, I know her mind is somewhere else.

Usage 2: My professor is often *distrait* and disengaged, so I find it difficult to approach him with my questions.

Usage 3: Sarah is the typical *distrait* artist; her mind is always thinking of a new project, and she always seems a little spacey.

DIURNAL (adj)   [dahy-UR-nl]

Meaning: on a daily basis

Usage1: Jack made the *diurnal* migration from his house to the office and back again.

Usage 2: The *diurnal* sleep-wake cycle is a source of endless speculation and research.

Usage 3: After infancy, the *diurnal* patterns of young children become predictable and continue over the lifespan.

Usage 4: Each morning, Ella's cat was at the front door expecting his *diurnal* ritual of eating and sleeping to begin.

DOCKET (n)   [DOK-it]

Meaning: program as for trial; book where such entries are made; agenda or schedule, usually in court

Usage 1: Usually the *docket* is full on Monday mornings after a weekend full of criminal activity and arrests.

Usage 2: My *docket* today is open, though I have lots of paperwork to complete before the end of the day.

Usage 3: Due to Bill's dermatologist being in such high demand, his *docket* is usually full six months ahead of time.

Usage 4: The attorney did his best to avoid having the case added to the *docket*.

Usage 5: Today, our *docket* includes grocery shopping, a birthday party, and yard work.

DODDERING (adj)   [DOD-er-ing]

Meaning: shaky; mentally or physically feeble or infirm due to old age

Usage 1: The *doddering* old man cursed at me wildly before giving me a smile.

Usage 2: Laura didn't like visiting nursing homes, where the *doddering* residents reminded her of impending old age.

Usage 3: Though Mr. Fitz is a *doddering* old fellow of eighty-five, he continues to live alone and volunteer in the community whenever he can.

Usage 4: The political appeared in a public engagement several years ago, and even at that time he was a doddering man with slurred speech.

DOLT (n)   [dohlt]

Meaning: stupid person

Usage 1: He is truly a *dolt* if he thinks he can find anyone smarter or funnier than Sara.

Usage 2: Only a *dolt* would hide his life savings under his mattress.

Usage 3: This test must have been written for a *dolt*; the questions are incredibly easy.

Usage 4: The media portrayed the politician to look like a *dolt* and made fun of him on a regular basis.

Usage 5: Some cat-lovers think all dogs are *dolts*, but some dogs are just as smart as cats.

DOSSIER (n)   [DOS-ee-ey]

Meaning: file of information about a subject

Usage 1: I have several *dossiers*, one on each of my patients.

Usage 2: The lawyer always seemed to be carrying *dossiers*, as he was constantly on his way to one hearing or another.

Usage 3: You can say whatever you want about Tony, but his *dossier* is clean and crime-free.

Usage 4: The attorney approached the judge, *dossier* on his client in hand.

DOUR (adj)   [d*oo* r]

Meaning: sullen; harsh, forbidding, or stubborn

Usage 1: I often pride myself on being *dour*, though sometimes it can make relationships with other people difficult.

Usage 2: The young horse was being *dour* as he reared up at his owner and refused to trot when asked.

Usage 3: He is a *dour* child; he does the opposite of what his mother says and always insists on having his way.

DRACONIAN (adj)   [drey-KOH-nee-*uh* n]

Meaning: very severe or exceedingly harsh, oppressive, or strict

Usage 1: Mr. Brown was known all over the school for his *draconian* punishments; no student wanted to act up in his class.

Usage 2: Draconian cuts in taxes ruled the news the day after the income tax rate was slashed in half.

Usage 3: In a *draconian* attempt at winning the race, the driver veered in front of his opponent and slammed on the brakes.

Usage 4: Draconian consequences, such as spanking, were much more widely accepted in the past.

DROSS (n)   [draws]

Meaning: refuse; rubbish; worthless impurities; waste or impure matter which is often thrown off

Usage 1: The consignment store held many interesting items if customers were willing to comb through the dross.

Usage 2: Separating the *dross* from the gold is a process that can apply to many areas of life.

Usage 3: "Who's listening to that *dross*?" asked the elderly man as the teenager blasted rap music through his car speakers.

DRUDGERY (n)   [DRUHJ-*uh*-ree]

Meaning: menial work; tedious work

Usage 1: I manage to cope with the *drudgery* until five o'clock, when I gather my coat and make a beeline for the door.

Usage 2: Clint made his way through the *drudgery* of an office job for thirty years until retirement.

Usage 3: All jobs have an aspect of *drudgery*; it is finding enjoyment despite the tedium that is key.

Usage 4: The *drudgery* of a daily routine can be mind numbing but also comforting.

Usage 5: Toni found practicing the piano to be *drudgery*, but was glad she spent the time when the day of her recital came around.

DUBIOUS (adj)   [DOO-bee-*uh* s]

Meaning: questionable; fraught with doubt or uncertainty

Usage 1: Brandi's *dubious* claims to her parents that she was out late studying were well thought out, but didn't fool anyone.

Usage 2: I was quite *dubious* that the gentleman who asked for my number had any intent of calling me.

Usage 3: The politician was known for engaging in many *dubious* money-making schemes.

DULCET (adj)   [DUHL-sit]

Meaning: sweet sounding; melodious and pleasing to the ear

Usage 1: Leroy still found the voice of his wife *dulcet* after all these years.

Usage 2: A skilled cello player can create the most *dulcet* tones, despite the cello's size.

Usage 3: At dinnertime, I find it calming to listen to *dulcet* music on the radio.

Usage 4: Patty thought her dogs had *dulcet* barks, but her neighbors were very annoyed at the sounds.

Chapter **24**

Ebb – Gadfly

This chapter covers the following words, each with its part of speech, pronunciation, and descriptive meaning.

Usage of the word is also illustrated in three to five sample sentences.

ebb	expiate	frugality
ecclesiastic	expository	frustrate
ecologist	expunge	fulminate
efface	extemporaneous	fulsome
effeminate	extraneous	furor
effete	extrinsic	furtive
effluvium	extrude	fusillade
egoism	exuberant	gadfly
egregious	fallacy	
ellipsis	flippancy	
embattled	foil	
euphoria	foist	
euthanasia	forte	
evanescent	fortuitous	
exchequer	fractious	
excoriate	fraudulent	
exegesis	frenetic	
exiguous	fresco	
exonerate	frieze	
expatiate	frivolous	
expatriate	froward	

EBB (v)   [eb]

Meaning: lessen; to recede, weaken, or decline

Usage 1: Throughout the day, Angie watched the tide *ebb* and flow as she sat on the shore and contemplated her life.

Usage 2: As a freelancer, my work seems to *ebb* when I need money the most, and increases when I have the least amount of time.

Usage 3: As Tim aged out of adolescence, his appetite *ebbed* to the point he was eating three regular meals a day.

Usage 4: The novel initially was fast-paced and interesting, but it *ebbed* around the middle that made it difficult to keep reading.

Usage 5: When she entered college and had to take genetics class, Stephanie's interest in biology began to *ebb*.

ECCLESIASTIC (adj)   [ih-klee-zee-AS-tik]

Meaning: pertaining to the church; of the church or Christian religion

Usage 1: As a teenager, Joan attended numerous *ecclesiastic* conferences complete with charismatic singing and fervent prayer.

Usage 2: An *ecclesiastic* follower of Paul, Gordon devoted his entire thesis to a dissection of the letter to the Ephesians.

Usage 3: My *ecclesiastic* sister always insisted that we go to church, even if we were on vacation.

ECOLOGIST (n)   [ih-KOL-*uh*-jist]

Meaning: person who studies the relationship between organisms and the environment

Usage 1: My father, an *ecologist*, was always forcing us to take vacations to the outdoors and go on hunts for small bugs and strange plants.

Usage 2: The house was an *ecologist's* dream - it was made entirely from sustainable materials, was surrounded by native plants, and sat next to the clear ocean.

Usage 3: My best friend is an *ecologist*, which is a nice idea but the constant reminders to recycle can become annoying.

Usage 4: My professor was an avid *ecologist* who inspired all of his students to become more aware of the impact their mere existence had on their environments.

EFFACE (v)   [ih-FEYS]

Meaning: rub out; erase or get rid of

Usage 1: Gretchen and Holly had a friendship that distance and time could not *efface*; they were close even until Gretchen's death.

Usage 2: The rebels' plans to *efface* the government were thwarted when the message was intercepted by the police.

Usage 3: It was never the intent of the university to *efface* ethnic differences, but to acknowledge and respect those differences.

EFFEMINATE (adj)   [ih-FEM-*uh*-nit]

Meaning: having womanly traits

Usage 1: In some cities, it is perfectly accepted for men to have *effeminate* characteristics such as good fashion sense and interest in gossip and movies.

Usage 2: Despite his *effeminate* voice, Jeffrey eventually became a relatively well-known alto singer.

Usage 3: I was surprised that Dr. Glassman, a broad-shouldered man with a deep voice, would give such effeminate handshakes.

Usage 4: Some women find men with *effeminate* qualities, such as sensitivity, to be extremely attractive.

EFFETE (adj)   [ih-FEET]

Meaning: worn out; barren; exhausted; depleted of vitality or force

Usage 1: The small *effete* town was slowly dying away as the population aged and young people moved to larger cities.

Usage 2: After years of growing vegetables in the same garden, the *effete* soil may need a year or two to strengthen and rebuild its nutrients.

Usage 3: After a full day of swimming and a birthday party, the *effete* toddler took a long afternoon nap.

EFFLUVIUM (n)   [ih-FLOO-vee-*uh*m]

Meaning: noxious smell; odorous fumes

Usage 1: As Carly stepped into the woods, the *effluvium* coming from the brush let her know that something had died there recently.

Usage 2: I despise taking out the trash, as every time I open the lid to the dumpster the *effluvium* seems to hit me in the face.

Usage 3: Bacteria, though sometimes beneficial to humans, carries a certain *effluvium* which is generally unpleasant.

Usage 4: After the family had been out of town for several days, the *effluvium* coming from the cat's litter box was overwhelming.

EGOISM (n)   [EE-goh-iz-*uh* m]

Meaning: belief that one should be interested in one's self rather than in others; self-interest rather than the interest in others

Usage 1: My cat's *egoism* leads her to wake me up when she is hungry and walk all over my keyboard when she wants to be petted.

Usage 2: *Egoism* is normal and expected for young children, as they are only starting to understand the impact of their decisions and actions on others.

Usage 3: Some say *egoism* and altruism are the same things, as altruism usually leaves the giver with a cozy feeling inside.

Usage 4: Valerie's *egoism* is very high and has impaired her relationships with family and friends.

Usage 5: Larry tended to explain himself in terms of his *egoism*, which was often a turn-off for women.

EGREGIOUS (adj)   [ih-GREE-j*uh* s]

Meaning: notorious; outrageously bad or shocking; causing great disgust

Usage 1: The woman was finally arrested after police had enough evidence to believe she was the one who committed the *egregious* murders.

Usage 2: The *egregious* tax hikes the government implemented last week will negatively affect everyone.

Usage 3: Terra was known for spreading *egregious* rumors about her coworkers around the office, and no one trusted her.

Usage 4: The *egregious* violations of hospital policy resulted in Bert being placed on leave without pay.

Usage 5: Karen's husband was finally tired of her *egregious* lies and notified her he was seeking divorce.

ELLIPSIS (n)   [ih-LIP-sis]

Meaning: omission of words understood from a context as in 'if (it is) possible'; the omission of a phrase that can be inferred

Usage 1: Children often have trouble with *ellipsis*, as they do not have enough experience to infer what is not being said.

Usage 2: One of the criticisms of the author's latest non-fiction book is the overuse of the *ellipsis*, as he expects readers to know what he is thinking.

Usage 3: Shelly used *ellipsis* in her diary to indicate the unspoken in case her mother or brother was to find the entries.

EMBATTLED (adj)   [em-BAT-ld]

Meaning: (of army, etc) ready for battle; in a state of defense

Usage 1: After his traumatic experiences in battle, the veteran had an *embattled* air about him, always on guard and hyper vigilant.

Usage 2: The *embattled* troops were dressed and at attention, ready for any attacks that may come their way.

Usage 3: Christian liberals have felt *embattled* over the past decades due to criticisms from conservatives about the authenticity of their religious beliefs.

Usage 4: The *embattled* nation was prepared for warfare, even though there was no one to fight.

Usage 5: After her overnight in jail, Rachel entered the school *embattled* for the onslaught of rumors she knew were coming.

EUPHORIA (n)   [yoo-FAWR-ee-*uh*]

Meaning: feeling of great happiness and well-being (sometimes exaggerated); feeling of great joy

Usage 1: Dana was overcome with feelings of *euphoria* following the birth of her first child.

Usage 2: I was in a state of *euphoria* for several days when I was offered a well-paying job after years of searching.

Usage 3: Mark was in a state of *euphoria* when he found out he won a raffle for a trip to Europe.

Usage 4: The winning candidate's happiness was only a short-term *euphoria*; the next day he realized this meant he had to get to work.

Usage 5: There are lots of ways to reach a state of *euphoria* without drugs or alcohol.

EUTHANASIA (n)   [yoo-th*uh*-NEY-zh*uh*]

Meaning: mercy killing; the act of painlessly ending the life of a person suffering from terminal illness

Usage 1: The topic of euthanasia is one of great debate, as some believe death should occur naturally instead.

Usage 2: It's difficult to believe that those who oppose the gentle act of *euthanasia* are the same people who support the death penalty.

Usage 3: After days of not eating, the elderly cat was given *euthanasia* so she could die in peace.

Usage 4: Close family members of people who are experiencing great pain and suffering are more likely to support *euthanasia*.

EVANESCENT (adj)   [ev-*uh*-NES-*uh* nt]

Meaning: fleeting; vanishing into air, like a vapor

Usage 1: Soon after I wake up in the mornings, my *evanescent* dreams slip away.

Usage 2: In the fading sunlight, the *evanescent* bubbles seemed to disappear into the air.

Usage 3: In the prodromal phase of a psychotic disorder, there are often *evanescent* hallucinations that are mildly bothersome but not impairing.

Usage 4: One of the reasons I love listening to classical music is the delicate, *evanescent* sound that is so different from other music on the radio.

EXCHEQUER (n) [EKS-chek-er]

Meaning: treasury or place to store money

Usage 1: The *exchequer* run by our family became much wealthier after my investment banker of a grandfather died.

Usage 2: Out of the town *exchequer* came funds to revitalize downtown and turn it into apartment buildings and a plaza.

Usage 3: Chancellor of the *exchequer* is an admired position, known for proper conduct surrounding all things financial.

EXCORIATE (v) [ik-SKAWR-ee-eyt]

Meaning: scold with biting harshness; strip the skin off; criticize severely and harshly

Usage 1: I wasn't prepared for my professor to *excoriate* my first essay so severely.

Usage 2: The late night news showed two opposing candidates *excoriating* each other's personal lives to the core.

Usage 3: After her group of friends *excoriated* her for months, Amber finally decided to cut herself off from them and spend time with people who didn't criticize her constantly.

Usage 4: The editorial *excoriated* the local police department for allowing the shootings and attempted assaults to continue.

Usage 5: Before you *excoriate* your brother for taking your belongings, make sure you know it was actually him who did it.

EXEGESIS (n) [ek-si-JEE-sis]

Meaning: explanation of a text, particularly a religious one

Usage 1: In seminary, I felt as if I were writing an *exegesis* almost every day.

Usage 2: He is a natural-born scholar, and for fun will write an *exegesis* about the latest scripture he has read.

Usage 3: I like this Bible because of the helpful *exegesis* that is attached to each passage.

Usage 4: The opposite of *exegesis* is eisegesis, in which the reader interprets text based on his or her own experiences.

EXIGUOUS (adj) [ig-ZIG-yoo-*uh* s]

Meaning: small; minute; meager or scanty

Usage 1: One reason Jim felt the need to over explain himself was that his education was *exiguous*, consisting of only one semester at the state college.

Usage 2: The *exiguous* stash in my pantry consisted of only two cans of beans and a box of noodles.

Usage 3: Mark's *exiguous* list of places to visit while in France left him lots of time to act spontaneously and do whatever he liked in that moment.

Usage 4: After the *exiguous* town was approved for a million-dollar improvement, citizens began attending town hall meetings with ideas for the revitalization.

Usage 5: For her fiftieth birthday, Pearl lost thirty pounds and celebrated by buying an *exiguous* bikini.

EXONERATE (v) [ig-ZON-*uh*-reyt]

Meaning: acquit; exculpate; to relieve someone of a load or accusation

Usage 1: Hoping she could be *exonerated* from her past, Lisa got a new job and a new place to live on the other side of the county.

Usage 2: My dog Lucky looked at me with those big brown eyes, and I found it difficult not to *exonerate* him from gobbling up the fried chicken I had left on the counter.

Usage 3: After twenty years in prison, Mr. Jackson was *exonerated* when DNA evidence showed that he was not guilty of the murder.

EXPATIATE (v)   [ik-SPEY-shee-eyt]

Meaning: write or speak at length

Usage 1: The politician enjoyed *expatiating* on the current state of the union to anyone who would listen.

Usage 2: Carla felt there was no need to *expatiate* on the changes that had occurred in her life; anyone could see that she was suddenly living alone.

Usage 3: My gym teacher is a health nut, and we often listen to him *expatiate* on the dangers of fast food and white flour.

Usage 4: My grandmother is such a sweet person, but the fact that she can *expatiate* for a half-hour about what she had for dinner is exhausting.

EXPATRIATE (n)   [eks-PEY-tree-it]

Meaning: exile; someone who has withdrawn from his native land; one who has moved to a foreign land

Usage 1: After the drastic changes in government, the number of *expatriates* leaving the country soared.

Usage 2: In my opinion, companies that have moved overseas due to cheap labor are *expatriates* that do not deserve my business.

Usage 3: I think my little dog wants to be an *expatriate*; every time I open the door he darts out and won't come home on his own.

Usage 4: The American moved to France as a college student after he met his future wife, yet his family calls him an *expatriate*.

EXPIATE (v)   [EK-spee-eyt]

Meaning: make amends for (a sin); to make up for following a wrongdoing

Usage 1: After Chris' long apology, his wife was able to *expiate* him for his mistakes.

Usage 2: I am a sensitive person, and it's difficult for me to *expiate* myself when I do something wrong even if others forgive me.

Usage 3: The adolescent girl refused to *expiate* for staying out past her curfew, and continued to defy her parents' rules.

Usage 4: After cheating on the exam, Phil felt so strongly that he needed to expiate himself that he confessed to his teacher.

Usage 5: Some parents feel strongly that their children should *expiate* violations of household rules, but it is often better to let the children decide on their own when to ask for forgiveness.

EXPOSITORY (adj)   [ik-SPOZ-i-tawr-ee]

Meaning: explanatory; serving to give a detailed explanation of

Usage 1: Trish submitted an *expository* essay about cell development and how even microorganisms can affect the entire planet.

Usage 2: The high school debate club spent hours having *expository* discussions about topics from abortion to technology.

Usage 3: The best-selling author wrote long *expository* paragraphs about the relationships between couples to explain their current dynamics.

Usage 4: As a child, Owen would read *expository* volumes of books such as the encyclopedia in his free time.

Usage 5: In the *expository* pamphlet about Mormonism, you will find information about the origins and how to join.

EXPUNGE (v)   [ik-SPUHNJ]

Meaning: cancel; remove; erase or omit, as from a record

Usage 1: Following the decades long civil war, citizens were hoping that the new government would *expunge* the nation's violent history.

Usage 2: Due to the lack of preparation given to the prosecution's attorney, the evidence was *expunged* from the record.

Usage 3: Following the horrible divorce, Jeremy wanted to *expunge* the past three years of his life from his memory.

Usage 4: Mari's only intent was to *expunge* the myth that Islam is a religion of violence and replace it with the truth that it is a religion of peace.

EXTEMPORANEOUS (adj)   [ik-stem-p*uh*-REY-nee-*uh* s]

Meaning: impromptu; immediate; carried out without preparation; spontaneous

Usage 1: Paul's *extemporaneous* monologues at dinner parties were often met with yawns and lots of eye rolling.

Usage 2: At my church, members are encouraged to engage in *extemporaneous* prayer rather than adhering to a strict liturgy.

Usage 3: Nate was incredibly smart and well-read, and had a talent for making *extemporaneous* speeches on a whim throughout college.

EXTRANEOUS (adj)   [ik-STREY-nee-*uh* s]

Meaning: superfluous; not an essential or vital part of something

Usage 1: Frank was keeping to a budget, and eliminated any and all *extraneous* items from his grocery list.

Usage 2: If you've ever looked at the national budget, you'll see hundreds of *extraneous* items that, in my opinion, should be removed.

Usage 3: Once Charles had children, he rarely had time to do any *extraneous* activities such as reading and playing golf.

Usage 4: My professor prefers our essays to get right to the point, and will mark down our scores if we provide too much *extraneous* information.

Usage 5: I don't mind *extraneous* information when I'm having an informal dinner, but at a corporate meeting I prefer to stay on topic.

EXTRINSIC (adj)   [ik-STRIN-sik]

Meaning: not essential; extraneous; separable from the person or thing itself; external

Usage 1: Dogs and other pets will usually change their behaviors for *extrinsic* rewards, such as treats or rubs on the head.

Usage 2: As a self-centered adolescent, Sally often found it difficult to understand that sometimes the needs of the *extrinsic* world were greater than her own.

Usage 3: *Extrinsic* aspirations, such as wealth and fame, seem glamorous, but it is the intrinsic ones like strong relationships that are truly rewarding.

Usage 4: The author commonly uses *extrinsic* information that isn't really relevant to the topic to fill up extra pages.

EXTRUDE (v)   [ik-STROOD]

Meaning: force or push out

Usage 1: The metal jeweler carefully *extruded* the shapes from the flat metal circle, creating the image of a raised flower.

Usage 2: I always *extrude* the toothpaste from the tube by squeezing the bottom, but my husband insists on squeezing it in the middle.

Usage 3: At age 11, Lora had four teeth *extruded* in order to prepare her mouth for braces two years later.

Usage 4: The skilled teacher was able to *extrude* the student's ultimate points from the poorly written essay.

EXUBERANT (adj)   [ig-ZOO-ber-*uh* nt]

Meaning: abundant; effusive; lavish or enthusiastic in energy

Usage 1: The puppy's *exuberant* personality gradually tapered off as he reached one year of age.

Usage 2: Toddlers seem to be *exuberant* about the smallest things, including inconsequential toys and candy.

Usage 3: Stella's *exuberant* lifestyle made her extremely popular with those who enjoy parties and social events.

Usage 4: Some years I have trouble growing vegetables in my garden, but this year the growth of my tomatoes and squash is simply *exuberant*.

Usage 5: The *exuberant* energy of the new college president contributed to the increasing numbers of donors giving to new projects.

FALLACY (n)   [FAL-*uh*-see]

Meaning: mistaken idea based on flawed reasoning; mistaken belief or false notion

Usage 1: Lee failed his exam because of the *fallacy* of believing that guessing is better than trying to answer the questions correctly.

Usage 2: There is a high risk of *fallacy* when evaluating one's own appearance, as we tend to be very self- critical and see flaws in our appearances that others do not see.

Usage 3: I've never bought into the *fallacy* that money can buy happiness, because there are plenty of wealthy people who seem miserable.

Usage 4: Young children often believe *fallacies*, including that Santa Claus exists and reindeer can fly.

Usage 5: He is a skeptical person, and therefore believes that most assumptions and beliefs people have are *fallacies*.

FLIPPANCY (n)   [FLIP-*uh* n-see]

Meaning: trifling gaiety; inconsiderate pertness; taking something too lightly

Usage 1: The *flippancy* with which her friends treated the conversation about death made Nora feel awkward.

Usage 2: The priest felt it was highly inappropriate for parishioners to treat the sacraments with such *flippancy*.

Usage 3: Clara's family has always had plenty of money, so the *flippancy* of their shopping sprees and major purchases makes sense.

Usage 4: Trish, a vegetarian, always becomes annoyed whenever others treat her diet with *flippancy* by asking her if she eats fish.

Usage 5: The *flippancy* that teenage girls often exhibit toward their parents changes once they realize how important family relationships really are.

FOIL (n)   [foil]

Meaning: character who contrasts with another character

Usage 1: My twin sister is often my *foil*; when I am stressed out she calms me down.

Usage 2: One of the most basic and common literary devices is the use of a *foil*, which accentuates qualities of both characters.

Usage 3: Anyone who has read the Harry Potter series knows that evil Voldemort is the *foil* of well-meaning Dumbledore.

FOIST (v)   [foist]

Meaning: insert improperly; palm off; to pass off something fake as genuine

Usage 1: The pawn shop owner regularly *foists* off fake diamonds to customers.

Usage 2: As a young child, Sara had religious values *foisted* upon her and now declares herself an atheist.

Usage 3: The tour guide leading the group of Americans around in Rome warned them not to let anyone *foist* any false or inferior goods on them.

Usage 4: Even after we had all decided not to invite our acquaintance to dinner, Jeff *foisted* him into the restaurant.

Usage 5: There are hundreds of people out there who will try to *foist* copied works of art on eager buyers.

FORTE (n)   [FAWR-tey]

Meaning: strong point, special talent or strength

Usage 1: It's too bad that taking care of others isn't Esther's *forte* - she already has three children.

Usage 2: The dog's *forte* definitely wasn't listening, as he was fifteen years old and had never learned to come when called.

Usage 3: I often think of cooking as my *forte*, because my family compliments me every time I make a meal.

Usage 4: Jan's *forte* is soccer, and she is practicing all the time in hopes of earning a scholarship next year.

Usage 5: Due to her *forte* as a writer, Olivia began working from home as a freelancer.

FORTUITOUS (adj)   [fawr-TOO-i-t*uh* s]

Meaning: accidental; by chance; happening by accident or chance

Usage 1: In a *fortuitous* meeting, Nigel and Stan realized they were cousins.

Usage 2: My husband and I met ten years ago in a *fortuitous* encounter at a bookstore.

Usage 3: Val was denied admission into the university, but by *fortuitous* chance she met the admissions director at the gym and one week later received a letter of acceptance.

Usage 4: Frazier quit his job at the firm to become self-employed, a *fortuitous* decision considering the firm fired half of its employees one month later.

Usage 5: By *fortuitous* circumstances our town home was sold the same day we found the house of our dreams.

FRACTIOUS (v)   [FRAK-sh*uh* s]

Meaning: unruly; inclined to make trouble

Usage 1: Her *fractious* dogs constantly run through my flower gardens and steal my tennis balls.

Usage 2: When my grandfather and his brothers get together they always end up fighting like a group of *fractious* children.

Usage 3: The *fractious* political era is marked by government shut-downs and unapproved budgets.

Usage 4: Rosie's first husband was *fractious* and overbearing, but her second husband is terribly shy and meek.

Usage 5: It can become quite *fractious* in a psychiatric hospital, where patients with mental disorders don't have full control over what they are doing or saying.

FRAUDULENT (adj)   [FRAW-j*uh*-l*uh* nt]

Meaning: cheating; deceitful, dishonest, or deceptive

Usage 1: His *fraudulent* scheme to evade taxes was interrupted when the IRS auditor appeared at his door.

Usage 2: The artwork was submitted with a *fraudulent* certificate of authenticity, which the expert immediately pointed out.

Usage 3: The *fraudulent* signature appeared the same as the real one, but the ink dated to ten years after the author had died.

FRENETIC (adj)   [fru*uh*-NET-ik]

Meaning: frenzied; frantic; wildly excited or active

Usage 1: The little girl's *frenetic* dance received a round of applause at the end of the show.

Usage 2: Instead of making him sleepy, the medicine put Ben in a wild, *frenetic* state.

Usage 3: I woke up in the middle of the night to see Sheila painting the walls of the kitchen at a *frenetic* pace.

FRESCO (n)   [FRES-koh]

Meaning: painting on plaster (usually fresh); a technique that was popular during the Renaissance period in which artists painted on plaster

Usage 1: A local artist painted a *fresco* of the prodigal son on the back wall of the sanctuary.

Usage 2: Giotto's *frescoes* in Italy are painted with pure tones of color and can evoke an emotional response from the most stoic viewer.

Usage 3: Frescoes are coming back into fashion, as more artists are learning about painting on plaster and various other Renaissance techniques.

Usage 4: Most people aren't familiar with the technique of applying *frescoes*, in which layers of paint are applied to fresh plaster.

FRIEZE (n)   [freez]

Meaning: ornamental band on a wall; decorative band on a wall

Usage 1: The architect's style was punctuated by *friezes* of various sizes and shapes.

Usage 2: As an art history major, I would spend hours outside of buildings, examining and sketching the *frieze* at the top of the columns.

Usage 3: A portion of the *frieze* from the Greek revival column was given to the museum last year.

FRIVOLOUS (adj)   [FRIV-*uh*-lu*uh* s]

Meaning: lacking in seriousness; self-indulgently carefree; relatively unimportant; having no serious value

Usage 1: Jackie would rather spend her money on *frivolous* purchases like lipstick rather than food or other things she really needs.

Usage 2: Frivolous lawsuits are what pay the majority of Randy's mortgage, though every once in a while he is assigned an important case.

Usage 3: It is ridiculous that when the economy is in such a poor state, Bart wants to spend his money on frivolous items such as video games.

FROWARD (adj)   [FROH-werd]

Meaning: stubbornly disobedient or contrary

Usage 1: In my school, *froward* students are always sent to the principal's office when they get in trouble.

Usage 2: Even though our office has a laidback atmosphere, froward pranks are not appreciated.

Usage 3: Tess's *froward*, unruly children were a constant source of gossip in the neighborhood.

Usage 4: There is a clear difference between a teenager who is simply *froward* and one who has documented mental illness causing oppositional behavior.

FRUGALITY (n)   [froo-GAL-i-tee]

Meaning: thrift or sparingness

Usage 1: Ursula's *frugality* throughout the month meant she could splurge on a fancy dinner and new outfit at the end of the month.

Usage 2: My mother always valued *frugality*; we were never able to have expensive groceries and usually wore clothes from consignment stores.

Usage 3: When traveling abroad, *frugality* is key because added taxes and costs can become expensive.

Usage 4: Due to their constant fights about never having enough money, Ann and Jerry decided to try *frugality* as a way to save their marriage.

Usage 5: Frugality is near impossible if you live in Hollywood.

FRUSTRATE (v)   [FRUHS-treyt]

Meaning: thwart; defeat; to prevent from accomplishing a purpose

Usage 1: I become *frustrated* when others are late for meetings and don't answer my calls.

Usage 2: Robocalls *frustrate* most of us, as they feel like a huge waste of time.

Usage 3: Not being able to get his way all the time *frustrates* children like Colt, who are used to dictating their own lives.

Usage 4: Republicans deliberately *frustrate* the budgetary approval process in an attempt to convince Democrats to revise it.

FULMINATE (v)   [FUHL-m*uh*-neyt]

Meaning: thunder; explode; to issue an explosive verbal attack

Usage 1: Victor and his friends *fulminate* all the time about the new coach, but I think the team is doing well.

Usage 2: This year, I was too busy to *fulminate* about the fact that none of my children even called me on Mother's Day.

Usage 3: The debate was made up of six potential candidates, each one *fulminating* about the other five.

FULSOME (adj)   [FOO L-s*uh* m]

Meaning: disgustingly excessive; excessively or sickeningly flattering

Usage 1: The *fulsome* flattery Isaac gave his date felt awkward and insincere.

Usage 2: The university president showered *fulsome* praises on his faculty in an attempt to make them feel appreciated.

Usage 3: The *fulsome* compliments issued by the CEO actually insulted the benefactor.

FUROR (n)   [FYOO R-awr]

Meaning: frenzy; violent anger or rage

Usage 1: The bad referee calls at the championship game put fans of the losing team in an absolute *furor*.

Usage 2: I was in a *furor* when I discovered that my tires had been slashed and my car was keyed.

Usage 3: Anthony couldn't understand his wife's *furor* when he suggested that she quit her job to become a homemaker.

Usage 4: The most recent healthcare bill has created such a *furor* in the nation's capital that police have been called to control the crowds.

Usage 5: The *furor* outside the courtroom is in response to the murder trial.

FURTIVE (adj)   [FUR-tiv]

Meaning: stealthy; sneaky or having hidden motives or purposes

Usage 1: The cat's *furtive* steps over the rug led her to the small bug resting in the corner.

Usage 2: Furtive conversations between top administrators were discovered, putting both careers in jeopardy.

Usage 3: The romantic relationship between Mary and George was certainly private, but I don't think it was considered *furtive* as everyone knew about it.

Usage 4: The small child hid behind the curtain while playing hide and seek and gave a *furtive* giggle.

FUSILLADE (n)   [FYOO-s*uh*-leyd]

Meaning: simultaneous firing or outburst (of missiles, questions, etc.); a discharge from several firearms at the same time

Usage 1: The tragedy of last week's *fusillade* in the projects continues to be discussed on the local news.

Usage 2: During my first time at a firing range, the *fusillade* all around me gave me nightmares for days.

Usage 3: I heard one shot, then another, and then a *fusillade* that lasted for a full minute.

GADFLY (n)   [GAD-flahy]

Meaning: animal-biting fly; an irritating person; a person who irritates or annoys by persistent criticism

Usage 1: Following the baseball team's loss, the sportscaster was a complete *gadfly* during interviews.

Usage 2: Carla can be a real *gadfly* when her husband refuses to do things exactly as she wants them to be done.

Usage 3: My brother can be such a *gadfly* when he constantly bothers me with questions and remarks.

Chapter **25**

Gaffe – Indemnify

This chapter covers the following words, each with its part of speech, pronunciation, and descriptive meaning.

Usage of the word is also illustrated in three to five sample sentences.

gaffe	hydrophobia	incommodious
garner	hypochondriac	incontinent
garnish	hypocritical	incorrigible
garrulity	idiosyncratic	increment
genuflect	implacable	incrustation
germinal	implicate	incubus
gerontocracy	importune	incursion
gerrymander	impregnable	indemnify
gesticulation	impromptu	
gibberish	impropriety	
giddy	improvise	
girth	impudence	
glacial	impugn	
harping	incandescent	
harrow	incarcerate	
homeostasis	incendiary	
hone	incessant	
hortatory	incidental	
hostility	incipient	
hurtle	inclement	
husbandry	incognito	

GAFFE (n)   [gaf]

Meaning: a social or diplomatic blunder or mistake

Usage 1: Though it can be difficult to pronounce, please don't commit the *gaffe* of butchering the company president's name.

Usage 2: It was Tina's first formal dinner, and she committed many *gaffes* including serving herself from the platter and clearing her own place at the table.

Usage 3: At the tennis match, Henry committed a *gaffe* by forgetting to shake his opponent's hand following the game.

Usage 4: I didn't mean to commit such a *gaffe*, but it's hard for me to remember all the rules of etiquette.

Usage 5: I committed the technological *gaffe* of texting my friend goodbye.

GARNER (v)   [GAHR-ner]

Meaning: gather; store up; to accumulate a supply of something

Usage 1: Cheryl spent most of the week *garnering* enough signatures on her petition to submit it to the city council.

Usage 2: Everyday, the farmer would wake up early to *garner* the grain for the day and put it away in storage.

Usage 3: John *garnered* the wages he had earned over the last month and used them all to pay for his wife's medical bills.

GARNISH (v)   [GAHR-nish]

Meaning: decorate; to enhance the appearance of something by adding decoration

Usage 1: Her coat was *garnished* by a fur collar, which added the impression of wealth to her entire outfit.

Usage 2: The potato salad was *garnished* with parsley to make it appear fancier.

Usage 3: Sheila is a cake designer and spends her days *garnishing* cakes with frosting, flowers, and other decorations.

Usage 4: The dress was simple, but Katie *garnished* her appearance by adding a bold necklace and high heels.

Usage 5: Bloody Mary cocktails are almost always *garnished* with celery or some other vegetable.

GARRULITY (n)   [guh-ROO-li-tee]

Meaning: the quality or state of being very talkative

Usage 1: The *garrulity* of teenage girls surprises me; they can talk to each other on the phone for hours.

Usage 2: Ted's *garrulity* often led to glassy stares and stifled yawns after he spoke for minutes without stopping for a breath.

Usage 3: Though the professor is very smart, she often resorts to *garrulity* when she doesn't know much about the subject.

Usage 4: After the toddler's second birthday, he began speaking all the time and was known in the family for his *garrulity*.

GENUFLECT (v)   [JEN-yoo-flekt]

Meaning: bend the knee as in worship; to kneel on one knee and then rise again; to show deference or servility

Usage 1: Every Sunday during confession, we *genuflect* before the altar at church.

Usage 2: In order to win the political race, the candidate had to *genuflect* to the left and win supporters' trust.

Usage 3: As the queen approached, the audience *genuflected* in reverence and did not rise until she had passed.

Usage 4: As a pious Christian, Belle always *genuflected* whenever she entered the sanctuary.

GERMINAL (adj) [JUR-m*uh*-nl]

Meaning: pertaining to a germ; in the earliest stages of development; creative or productive

Usage 1: In the *germinal* phases of her career as a veterinarian, Nadia rescued sick birds and kittens and nursed them back to life.

Usage 2: Germinal reproduction is characterized by the first stages of budding.

Usage 3: The *germinal* stages of the Christian church can be traced back to thousands and thousands of years before Christ.

GERONTOCRACY (n) [jer-*uh* n-TOK-r*uh*-see]

Meaning: government or council composed of old people

Usage 1: The Presbyterian church is modern in some ways, but most decisions are still made by *gerontocracies*.

Usage 2: Despite all the advances of the modern Western world, the United States is still mostly a *gerontocracy*.

Usage 3: The benefits of a *gerontocracy* are that members have experience and power.

Usage 4: The Catholic church is truly a *gerontocracy*, but not even the women seem to mind.

GERRYMANDER (v) [JER-i-man-der]

Meaning: change voting district lines in order to favor a political party; dividing of a district in a way that gives a political party a majority while concentrating the voting strength of the opposing party into few districts

Usage 1: The incumbent *gerrymandered* so he could win each election the past twenty years.

Usage 2: The large number of Republican officials running our city *gerrymandered* so they could win the election.

Usage 3: Students running for student council cannot *gerrymander*, as each student is given an equal vote rather than being part of a district.

GESTICULATION (n) [je-stik-y*uh*-LEY-sh*uh* n]

Meaning: motion; an excited or expressive gesture

Usage 1: Italian conversations are often accompanied by wild *gesticulations*.

Usage 2: Even though I couldn't hear what he was saying, Mike used *gesticulations* in way that showed me he was furious.

Usage 3: In the middle of the soccer match, referees began using furious *gesticulations* at two of the players who had committed serious violations.

Usage 4: Yvonne was a quiet woman who did not use *gesticulations*, though her facial expressions always got the points across.

GIBBERISH (n) [GIB-er-ish]

Meaning: babbling; foolish, confused, or meaningless words

Usage 1: Lillian often talks *gibberish* in her sleep and we have no idea what she is saying.

Usage 2: Toddlers know exactly what they are saying, but to most of the world it sounds like *gibberish*.

Usage 3: I think the politician's argument is complete *gibberish*; it doesn't make any sense.

Usage 4: Though turkeys seem to understand the *gibberish* they mutter to each other, no one else understands.

GIDDY (adj) [GID-ee]

Meaning: light-hearted; dizzy; playful and silly; showing great happiness and joy

Usage 1: Sandra was absolutely *giddy* after accepting John's marriage proposal.

Usage 2: The young newlyweds were *giddy* on their honeymoon, laughing and talking late into the night.

Usage 3: My horse becomes *giddy* anytime I approach him with an apple in my hand.

Usage 4: Even though they like to appear serious, Rhonda's two teenage boys often engaged in *giddy* conversation late at night.

Usage 5: The couple who won the state lottery was *giddy* with joy for weeks afterward.

GIRTH (n)   [gurth]

Meaning: distance around something; circumference; the size of something measured around the middle

Usage 1: As he has approached middle age, his *girth* has expanded.

Usage 2: The old oak tree in our front yard is almost three yards in *girth*.

Usage 3: Though Barb comes from a family of petite women, she is a woman of large *girth*.

Usage 4: As the dog aged, her *girth* became more and more pronounced until the veterinarian finally had to put her on a diet.

Usage 5: The *girth* of a hot air balloon looks small when it is in the sky, but when it is on the ground you can see how huge it truly is.

GLACIAL (adj)   [GLEY-sh*uh* l]

Meaning: like a glacier; extremely cold and devoid of warmth or cordiality

Usage 1: Pearl's *glacial* stares in my direction told me I had upset her in some way.

Usage 2: After the couple's divorce, they exchanged *glacial* messages about how to divide up their belongings.

Usage 3: Vermont in February can be completely *glacial*; not only does it snow constantly, but the wind is freezing.

HARPING (n)   [HAHR-ping]

Meaning: tiresome dwelling on a subject; persisting on discussing something others don't want to discuss

Usage 1: Why does she keep *harping* on a fight we had five years ago?

Usage 2: Sylvia's mother is *harping* on the high prices of milk and bread.

Usage 3: I know we are poor, so I don't know why she keeps *harping* on the fact.

Usage 4: Michelle keeps *harping* on the fact that I failed my science class, but doesn't she know she failed hers too?

Usage 5: Phoebe was *harping* for hours on the fact that the ice cream shop was closed on the hottest day of the year.

HARROW (v)   [HAR-oh]

Meaning: break up ground after plowing; to draw a tool over the ground to break up weeds; torture; to bother or stress

Usage 1: Cora and Jessica *harrowed* the new girl at school everyday until the girl broke down in sobs.

Usage 2: We spent the summer cutting down trees, *harrowing* the soil, and planting crops.

Usage 3: A farmer's life is characterized by *harrowing*, sowing, and harvesting.

HOMEOSTASIS (n)   [hoh-mee-*uh*-STEY-sis]

Meaning: tendency of a system to maintain relative stability; the tendency of a living organism to maintain internal stability to compensate for environmental changes

Usage 1: Cellular *homeostasis* in the immune system is important for a well-balanced person to fight off disease.

Usage 2: Homeostasis can sometimes refer to the psychological tendency to find balance after a major stressor has been removed.

Usage 3: An animal population reaches *homeostasis* if an equal number of births and deaths occur.

HONE (v)   [hohn]

Meaning: to sharpen; to improve or make more effective

Usage 1: In Ellie's senior English class, her teacher's high expectations helped her *hone* her writing skills.

Usage 2: By meeting lots of women through the dating website, Bert was able to *hone* his relationship skills and finally meet a woman he loved.

Usage 3: Jeff loves to whittle small animal carvings, and everyday *hones* his carving knives to make sure their cuts are precise.

Usage 4: If you want to *hone* your piano skills, you have to practice every day.

Usage 5: Parenthood has *honed* my patience much more than I ever thought possible.

HORTATORY (adj)   [HAWR-t*uh*-tawr-ee]

Meaning: encouraging; tending or aiming to exhort or praise

Usage 1: The politician's message was *hortatory* only in words, as his eyes were cold and showed no sign of friendliness.

Usage 2: The legislative bill contains lots of *hortatory* language, but lacks true meaning or structure.

Usage 3: Lloyd often told *hortatory* stories about his own grandfather, who he clearly admires more than any other man.

Usage 4: The *hortatory* stories that come out of the preschooler's mouth are just wishful thinking.

HOSTILITY (n)   [ho-STIL-i-tee]

Meaning: unfriendliness; hatred; strong resistance to a plan, idea, person, or project

Usage 1: Fred expressed blatant *hostility* toward the man who would marry his ex-wife.

Usage 2: The neighbor's dog is usually tame, but whenever I walk my new puppy the dog barks with *hostility*.

Usage 3: The committee's plan to reduce the company's workforce by a quarter was met with strong *hostility*.

HURTLE (v)   [HUR-tl]

Meaning: crash; rush; to move with great speed and a rushing noise

Usage 1: The overnight train *hurtled* through the darkness as we traveled from Paris to Heidelberg.

Usage 2: The motorbikes *hurtled* down sidestreets and alleys, trying to escape the police.

Usage 3: The young dog *hurtled* down the road toward the cat, who simply gazed at him from the inside of the window.

Usage 4: Manny loves going to water parks and *hurtling* down the huge slides without fear.

HUSBANDRY (n)   [HUHZ-b*uh* n-dree]

Meaning: frugality; thrift; the act of cultivating crops and breeding livestock

Usage 1: My grandpa loved talking about *husbandry* to whoever would listen, as his entire life revolved around feedings and harvests.

Usage 2: Dora considered obtaining a degree in *husbandry*, as there is a real science to understanding crops and livestock.

Usage 3: Many nomadic tribes know more than any of us about *husbandry* and the best ways to nurture livestock.

HYDROPHOBIA (n)   [hahy-dr*uh*-FOH-bee-*uh*]

Meaning: an abnormal fear of water, as a symptom of rabies

Usage 1: I knew the dog had a case of *hydrophobia* when he refused to go near the lake, whereas last week he was jumping in with glee.

Usage 2: This week marked the first instance of *hydrophobia* in the state, as a bat tested positive for rabies.

Usage 3: One of the most dreaded and fatal diseases in the animal world is rabies, marked by *hydrophobia* and foaming at the mouth.

Usage 4: To avoid the trouble of *hydrophobia*, we make sure to have our cat vaccinated every year.

Usage 5: There was a news story about a dog in our neighborhood showing signs of *hydrophobia*.

HYPOCHONDRIAC (n)   [hahy-p*uh*-KON-dree-ak]

Meaning: a person who is constantly under the conviction that he or she is or is likely to become ill, despite no medical evidence for these beliefs

Usage 1: Chris is such a *hypochondriac*; every time I see him he thinks he has cancer or some other fatal disease.

Usage 2: I've had a lot of medical appointments, but I'm no *hypochondriac*; all my annual appointments seem to fall around the same time each year.

Usage 3: Some people call *hypochondriacs* "health worriers" because that's all they do, all the time - worry about their health.

Usage 4: Lynn would never call herself a *hypochondriac*, but I've never heard of anyone going to the doctor so much.

Usage 5: With the rise in technology, *hypochondriacs* now only have to go online to diagnose themselves with various rare ailments.

HYPOCRITICAL (adj)   [hip-*uh*-KRIT-i-k*uh* l]

Meaning: pretending to be virtuous; deceiving; having actions or words that go against someone's beliefs

Usage 1: The church is often criticized for being *hypocritical*, especially when the gospel of love is preached yet homosexual marriages are banned.

Usage 2: Tom committed the *hypocritical* action of having an affair with his secretary while always claiming to have strict moral values.

Usage 3: Jed made the *hypocritical* remark that he loved all food, but really couldn't stand Nancy's apple pie.

Usage 4: Chuck felt very *hypocritical*, as he was always telling his wife to save money yet he just bought himself a new TV.

Usage 5: I hate when I get that *hypocritical* feeling of doing something I know I just told someone else not to do.

IDIOSYNCRATIC (adj)   [id-ee-oh-sin-KRAT-ik]

Meaning: eccentric; peculiar to a specific individual

Usage 1: She has an *idiosyncratic* manner of using words improperly.

Usage 2: I have been told I have *idiosyncratic* views, as I lead a life made up of periods of intense creativity and mental acuity.

Usage 3: The *idiosyncratic* positions of our congregation's pastor on the rights of homosexuals are not easily accepted by his church-goers.

Usage 4: The psychiatrist received training in analysis as a student, which these days is preserved for only the most *idiosyncratic* mental health professionals.

IMPLACABLE (adj)   [im-PLAK-*uh*-b*uh* l]

Meaning: Not being able to be calmed or pacified

Usage 1: Right after she was in a car accident, Claire was so upset and *implacable* it took two hours for her to calm down.

Usage 2: The screaming child who wanted a chocolate bar was *implacable* and would not listen to his father's reasonable words.

Usage 3: Trish had an *implacable* hatred of anyone who ate meat, and she therefore found making friends to be quite difficult.

IMPLICATE (v) [IM-pli-keyt]

Meaning: incriminate; show to be involved; to show a connection to a crime

Usage 1: The prosecution *implicated* the defendant when they showed that the hat left at the scene of the crime belonged to the accused murderer.

Usage 2: The handkerchief was left there to *implicate* me as having a role in the crime, but I promise I was never there.

Usage 3: Thanks to decades of research and major technological advances, specific genes can now be *implicated* to cause certain diseases or disorders.

Usage 4: Why are you *implicating* that I actually had something to do with the missing books?

Usage 5: By dropping hints and making suggestions, Carla subtly *implicated* Dora as the one who was behind the whole scheme.

IMPORTUNE (v) [im-pawr-TOON]

Meaning: beg persistently; to ask someone for something repeatedly in an annoying way

Usage 1: I was *importuned* all day to paint my little sister's nails, so I finally agreed if she would stop bothering me.

Usage 2: After *importuning* his father for a month about a new dog, the boy was taken to the pound and allowed to pick out a new puppy.

Usage 3: Dr. Savage was *importuned* for weeks to speak at a conference, and I think she agreed just to keep them from calling her repeatedly.

IMPREGNABLE (adj) [im-PREG-n*uh*-b*uh* l]

Meaning: invulnerable; not able to be destroyed or captured

Usage 1: The *impregnable* fortress stayed in tact throughout all of the Middle Ages.

Usage 2: The cohesive and strong government was considered *impregnable,* as despite numerous coups it remained in tact.

Usage 3: My mother's refusal to yield to any of her children's requests was simply *impregnable*; I don't remember her ever giving in to any of us.

Usage 4: Dawn's *impregnable* spirit is admirable; she refuses to stay in bed even though she is receiving chemotherapy.

Usage 5: Their *impregnable* relationship is built upon fifty years' worth of trust and experience.

IMPROMPTU (adj) [im-PROMP-too]

Meaning: extemporaneous; without previous preparation; off hand; on the spur of the moment; done without thought or plan

Usage 1: The *impromptu* wedding consisted of a denim sundress, a grocery store cake, and a simple gold ring.

Usage 2: Sometimes *impromptu* parties are much more fun than those that take weeks to plan.

Usage 3: Wanda's *impromptu* outfit was thrown together at the very last minute.

Usage 4: Julie, Andrea, and I gathered yesterday for an *impromptu* lunch meeting.

IMPROPRIETY (n)   [im-pr*uh*-PRAHY-i-tee]

Meaning: improperness; unsuitableness; unacceptable or inappropriate behavior, character, or language

Usage 1: Linda's latest *impropriety* occurred when she wore her own wedding dress to Lucinda's wedding.

Usage 2: I can't believe Rod had the nerve to commit the *impropriety* of making out with his new girlfriend right in front of his former mother-in-law!

Usage 3: Stories and rumors about sexual *impropriety* eventually led to the minister stepping down from the pulpit.

IMPROVISE (v)   [IM-pr*uh*-vahyz]

Meaning: to do something on the spur of the moment

Usage 1: I have played the saxophone for years, and have gotten to the point that I enjoy *improvising* when I don't have my music in front of me.

Usage 2: Right before meeting with her supervisor, Tanya remembered she was supposed to come prepared with a case study, and instead had to *improvise*.

Usage 3: Stella forgot about her class presentation on mitosis, but managed to *improvise* her way through it.

Usage 4: I don't own much piano sheet music, but I *improvise* often.

Usage 5: Rather than use a cookbook, Juliette usually *improvised* and ended up creating dozens of delicious recipes on her own.

IMPUDENCE (n)   [IM-py*uh*-d*uh* ns]

Meaning: impertinence; insolence; offensively bold behavior

Usage 1: Bert constantly insults other people without regard and doesn't seem to understand his own *impudence*.

Usage 2: The toddler's *impudence* was clear when he smacked his own mother right in the face.

Usage 3: Francesa had the *impudence* to bring her new boyfriend with her to graduation.

Usage 4: Jacob's *impudence* during the town council meeting led to his being asked to leave by the local police.

IMPUGN (v)   [im-PYOON]

Meaning: contradict (often in an insulting way); challenge; gainsay; to call into question; to dispute the truth, validity, or honesty of a statement or motive

Usage 1: Many historical figures have *impugned* the Church for resisting change and being self-righteous.

Usage 2: The king's title was *impugned* only by those brave enough to speak out against what they believed to be unjust treatment of the poor.

Usage 3: I do not claim to *impugn* their intentions, but the end result is clearly wrong.

Usage 4: Mr. Hill *impugned* Rebecca so severely in front of us that it's no wonder Rebecca didn't come to school today.

Usage 5: Professor Jackson was *impugned* by his students after he deliberately changed the format of the exam right after he distributed a study guide based on the old format.

INCANDESCENT (adj)   [in-k*uh* n-DES-*uh* nt]

Meaning: strikingly bright; shining with intense heat; to create light when heated

Usage 1: Incandescent light bulbs are slowly being replaced by LED bulbs.

Usage 2: The *incandescent* lamp lit the entire cabin, while Marsha strained to stay awake until she could finish the book.

Usage 3: There are some small fish that are naturally *incandescent*, and seem to be glowing from the inside out.

Usage 4: She saw an *incandescent* glow coming from the living room, and upon going downstairs saw that it was her father, reading by candlelight.

INCARCERATE (v)   [in-KAHR-s*uh*-reyt]

Meaning: imprison; to put someone in prison

Usage 1: Donna's father has been *incarcerated* since she was four years old, and she only sees him during visitation once a week.

Usage 2: The police threatened to *incarcerate* the young teenager for jaywalking, even though he wasn't aware he had done anything wrong.

Usage 3: Jeff was *incarcerated* for a brief time when he was in college, but this has since been erased from his record.

INCENDIARY (n)   [in-SEN-dee-er-ee]

Meaning: arsonist; a person who starts fires, or a person who agitates others

Usage 1: After lighting his apartment building on fire twice, the little boy was known for being quite an *incendiary*.

Usage 2: The outside *incendiaries* who are stuck on overthrowing the government have been conducting protests all week long.

Usage 3: Barry, an *incendiary*, was sent to prison for setting his ex-wife's car on fire.

Usage 4: Terrance's *incendiary* tendencies do not bode well for his future, as he's already been to juvenile detention twice.

Usage 5: My mother used to joke that I would become an *incendiary*, but thankfully I became a fireman instead.

INCESSANT (adj)   [in-SES-*uh* nt]

Meaning: uninterrupted; unceasing; continue without stopping or pause

Usage 1: The *incessant* noise from the repair crew was interfering with the baby's afternoon nap.

Usage 2: All I wanted was to get away from the *incessant* emails and phone calls at work.

Usage 3: The rehearsals leading up to opening day became so *incessant* I was singing and reciting lines in my sleep.

Usage 4: The *incessant* buzzing from mosquitoes around my ears finally prompted me to go back inside.

INCIDENTAL (adj)   [in-si-DEN-tl]

Meaning: not essential; minor; accompanying but not a major part of something

Usage 1: We can absorb *incidental* costs such as parking and subway fees, but need to budget carefully for meals and hotels.

Usage 2: There were many *incidental* findings in the legal case that were not ultimately brought before the jury.

Usage 3: The link between the CEO and his secretary could no longer be called *incidental*.

INCIPIENT (adj)   [in-SIP-ee-*uh* nt]

Meaning: beginning; in an early stage; beginning to come into being or become apparent

Usage 1: In the *incipient* stages of her pregnancy, Lucy could tell small changes in how her clothes fit and how tired she was at the end of the day.

Usage 2: Even though I just met her today, I have an *incipient* dislike for her.

Usage 3: The artist often did not know what the end product would be when his paintings were in the *incipient* stages.

INCLEMENT (adj)   [in-KLEM-*uh* nt]

Meaning: stormy; unkind; physically severe, as in weather; having rain or storms

Usage 1: The golf match was postponed due to *inclement* weather throughout the whole weekend.

Usage 2: The *inclement* weather policy stated that school would open two hours late if roads were icy.

Usage 3: On my wedding day, the sun was shining and there was no risk of *inclement* weather.

Usage 4: Summertime in the South is marked by days of beautiful, unrelenting sunshine interrupted by severe storms and *inclement* weather.

Usage 5: Hail, lightning storms, and snow are all examples of *inclement* weather.

INCOGNITO (adj)   [in-kog-NEE-toh]

Meaning: with identity concealed; using an assumed name; with one's true identity kept secret

Usage 1: Because she is an attorney for such a high-profile case, Charlotte travelled *incognito* by dying her hair and wearing sunglasses.

Usage 2: If Mr. Smith wants to remain *incognito*, he needs to stop telling people all about his childhood and where he comes from.

Usage 3: These days, people think they are *incognito* and can say whatever they want on social media sites, but they can be tracked down quickly.

Usage 4: After rumors started spreading around the hospital that she was having an affair with the nurse, Dr. Shapiro went *incognito* around town by frequenting places she didn't normally go.

INCOMMODIOUS (adj)   [in-k*uh*-MOH-dee-*uh* s]

Meaning: not spacious; inconvenient or uncomfortable

Usage 1: This chair is incredibly *incommodious*; the back is hard and the seat almost touches the floor.

Usage 2: Even though her new car was cute, Charla admitted that its size made it quite *incommodious*.

Usage 3: After being used to his own office for years, Cliff found his tiny cubicle *incommodious*.

INCONTINENT (adj)   [in-KON-tn-*uh* NT]

Meaning: lacking self-restraint; licentious; unrestrained; uncontrolled

Usage 1: The young puppy was not yet housebroken, and became *incontinent* all over the floor while they were out.

Usage 2: Ralph is truly an *incontinent* man; he gives way to any sort of pleasure that comes his way without stopping or thinking about it.

Usage 3: When he drinks, Chase becomes *incontinent* and often gets himself in serious trouble because he can't make rational decisions.

Usage 4: Though Vivi has been toilet-trained for about a year, sometimes she is still *incontinent* in the middle of the night.

Usage 5: Incontinent incidents, joint pain, and overall tiredness come with old age.

INCORRIGIBLE (adj)   [in-KAWR-i-j*uh*-b*uh* l]

Meaning: not correctable; incapable of being reformed or corrected

Usage 1: Those little twins are simply *incorrigible* - they throw tantrums constantly and hit each other and their parents when they don't get their way.

Usage 2: Unfortunately, the forensic psychologist decided that the convicted felon was *incorrigible*, as he conveyed no regrets for his actions.

Usage 3: We had to give the puppy away, as it was simply *incorrigible* and chewed on everything in sight.

INCREMENT (n)   [IN-kr*uh*-m*uh* nt]

Meaning: a small increase, gain, or augmentation

Usage 1: When completing a big project, it is helpful to break it down into small *increments*.

Usage 2: After years in therapy, Shauna noticed *increments* in the ways she related to people and dealt with her anxiety.

Usage 3: Johnny's allowance increased by five-dollar *increments* over the course of a year.

Usage 4: The bank teller counted out the foreign currency in *increments* of ten euros.

Usage 5: The little girl was just learning to count, but could already count in *increments* of twos and threes.

INCRUSTATION (n)   [in-kruh-STEY-sh*uh* n]

Meaning: hard coating or crust; a coating of a hard material, such as a decorative technique or a scab

Usage 1: The platter was full of nuts and dried fruit with an *incrustation* of crystallized honey.

Usage 2: My cat returned home in the morning, and I could tell she had been in a fight by the *incrustation* over a cut on her left ear.

Usage 3: The caramel dessert was delicious, from the creamy center to the outer *incrustation* of brown sugar.

Usage 4: The cheesecake looked too beautiful to eat, with a thin *incrustation* of honey all along the edge.

INCUBUS (n)   [IN-ky*uh*-b*uh* s]

Meaning: burden; mental care; a disturbing nightmare; an evil spirit or fiend

Usage 1: Following the trauma of a severe car accident, Kelsey had a horrible *incubus* from which she awoke sweating and screaming.

Usage 2: Patti said the experience wasn't caused by anything other than an evil *incubus* wanting to destroy the children's lives.

Usage 3: The greedy *incubus* who ruled over the land destroyed fields, took money from the poor, and burned cities to the ground.

INCURSION (n)   [in-KUR-zh*uh* n]

Meaning: a raid or invasion; aggressive entrance into foreign territory; an entering into

Usage 1: The *incursion* into enemy territory took all of the residents by surprise.

Usage 2: Larry's *incursion* into theater was marked by his role as the lead in Hamlet.

Usage 3: Due to the high level of conflict between the two nations, there are frequent *incursions* from either side throughout the summer.

Usage 4: The unexpected *incursion* into the native settlers' camp was met with bows and arrows and cries of warfare.

Usage 5: The boys decided to plan an *incursion* in the middle of the night to disrupt the girls' sleepover in the tree-house.

INDEMNIFY (v)   [in-DEM-n*uh*-fahy]

Meaning: make secure against loss; compensate for loss; to give or promise to give the cost of possible future damage, loss, or injury

Usage 1: In marriages, neither party offers to *indemnify* the other - it is an act of trust to share a life and banking account with another.

Usage 2: It is ridiculous to even consider buying an insurance policy if it does not *indemnify* the insured against loss or liability.

Usage 3: When Lisa was buying her first home, she was overwhelmed with the homeowner's policy she was required to buy and the fact that it *indemnified* her against all manner of things.

Usage 4: Thankfully, I was *indemnified* by returning that ugly Christmas sweater to the store and getting store credit.

Chapter **26**

Indiscriminate – Motley

This chapter covers the following words, each with its part of speech, pronunciation, and descriptive meaning.

Usage of the word is also illustrated in three to five sample sentences.

indiscriminate	lithe	mollycoddle
indomitable	loath	monarchy
inebriety	longevity	monolithic
ineluctable	loquacious	moratorium
inerrability	lucre	mordant
inexorable	lugubrious	moribund
infantile	lumen	mortify
infernal	lustrous	motley
infinitesimal	marital	
influx	matriarch	
jabber	matrix	
jaded	maudlin	
jargon	mete	
jaundiced	millinery	
kaleidoscope	mirth	
ken	miscegenation	
lascivious	misogamy	
laudatory	misogynist	
laxative	mitigate	
lexicographer	modicum	
libido	modulation	

INDISCRIMINATE (adj)   [in-di-SKRIM-*uh*-nit]

Meaning: choosing at random; confused; not making or based on careful distinctions

Usage 1: The attorney was rather *indiscriminate* in choosing who would testify at the trial.

Usage 2: Even though she is on a diet, Jane made *indiscriminate* choices at the buffet and ended up eating fried chicken and chocolate cake.

Usage 3: When it comes to fashion, I am *indiscriminate*, as I never know how to match my outfit.

Usage 4: It seems to me that the volleyball team is made up of *indiscriminate* members, as some are very good but others look like they've never seen a net.

INDOMITABLE (adj)   [in-DOM-i-t*uh*-b*uh* l]

Meaning: unconquerable; unyielding; incapable of being overcome or subdued

Usage 1: He truly is an *indomitable* leader, as his guidance prevailed even in the most intense and stressful circumstances.

Usage 2: The *indomitable* tennis star crushed her opponent in the first two sets.

Usage 3: The little boy's *indomitable* spirit carried him through two courses of chemotherapy for a rare form of cancer.

Usage 4: The Olympic star's *indomitable* spirit was partially the reason she won the gold medal.

INEBRIETY (adj)   [in-i-BRAHY-i-tee]

Meaning: habitual intoxication; the state of being drunk or intoxicated

Usage 1: When Bob is in a state of *inebriety*, he thinks everything is funny.

Usage 2: In her *inebriety*, Carla mistook Jim for her husband and tried to leave the party with him.

Usage 3: Though he tried to compose himself, Patrick's *inebriety* was apparent to anyone who came within ten feet of him.

INELUCTABLE (adj)   [in-i-LUHK-t*uh*-b*uh* l]

Meaning: irresistible; inevitable; not to be avoided or escaped

Usage 1: It was devastating news to hear that Rich was diagnosed with this type of cancer, as it is known for its quick and *ineluctable* decline.

Usage 2: Their *ineluctable* relationship was one of fairytales, as the couple met when they were in Kindergarten and courted all through school.

Usage 3: After the smells of chocolate chip cookies wafted through the house, it was *ineluctable* that the children would soon gather in the kitchen.

Usage 4: Val knew there was no sense in trying to escape her parents' *ineluctable* consequences after she broke curfew.

Usage 5: Mental illness runs in my family, so it was *ineluctable* that I would also suffer from at least a mild form of depression.

INERRABILITY (n)   [in-ER-*uh* bil-i-tee]

Meaning: infallibility; freedom or exemption from error

Usage 1: The *inerrability* of the pastor led to many heated discussions and conflicts as various congregation members challenged his views.

Usage 2: Many people believe that great historical political figures are known for their *inerrability*, as they are often regarded as well-knowing and never wrong.

Usage 3: The *inerrability* of the customer is always the number one principle to adhere by when you are working in retail.

Usage 4: In his complacency, Trey was convinced that his *inerrability* meant he was always right.

INEXORABLE (adj)   [in-EK-ser-*uh*-b*uh* l]

Meaning: relentless; unyielding; implacable; not capable of being persuaded

Usage 1: The *inexorable* pleas by the little boy finally led to her giving in to him and buying him a candy bar.

Usage 2: Paper records are in an *inexorable* decline, as electronic medical records are being implemented all over the country.

Usage 3: Health insurance companies often require *inexorable* prerequisites in order to cover people.

INFANTILE (adj)   [IN-f*uh* n-tahyl]

Meaning: childish; suggesting a lack of maturity

Usage 1: The high school students acted *infantile* when they were told that the rules regarding lunchtime were changed.

Usage 2: Scarlet fever is typically thought of as an *infantile* illness, though I have seen several adults come down with it.

Usage 3: The young couple's relationship was quite *infantile*, as she pouted when she didn't get her way and he often threw temper tantrums when he was upset with her.

Usage 4: That tantrum you threw in front of everyone at the store was absolutely *infantile*.

Usage 5: I wonder what Caleb said to Sylvie to make her act so *infantile* in front of all of their friends.

INFERNAL (adj)   [in-FUR-nl]

Meaning: devilish; relating to hell or the lower world of the dead

Usage 1: Ted was so opposed to slavery in principle that he often referred to it as an '*infernal* practice.'

Usage 2: The *infernal* tones of the novel gave it a somber and disturbing tone.

Usage 3: Christian writing often alludes to heaven but also makes *infernal* references, as both worlds are part of the Christian belief system.

Usage 4: I was raised in the church, and often pondered everyone's heavenly or *infernal* futures.

INFINITESIMAL (adj)   [in-fin-i-TES-*uh*-m*uh* l]

Meaning: very small; immeasurably or incalculably minute

Usage 1: Though the kitchen floor appeared clean, Jack could still see the *infinitesimal* number of crumbs gathered in the corners.

Usage 2: One snowflake is *infinitesimal*; thousand of snowflakes create a snowfall.

Usage 3: There is an *infinitesimal* amount of peanut butter in the jar, so why don't you just throw it away?

INFLUX (n)   [IN-fluhks]

Meaning: flowing into; a mass arrival or incoming

Usage 1: At the beginning of the school year, there is an *influx* of new students who moved over the summer.

Usage 2: The days before Christmas see an *influx* in sales for toy stores.

Usage 3: There has been an *influx* in the number of calls to our customer service department due to the recent malfunction in the product.

Usage 4: Flu season usually is commensurate with an *influx* of patients coming to urgent care.

Usage 5: The recession led to an *influx* of people wanting to join credit unions rather than banks.

JABBER (v)   [JAB-er]

Meaning: chatter rapidly or unintelligibly; to engage in excited, fast, and sometimes nonsensical talk

Usage 1: After his first day of kindergarten, the five-year-old *jabbered* all the way home about his new friends.

Usage 2: My mother has a real talent for *jabbering* on for hours while really saying nothing.

Usage 3: The twins can *jabber* for hours to each other in their secret language that only they understand.

Usage 4: My uncle is the most talkative person you've met, and can *jabber* with anyone he meets.

JADED (adj)   [JEY-did]

Meaning: fatigued; surfeited; made dull, apathetic, or cynical by experience or overworking

Usage 1: After series of nasty breakups, Clark became *jaded* and found fault with every woman he went on a date with.

Usage 2: Emily was a *jaded* social worker, always finding fault in the families that she worked with.

Usage 3: Maybe I'm becoming too *jaded* about the state of our youth these days, as I constantly find problems with the way they relate to me.

JARGON (n)   [JAHR-g*uh* n]

Meaning: technical terminology; gibberish; the language of a particular trade or group

Usage 1: Please drop the medical *jargon* and just explain to us what the treatment for this type of cancer will be.

Usage 2: When talking with clients, it is important to remember they probably won't understand all the psychological *jargon* you usually use.

Usage 3: Internet *jargon* is constantly changing and I often have no idea what those terms mean.

Usage 4: The woman politely asked the doctor to drop the medical *jargon* and tell her in laymen's terms what was wrong with her son.

Usage 5: My husband, an accountant, often lapses into financial *jargon* that no one in our family understands.

JAUNDICED (adj)   [JAWN-dist]

Meaning: Exhibiting envy, prejudice, or hostility

Usage 1: George was *jaundiced* toward the medical field after a botched surgery left his father comatose.

Usage 2: Lauren became quite *jaundiced* toward her neighbor, who seemingly had a perfect marriage, job, and family.

Usage 3: I have to admit that even I was *jaundiced* toward the mayor's wife, who always seemed to be going to fancy parties and wearing expensive clothes.

Usage 4: After Sara was turned down for the supervisor position, she became *jaundiced* toward all of her coworkers.

KALEIDOSCOPE (n)   [k*uh*-LAHY-d*uh*-skohp]

Meaning: a toy consisting of a tube with mirrors and glass that can be turned to create different patterns and colors

Usage 1: The little boy was fascinated with his first *kaleidoscope* and the way the colors and lights changed.

Usage 2: The sunset was simply breathtaking, as the way it shone through the gardens created a *kaleidoscope* of colors and shades.

Usage 3: By rotating the stage and the lights, the crew was able to create a *kaleidoscope* effect.

KEN (n)   [ken]

Meaning: range of knowledge; the range of what one knows

Usage 1: Jack's *ken* ranges from how to cook the perfect pancake to the exact pieces of legislation Lyndon Johnson passed while he was in office.

Usage 2: My *ken* as it relates to social work has come in handy many times since I've begun providing individual therapy to clients.

Usage 3: Though your *ken* of biological sciences is now narrow, by the time you graduate you will know more than you ever thought possible.

Usage 4: Ella's knowledge of medieval poetry is quite impressive, though this *ken* has not yet led to a successful career.

Usage 5: The dermatologist suggested sending the specimen off to a lab, as determination of skin cancer was well beyond his *ken*.

LASCIVIOUS (adj)　[l*uh*-SIV-ee-*uh* s]

Meaning: Expressing lust or uncontrollable sexual desire

Usage 1: The old man was asked to leave the bar after he gave a group of young girls *lascivious* looks.

Usage 2: William is an unhappy man with a greedy and *lascivious* character.

Usage 3: Carol and Ron have been married for years, but I sometimes catch him giving her a wink or a lascivious look.

LAUDATORY (adj)　[LAW-d*uh*-tawr-ee]

Meaning: Expressing praise through speech or actions

Usage 1: The president was *laudatory* of the valedictorian's contributions to this year's graduating class.

Usage 2: I know Chandler is a smart child, but must his parents always be so *laudatory* about him?

Usage 3: My grandfather's headstone contains a *laudatory* epithet about his mission and volunteer work in the community.

Usage 4: The professor was *laudatory* of his students, as they all worked very hard together to write and produce an entire play.

LAXATIVE (adj)　[LAK-s*uh*-tiv]

Meaning: stimulating the evacuation of the bowels

Usage 1: Some people with eating disorders take *laxatives* as a way of purging their systems of any extra food or waste.

Usage 2: Caffeine is often thought of as a *laxative,* which is one reason people drink caffeinated coffee in the morning.

Usage 3: In case of constipation, treatment usually consists of *laxatives* and increasing daily intake of fiber.

LEXICOGRAPHER (n)　[lek-si-KOG-r*uh*-fer]

Meaning: a person who writes or compiles a dictionary

Usage 1: The famous *lexicographer* constantly collects new words and writes down snippets of comments he hears in conversations.

Usage 2: The Latin scholar and *lexicographer* spent his career studying the ancient language and providing interpretations for others.

Usage 3: Dictionaries are often written and compiled by *lexicographers* rather than language experts, who would be able to give more insight into word usage.

Usage 4: Dan always dreamed of becoming a *lexicographer,* as he always loved words and their various meanings.

LIBIDO (n)   [li-BEE-doh]

Meaning: emotional urges behind human activity; emotional energy of biological desires, particularly sexual desire

Usage 1: Van expected his *libido* to decrease as he aged, but after he remarried he found that it only increased over time.

Usage 2: Impotence is different from low *libido*, as impotence refers to the inability to perform sexually while low libido is the absence of the actual desire.

Usage 3: A woman's *libido* is more difficult to measure than a man's, as it usually includes the desire to connect emotionally with her partner.

LITHE (adj)   [lahy*th*]

Meaning: having a graceful, flexible body

Usage 1: Yoga has kept Grace's *lithe* body in shape throughout her sixties.

Usage 2: The *lithe* ballerina jumped and twirled her way through the entire piece.

Usage 3: The *lithe* cat jumped from floor to couch without making a sound.

Usage 4: I used to be much more *lithe* than I am now, as I can't even touch my toes anymore.

Usage 5: She is as *lithe* as a cat, as she can jump and skip across the ice like it's nothing.

LOATH (adj)   [loh*th*]

Meaning: disinclined; unwilling or reluctant

Usage 1: After a night of socializing and spending time with friends, Harriet was *loath* to leave the party.

Usage 2: Though it was obvious to everyone around him, Darrel was *loath* to admit that he was drunk.

Usage 3: The politician was *loath* to face up to the fact that he had accepted bribes from companies in return for passing legislation in their favor.

Usage 4: I am *loath* to admit my mistakes, though sometimes it's necessary.

Usage 5: During the child custody case, the social worker was *loath* to testify against a mother she had just spoken with that morning.

LONGEVITY (n)   [lon-JEV-i-tee]

Meaning: long life; the amount of time one's life or term of service lasts

Usage 1: My *longevity* with the state is 27 years; three more years and I'll be able to retire.

Usage 2: Crystal often pondered the *longevity* of her marriage to Rodney, as they fought all the time yet never considered divorce.

Usage 3: The panda bear held a record for *longevity* in that particular zoo, as she had been there five years longer than any other panda before her.

Usage 4: In general, women have greater *longevity* than men.

LOQUACIOUS (adj)   [loh-KWEY-sh*uh* s]

Meaning: talkative; enjoying conversation and talking

Usage 1: Cybil's *loquacious* phone calls every night leave me exhausted, even though I never say a word.

Usage 2: Even as a child, Tom was known for being *loquacious*, as he could talk for hours without taking a break.

Usage 3: You can tell Jon has had a few drinks because he becomes *loquacious*.

Usage 4: Jillian is the most *loquacious* person I know, and she can find things to talk about where there are none.

Usage 5: I have never been a *loquacious* person; I'm quiet and more reserved than most.

LUCRE (n)   [LOO-ker]

Meaning: Riches, money, or profits, especially regarded as gained in a dishonorable way

Usage 1: After the lawsuit, neither party was given the *lucre* as they were both penalized for disorderly conduct.

Usage 2: Fifi told Jillian that she didn't want her filthy *lucre*, which was earned through underhanded bribes.

Usage 3: The *lucre* was obtained during nights of cigar-smoking and poker in the back room.

Usage 4: Marva refused to accept any of what she considered to be filthy *lucre*, even though it would have made her rich.

LUGUBRIOUS (adj)   [loo-GOO-bree-*uh* s]

Meaning: mournful; sad or depressed, as in mood or affect

Usage 1: Cherry looked *lugubrious* every time I saw her in the weeks after her father died.

Usage 2: The baritone's voice was *lugubrious* and somber, yet strikingly beautiful.

Usage 3: At the funeral, I couldn't help but glance at each person's *lugubrious* expression.

Usage 4: The *lugubrious* child never wanted to go outside and play; he just sat inside and stared out the window.

Usage 5: Sandy looks so *lugubrious* because she just lost her job and broke up with Jake last week.

LUMEN (n)   [LOO-m*uh* n]

Meaning: unit of light energy (one candle's worth); the measure of brightness from a light source

Usage 1: A 100-watt light bulb contains 1,200 *lumens*.

Usage 2: Brightness measures the total amount of light projected by something in *lumens*.

Usage 3: When you shop for light bulbs, make sure to compare the *lumens* to ensure you are buying the amount of light you want.

Usage 4: Building design teams can give occupants sufficient light outside after dark by using fixtures with a high number of *lumens*.

LUSTROUS (adj)   [LUHS-tr*uh* s]

Meaning: shiny and bright

Usage 1: Shampoo commercials always show *lustrous*, strong hair as proof that their products work.

Usage 2: The horse's *lustrous* black coat was brushed everyday by his faithful owner.

Usage 3: The walkway leading up to the front door of the mansion was composed of smooth, *lustrous* stones.

MARITAL (adj)   [MAR-i-tl]

Meaning: related to marriage

Usage 1: They were the pictures of *marital* bliss - holding hands, taking late night walks, and frequent vacations.

Usage 2: Derek is known all over town for his *marital* infidelity and lies.

Usage 3: The *marital* relationship is a complicated one - who expects anyone to live with someone for the rest of their lives and always be happy about it?

Usage 4: Even though Bruce has denounced his religious upbringing years ago, he highly values *marital* fidelity and altruism.

Usage 5: Tony and Jess composed their own *marital* vows rather than reciting more traditional ones.

MATRIARCH (n)   [MEY-tree-ahrk]

Meaning: woman who rules a family or larger social group; a woman who is the head of a family or a powerful mother figure

Usage 1: Rose Kennedy, the mother of President and Bobby Kennedy, was a great example of a *matriarch*.

Usage 2: My grandmother, the *matriarch* of our Italian family, loves cooking for twenty people every week.

Usage 3: Christina, the *matriarch* of the family, was diagnosed with cancer last week and her family is at a loss at what to do when she is sick.

MATRIX (n)   [MEY-triks]

Meaning: point of origin; array of numbers or algebraic symbols; mold or die; a situation or surrounding substance within which something else originates, develops, or is contained

Usage 1: Donny likes to organize a list like a *matrix*, in which there are numerous rows and columns each representing the intersection of other pieces of information.

Usage 2: Cement is made up of the *matrix*, which is the lime, and the aggregate, the hard stone embedded in the lime.

Usage 3: The construction team uses a *matrix* made of local materials, but the stone they add to it is from anywhere.

Usage 4: My husband is a former bricklayer, so he knows all about the *matrix* and the aggregate.

MAUDLIN (adj)   [MAWD-lin]

Meaning: effusively sentimental; tearfully sentimental; weak and silly

Usage 1: The gypsy's method of collecting change is to approach tourists with a *maudlin* tone and tell a story about a sick child.

Usage 2: Graduation night is supposed to be exciting, so why are you getting so *maudlin* about it?

Usage 3: Trisha couldn't help herself; she was so overcome with the *maudlin* tone of the wedding that she began sobbing uncontrollably.

METE (v)   [meet]

Meaning: to hand out, distribute, or measure

Usage 1: Professor Thomas was an extreme conservationist, and counted each photocopy he made and *meted* them out carefully.

Usage 2: At the store, it seemed like everywhere he looked Sonny saw physical discipline *meted* out on young children.

Usage 3: The midwife was *meted* out a sentence of a $200 fine due to practicing without a medical license.

MILLINERY (n)   [MIL-*uh*-ner-ee]

Meaning: shop that sells women's hats; women's hats and headdresses

Usage 1: The art of *millinery* is underappreciated these days, as dress has become more and more casual.

Usage 2: The Industrial Revolution and the rise of the factory worker led to fewer *millineries* and locally- owned hat shops.

Usage 3: Sara went to the local shop to purchase *millinery* for her church outfits.

Usage 4: My grandmother still has a closet full of *millinery*, though she never wears any of it anymore.

Usage 5: I miss the days of hoop skirts, *millinery*, and courtship.

MIRTH (n)   [murth]

Meaning: merriment; laughter or amusement

Usage 1: The sounds of children's *mirth* echoed through the hallways on the last day of school.

Usage 2: As my father told the joke, I could read the *mirth* in his eyes even though the rest of his face and body appeared serious.

Usage 3: I love Christmas, if not for the presents for the *mirth* expressed around the world on that day.

Usage 4: Following the birth of their first child, sounds of *mirth* could be heard through the door of the delivery room.

Usage 5: My childhood is marked by periods of *mirth* and a general sense of security.

MISCEGENATION (n)   [mi-sej-*uh*-NEY-sh*uh* n]

Meaning: intermarriage between persons of two different races; marriage or sexual relations between a man and woman of different races

Usage 1: At one time, *miscegenation* was a crime which carried serious consequences.

Usage 2: Miscegenation was included in the Bible as a crime punishable by God, as God did not intend for members of different tribes to reproduce.

Usage 3: Prior to emancipation, *miscegenation* occurred more frequently than we know now, and was often overlooked if the male counterpart was wealthy or in a position of power.

Usage 4: Miscegenation is no longer out of the ordinary, but only fifty years ago it was considered obscene in some parts of the country.

MISOGAMY (n)   [mi-SOG-*uh*-mee]

Meaning: Hatred of or opposition to marriage

Usage 1: Three divorces later, Sherree began to understand why some people support *misogamy*.

Usage 2: Leroy's *misogamy* comes from the fact that his parents were married for fifty years yet neither of them ever seemed happy.

Usage 3: Misogamy is much more common in males than females, for males feel that traditional forms of marriage are confining and restrictive.

Usage 4: Misogamy is becoming increasingly unpopular, as people start to realize the values of marriage.

Usage 5: Eddie used to believe in *misogamy*, but now that many states allow same-sex unions his views have changed.

MISOGYNIST (n)   [mi-SOJ-*uh*-nist]

Meaning: hater of women; someone who hates women

Usage 1: Todd is such a *misogynist*; he's always making snide comments about his wife or women in the office when he thinks they can't hear.

Usage 2: Ralph doesn't realize he is a *misogynist*, but his sarcastic remarks about how stupid and manipulative women are make it clear to everyone else.

Usage 3: This office has no tolerance for *misogynists*, as all the employees are female.

Usage 4: I finally had to quit my job after years of putting up with that *misogynist*, who constantly belittled all the women in the office.

MITIGATE (v)   [MIT-i-geyt]

Meaning: appease; moderate; to make something less severe, harsh, or painful

Usage 1: Thanks to the pharmaceutical interventions of the 21st century, there are numerous drugs used to mitigate pain.

Usage 2: The detrimental effects of warfare were *mitigated* by reconstruction efforts coordinated by the federal government.

Usage 3: In trying to *mitigate* the effects of her son's depression, Judy bought a new puppy and made all of her son's favorite foods.

Usage 4: The anti-nausea medication will *mitigate* the effects of the chemotherapy.

MODICUM (n)   [MOD-i-k*uh* m]

Meaning: a very small amount or limited quantity

Usage 1: I am lactose intolerant, but when I eat spaghetti I like a *modicum* of cheese on top.

Usage 2: Zoe doesn't really like Tom, so the compliment he gave her today about her voice gave her a *modicum* of confidence.

Usage 3: We all felt a *modicum* of relief after realizing our presentation would be after lunch, but still felt nervous.

Usage 4: The employees at my company gave a *modicum* of their monthly earnings which totaled enough to fund the project.

Usage 5: The politicians didn't give even a *modicum* of grace to each other during the debate.

MODULATION (n)   [moj-*uh*-LEY-sh*uh* n]

Meaning: toning down; changing from one key to another; a variation in pitch or stress in speech

Usage 1: My roommate is a speech therapist, so I am always self-conscious about my pronunciation and *modulation* when I talk.

Usage 2: Her voice was capable of precise *modulation*, which led her to major roles in musicals and other performances.

Usage 3: Periodic *modulation* of psychiatric medications is sometimes necessary when treating a serious mental illness.

Usage 4: The *modulation* in her voice was clear when she was very stressed or anxious.

MOLLYCODDLE (v)   [MOL-ee-kod-l]

Meaning: to pamper or coddle; to indulge excessively

Usage 1: Pamela was raised as an only child in a wealthy home, and was *mollycoddled* constantly by her parents.

Usage 2: When he entered college, Cameron was surprised to find that his professors were not interested in *mollycoddling*, but expected him to meet deadlines and study for exams.

Usage 3: We try not to *mollycoddle* our children, because we think they need to have natural consequences for their behaviors.

MONARCHY (n)   [MON-er-kee]

Meaning: a government ruled by a single person, usually in a hereditary role

Usage 1: England's *monarchy* has a certain dignity about it and shows no signs of changing.

Usage 2: There is a difference between an absolute *monarchy* and the monarchies of today, in which citizens have a say in the decision-making process.

Usage 3: Frank is completely against *monarchies* and believes they exist only because no one has the courage to question them.

Usage 4: I've always felt there is something worth preserving about a *monarchy*.

Usage 5: Though many people criticize them, the *monarchies* of today are often glorified in pictures of entertainment magazines.

MONOLITHIC (adj)   [mon-*uh*-LITH-ik]

Meaning: solidly uniform; unyielding; something that is large or massive, or something that is made of a large block of stone

Usage 1: The *monolithic* structure is thought to have been made by the Druids, and still stands today.

Usage 2: The *monolithic* corporation has over ten thousand employees and has offices all over the world.

Usage 3: The *monolithic* sculpture, though massive, stood in the middle of the park and was a topic of conversation for most people who walked by.

Usage 4: The media is a *monolithic* existence that rules all of our lives.

MORATORIUM (n)   [mawr-*uh*-TAWR-ee-*uh* m]

Meaning: legal delay of payment; a temporary prohibition of an activity

Usage 1: The county has declared a *moratorium* on water use until the new budget is passed.

Usage 2: Thanks to the new president, there is a *moratorium* in place that delays student loan payback.

Usage 3: Due to various complaints received by the medical ethics board, there is a *moratorium* on all cloning experiments.

MORDANT (adj)   [MAWR-dnt]

Meaning: biting; stinging; very sarcastic or painful wit or speech

Usage 1: Kyle says he just has a sarcastic sense of humor, but his *mordant* tone suggests that he is being cruel.

Usage 2: Mordant comedy often is very popular, as very few people have the courage to make those types of remarks themselves.

Usage 3: Mordant sarcasm is common at my workplace, though I feel uncomfortable with it and often just keep my mouth shut.

Usage 4: Nat has a sick sense of humor; he likes the *mordant* characters in books and movies the most.

Usage 5: Her *mordant* sense of humor sometimes catches all of us off guard.

MORIBUND (adj)   [MAWR-*uh*-buhnd]

Meaning: at or near death; lacking in life and vitality

Usage 1: Mike's *moribund* appearance told me that he would die in the next few days.

Usage 2: Rather than remember my grandmother in her *moribund* state at the end of her life, I choose to remember the times she was energetic and full of life.

Usage 3: The *moribund* nation is practically destroyed; its government has fled, houses are burned, and the land is littered with bodies of people and animals.

Usage 4: The *moribund* figure keeps appearing in my nightmares, even though I don't know who it is or why it is showing up.

MORTIFY (v)   [MAWR-t*uh*-fahy]

Meaning: punish the flesh; to cause someone to feel ashamed, embarrassed, or humiliated; to practice self- denial

Usage 1: Chester was completely *mortified* when his mother came into his class in the middle of the day to bring him his lunchbox.

Usage 2: Ashley was *mortified* when Ashley's boyfriend called and her grandmother told him Ashley was using the toilet.

Usage 3: I was never more *mortified* than when I fell down the stairs of the stage after giving my presentation to a hundred of my peers.

Usage 4: Though not socially accepted, some individuals in the Roman Catholic Church *mortify* the flesh even today as a way of denying themselves pleasure.

Usage 5: Angela's family was very religious when she was growing up, and it wasn't uncommon for her parents to *mortify* their children by disciplinary practices such as making them kneel for hours.

MOTLEY (adj)   [MOT-lee]

Meaning: multi-colored; varied in appearance or character; disparate or mixed

Usage 1: The *motley* group of kids was made up of girls and boys of all colors, all of whom were friends and didn't seem to mind their differences.

Usage 2: We went to the animal shelter to pick out a cat and were met with a *motley* group of kittens ranging from solid white to calico.

Usage 3: The city's *motley* flag was composed of purple, green, yellow, red, and orange, and lacked any sort of central theme.

Chapter 27

Mulct – Petrify

This chapter covers the following words, each with its part of speech, pronunciation, and descriptive meaning.

Usage of the word is also illustrated in three to five sample sentences.

mulct	overhaul	penumbra
muse	overt	penurious
mutter	overwrought	perception
myriad	pageant	peregrination
nautical	paradigm	peripheral
navigable	paranoia	perspicuous
nepotism	paraphernalia	pertinacious
nib	pariah	pest
nicety	parochial	pestilential
niggardly	parquet	petrify
nirvana	parsimonious	
objective	pastiche	
obloquy	patina	
obscure	patois	
obsession	peccadillo	
obtrusive	pecuniary	
optometrist	pedagogue	
ordination	pedant	
ossify	pejorative	
oust	pellucid	

MULCT (v)   [muhlkt]

Meaning: To punish by a fine or by depriving a person of something by fraudulent means

Usage 1: The government sometimes *mulcts* taxpayers for reasons such as infrastructure.

Usage 2: Rosa wasn't paying attention when Farrah *mulcted* her out of $10,000.

Usage 3: The automobile repairman was soon found guilty for *mulcting* his customers out of thousands of dollars for selling damaged parts as new ones.

MUSE (v)   [myooz]

Meaning: to ponder; to have deep thoughts; to meditate

Usage 1: In between studying, Shelly often *mused* about what her life would be like after she graduated.

Usage 2: Chandra and William spent hours *musing* over their unborn child and making up stories about what their life as a family would be like one day.

Usage 3: The artist *mused* over his blank canvases until inspiration struck, which sometimes took weeks.

Usage 4: Olivia *mused* over her paper for several minutes before composing a letter to her mother.

Usage 5: Renoir's famous sculpture shows a man *musing* over something of seemingly utmost importance.

MUTTER (v)   [MUHT-er]

Meaning: murmur or grumble; to speak or chatter in a low voice or in a way that is hard to hear

Usage 1: Though Patti was *muttering* under her breath, I could tell she was saying something mean about her peers.

Usage 2: The homeless lady walked along the sidewalk, *muttering* to herself about aliens and the end of the world.

Usage 3: As Brent was told to take a number and wait in line, he walked out of the doughnut shop while muttering to himself about fast food.

MYRIAD (n)   [MIR-ee-*uh* d]

Meaning: A countless or extremely great number

Usage 1: There are a *myriad* of ant species, from tiny ones to ones that are inches long.

Usage 2: I have a *myriad* of reasons for not wanting to go to the party, the fact that your mother will be there is only one of them.

Usage 3: Our new home has a *myriad* of pine trees in the front yard, which we plan to cut down later this year.

Usage 4: Her closet is full of a *myriad* of blouses and skirts.

NAUTICAL (adj)   [NAW-ti-k*uh* l]

Meaning: Relating to or characteristic of ships, sailors, or navigation in the water

Usage 1: The *nautical* breeze blowing off the lake onto the passengers in the sailboat felt heavenly on the humid day.

Usage 2: The little boy looked so cute in his *nautical* outfit, complete with a sailor's hat and pants.

Usage 3: The measure of *nautical* miles is used to describe distance and speed on the water.

NAVIGABLE (adj)   [NAV-i-g*uh*-b*uh* l]

Meaning: wide and deep enough to allow ships to pass through; able to be steered or directed

Usage 1: The *navigable* waters made it easy for trade ships to get in and out of the port.

Usage 2: Though the uppermost portions are narrow, the river widens further south and becomes more *navigable*.

Usage 3: The river that flows through the center of the city is surprisingly *navigable*.

Usage 4: Even though the waters are deep and *navigable*, the ship still managed to hit an iceberg.

Usage 5: Jack found the small, narrow lake *navigable*, as it was just wide enough to accommodate his canoe.

NEPOTISM (n)   [NEP-*uh*-tiz-*uh* m]

Meaning: favoritism (to a relative); giving relatives special treatment in the workplace

Usage 1: My boss's use of *nepotism* is disgusting; he has already given high-paid positions to both his children and a nephew.

Usage 2: Nepotism ran rampant in ancient Rome and Greece, where family members were regularly given appointments of high power.

Usage 3: Democracy signaled the end of most forms of *nepotism*, though it is still seen today in political family legacies in America.

Usage 4: Nepotism runs rampant in the state government, where family members fill up committee seats and children follow in the footsteps of their fathers.

NIB (n)   [nib]

Meaning: the bill or beak of a bird; the point or end of a pen

Usage 1: Before modern pens were invented, anyone who wrote had to dip the *nib* in a bottle of ink in order to write anything.

Usage 2: Calligraphists know the importance of a high-quality *nib* to the art of writing.

Usage 3: The cardinal jabbed his *nib* into the suet to get to a particular seed.

NICETY (n)   [NAHY-si-tee]

Meaning: precision; minute distinction; something calling for delicacy, accuracy, or precision in handling

Usage 1: The logger took pride in his works of great *nicety*, in which he felled trees in precise, exact rows.

Usage 2: The cookbook holder has the *nicety* of giving room for the entire book while also protecting the pages.

Usage 3: One of the *niceties* of this particular set of knives is the precision with which they cut.

Usage 4: The captain showed off the *niceties* of his gun, which quickly broke three holes in the bulls eye.

Usage 5: I am not used to such *niceties* as cheese graters and automatic coffee grinders.

NIGGARDLY (adj)   [NIG-erd-lee]

Meaning: not willing to spend money; parsimonious; grudging and petty in giving or spending

Usage 1: Charles can be so *niggardly* when he leaves a five percent tip for the waiter.

Usage 2: The *niggardly* old couple rarely went out to eat and often ate white bread and peanut butter at home.

Usage 3: The *niggardly* city council refused to consider any alterations to the budget.

Usage 4: Jim can be a *niggardly* spender, as he grumbles every time he has to reach for his wallet.

NIRVANA (n)   [nir-VAH-n*uh*]

Meaning: A place or state of being in complete peace and happiness

Usage 1: Jillian's idea of *nirvana* is an ice cream shop inside of Disneyworld.

Usage 2: In Buddhist teachings, the ultimate goal of life is *Nirvana*, the ultimate peace.

Usage 3: After winning the election by a landslide, the Democrats were in *nirvana* for the rest of the evening.

OBJECTIVE (n)   [*uh* b-JEK-tiv]

Meaning: A goal or something to aim for

Usage 1: The *objectives* of this meeting are to define the limits of the budget and brainstorm about ways to conserve energy.

Usage 2: Dr. Smith always explained that the most important *objective* of the course is to understand physics, not to just pass the tests.

Usage 3: *Objectives* of traffic control include directing vehicles in ways that eliminate accidents and encourage a flow of traffic.

Usage 4: Most parents' main *objective* in the first few months is to train their infants to sleep through the night.

Usage 5: That dog's sole *objective* is to steal any food that is lying around.

OBLOQUY (n)   [OB-*luh*-kwee]

Meaning: strong words spoken against someone; tirade; verbal abuse or disgrace resulting from such abuse

Usage 1: Jess sometimes resorts to *obloquy* such as telling lies about some of the teachers.

Usage 2: Some of the *obloquy* heaped upon the president was well-deserved, as he is a cold-hearted, insensitive individual.

Usage 3: The politician fled from office, afraid of the outpouring of *obloquy* that he feared would soon occur.

Usage 4: Because of the widespread *obloquy* in the high school, classes were cancelled for an entire afternoon so the principal could address the student body together.

OBSCURE (v)   [*uh* b-SKYOO R]

Meaning: darken; make unclear; to make confusing or hard to see

Usage 1: Tad *obscured* the fact that he didn't fully understand the topic by using long, complicated words in his essay.

Usage 2: The assassination by the political party was *obscured* by the media, who passed the murder off onto a layperson.

Usage 3: During an eclipse, the sun is *obscured* during the day, causing darkness when there is usually light.

OBSESSION (n)   [*uh* b-SESH-*uh* n]

Meaning: fixed idea; continued brooding; a focus on one thing with little interest in anything else

Usage 1: When Sasha was a young girl, she had an *obsession* with horses and dolphins.

Usage 2: Jack's *obsession* with fast cars is the reason for all the posters and calendars.

Usage 3: Shelly has an *obsession* with cooking, as you can see by her stacks of cookbooks and hundreds of utensils.

Usage 4: Your *obsession* with that television show is really ruining your social life.

OBTRUSIVE (adj)   [*uh* b-TROO-siv]

Meaning: displeasingly noticeable; noticeable and undesirable; sticking out or in the way

Usage 1: Generally Jocelyn was happy with her appearance, but if she could change one thing it would be the *obtrusive* mole on her nose.

Usage 2: After the ice storm, the city was full of *obtrusive* trees that had fallen down and blocked the roads.

Usage 3: One of my pet peeves is *obtrusive* people trying to butt ahead of me in line at the store.

OPTOMETRIST (n)   [op-TOM-i-trist]

Meaning: A person who is trained to examine eyes for defects, diagnose problems or impairments, and prescribe lenses or other forms of treatment

Usage 1: I make an appointment with my *optometrist* every year to see if I need a new prescription for eyeglasses.

Usage 2: Mary has been seeing an *optometrist* for decades, ever since she got glasses at seven years old.

Usage 3: The *optometrist's* office is always calming to me; it is dark and quiet and no one ever gives me a shot.

Usage 4: My father refuses to go to the *optometrist*, and insists his vision is getting better, not worse.

Usage 5: Charlotte thought about studying to become an *optometrist*, but decided to become a dentist instead.

ORDINATION (n)   [awr-dn-EY-sh*uh* n]

Meaning: ceremony making someone a minister; the act of consecration to the ministry

Usage 1: After years of studying at seminary, the day of Andy's *ordination* finally arrived.

Usage 2: A future minister's *ordination* is a significant ceremony, and often many family members and friends are invited.

Usage 3: In a presbytery, the *ordination* and induction of ministers occurs several times a year.

Usage 4: Chuck's *ordination* was followed by a party celebrating his welcome into ministry.

OSSIFY (v)   [OS-*uh*-fahy]

Meaning: to become bony or change into bony tissue, or to stop developing or become stagnant

Usage 1: When tissue becomes bony, it has started to *ossify*.

Usage 2: It was clear the newspaper business was beginning to *ossify* when sales plummeted and some of the staff was laid off.

Usage 3: The churches in New England have *ossified* significantly, with only a few in the bigger cities experiencing any growth in the last few years.

Usage 4: When couples feel their marriages begin to *ossify*, it is time to take a vacation or do something to create growth.

Usage 5: The political institutions that were implemented decades ago have begun to *ossify*, and need some young members to spur change.

OUST (v)   [oust]

Meaning: expel; drive out; to get rid of something or someone

Usage 1: My boss is so obnoxious and mean, I wish she could be *ousted*.

Usage 2: Even the uprising and the protests failed to *oust* the current ruler.

Usage 3: In too many situations the natives have been *ousted* in favor of foreign invaders.

Usage 4: The incumbent was *ousted* from office by a flashy, energetic competitor.

OVERHAUL (v)   [oh-ver-HAWL]

Meaning: to thoroughly examine and make necessary repairs, or to catch up with something

Usage 1: My auto mechanic reported to me that my transmission needed a complete *overhaul*, and would cost me thousands.

Usage 2: Hospital administration announced that the system for training staff was undergoing an *overhaul*, and all employees would be required to be retrained soon.

Usage 3: I hired an HVAC company to *overhaul* our cooling system, as we were paying high energy bills but our house never felt cool.

Usage 4: The government decided to do a complete *overhaul* of the budget, rather than negotiate parts that already existed.

Usage 5: Let's do an *overhaul* of the kitchen; I'm tired of all the appliances and want to replace the cabinets and flooring.

OVERT (adj) [oh-VURT]

Meaning: open to view; public; not secret; clear and out in the open

Usage 1: Marsha and Peter are known for their *overt* displays of affection and have to be asked often to be more discreet.

Usage 2: Phoebe gave a small smile to the new guest, but showed no *overt* signs of recognizing who he was.

Usage 3: We don't own anything valuable, so there was no *overt* reason for anyone to break into our home.

OVERWROUGHT (adj) [OH-ver-RAWT]

Meaning: extremely agitated; hysterical; overcome with emotion or in a high state of anxiety

Usage 1: Raven was *overwrought* with anxiety at the thought of her husband being sent off for a year long deployment.

Usage 2: The death of her grandmother left Barb *overwrought* with grief.

Usage 3: In the weeks leading up to her medical exam, Christie was *overwrought* with anxiety and was unable to sleep or eat.

PAGEANT (n) [PAJ-*uh* nt]

Meaning: a splendid public show and procession; a beauty contest, or an elaborate form of entertainment consisting of historical themes and costumes

Usage 1: After a childhood of makeup and *pageant*, Whitney refuses to dress up for any occasion and only wears baggy clothing.

Usage 2: The Miss America beauty *pageant* is the epitome of unhealthy body types.

Usage 3: The Renaissance *pageant* consisted of plays, fake fights, and a dinner.

PARADIGM (n) [PAR-*uh*-dahym]

Meaning: model; example; pattern; a widely accepted belief or concept

Usage 1: Despite some opposition from conservative groups, the *paradigm* of evolution is taught in most schools today.

Usage 2: It is hard to believe that only a few hundred years ago no one was even aware of the *paradigm* that the world is round.

Usage 3: The western *paradigm* of economic productivity and well-being is widely accepted throughout the United States.

PARANOIA (n) [par-*uh*-NOI-*uh*]

Meaning: psychosis marked by delusions of grandeur or persecution; a mental disorder with delusions or extreme irrational fear or distrust of others

Usage 1: The young girl's *paranoia* about others hurting her impaired her ability to go outside of the house.

Usage 2: Jacob has *paranoia* about the government stealing his personal information and using it for their benefit.

Usage 3: Due to her *paranoia*, Teresa thinks everyone is out to get her.

Usage 4: Late at night, when I am alone in the house, my *paranoia* gets the better of me and I think I hear people outside of the windows.

Usage 5: The widespread *paranoia* of the times led many people to build bomb-shelters and collect enough food to last a year.

PARAPHERNALIA (n) [par-*uh*-fer-NEYL-y*uh*]

Meaning: equipment; odds and ends; personal belongings or the things needed do a task

Usage 1: After I had my first baby, I lugged baby *paraphernalia* such as bottles, toys, and diapers everywhere I went.

Usage 2: As an artist, I spend most of my money on paint, brushes, and other art supplies and *paraphernalia*.

Usage 3: The doctor rummaged through the drawer among stethoscopes and other medical *paraphernalia* before finding the tool he needed.

Usage 4: His is a system of worship that requires no religious *paraphernalia* such as crosses or rosary beads.

PARIAH (n)   [puh-RAHY-uh]

Meaning: A person who is rejected from society; an outcast

Usage 1: After cheating on her husband, Melissa became the *pariah* of the family.

Usage 2: Any organization that refuses to hire racial minorities or women is a *pariah* in today's society.

Usage 3: Rose felt like a *pariah* after all those dirty rumors spread through the school.

PAROCHIAL (adj)   [puh-ROH-kee-uh l]

Meaning: narrow in outlook; provincial; having a limited or narrow scope; of or relating to the church parish

Usage 1: James' worldview is extremely limited and *parochial*, as he has never ventured outside of his small hometown until now.

Usage 2: The *parochial* church council meets biweekly to discuss items of interest relating to the congregation.

Usage 3: His *parochial* upbringing instilled in him a strong sense of moral values.

Usage 4: The *parochial* minds of the town leaders unfortunately keep the laws stuck in the last century.

Usage 5: The *parochial* clergy must be married when they are appointed, but if their spouses die they are not allowed to marry again.

PARQUET (n)   [pahr-KEY]

Meaning: A floor made of geometric pieces of wood to create designs for decorative effect

Usage 1: The mansion's entire first level was covered in intricate *parquet* that was simply dazzling.

Usage 2: When Nina redecorated her house, she decided to take out the carpet and replace it with *parquet* flooring.

Usage 3: My dream home has *parquet* throughout the entire house.

Usage 4: The *parquet* appeared delicate, so guests often took off their shoes before entering without being asked.

PARSIMONIOUS (adj)   [pahr-suh-MOH-nee-uh s]

Meaning: stingy; excessively frugal; cheap or extremely reluctant to spend money

Usage 1: I hate selling items at flea markets, because the *parsimonious* customers who come through always try to haggle.

Usage 2: My great-uncle was the most *parsimonious* man you'd ever met, as he'd try to argue for a discount even at department stores.

Usage 3: I'm afraid that when Josh gets older, he will be a *parsimonious* old man who watches every dime.

PASTICHE (n)   [pa-STEESH]

Meaning: imitation of another's style in musical composition or in writing; a work of art made from various pieces, or a work of art made to resemble works of other artists

Usage 1: Nora's unacceptable *pastiche* was completely out of character and not true to her characteristic style at all.

Usage 2: Melody loves to write her short stories as early-twentieth century *pastiches*.

Usage 3: The musical comedy is a perfect *pastiche* of a silent film made in the 1920's.

Usage 4: Abstract art has quickly become a *pastiche*, as many artists try to mimic Picasso and his contemporaries.

Usage 5: My father was a great fan of Beethoven, so it's no surprise that all the music he composed were pastiches of the great pianist.

PATINA (n)   [PAT-n-*uh*]

Meaning: green crust on old bronze works; tone slowly taken by varnished painting; a crust or film that occurs due to use or exposure to oxygen

Usage 1: Some people like the greenish *patina* that shows up on copper after several years.

Usage 2: The warm color of the silver may be attributed to *patina*, but I think it was the artist's intent.

Usage 3: Though *patina* sometimes gets in the way of the art, it can enhance the tints the artist originally placed there.

Usage 4: The bronze medallion on the necklace was made more beautiful by the *patina* that grew with time.

PATOIS (n)   [PAT-wah]

Meaning: local or provincial dialect; a form of language differing from the accepted standard, such as a local dialect

Usage 1: Phyllis often spoke in a *patois* of the people of eastern North Carolina, as that is where she grew up.

Usage 2: In northern Italy, you will hear a French *patois* mixed with Italian vocabulary.

Usage 3: When I went down to New Orleans, I was impressed by the beauty of the creole *patois* that many of the folks outside the city seemed to use.

Usage 4: Though I formally studied French in school, the *patois* of the region was difficult for me to understand.

PECCADILLO (n)   [pek-*uh*-DIL-oh]

Meaning: slight offense; a small or unimportant sin or wrongdoing

Usage 1: Cindy was apologetic for the *peccadillo* of forgetting to close the door behind her even though Julie didn't seem to care.

Usage 2: Often people seem to feel uncomfortable around Oscar, who apologizes constantly for *peccadillos* that others wouldn't even bother with.

Usage 3: Even though it didn't seem to bother anyone else, I am very ashamed of this little *peccadillo* of mine.

PECUNIARY (adj)   [pi-KYOO-nee-er-ee]

Meaning: something relating to money

Usage 1: Jayden's *pecuniary* interests usually take precedence over everything else, including his family.

Usage 2: The *pecuniary* gain or loss is always the focus of the budget meetings at church.

Usage 3: Some corporate executives are driven by *pecuniary* motives in business, while others truly want to make a positive difference in the world.

Usage 4: The veterinarian's priorities are certainly *pecuniary*, as she often suggests expensive tests and exams that probably aren't really necessary.

Usage 5: Due to her *pecuniary* preferences, Jamie decided to seek out a career in the banking sector.

PEDAGOGUE (n)   [PED-*uh*-gog]

Meaning: a strict teacher or educator

Usage 1: The teacher is known for being a *pedagogue*, as she makes any child who misbehaves stand in the corner for hours.

Usage 2: In the 19th century, *pedagogues* were frequently employed to educate the children of wealthy families and to correct any misbehavior.

Usage 3: Mr. Smith is an old-fashioned *pedagogue* who lectures for hours.

Usage 4: The old *pedagogue* was strict until his last day of teaching, when he dismissed us five minutes early.

Usage 5: A *pedagogue* often gives too much attention to formal rules instead of encouraging discussion and creative thinking.

PEDANT (n)   [PED-nt]

Meaning: scholar who overemphasizes book learning or technicalities; someone who is overly concerned with rules and book learning

Usage 1: Some academics are still *pedants*, but often you will find many who are more relaxed.

Usage 2: My mother, a teacher, is more of a *pedant* at home with me and my siblings than at school, where she lets her students off the hook all the time.

Usage 3: The old *pedant* assigned hundreds of pages of reading to students in his classes.

Usage 4: Even though Gracie is usually fun to be around, she is a *pedant* when it comes to academics and learning.

PEJORATIVE (adj)   [pi-JAWR-*uh*-tiv]

Meaning: negative in connotation; having a negative or belittling effect

Usage 1: After a semester's worth of his teacher's *pejorative* comments, Andy finally gave up and stopped trying altogether.

Usage 2: The newspaper used the *pejorative* term "wasteland" when referring to the impoverished area of the city.

Usage 3: It is increasingly common to use *pejorative* terms to describe Muslims, though most of them have done nothing to deserve it.

PELLUCID (adj)   [p*uh*-LOO-sid]

Meaning: transparent; limpid; clear, simple, and easy to understand

Usage 1: The sample questions at the beginning of the test were *pellucid* in nature to build the confidence of the test takers.

Usage 2: The *pellucid* math question was answered easily by the little boy.

Usage 3: The *pellucid* waters served as an excellent place to practice my scuba-diving.

Usage 4: Roy has a *pellucid* way of writing, which has earned him jobs working as a journalist in many newspapers.

Usage 5: The singer is known for his *pellucid* tones and reverberating voice.

PENUMBRA (n)   [pi-NUHM-br*uh*]

Meaning: partial shadow (in an eclipse); the lighted area around the shadow of a moon or planet during an eclipse

Usage 1: The small *penumbra* during the eclipse allowed just enough light to guide my walk home.

Usage 2: The astronomer studies eclipses and their inevitable *penumbrae*.

Usage 3: There is a gradual increase in the *penumbra* from total darkness to some light from the beginning of the eclipse to the end.

Usage 4: The umbra and *penumbra* are separate parts of a shadow created by a light source after shining on an opaque object.

PENURIOUS (adj)   [p*uh*-NOO R-ee-*uh* s]

Meaning: Very poor or impoverished; mean; unwilling to spend money

Usage 1: The *penurious* folk on the streets of Atlanta always intimidate me when they ask for money.

Usage 2: My grandfather was such a *penurious* man that I never saw him smile.

Usage 3: Even though Charles is a generous man, his *penurious* upbringing has put him in the habit of spending very little money.

Usage 4: Your *penurious* habits are quite unattractive; can't you be nice to people once in awhile?

PERCEPTION (n)   [per-SEP-sh*uh* n]

Meaning: keen natural understanding; awareness, comprehension, or an understanding of something

Usage 1: My *perception* of the doctor is that he cares more about the patients' money than he does about his patients.

Usage 2: Mental illness is often discussed in terms of *perceptions* of reality.

Usage 3: My toddler's *perception* of who is powerful is much different than my own.

Usage 4: When I woke up in the middle of the night and thought it was morning, my *perception* of time was erroneous.

Usage 5: The detective's quick and accurate *perception* rescued him from many dangerous situations and solved numerous crimes.

PEREGRINATION (n)   [per-i-gr*uh*-NEY-sh*uh* n]

Meaning: a long and winding journey; a long walk or trek; a course of travel

Usage 1: The *peregrination* across Ireland from one pub to the next sounds like my idea of the perfect vacation.

Usage 2: When he graduated from high school, my father made the *peregrination* from Vermont to California all on foot.

Usage 3: Nomads spend their entire lives completing one long *peregrination*.

PERIPHERAL (adj)   [p*uh*-RIF-er-*uh* l]

Meaning: marginal; outer; of indirect importance; not central; just outside of the main focus

Usage 1: Jenny's *peripheral* vision is very poor, which is why she must turn directly toward you in order to see your face.

Usage 2: The young man moved into her *peripheral*, and she could sense him just beside her.

Usage 3: Mary thought she caught sight of him in her *peripheral* vision, but when she turned she didn't see anything at all.

Usage 4: It is important to have your *peripheral* vision when driving, as you must be able to see cars beside you as well as in front of you.

Usage 5: Though the main topic of the meeting was the budget, *peripheral* matters were discussed as well.

PERSPICUOUS (adj)   [per-SPIK-yoo-*uh* s]

Meaning: having insight; penetrating; astute; easily understood; clear in statement or expression

Usage 1: James' style is *perspicuous*, which is one reason I can read his stories without much difficulty.

Usage 2: That particular rendition of the political race was more popular than the rest, as it provided a more *perspicuous* explanation than others.

Usage 3: When Rose first began public speaking she spoke too quickly, but now she is careful that her words are slow and her presentations *perspicuous*.

PERTINACIOUS (adj)   [pur-tn-EY-sh*uh* s]

Meaning: stubborn and persistent; determined

Usage 1: The car salesman's *pertinacious* attitude helped him become the top salesperson in the entire district.

Usage 2: Ursula is determined and *pertinacious,* and finds a way to get anything that she wants.

Usage 3: David is charming but *pertinacious,* which is one reason why women find him so irresistible.

PEST (n)   [pest]

Meaning: An annoying person or thing

Usage 1: Clarence can be such a *pest* when he doesn't immediately get what he wants.

Usage 2: In the middle of summer, my yard is full of mosquitoes and other little *pests.*

Usage 3: We finally decided to call the *pest* control company when tiny flies buzzed in our ears all night long.

Usage 4: The little *pest* kept buzzing around my head as I ran that I finally stopped in my tracks.

Usage 5: I can't stand little dogs; I think the *pests* are more annoying than anything else.

PESTILENTIAL (adj)   [pes-tl-EN-sh*uh* l]

Meaning: causing plague; baneful; likely to cause widespread and deadly infection

Usage 1: The *pestilential* virus spread quickly throughout the small African nation, leaving many young and elderly people in its wake.

Usage 2: All of the children raised in that area were warned to stay out of the *pestilential* swamp, where diseased mosquitoes are rampant.

Usage 3: The *pestilential* atmosphere of the country was one of violence and cold heartedness.

Usage 4: Andrew spent three months in Africa, battling *pestilential* illnesses and infections.

Usage 5: Schools were cancelled until the *pestilential* outbreak could be gotten under control.

PETRIFY (v)   [PE-tr*uh*-fahy]

Meaning: To cause extreme fear, or to change organic matter into stone

Usage 1: The geologists were thrilled to find a group of *petrified* fossils deep in the earth during a dig.

Usage 2: Clara was absolutely *petrified* when she woke in the middle of the night and thought she saw a ghost.

Usage 3: Peter was so *petrified* by what Anna said in front of his wife that he turned white and had to sit down.

This page is intentionally left blank

Chapter **28**

Pharisaical – Requiem

This chapter covers the following words, each with its part of speech, pronunciation, and descriptive meaning.

Usage of the word is also illustrated in three to five sample sentences.

pharisaical	queasy	rendition
philanderer	quietude	reparable
posture	quintessence	repartee
precedent	quorum	repercussion
proponent	raconteur	repertoire
prosaic	raspy	replica
protean	raucous	reprieve
protuberance	ravenous	requiem
proviso	realm	
provoke	rebuttal	
proxy	recidivism	
prune	rectitude	
prurient	redoubtable	
pseudonym	refectory	
psychopathic	refraction	
puerile	refulgent	
pugilist	regatta	
purveyor	regime	
putrid	regnant	
pyre	reiterate	
pyromaniac	remediable	

PHARISAICAL (adj)   [far-*uh*-SEY-ik l]

Meaning: Emphasizing the observance of ritual or practice over meaning; self-righteous

Usage 1: Many of Jesus' *pharisaical* teachings were meant to emphasize the importance of intent before ritual.

Usage 2: Sara is rather *pharisaical* in the way she understands religion; she thinks that as long as she does good deeds she will be saved no matter the state of her heart.

Usage 3: The politician was known by many for his *pharisaical* words, as he preached one thing but often did another.

Usage 4: Pharisaical legalism ruled the religious atmosphere during Jesus' time, which is why Christ's teachings about grace were so radical.

Usage 5: Don't be so *pharisaical*; just because I think Randy is cute doesn't mean I've cheated on Bob.

PHILANDERER (n)   [fi-LAN-dr*uh* r]

Meaning: faithless lover; a flirt, particularly male; someone who plays at courtship

Usage 1: Even though Travis says he wants to settle down, his frequent dates indicate he is a *philanderer* at heart.

Usage 2: The *philanderer* never showed up at a function with the same woman on his arm.

Usage 3: Ralph is such an obnoxious *philanderer*; he leads women on and then breaks their hearts without remorse.

Usage 4: Her husband likes to think he is a *philanderer*, but no one really thinks he's serious when he flirts.

Usage 5: That tomcat is such a *philanderer*, I must have seen a dozen female cats walk by the house tonight.

POSTURE (v)   [POS-cher]

Meaning: act artificially; to strike a pose or position; to develop a policy or stance for something

Usage 1: When he became angry, the teenage boy would often *posture* in a threatening manner toward his peers.

Usage 2: The ballerinas *postured* in a graceful design on the stage.

Usage 3: The politician *postures* that global warming is a danger to all living beings on the planet, and must be addressed immediately.

Usage 4: The company *postured* that the former employee's claims were untrue.

PRECEDENT (adj)   [pri-SEED-nt]

Meaning: something preceding in time that may be used as an authority or guide for future action; coming before something else in time; being used as the authority or a guide for the future

Usage 1: The *precedent* case established the general awareness that the conservation judge was not in favor of women's rights.

Usage 2: A *precedent* action usually indicates that future actions will follow in its shadow.

Usage 3: Jill's *precedent* relationship was truly disastrous, and I hope she learned from that experience.

Usage 4: If you establish the *precedent* that ice cream before dinner is acceptable, your children will expect it every night.

PROPONENT (n)   [pr*uh*-POH-n*uh* nt]

Meaning: supporter; backer; opposite of opponent; someone who supports or is in favor of something, or who advocates for a cause

Usage 1: Even though he is usually a conservative thinker, Mr. Johnston is a *proponent* of abortion and legalization of marijuana.

Usage 2: Jonathan became a *proponent* of gun reform after all the shootings that occurred in schools out west.

Usage 3: I am a *proponent* of children being returned to their parents, but only if the parents undergo rigorous therapy and treatment.

PROSAIC (adj) [proh-ZEY-ik]

Meaning: dull and unimaginative; factual; boring, ordinary, plain, or common

Usage 1: Sometimes Ellen felt as if her life was full of *prosaic* motions - running errands, giving baths, and cooking dinner.

Usage 2: While I love going on vacation, sometimes the *prosaic* rhythm to everyday life can be comforting.

Usage 3: Howard is an ordinary, *prosaic* man; don't you want someone more exciting?

Usage 4: During my trip to Italy, I kept a journal about my experiences but my *prosaic* language didn't come close to capturing the sights and sounds.

Usage 5: Prosaic day-to-day concerns of my life include doing laundry and making sure we have enough bread for sandwiches.

PROTEAN (adj) [PROH-tee-*uh* n]

Meaning: versatile; able to take on many shapes; complex, varied, or changing easily

Usage 1: The *protean* lizard quickly changed from red to green when it crawled upon a leaf.

Usage 2: Protean behavior is behavior that is easily corrected.

Usage 3: The *protean* nature of careers in the 21st century means that people often work in several different fields before retiring.

Usage 4: The *protean* subject of digital technology is difficult to comprehend, as it changes by the day.

PROTUBERANCE (n) [proh-TOO-ber-*uh* ns]

Meaning: protrusion; bulge; something that bulges or sticks out from something else

Usage 1: The *protuberance* of teeth in the gums is one reason many babies seem to be fussy for no reason.

Usage 2: The *protuberance* on top of that bird's head is probably due to evolution.

Usage 3: The rhinoceros gestured toward the visitors with his huge, pointed *protuberance*.

Usage 4: The extension hooked onto the *protuberance* of the pipe to create a seal.

Usage 5: Many species of dinosaurs had horny *protuberances* at various places of their bodies to act as protection during a brutal time.

PROVISO (n) [pr*uh*-VAHY-zoh]

Meaning: a stipulation; a condition attached to an agreement

Usage 1: When we sold our house, we did so with the *proviso* that we would find another home to move into by the closing date.

Usage 2: Without a *proviso* stating that American presidents must have United States citizenship, it is possible that a foreigner could take office.

Usage 3: In my grandmother's will, she divided her estate equally among us with the *proviso* that we were all still alive.

Usage 4: The last *proviso* of the state constitution ensures that all residents will be given fair treatment in court.

PROVOKE (v) [pr*uh*-VOHK]

Meaning: stir to anger; cause retaliation; to intentionally irritate or anger; to annoy

Usage 1: Young children often *provoke* their peers with the intent of getting a reaction.

Usage 2: Miriam and her twin sister *provoked* each other all evening long, until both left the restaurant in a huff.

Usage 3: My neighbor has been trying to *provoke* me all summer long, with his irritating comments about my yard and his looks of disapproval in my general direction.

PROXY (n)   [PROK-see]

Meaning: authorized agent; a substitute for someone else, the authority to stand in for someone else, or a document for a person to vote on someone else's behalf

Usage 1: Because the lead actress became ill hours before opening night, a *proxy* took her place and dazzled the audience.

Usage 2: In her legal documents, you will find that Jan included a *proxy* stating that her son can make decisions about her health care in case she is not able to do so.

Usage 3: The paraplegic obtained a *proxy* stating that though he was registered to vote, he would have to have a proxy actually cast his ballot.

PRUNE (v)   [proon]

Meaning: cut away; trim; to cut off the excess or dead parts of something

Usage 1: The previous homeowners did not do yard work, so we spent weeks *pruning* the azaleas and other bushes.

Usage 2: Olivia is a perfectionist and spends hours *pruning* her rose bushes.

Usage 3: After the company went bankrupt, upper management was forced to *prune* one-third of all its employees.

Usage 4: When growing fruit trees, it is important to remember to *prune* them in mild weather or moderate frosts.

Usage 5: If you don't *prune* those climbing plants, they will take over your trellis.

PRURIENT (adj)   [PROO R-ee-*uh* nt]

Meaning: having or causing lustful thoughts and desires; lewd, or related to an excessive interest in sex

Usage 1: Luke gave the young woman seated across from him a *prurient* glance, and waited to see if she would respond.

Usage 2: The *prurient* magazines were tactfully hidden in the top row of the magazine rack.

Usage 3: Some colleges these days are known for their *prurient* immorality, which is attractive to some but is distasteful to others.

Usage 4: Your *prurient* comments often make others feel uncomfortable, so try to be more respectful in what you say.

PSEUDONYM (n)   [SOOD-n-im]

Meaning: pen name; a fake name, often used for writers

Usage 1: Many children are disappointed to learn that Dr. Seuss was a *pseudonym*, and his real name was actually quite plain.

Usage 2: The advantage to using a *pseudonym* is that it acts as a mask you can always hide behind.

Usage 3: The author used a *pseudonym* to hide her identity, and often marveled that her close friends never figured out who she was.

Usage 4: Her *pseudonym* is simply her middle and first names reversed, so it's not difficult to figure out who she is.

PSYCHOPATHIC (adj)   [sahy-k*uh*-PATH-ik]

Meaning: pertaining to mental derangement; suffering from a mental disorder

Usage 1: My great-grandmother spent the last twenty years of her life in a *psychopathic* hospital, though what disorder she suffered from I do not know.

Usage 2: He is so obsessed with video games it's almost *psychopathic* in nature.

Usage 3: Meredith works with children who have *psychopathic* disorders and must enter the hospital for treatment.

PUERILE (adj)   [PYOO-er-il]

Meaning: Characteristic of a child, especially childish behavior

Usage 1: Rodney's *puerile* pranks are getting old, as they have quickly gotten annoying.

Usage 2: Junior's *puerile* jokes are not only inappropriate, but are much more childish than his normal way of relating.

Usage 3: You can tell Jon has had a few drinks because of his *puerile* behavior.

Usage 4: Your *puerile* attitude toward long term relationships makes it clear that you will never be married for long.

Usage 5: In a *puerile* manner, the boy begged and pleaded with his mother for a candy bar.

PUGILIST (n)   [PYOO-j*uh*-list]

Meaning: a person who boxes; a boxer

Usage 1: Henry's father was a boxer, and I think that's where he learned how to fight like a *pugilist*.

Usage 2: The little boy looks just like a miniature *pugilist* when he raises his hands and growls like that.

Usage 3: Maury was a *pugilist* with the clear signs of a boxer - a crooked nose that clearly had been broken several times.

Usage 4: The *pugilists* hopped around the ring, looking for open areas in each other's bodies to take a hit.

Usage 5: Carl always seems ready for a fight; I think he would make a prize winning *pugilist*!

PURVEYOR (n)   [per-VEY-er]

Meaning: furnisher of foodstuffs; caterer; a person or organization that gives out food, supplies, or ideas

Usage 1: The American Red Cross is one example of a well-known *purveyor* with a great reputation.

Usage 2: George is the *purveyor* of the neighborhood; as soon as he sees someone in need, he is the first one to offer food or supplies.

Usage 3: The urban areas of our cities are full of well-intentioned *purveyors* trying to make a difference in the lives of the homeless.

Usage 4: My aunt is a *purveyor* for hungry animals, and is always buying food so she can feed them on her front porch.

PUTRID (adj)   [PYOO-trid]

Meaning: foul; decayed; something disgusting, rotting, or smelly

Usage 1: Laura quickly lifted the lid of the trashcan and threw in her plate before she could catch a whiff of the *putrid* smell.

Usage 2: As soon as I stepped into the woods and smelled the *putrid* scent, I knew the cat had killed another rodent.

Usage 3: We had forgotten to clean our refrigerator before our vacation, and we were greeted with *putrid* smells of old leftovers upon our return.

PYRE (n)   [pahy*uh* r]

Meaning: heap of combustible material, esp. for burning a corpse; a pile of wood meant to be burned; a fire used to burn a corpse at a funeral

Usage 1: The grotesque *pyre* was set aflame, erasing the corpses of hundreds of victims.

Usage 2: Sherry wanted to be buried in a casket rather than have her body placed in a funeral *pyre*.

Usage 3: During the Holocaust, the Nazis often built *pyres* to get rid of the bodies of the Jews who were exterminated.

PYROMANIAC (n)   [pahy-r*uh*-mey-NEE-ak]

Meaning: person with an insane desire to set things on fire; a person with a persistent compulsion to start destructive fires

Usage 1: Bart, a *pyromaniac*, has served three separate sentences for burning houses and cars.

Usage 2: Just because a child is interested in matches doesn't mean he is going to become a *pyromaniac*.

Usage 3: I wonder what it's like to be a *pyromaniac*; wouldn't you be afraid of all the damage you cause?

Usage 4: The ten year old eventually became a *pyromaniac*, and said he was compelled to do it to relieve stress.

Usage 5: *Pyromaniacs* often are compassionate people, but for some reason have a compulsion to start random fires.

QUEASY (adj)   [KWEE-zee]

Meaning: easily nauseated; squeamish; over-scrupulous; delicate; having an uneasy feeling in one's stomach; slightly worried about something

Usage 1: Just the thought of blood made Jared *queasy*, which is why he never became a doctor.

Usage 2: The continuous rocking of the fishing boat started to make me feel *queasy*, so I moved closer to the side.

Usage 3: Even though she was passionate about the subject, Val felt *queasy* at the thought of giving a speech about it in front of all her colleagues.

QUIETUDE (n)   [KWAHY-i-tood]

Meaning: tranquility; a state of being quiet, calm, and restful

Usage 1: Though I like talking with friends, I also enjoy periods of *quietude*.

Usage 2: Max says that during *quietude* he can reflect on his own thoughts and attitudes.

Usage 3: Toddlers and young children often don't understand the value of *quietude*, and want to play or talk all of the time.

Usage 4: Early morning is the best time to find *quietude* in my house.

Usage 5: After weeks of hearing the tractors and jackhammers repave the road outside my house, I had a new appreciation for *quietude*.

QUINTESSENCE (n)   [kwin-TES-*uh* ns]

Meaning: purest and highest embodiment; a classic example of a characteristic or personae

Usage 1: Ellie is the *quintessence* of a good hostess; she turns down the sheets and makes sure her guests always have something delicious to eat.

Usage 2: The *quintessence* of the Christian religion is forgiveness and grace.

Usage 3: Jack always carries his calculator and pocket protector and talks about numbers constantly - the *quintessence* of a mathematician.

Usage 4: The *quintessence* of summertime is drinking iced tea outside and watching lightning bugs.

Usage 5: Mary always insisted that the *quintessence* of childhood is eating popsicles and playing under shady trees.

QUORUM (n)   [KWAWR-*uh* m]

Meaning: the minimum number of members of a society or organizations necessary to conduct a meeting

Usage 1: At our congregational meetings, pastors always hold votes immediately after the service so a *quorum* is always met.

Usage 2: The meeting was dismissed early because it was clear a *quorum* would not be met that day.

Usage 3: In the bylaws, it clearly states that five out of eight committee members must be present in order to form a *quorum*.

Usage 4: The chairman waited to start the meeting until a *quorum* was formed, as there were several important issues to vote on.

RACONTEUR (n)   [rak-*uh* n-TUR]

Meaning: storyteller; a person who tells anecdotes in a skillful and amusing way

Usage 1: My uncle is known far and wide for being a *raconteur*, as he can make the most plain story sound fascinating.

Usage 2: Pat is often the center of social gatherings, as he is a *raconteur* of stories from his childhood in the South.

Usage 3: Hearing him talk about his breakfast as the most interesting thing in the world, I think Bobby might grow up to be a *raconteur*.

Usage 4: I've always wanted to be a *raconteur*, but I have never been able to openly express myself in public.

RASPY (adj)   [RAS-pee]

Meaning: grating; harsh; rough or irritated

Usage 1: The smoker had a *raspy* voice, making her sound much older than she actually was.

Usage 2: After a late night out, in the morning my voice is always *raspy*.

Usage 3: Charles barely spoke, and when he did it was in the form of a *raspy* whisper.

RAUCOUS (adj)   [RAW-k*uh* s]

Meaning: harsh and boisterous; loud and disorderly

Usage 1: The fraternity was known not only for its handsome recruits but for its *raucous* parties.

Usage 2: I try to avoid going to the beach around the Fourth of July, when the crowds are the most *raucous*.

Usage 3: Billie loves their music, but the *raucous* concerts usually keep her from going.

Usage 4: Polly finally had to knock on her neighbors' door in the middle of the night to ask them to quiet down and stop their *raucous* behavior.

Usage 5: I have four sons under the age of ten, so I'm used to a *raucous* household.

RAVENOUS (adj)   [RAV-*uh*-n*uh* s]

Meaning: rapacious; extremely hungry or famished

Usage 1: I'm so *ravenous* I think I could eat an entire pizza.

Usage 2: Shelly always feels *ravenous* after swim practice, where she burns lots of calories very quickly.

Usage 3: I don't understand how teenage boys can be so *ravenous* all of the time!

Usage 4: Every morning when I wake up, I'm *ravenous* no matter how much I ate the evening before.

REALM (n)   [relm]

Meaning: sphere of influence; a kingdom, or field or domain of activity or interest

Usage 1: The *realm* of physics has never really interested me, as I am more engaged by language arts and creativity.

Usage 2: The residents living in the *realm* were submissive to the king's demands.

Usage 3: In the *realm* of dreams, I often think about long-lost friends I once had in childhood.

REBUTTAL (n)   [ri-BUHT-l]

Meaning: a refutation or contradiction, especially pertaining to law; a form of evidence presented to contradict or nullify other evidence presented by an adverse party

Usage 1: After the politician made his remarks, the opposing candidate returned with his *rebuttal*.

Usage 2: Clara's teenage girl was constantly offering *rebuttals* to the things her mother said.

Usage 3: The prosecution offered a series of *rebuttals* against the defendant's claim that he was not the murderer.

Usage 4: John offered his most passionate *rebuttal* in the closing statement.

Usage 5: The little girl's *rebuttal* of her mother's accusation that she ate the cake was hard to believe, as the girl had chocolate all over her face.

RECIDIVISM (n)   [ri-SID-*uh*-viz-*uh* m]

Meaning: habitual return to crime; committing new offenses after being punished for a crime

Usage 1: Unfortunately, the rate of *recidivism* in young males is very high even after they are released from jail.

Usage 2: Though many rehabilitation programs seem to work in the short term, *recidivism* is very common among those with substance use problems.

Usage 3: The problem of *recidivism* is a big one in the United States, as it proves that the current criminal justice system doesn't fix the problem, it only prolongs it.

Usage 4: Recidivism is a major problem for teenagers who are involved in gangs and drug use.

RECTITUDE (n)   [REK-ti-tood]

Meaning: moral virtue; correctness of judgment; moral uprightness or righteousness

Usage 1: Patty's *attitudes* on financial rectitude are getting tiresome, as she always seems that she knows more than other people.

Usage 2: Christians assert that moral *rectitude* is the result of following the teachings of Jesus Christ.

Usage 3: Those who claim to be supporters of moral and patriotic *rectitude* should examine their own contributions to overseas spending.

REDOUBTABLE (adj)   [ri-DOU-t*uh*-b*uh* l]

Meaning: formidable; causing fear or awe

Usage 1: The *redoubtable* fireworks caused a wave of gasps to go through the crowd.

Usage 2: Dr. Lewis is the most *redoubtable* professor on campus; when anyone sees him coming they get quiet and look down at the ground.

Usage 3: My grandmother was a *redoubtable* old woman with strict rules but a warm, kind heart.

Usage 4: As she watched the *redoubtable* meteor shower from her window, Reba's eyes widened in awe.

Usage 5: Frank's *redoubtable* figure towers over most people at six and a half feet tall.

REFECTORY (adj)   [ri-FEK-t*uh*-ree]

Meaning: a dining hall in a college, monastery, or other facility

Usage 1: Every morning, before our 8 AM classes we sluggishly made our way to the *refectory* for some cereal and coffee.

Usage 2: The walls of the spacious *refectory* hall in the prestigious university were covered in plaques, so diners could admire the wealth of alumni as they ate.

Usage 3: The *refectory* of the monastery is usually very quiet, even at meal times.

Usage 4: One of my favorite times of day is early morning, when I grab a cup of coffee at the *refectory* and sit quietly for a while.

REFRACTION (n)   [ri-FRAK-sh*uh* n]

Meaning: The bending of a light or sound wave

Usage 1: Adam stared at the prism's *refraction* of the sunlight as it cast upon the far wall.

Usage 2: The law of the *refraction* of light states that when light passes from a fast medium to a slow medium it is bent.

Usage 3: Don's book about *refraction* is dry, but the pictures of rainbows and prisms are fascinating.

Usage 4: Rainbows are always perfect bands because they are a result of *refraction* when light bends after a rainstorm.

REFULGENT (adj)   [ri-FUHL-j*uh* nt]

Meaning: gleaming; shining, glowing, or radiant

Usage 1: The *refulgent* room sparkled with light.

Usage 2: After Jonathan scrubbed the bathroom clean, the *refulgent* floor reflected the sunlight.

Usage 3: Ashley's *refulgent* smile made it clear to all that she was in love.

REGATTA (n)   [ri-GAT-*uh*]

Meaning: A boat race or series of boat races

Usage 1: The *regatta* drew thousands to the port as the ships took off.

Usage 2: The town's beauty is particularly evident every summer during the annual *regatta*, when participants come from all around to race their boats around the island.

Usage 3: Darren has only had one sailing lesson, but he's already talking about entering his first *regatta*.

Usage 4: It was a beautiful day in May, perfect for watching the *regatta* as it raced through the lake.

Usage 5: We built a *regatta* of boats out of all the old newspapers.

REGIME (n)   [r*uh*-ZHEEM]

Meaning: method or system of government; a group that is in control and has power; an accepted way that things are done

Usage 1: The Russian *regime* has made the news almost daily lately due to the conflict with the Ukraine.

Usage 2: Peter's autocratic *regime* didn't last very long at his company, which was made up of employees with strong opinions.

Usage 3: The unstable nation is currently ruled by a military *regime* that has no control over its citizens.

Usage 4: The *regime* of Queen Elizabeth II has lasted six decades.

REGNANT (adj)   [REG-n*uh* nt]

Meaning: predominant; prevalent; sovereign; reigning, ruling, or of greatest power

Usage 1: The queen *regnant* was a quiet, gentle person who was gracious to all of her subjects.

Usage 2: If the board's idea should become *regnant*, make sure they give me credit.

Usage 3: Ancient Rome is full of *regnant* men, some of whom were kind and others who were ruthless.

REITERATE (v)   [ree-IT-*uh*-reyt]

Meaning: To repeat something again

Usage 1: Clarence *reiterated* his argument to the point that Josh finally interrupted him.

Usage 2: Though I have already reviewed why I believe we should proceed with the budget, let me *reiterate* my reasons again.

Usage 3: The most *reiterated* question that arose during the meeting was to ask when the next break would be.

REMEDIABLE (adj)   [ri-MEE-dee-*uh-buh* l]

Meaning: reparable; able to be repaired, cured, or treated

Usage 1: Thankfully, the hearing loss that Pat has had lately is *remediable* with surgery.

Usage 2: Following the court's ruling last week, all the charges taken out of the bank customers' accounts are *remediable*.

Usage 3: Remediable causes of intestinal upset include parasites, stomach viruses, and an imbalance of bacteria.

Usage 4: After twenty years of fighting, Claire wondered if her marriage to Greg was *remediable*.

Usage 5: The little boy cried after breaking the crayon and realizing the damage was not *remediable*.

RENDITION (n)   [ren-DISH-*uh* n]

Meaning: artistic interpretation of a song, etc; an interpretation or translation of something

Usage 1: Chuck's latest *rendition* of 'Happy Birthday' is always a treat to hear.

Usage 2: A jazzy, soulful *rendition* of that song had the crowd clapping and dancing by the end.

Usage 3: Larry's *rendition* of the Declaration of Independence always drew a crowd.

Usage 4: The *rendition* of the popular Broadway musical was one of the best so far.

Usage 5: The three-year-old's *rendition* of "Twinkle Twinkle Little Star" was recorded over and over again by her parents and grandparents.

REPARABLE (adj)   [REP-er-*uh-buh* l]

Meaning: able to be repaired, mended, or remedied

Usage 1: The damage to your sweater is *reparable*; let me use some of my magic stain remover.

Usage 2: Though they quarrel often, the couple's fights are always *reparable*.

Usage 3: Jack knew the friendship was beyond *reparable* when he tried to apologize but was turned away.

REPARTEE (n)   [rep-er-TEE]

Meaning: a quick, amusing reply in a conversation; fast-paced, witty conversation

Usage 1: Angela and Dave enjoy *repartee* in which wit and sarcasm reign.

Usage 2: Allie's sense of humor is a perfect match for Frank's love of *repartee*.

Usage 3: The dialogue of the play is full of *repartee* that is easy to miss unless you are paying close attention.

Usage 4: Jack and Adam often left others confused when they conversed in *repartee*.

REPERCUSSION (n)   [ree-per-KUHSH-*uh* n]

Meaning: rebound; reverberation; the reaction to another event or action

Usage 1: The *repercussion* in public school for gang talk or signs is a week of suspension.

Usage 2: If you want to tell Landon all about his wife's affair, then you will have to suffer the *repercussions* as well.

Usage 3: Paul was caught stealing a jacket from the store, and now must experience the *repercussions* that come along with that.

REPERTOIRE (n)   [REP-er-twahr]

Meaning: The collection of music, plays, dances, or pieces that a performer knows or is prepared to perform

Usage 1: Carl was a Boy Scout, and has a *repertoire* for tying knots that is rather impressive.

Usage 2: Japanese and Chinese calligraphists must have an extensive *repertoire* of exquisite symbols.

Usage 3: His *repertoire* includes musical numbers from a variety of different Broadway shows.

Usage 4: Now that you have successfully made a souffle, you can add it to your *repertoire*.

Usage 5: The musician's *repertoire* included violin, piano, organ, and flute.

REPLICA (n)   [REP-li-k*uh*]

Meaning: A nearly-exact copy of something

Usage 1: There is a large market for works of art that are *replicas* of famous pieces.

Usage 2: This jacket is an exact *replica* of Michael Jackson's, and makes me feel like I'm a rock star.

Usage 3: These two purses are so much alike, it's hard for me to tell which is genuine and which is a *replica*.

Usage 4: This painting is an exact *replica* of an original Leroy Neiman print, but the poor signature gives it away.

REPRIEVE (n)   [ri-PREEV]

Meaning: temporary stay or suspension of a punishment; a permanent or temporary escape from punishment or consequences

Usage 1: Lily's mother gave her a *reprieve* from being grounded so Lily could go to her senior prom.

Usage 2: Josh has been doing an awful job at work, but his boss has given him a *reprieve* even though he should be fired.

Usage 3: Teddy normally watches television after dinner, but due to his wife's anger he did the dishes and hoped for a *reprieve*.

Usage 4: Martha was in a good mood, so she issued her sons a *reprieve* even though they broke one of her favorite lamps.

Usage 5: My dog ate the entire birthday cake, but it's so much easier to give him a *reprieve* than to punish him.

REQUIEM (n)   [REK-wee-*uh* m]

Meaning: mass for the dead; dirge; song, chant, or poem for someone who died

Usage 1: Church music history is full of *requiems* dedicated to people who died.

Usage 2: This particular *requiem* has nothing to do with death, but is in commemoration of the Bible.

Usage 3: The tradition of composing a *requiem* when someone passes has largely disappeared, but we still have the music of the past to serve as comfort.

Usage 4: The old *requiem* was slow and contemplative, which was suitable when considering it was written for a person who died.

This page is intentionally left blank

Chapter **29**

Requite – Tarry

This chapter covers the following words, each with its part of speech, pronunciation, and descriptive meaning.

Usage of the word is also illustrated in three to five sample sentences.

requite	subtlety	sycophant
reverie	succinct	sylvan
rueful	suffragist	symbiosis
sedative	suffuse	synchronous
segregate	sumptuous	synthetic
semblance	superannuated	taint
severance	supercilious	tantamount
static	supererogatory	tarry
steadfast	superfluous	
stellar	supernumerary	
stockade	supplant	
stodgy	suppliant	
stratagem	suppress	
stringent	surfeit	
stultify	surmount	
stygian	surreptitious	
subaltern	surveillance	
suborn	suture	
subservient	swelter	
subsistence	swindler	
subsume	sybarite	

REQUITE (v)   [ri-KWAHYT]

Meaning: revenge; to correct a wrong; to return or repay for a benefit

Usage 1: As a way of *requiting* the fire department for their hard work, I'd like to bring them breakfast tomorrow.

Usage 2: The elderly ladies are quick to *requite* a kindness, and often repay in cookies or hand-sewn crafts.

Usage 3: At the slot machines, I was hoping to win enough money to *requite* my friends for all the money they loaned me over the year.

REVERIE (n)   [REV-*uh*-ree]

Meaning: musing; a state in which someone is lost in thoughts and daydreams

Usage 1: The teacher found me in a brief *reverie* when she called on me in class.

Usage 2: Mishka was always a daydreamer; if you couldn't find her right away you could bet she was in the middle of a *reverie* somewhere.

Usage 3: While she waited for her order at the coffee shop, Gail had a *reverie* about herself and the handsome barista.

Usage 4: Angela was in the middle of a *reverie* about winning an Olympic gold medal when she missed the gunshot signaling the beginning of the race.

Usage 5: Before drifting off to sleep, I often spend a few minutes in a state of *reverie*.

RUEFUL (adj)   [ROO-f*uh* l]

Meaning: Expressing sorrow or regret

Usage 1: Jane had a *rueful* expression on her face as she left the principal's office after being admonished for cheating.

Usage 2: The little girl had a *rueful* expression on her face when her mother walked into the bedroom and saw the crayon markings on the wall.

Usage 3: The basketball coach wore a *rueful* smile after the game in which his players missed numerous shots and caused more fouls than they ever had before.

Usage 4: The puppy wore a *rueful* expression after his owner discovered his new pair of shoes, torn to bits.

SEDATIVE (n)   [SED-*uh*-tiv]

Meaning: calming drug or influence; a substance that induces sleep or relaxation by reducing irritability or excitement

Usage 1: When the patient came into the hospital thrashing back and forth, he was given a *sedative* to calm him down.

Usage 2: The little boy was given a *sedative* during surgery, so he stayed asleep at least an hour after the doctor was finished.

Usage 3: After two weeks of insomnia and being unable to sleep, I asked my doctor for a *sedative*.

SEGREGATE (v)   [SEG-ri-geyt]

Meaning: separate; set apart from the rest of each other; isolate or divide

Usage 1: Before the 1960's, racial minorities were *segregated* from whites in even the most urban areas.

Usage 2: Due to recent recycling laws, all plastics and cans need to be *segregated* from ordinary trash.

Usage 3: During meiosis, alleles are *segregated* into two groups and transmitted independently.

Usage 4: Due to the rumors and fights that recently occurred, the high school opted to *segregate* classes by gender.

Usage 5: The veterinary clinic *segregates* healthy cats from sick ones to avoid the spread of disease.

SEMBLANCE (n)　[SEM-bl*uh* ns]

Meaning: guise; the outward appearance or apparent form of something, especially when the reality is different

Usage 1: In spite of falling headfirst down the stairs, Crystal managed to raise her head for some *semblance* of pride.

Usage 2: After her young children went to bed, Jackie tried to create some *semblance* of order in her home.

Usage 3: Nora's stories always bear some *semblance* to the truth, but she tends to leave out information sometimes.

SEVERANCE (n)　[SEV-er-*uh* ns]

Meaning: partition; separation; the act of ending employment, a relationship, or connection

Usage 1: After he was notified of his *severance,* Jack moved cross-country and started a band.

Usage 2: The pastor's *severance* from the church he had served for ten years was difficult, but was a relief for all who were involved in the decision.

Usage 3: The *severance* of ethics from the field of politics is one that occurred many years before the current presidency.

Usage 4: My father-in-law was told about his *severance* after twenty-seven years of service for the same company.

Usage 5: Laura and Mark's *severance* fortunately does not seem to have negatively impacted their children.

STATIC (adj)　[STAT-ik]

Meaning: unchanging; lacking development; showing little or no change; an electric charge

Usage 1: *Static* charge is at work when someone's hair stands up after being rubbed on a balloon.

Usage 2: The *static* nature of cats during summer days is the epitome of relaxation.

Usage 3: The *static* views of the political party have remained unchanged for decades.

Usage 4: I dislike change, and would be happy if everything in my life was *static* forever.

STEADFAST (adj)　[STED-fast]

Meaning: loyal; unswerving; resolutely firm and unwavering

Usage 1: Millie's *steadfast* views on child rearing could not be swayed, even by her own mother.

Usage 2: John's *steadfast* belief in God has carried him through many difficult times.

Usage 3: Jeffrey's *steadfast* and practical financial habits paid off when he was able to retire early due to a large savings account.

STELLAR (adj)　[STEL-er]

Meaning: pertaining to the stars; of or relating to the stars; exceptionally good or outstanding

Usage 1: Patricia's *stellar* performance at her senior recital earned her a standing ovation.

Usage 2: Out in the country, I enjoy looking at the *stellar* sky and all the infinite bodies it holds.

Usage 3: Because of her *stellar* grades over the course of the semester, Vicki's father treated her to a new bicycle.

Usage 4: The *stellar* guitarist received lots of tips from passersby throughout the day.

Usage 5: The *stellar* constellations never cease to amaze me with their never-ending combinations.

STOCKADE (n)　[sto-KEYD]

Meaning: wooden enclosure or pen; a line of tall posts that are set in the ground and used as a barrier to protect or defend a place

Usage 1: The little boy pretended that the couches were *stockades* protecting him from the enemy soldiers.

Usage 2: Stockades were common in the 18th and 19th centuries, when horses were the only form of transportation and shelter had to be constructed on the fly.

Usage 3: The group of buildings was enclosed in a *stockade*, clearly defining the territory.

Usage 4: My unfriendly next-door neighbors put up a *stockade* around their house this weekend to keep out unwanted visitors.

Usage 5: The community was surrounded by a tall *stockade,* and a secret code was needed to pass through the gate at the entrance.

STODGY (adj)   [STOJ-ee]

Meaning: stuffy; boringly conservative; too dull or boring to be interested; having old-fashioned opinions and beliefs

Usage 1: The *stodgy* information in today's lecture almost put me to sleep.

Usage 2: Usually the author's novels have interesting, engaging plots, but this particular one is quite *stodgy.*

Usage 3: The *stodgy* conversation over dinner tonight made me rethink who I want to spend my time with.

Usage 4: Continuing education credits don't need to be *stodgy*, but they often lack excitement or dynamo.

Usage 5: The *stodgy* old man glared at the affectionate young couple with disapproval.

STRATAGEM (n)   [STRAT-*uh*-j*uh* m]

Meaning: clever trick; a plan or scheme intended to outwit an opponent or achieve a purpose

Usage 1: Rick's *stratagem* at paintball is to lay low for the first half of competition, then attack the opponent with a vengeance.

Usage 2: Carl's *stratagem* for the scavenger hunt was to focus as much as possible on the clues and send the fastest people on his team out front.

Usage 3: During medieval warfare, *stratagem* often consisted of approaching the enemy at the right place and time.

STRINGENT (adj)   [STRIN-j*uh* nt]

Meaning: binding; rigid; strict, precise, and exacting, as of regulations, requirements, or conditions

Usage 1: The local town's laws about alcohol consumption are so *stringent* that many people go to the next town over to drink.

Usage 2: My mother had very *stringent* rules at home, and I never dared to break any of her rules.

Usage 3: Stringent penalties are often the only reason people refrain from speeding when they see a police officer on the road.

Usage 4: Your *stringent* policies on dating will never help you find a suitable spouse.

Usage 5: Even though the students complained nonstop about the high school's *stringent* dress-code policies, they all adhered to it.

STULTIFY (v)   [STUHL-t*uh*-fahy]

Meaning: to cause to seem foolish or useless; cause to lose enthusiasm and initiative, especially as a result of a tedious or restrictive routine

Usage 1: The lack of consumer demand *stultified* any hint of economic development in the city.

Usage 2: Mark grew up on a farm in rural Kansas, and often refers to how his upbringing *stultified* his childhood.

Usage 3: The professor's boring tone and mundane lectures *stultified* any interest the students may have had in American history.

Usage 4: After a few months, the mundane tasks of caring for a puppy *stultified* Lin's interest in having a dog.

Usage 5: After the doctoral student's reading of his dissertation, his peers and professors *stultified* him by asking challenging questions and frowning at his answers.

STYGIAN (adj) [STIJ-ee-*uh* n]

Meaning: Very dark or hellish

Usage 1: After years of serving his sentence at the county jail, Rudy had nightmares about that *stygian*, cold cell.

Usage 2: Whenever my grandmother asked me to get something from the cellar, I would beg my brother to accompany me to the *stygian* space under the house.

Usage 3: The *stygian* blackness of the cave was stifling, and I felt panic rise up quickly in the back of my throat.

SUBALTERN (n)   [suhb-AWL-tern]

Meaning: navy officer; subordinate; someone of lower status, particularly an officer

Usage 1: The force is composed of several superior officers and dozens of *subalterns*.

Usage 2: The young and energetic *subaltern* entered the militia as soon as he graduated from high school

Usage 3: The captain's daughter married a *subaltern* of the regiment, who was quickly accepted into the family.

Usage 4: The *subaltern* went against all sorts of protocols by stepping in front of his superior.

Usage 5: The private tutor was a *subaltern* who was hired to teach the children of the wealthy family.

SUBORN (v)   [*suh*-BAWRN]

Meaning: persuade to act unlawfully (especially to commit perjury); bribe or induce someone to commit an unlawful act such as perjury

Usage 1: At the trial, Lance was accused repeatedly of conspiring to *suborn* one witness after another.

Usage 2: Testimony from all the witnesses *suborned* that Dillon had forced his subordinates to write dishonest contracts.

Usage 3: Not only was Walter convicted of perjury, but he was found guilty of *suborning* others to do the same.

Usage 4: I truly hope that the defendant is found guilty after *suborning* all those innocent new hires.

Usage 5: The attorney was accused of *suborning* a witness during the previous trial.

SUBSERVIENT (adj)   [*suh* b-SUR-vee-*uh* nt]

Meaning: behaving like a slave; servile; obsequious; obeying others unquestioningly; less important or subordinate

Usage 1: In Isla's native culture, all children are expected to be *subservient* to their parents and other elders.

Usage 2: I wonder if Jill knows that her new husband expects her career to become *subservient* to his.

Usage 3: The *subservient* pupils did exactly as the teacher ordered them.

Usage 4: My dogs and I have an understanding; the little dog is *subservient* to the German Shepherd, but both obey me.

SUBSISTENCE (n)   [*suh* b-SIS-t*uh* ns]

Meaning: existence; means of support; livelihood; the action of maintaining or supporting oneself at a minimum level

Usage 1: Ned earned minimum income needed for *subsistence* by waiting tables while working on his music on the side.

Usage 2: Rachel and her family moved out of the city onto a farm in the middle of nowhere to discover the true meaning of *subsistence*.

Usage 3: The means of *subsistence* before the industrial age was confined to in-season produce and locally- raised meats and grains.

SUBSUME (v)   [s*uh* b-SOOM]

Meaning: encompass; absorb, contain, or include something into something else

Usage 1: The company decided to *subsume* the issues we were having with the computer system into the greater agency plan for upgrading the entire server.

Usage 2: The restaurant was initially taken over by another local chain, then *subsumed* by a national conglomerate.

Usage 3: Views on organic produce and locally-grown food have been gradually *subsumed* into the public attitude over the past two decades.

Usage 4: Because only two students signed up for the class, it was *subsumed* into the second section.

Usage 5: All the short stories were *subsumed* into a larger volume of the author's works.

SUBTLETY (n)   [SUHT-l-tee]

Meaning: perceptiveness; ingenuity; delicacy; having indirect or small distinctions

Usage 1: The *subtlety* of differences between tones in the painting created a fascinating, engaging work.

Usage 2: Only Deidre could pick up on the *subtlety* of her husband's discomfort, and excused herself before others could notice.

Usage 3: You lack *subtlety*, but your honesty and earnestness make up for it.

SUCCINCT (adj)   [s*uh* k-SINGKT]

Meaning: terse; compact; briefly and clearly expressed, particularly of something written or spoken

Usage 1: Bradley is usually *succinct*, but never rude or impolite.

Usage 2: When giving a presentation, it is important to remember that you should use short, *succinct* sentences to clearly get your points across to the audience.

Usage 3: The author's *succinct* style often resulted in criticism that her books read like newspaper articles.

SUFFRAGIST (n)   [SUHF-r*uh*-jist]

Meaning: advocate of voting rights (for women); a person who believes in extending the right to vote, especially to women

Usage 1: In her later years, Harriet Tubman became a *suffragist*, speaking out in favor of women's right to vote.

Usage 2: Many American *suffragists* spent time in prison for protesting and disturbing the peace of cities and towns, all for the sake of women's voting rights.

Usage 3: *Suffragists* of the 1800's are romanticized, though their experiences often ostracized them from their families and friends.

Usage 4: I think I would make a good *suffragist* because I believe in the right to vote and want others to believe, too.

Usage 5: *Suffragists* were unpopular for their stance on voting, particularly when it concerned women's rights.

SUFFUSE (v)   [s*uh*-FYOOZ]

Meaning: permeate; to cover or spread over (esp. with a color or a liquid); gradually spread through or over

Usage 1: The setting sun *suffused* the horizon with a beautiful orange glow.

Usage 2: The independent film we saw last weekend was a romance *suffused* with comedy.

Usage 3: Miriam's cheeks became *suffused* with color after the young man she was dating gave her a compliment.

Usage 4: The summertime rain shower traveled quickly, and *suffused* the entire city in a humid sheet of rain.

SUMPTUOUS (adj) [SUHMP-choo-*uh* s]

Meaning: lavish; rich; magnificent, costly, or very expensive

Usage 1: After the dinner came to an end, the entire table was laid out with numerous *sumptuous* desserts.

Usage 2: My dream is to live in a *sumptuous* mansion with a jacuzzi and pool.

Usage 3: Lillian's *sumptuous* tastes included fur coats, diamond necklaces, and frequent trips to the manicurist.

Usage 4: The *sumptuous* dress was made of silk and embroidered all over with rhinestones.

SUPERANNUATED (adj) [soo-per-AN-yoo-ey-tid]

Meaning: retired on pension because of age; obsolete through age or new technological or intellectual developments

Usage 1: The *superannuated* computing equipment took five times longer to process information than the newer system.

Usage 2: The teenager looked at my *superannuated* calculator with interest.

Usage 3: His *superannuated* views about women's inferiority to men are completely out of date.

Usage 4: After Cathy worked for the government for thirty-five years, she *superannuated* with a generous pension.

SUPERCILIOUS (adj) [soo-per-SIL-ee-*uh* s]

Meaning: arrogant; condescending; patronizing; behaving or looking as though one thinks one is superior to others

Usage 1: In the early 20th century, it was common in wealthy families to find the matriarch of the family accompanied by a *supercilious* lady's maid.

Usage 2: Due to her *supercilious* attitude, Lacey found it difficult to make or keep friends.

Usage 3: James took his *supercilious* date to the nicest restaurant in town, but she told him that nothing on the menu was good enough for her.

Usage 4: The *supercilious* glances Julie kept throwing my way made me feel as if I had done something wrong.

SUPEREROGATORY (adj) [soo-per-*uh*-ROG-*uh*-tawr-ee]

Meaning: superfluous; more than needed or demanded; performed to an extent beyond what is required

Usage 1: Kyle's *supererogatory* help on my essay helped me earn a good grade and a compliment from my professor.

Usage 2: It is a matter of discussion in the Christian church as to whether *supererogatory* prayers convince God to answer them more quickly.

Usage 3: His *supererogatory* spirit leads him to give generous tips, help strangers, and go above and beyond the call of duty at work.

Usage 4: The horse's *supererogatory* efforts earned him a gold medal after performing well beyond any other competitor.

Usage 5: Your *supererogatory* comments make it sound like you are insincere.

SUPERFLUOUS (adj) [soo-PUR-floo-*uh* s]

Meaning: unnecessary; excessive; overabundant; more than enough

Usage 1: It irritates me when telemarketers ask me for *superfluous* information about myself.

Usage 2: Sara didn't think the precautions her workplace took were *superfluous*, but did think that some were common sense and shouldn't have to be taught.

Usage 3: My basil plant has numerous *superfluous* shoots and leaves to the point that I am trying to give it away.

Usage 4: Over the holiday, police took *superfluous* caution to prevent car accidents by creating checkpoints.

SUPERNUMERARY (n)   [soo-per-NOO-m*uh*-rer-ee]

Meaning: person or thing in excess of what is necessary; present in excess of the normal or requisite number

Usage 1: I served as a *supernumerary* witness to the signing of the will.

Usage 2: *Supernumerary* rainbows and intense blue skies are common after intense volcanic activity.

Usage 3: Because Jane had a *supernumerary* tooth growing through her gum, she had to have it removed.

SUPPLANT (v)   [*suh*-PLANT]

Meaning: usurp; replacing something forcefully or deceitfully

Usage 1: Though Mark worked as a researcher in the department for the past twenty years, a younger and more energetic professional *supplanted* his role.

Usage 2: After months of secret planning, the terrorists finally *supplanted* the government using firearms and force.

Usage 3: Chad was pleased when he successfully *supplanted* Terrie's boyfriend by convincing Terrie that she deserved better.

Usage 4: My grandfather always complains that old traditions are disappearing and being *supplanted* by new ones.

Usage 5: Digital photography has *supplanted* film photography in the past decade as technology has improved.

SUPPLIANT (adj)   [SUHP-lee-*uh* nt]

Meaning: entreating; beseeching; making a plea, especially to someone in power or authority

Usage 1: Trish is a *suppliant* young woman who relies on her parents for money.

Usage 2: The children's *suppliant* faces finally convinced their teacher to let them have fifteen extra minutes of recess.

Usage 3: The *suppliant* congregation knelt by the pews and asked a powerful God for forgiveness.

Usage 4: Bert's *suppliant* requests eventually led to his being promoted.

SUPPRESS (v)   [*suh*-PRES]

Meaning: stifle; prevent the development, action, or expression of; inhibit

Usage 1: Allie was terrified of public speaking, and could not *suppress* the waves of panic that continued to rise in her in the hours before her presentation.

Usage 2: The uprising of the minority class was forcibly *suppressed* by guns and violence.

Usage 3: Unfortunately, Margie's new medicine *suppresses* the benefits of the one that helps her most.

SURFEIT (v)   [SUR-fit]

Meaning: satiate; stuff; indulge to excess in anything; cause someone to desire no more of something as a result of having consumed or done it to excess

Usage 1: After a night of binge drinking, Lauren was *surfeited* with partying for at least a week.

Usage 2: Though the food was delicious, I quickly became *surfeited* with eating after three plates.

Usage 3: Paul never *surfeits* on too much beer and is always careful, as alcoholism runs in his family.

Usage 4: I lived in Florida for a year, and was *surfeited* with enough heat and humidity to last a lifetime.

Usage 5: When Shelley was sick she was *surfeited* with television, and now can't stand to turn it on.

SURMOUNT (v)   [ser-MOUNT]

Meaning: overcome a difficulty or obstacle

Usage 1: After three knee surgeries, Barb *surmounted* a triathlon and came in second place.

Usage 2: If you want to be an airplane pilot, you must *surmount* your fear of heights.

Usage 3: Josh has *surmounted* more challenges than most of us can imagine; he beat cancer, watched his father die, and had hip surgery.

Usage 4: My best friend *surmounted* a brain tumor last year, and showed me that she is the strongest person I know.

SURREPTITIOUS (adj)   [sur-*uh* p-TISH-*uh* s]

Meaning: furtive; hidden; done in secret or kept quiet; sneaky

Usage 1: The teenagers' *surreptitious* plan involved sneaking out in the middle of the night through their bedroom windows.

Usage 2: Though most people think Mary is a perfectly-behaved little girl, I have seen her *surreptitious* behaviors like taking cookies when she thought no one is looking.

Usage 3: Later, Patrick found out that Dion made a *surreptitious* recording of their conversation without Patrick's knowledge.

SURVEILLANCE (n)   [ser-VEY-l*uh* ns]

Meaning: watching; guarding; the close observation of someone, often to catch them doing something wrong

Usage 1: Because I'm under *surveillance,* I suspect that my landline is bugged and none of my conversations are private.

Usage 2: The private detectives made a living out of conducting *surveillance* on ordinary people whose spouses suspected them of extraordinary things.

Usage 3: The object of her *surveillance* was sitting at the back of the coffee shop, oblivious to her close observation.

Usage 4: Surveillance in parking lots isn't always reliable, as delay times are long and images are often fuzzy.

Usage 5: think *surveillance* is sometimes a good idea, particularly when you have teenagers who like to stay out late.

SUTURE (n)   [SOO-cher]

Meaning: stitches sewn to hold the cut edges of a wound or incision; material used in sewing; the joining together of two sides of a wound or incision; a seam formed when two parts unite

Usage 1: The doctor told me that the *sutures* should be taken out after about ten days.

Usage 2: The *suture* between the two bones on the back of the human head has evolved over millions of years.

Usage 3: After surgery, the dog's *sutures* healed nicely and dissolved on their own.

Usage 4: The *sutures* inserted by the medical resident will probably leave a scar.

SWELTER (v)   [SWEL-ter]

Meaning: be oppressed by heat; to be or feel uncomfortably hot; feel weak from great heat

Usage 1: The summers of southern Mississippi are known for their power to make grown men *swelter.*

Usage 2: Because of my fair skin, I have a low tolerance for the heat and tend to *swelter* in the summer sun.

Usage 3: The air conditioning in Lavonne's office was broken in July and her coworkers called out sick all month long so they wouldn't have to *swelter.*

SWINDLER (n)   [SWIND-ler]

Meaning: cheat; a person who cheats

Usage 1: The *swindler* won games all night until an observant person discovered his tricks.

Usage 2: You think he is a respectable and brilliant politician, but I see him as nothing but a *swindler*.

Usage 3: Mark is a notorious *swindler* who no one here trusts.

Usage 4: Chuck is known for being a *swindler* and can cheat anyone out of anything.

Usage 5: Gertrude's daughter is a little *swindler* who uses her charm and cuteness to get what she wants.

SYBARITE (n)   [SIB-*uh*-rahyt]

Meaning: lover of luxury; a person who is self-indulgent in their fondness for luxury

Usage 1: Farrah is such a *sybarite* that she buys furs year-round because she loves the feel of them.

Usage 2: The lifelong *sybarite* was crushed when she had to move out of her mansion into the tiny, one- bedroom apartment.

Usage 3: I never thought of myself as a *sybarite* until I had to switch from my favorite Italian wine to a cheaper version.

Usage 4: Sybarites irritate me, because who is to say what is worthy or luxurious?

SYCOPHANT (n)   [SIK-*uh*-f*uh* nt]

Meaning: servile flatterer; a person who praises powerful people in order to get their approval

Usage 1: Harry is such a *sycophant* he will say anything to get the professor to like him.

Usage 2: Only a true *sycophant* would compliment the company's president on her dry, monotone presentation.

Usage 3: Even though he wanted the job at the bank, Jackson was no *sycophant* and did not praise the supervisor's underhanded tactics.

SYLVAN (adj)   [SIL-v*uh* n]

Meaning: pertaining to the forest; associated with the woods; pleasantly rural or pastoral

Usage 1: I prefer our peaceful *sylvan* neighborhood to our former home in the city.

Usage 2: The trees and naturally wooded areas all add to the *sylvan* setting, though it would be nice to have a path to walk on.

Usage 3: The shady, *sylvan* glade made the perfect place to have a romantic picnic.

SYMBIOSIS (n)   [sim-bee-OH-sis]

Meaning: co-operation of persons or between animals or birds; a close and often long-term interaction between two or more biological species

Usage 1: In 1877, Albert Bernhard Frank investigated the *symbiosis* that exists between lichens and plants.

Usage 2: Symbiosis between fungi and plant roots nourishes the plants while feeding the fungi.

Usage 3: Mutualism is one type of *symbiosis*, in which each organism benefits from the relationship.

Usage 4: The *symbiosis* of the young couple's relationship is almost sickening; it's like they can't exist without each other.

Usage 5: In biology, we learned about *symbiosis* and the benefits it brings to the greater ecosystem.

SYNCHRONOUS (adj)   [SING-kr*uh*-n*uh* s]

Meaning: similarly timed; simultaneous with; existing or occurring at the same time

Usage 1: The *synchronous* lives of the twins were almost eerie; they were married on the same day and their children were born within a month of each other.

Usage 2: The athletes were *synchronous* as they jumped over hurdles, and were separated by only a quarter of a second at the finish.

Usage 3: The rise of the current political party was *synchronous* with a change in the nature of the public's positions on policy.

Usage 4: The swimmers were *synchronous* as they dove and flipped underwater.

SYNTHETIC (adj)   [sin-THET-ik]

Meaning: combining parts into a whole; the combination of two or more parts, whether by design or natural processes

Usage 1: I prefer clothing made of one hundred percent cotton to *synthetic* garments.

Usage 2: Food on the shelves of most American grocery stores are made of *synthetic* products such as chemically-made sweeteners.

Usage 3: Synthetic rubber has many advantages, though it is difficult to produce it on a commercial scale.

TAINT (v)   [teynt]

Meaning: to contaminate or corrupt; to decay or cause to be impure

Usage 1: Jake wasn't paying attention to sanitization when he was making beer, so it was *tainted* by bacteria in the middle of the process.

Usage 2: Even petty theft can *taint* a person's criminal record and prevent them from getting certain jobs in the future.

Usage 3: It was discovered last week that there was a terrorist plot to *taint* the city's water supply.

Usage 4: By cursing all the time, I'm afraid you might *taint* his language and mind.

Usage 5: After the murder, the victim's blood *tainted* his clothing.

TANTAMOUNT (adj)   [TAN-tuh-mount]

Meaning: equivalent in force, effect or value; equivalent in seriousness to; virtually the same as

Usage 1: The resignation of the company's CEO was *tantamount* to his admission of guilt.

Usage 2: Even though Sylvia was as gracious as ever, Paul knew her excuses were *tantamount* to a brush-off.

Usage 3: By ignoring the nation's pleas for help, the king interpreted this lack of inaction as *tantamount* to a declaration of neutrality.

Usage 4: Reading a novel from front to back is never *tantamount* to watching the movie.

TARRY (v)   [TAR-ee]

Meaning: dawdle; to delay, be late, or wait

Usage 1: Paula thought she and Bert had *tarried* too long, and proposed they get married this weekend.

Usage 2: To avoid any *tarrying*, I will get straight to the point.

Usage 3: Rick, if you *tarry* too much longer with the women I plan to leave this party without you.

This page is intentionally left blank

Chapter 30

Tatty – Zeal

This chapter covers the following words, each with its part of speech, pronunciation, and descriptive meaning.

Usage of the word is also illustrated in three to five sample sentences.

tatty	unaccountable	winsome
taut	unanimity	withstand
timid	unassailable	wont
tipple	unassuaged	
titular	veneer	wrath
toga	ventral	writhe
tome	virile	xenophobia
transfigure	virtuoso	yen
transitoriness	visage	zeal
trilogy	visceral	
trite	vivacious	
trivia	vociferous	
tumult	vogue	
turbulence	voluminous	
turgid	voluptuous	
tutelary	vortex	
ubiquitous	votary	
ulterior	voyeur	
ultimate	warrant	
ultimatum	wastrel	
umbrage	wean	

TATTY (adj)   [TAT-ee]

Meaning: shabby, decrepit, worn, or tawdry

Usage 1: The stadium was built ten years ago and is starting to look a little *tatty*.

Usage 2: For being a lawyer, your father's car sure does look *tatty*.

Usage 3: The pages of my favorite book are *tatty* during the most interesting parts.

Usage 4: Her *tatty* clothes made it clear that she hadn't done laundry in weeks.

TAUT (adj)   [tawt]

Meaning: Stretched with little or no give or flexibility

Usage 1: The tarp was *taut* across the top of the drum to prevent any water from seeping in.

Usage 2: As Mike sailed across the open seas, the strong wind pulled the sail *taut*.

Usage 3: Her *taut* smile indicated that she was not pleased at all to be at her ex-husband's wedding.

TIMID (adj)   [TIM-id]

Meaning: easily frightened; apprehensive; shy or fearful; showing a lack of courage or confidence

Usage 1: The *timid* child peeked out from around her mother's legs.

Usage 2: Andrea offered a *timid* handshake, and her hand was nearly crushed as her acquaintance grabbed it with fervor.

Usage 3: After a few dates, Randy's kisses became more eager and less *timid*.

Usage 4: No one ever sees our *timid* cat except us, as she hides in crevices much too small for her.

Usage 5: Don't be so *timid*, just say whatever is on your mind.

TIPPLE (v)   [TIP-*uh* l]

Meaning: imbibe; in the habit of drinking liquor; to drink alcoholic beverages habitually

Usage 1: The Italians tend to *tipple* throughout the day, whereas Americans like to drink just in the evening.

Usage 2: It's been just in the past few years that Walter has begun to *tipple* without restraint.

Usage 3: No matter if he is depressed or happy, Chris goes to the local bar to *tipple* on the weekends.

Usage 4: She *tippled* for many years until she was convicted of drinking while driving and was forced to get sober.

Usage 5: All the men in my family have *tippled* for as long as I can remember, and have at least one cocktail every day.

TITULAR (adj)   [TICH-*uh*-ler]

Meaning: nominal holding of title without obligations; holding or constituting a purely formal title or formal position without any real authority

Usage 1: The queen is the *titular* head of the Church of England, but doesn't hold any real political power anymore.

Usage 2: Titular bishops have headed the Catholic church for hundreds of years.

Usage 3: The *titular* king of Italy, though the head of a country at war, had a complete loss of control over his own people

Usage 4: Everyone called Howard 'the boss man,' but he knew this was a *titular* position as his wife made all the decisions.

TOGA (n)   [TOH-g*uh*]

Meaning: Roman outer robe; a cloth worn by citizens of ancient Rome which consisted of a loose, one-piece garment

Usage 1: For our production of Shakespeare's Julius Caesar, all of the male characters wore *togas*.

Usage 2: The *toga* was the most common garment worn in ancient Rome.

Usage 3: Clad in *togas*, the fraternity members ran across campus, through the fountains, and stopped under the windows of the sorority dorms.

Usage 4: In the theme of the party, all the guests wore *togas* held up at the shoulder with various devices.

TOME (n)   [tohm]

Meaning: large volume; a book, especially a heavy scholarly one

Usage 1: Kathy has been writing a *tome* on the oyster wars of North Carolina for years.

Usage 2: Nick is majoring in philosophy, and you can often find him lugging around *tomes* in his bookbag.

Usage 3: Instead of reading the latest bestsellers, Larry likes to come home from the library with *tomes* about history and religion.

TRANSFIGURE (v)   [trans-FIG-yer]

Meaning: transform outwardly, usually for the better; transform into something more beautiful or elevated

Usage 1: With her new hairstyle and make-up, Joan is completely *transfigured*.

Usage 2: The high school gymnasium was *transfigured* by disco balls and decorations.

Usage 3: Who would have thought that prayer could *transfigure* a person's soul so drastically?

TRANSITORINESS (n)   [TRAN-si-tawr-ee-nis]

Meaning: impermanence; the state of being temporary or not permanent; being transient

Usage 1: The *transitoriness* of Jack's job made it difficult for him to settle down and find a wife.

Usage 2: Lucy's *transitoriness* was difficult for her friends to follow, as one day she might live in an apartment and the next be staying with a friend across town.

Usage 3: I respect the *transitoriness* of the neighborhood cats, who are smart enough to reappear at houses frequently enough that most nights they eat three meals apiece.

Usage 4: Nomads' *transitoriness* contributes to their ability to live off the land without worrying about upkeep.

Usage 5: The *transitoriness* of the summer season in Vermont makes residents appreciate it even more.

TRILOGY (n)   [TRIL-*uh*-jee]

Meaning: group of three works; a set of three works of art or books that are connected

Usage 1: The famous *trilogy* was made into three movies.

Usage 2: The Hunger Games *trilogy* is one of the most well-known of the past ten years.

Usage 3: The artist created a *trilogy* of paintings conveying the stages of life before, during, and after birth.

Usage 4: I love reading *trilogies* because they usually connect so seamlessly.

Usage 5: Though the books were written as a *trilogy*, the movie industry managed to make them into a series of five films.

TRITE (adj)   [trahyt]

Meaning: hackneyed; commonplace; lacking in freshness or effectiveness because of constant use

Usage 1: The article consisted of a few *trite* phrases and was overall very dry.

Usage 2: I was bored quickly with the *trite* topics over dinner.

Usage 3: The speaker addressed a wide range of issues, some of which were *trite* and others engaging.

Usage 4: The *trite* tone the journalist used inevitably led to her disapproval by readers.

TRIVIA (n)   [TRIV-ee-*uh*]

Meaning: trifles; unimportant matters; details or prices of information of little importance or value

Usage 1: James has a great memory for *trivia* but never does well on exams.

Usage 2: We fill our minds with meaningless *trivia* about celebrities, television, and movie stars.

Usage 3: Things that may seem like *trivia* to you and I are quite important to others.

TUMULT (n)   [TOO-m*uh* lt]

Meaning: commotion; riot; loud confused noise caused by a large mass of people

Usage 1: Two seconds after the shooting, a *tumult* of shouting and screaming began.

Usage 2: When news spread that a bear had escaped from the zoo, the whole neighborhood was in a state of *tumult*.

Usage 3: The monkeys broke out in loud *tumult* when the tiger passed by.

Usage 4: Because they weren't told about the fire drill, a *tumult* broke out in the preschoolers' classroom.

Usage 5: Let's try to avoid a *tumult* by preparing everyone for the tornado.

TURBULENCE (n)   [TUR-by*uh*-l*uh* ns]

Meaning: state of violent agitation; instability, unsteadiness, or disorder

Usage 1: The *turbulence* of the plane was distressing, and many passengers clutched their armrests with white knuckles.

Usage 2: Lately, the *turbulence* of the nation's political climate has caused many citizens to flee.

Usage 3: Everyone on the block knows about the *turbulence* that characterizes Jessie and Zach's marriage - you can hear them screaming every night.

Usage 4: The *turbulence* that started at the school board meetings was due to the fact that the board made major changes in policies without warning.

TURGID (adj)   [TUR-jid]

Meaning: high sounding (of words); swollen, distended, congested; tediously pompous

Usage 1: The *turgid* river swept the logs along at a fast pace.

Usage 2: The *turgid* language made it hard to understand the author's point.

Usage 3: It is advisable to let the plants wilt before cutting them to avoid damage to the *turgid* leaves.

TUTELARY (adj)   [TOOT-l-er-ee]

Meaning: protective; pertaining to a guardianship; serving as protector, guardian, or patron

Usage 1: These African regions are watched over by *tutelary* spirits.

Usage 2: My *tutelary* saint was chosen for me on the day of my baptism.

Usage 3: On my first date, my *tutelary* brother served as the chaperone.

UBIQUITOUS (adj)   [yoo-BIK-wi-t*uh* s]

Meaning: omnipresent; present, appearing, or found everywhere

Usage 1: Grandpa's *ubiquitous* presence was felt by the whole family.

Usage 2: After she died, I felt my mother's *ubiquitous* spirit wherever I went.

Usage 3: No matter how far I got from civilization, the *ubiquitous* Internet was everywhere.

Usage 4: Christians believe in the *ubiquitous* spirit of God no matter where they go.

ULTERIOR (adj)   [uhl-TEER-ee-er]

Meaning: unstated; existing beyond what is obvious; intentionally hidden

Usage 1: I think Dave's *ulterior* motivation for washing his father's car has to do with his plan to ask his father if he can borrow the car tonight.

Usage 2: I have an *ulterior* interest in Kevin, but I don't let on because Tina likes him too.

Usage 3: The lawyer looked too closely for *ulterior* motives and missed the true reason for the murder - that the defendant was just plain evil.

ULTIMATE (adj)   [UHL-t*uh*-mit]

Meaning: final; not susceptible to further analysis; happening at the end of a process; the best imaginable

Usage 1: Dark chocolate cheesecake is the *ultimate* dessert.

Usage 2: The *ultimate* goal of working is making enough money to retire.

Usage 3: As the *ultimate* judge of the Constitution, the Supreme Court's decisions are final.

Usage 4: The *ultimate* sacrifice is laying down your life for someone else.

Usage 5: The *ultimate* decision-maker of punishment is my father, so you don't want to make him angry.

ULTIMATUM (n)   [uhl-t*uh*-MEY-t*uh* m]

Meaning: final warning; final demand or statement of terms

Usage 1: Julie gave her boyfriend an *ultimatum* - propose or leave.

Usage 2: After a week of calling out sick, the employee was given an *ultimatum* of returning to work or losing her job.

Usage 3: Ultimatums only get you the behavior you want, but never the attitude or motivation you desire.

Usage 4: Parents of toddlers find themselves offering *ultimatums* on a daily basis.

UMBRAGE (n)   [UHM-brij]

Meaning: resentment; harsh feelings; shade; offense or annoying remark

Usage 1: She took *umbrage* at Oliver's remarks, even though he didn't mean anything by them.

Usage 2: Paul gave *umbrage* to his ex-girlfriend every time he saw her.

Usage 3: We took *umbrage* to the fact that we were the last people to be seated.

UNACCOUNTABLE (adj)   [uhn-*uh*-KOUN-t*uh*-b*uh* l]

Meaning: Unable to be explained; not required to justify the actions of something

Usage 1: There remained the strange and *unaccountable* fact that the door was open when we got home, but nothing was taken.

Usage 2: Many health care providers are *unaccountable* for their patients' suffering.

Usage 3: My puppy is *unaccountable* for his actions; he is still learning.

Usage 4: At what age do you think a child is no longer *unaccountable* for what he does?

Usage 5: Am I *unaccountable*, or do you think I should make up for unintentionally hurting her feelings?

UNANIMITY (n)   [yoo-n*uh*-NIM-i-tee]

Meaning: complete agreement; agreement by all people involved

Usage 1: On this particular issue there is almost complete *unanimity*.

Usage 2: John Adams hoped for *unanimity* in his views on war with England, but was met with much resistance.

Usage 3: In a rare moment of *unanimity*, the siblings agreed to throw a party for their parents' anniversary.

Usage 4: Unanimity is sometimes a bad sign if everyone is agreeing to a bad idea.

UNASSAILABLE (adj)   [uhn-*uh*-SEY-*luh*-b*uh* l]

Meaning: not subject to question; not open to attack; unable to be attacked, questioned, or defeated

Usage 1: The athlete gained an *unassailable* lead early in the race.

Usage 2: The *unassailable* politician was terribly popular among young conservative voters.

Usage 3: If you plan to break curfew again, you had better have an *unassailable* excuse.

UNASSUAGED (adj)   [uhn-*uh*-SWEYJ d]

Meaning: unsatisfied; not soothed or relieved easily

Usage 1: Mary's *unassuaged* grief after her brother died lasted for months.

Usage 2: Despite all kinds of cold medications, my congestion remained *unassuaged*.

Usage 3: The protestors' anger was *unassuaged* even by the agreement the local executives reached.

Usage 4: The little boy's *unassuaged* distress when he was disciplined could be heard all over the neighborhood.

Usage 5: Because our pet dog's pain and discomfort were *unassuaged*, we had her put to sleep.

VENEER (n)   [v*uh*-NEER]

Meaning: thin layer; cover; thin decorative covering of wood applied to coarser wood or other materials

Usage 1: The woodworker carefully applied the *veneer* as a finishing touch on the jewelry box.

Usage 2: After years as a sculptor, Jane dabbled in the field of *veneer*, as she was always interested in the texture of different woods.

Usage 3: The *veneer* on the tiny box from Greece was placed there by a talented local artist.

VENTRAL (v)   [VEN-tr*uh* l]

Meaning: abdominal; relating to the underside of an animal or plant

Usage 1: The fish's *ventral* fin made swimming through murky water easier.

Usage 2: The spider's *ventral* section is made of a hard coating to protect it from enemies.

Usage 3: The *ventral* part of a snake is quite soft to help it slide along the ground.

Usage 4: On the *ventral* side of that leaf you will see this crop's first pepper.

VIRILE (adj)   [VIR-*uh* l]

Meaning: manly; having strength, energy, and a strong sex drive; full of strength

Usage 1: Lance's *virile* strength was apparent as he lifted twice his weight over his head.

Usage 2: Todd's *virile* scent drove her crazy.

Usage 3: The *virile* bull burst through the gates and ran straight for the flag.

Usage 4: There was a *virile* scent in the air at the boxing match, where men hit and punched each other nonstop.

Usage 5: The tomcat's *virile* tendencies led it to mark its territory and yowl late at night.

VIRTUOSO (n)   [vur-choo-OH-soh]

Meaning: highly skilled artist; a person highly skilled in music, art, or another creative pursuit

Usage 1: The young violin *virtuoso* held her own recital and received a standing ovation.

Usage 2: The celebrated clarinet *virtuoso* took a grand bow before starting to play.

Usage 3: At the end of the concert, the *virtuoso* played his own original piece of music.

Usage 4: As a child I wanted to become a piano *virtuoso*, but was never disciplined enough.

VISAGE (n)   [VIZ-ij]

Meaning: face; appearance; the form or proportions of a person's face; facial expression

Usage 1: Her *visage* made it clear that she was not pleased with how the evening was progressing.

Usage 2: She has an angular *visage*, but is actually quite pretty.

Usage 3: His *visage* reminded me of his father - strong jaw and nose, with soft eyes.

VISCERAL (adj)   [VIS-er-*uh* l]

Meaning: felt in one's inner organs; relating to deep inward feelings rather than intellect

Usage 1: When I see blood or vomit, I have an immediate *visceral* reaction and faint on the spot.

Usage 2: The voters' *visceral* fear of change was understandable in the wake of the last election, which resulted in a tyrant taking over the city.

Usage 3: Jennifer had a *visceral* feeling that Mike was not the one for her, but couldn't explain it in words.

VIVACIOUS (adj)   [vi-VEY-sh*uh* s]

Meaning: gay; full of life; attractively lively and animated, particularly a woman

Usage 1: My *vivacious* stepmother has too many friends to count.

Usage 2: If I were more *vivacious* I might be invited out, but I have always been a reserved person.

Usage 3: The *vivacious* movie star blew kisses and flirted shamelessly.

VOCIFEROUS (adj)   [voh-SIF-er-*uh* s]

Meaning: loudly vocal; noisy; vehement or clamorous of speech; expressing in a forceful way

Usage 1: His *vociferous* speech causes many to take offense.

Usage 2: Her *vociferous* statements about others' appearances are quite embarrassing; she is always criticizing someone.

Usage 3: The *vociferous* law student impressed many of his peers, but was not a favorite of his professors.

Usage 4: Your *vociferous* comments and rude stares have become quite embarrassing.

Usage 5: The speaker's *vociferous* manner of speaking offended many and caused many angry comments at the end.

VOGUE (n)   [vohg]

Meaning: popular fashion; prevailing fashion or style at a particular time

Usage 1: It's hard to remember when mullets and stretch pants were in *vogue*.

Usage 2: The fruity and sweet drinks so popular in the city are in *vogue*, much unlike my own favorite - craft beers.

Usage 3: The *vogue* these days is organic produce and local wines.

Usage 4: I look forward to the time when it is considered in *vogue* to go without makeup.

VOLUMINOUS (adj)   [v*uh*-LOO-m*uh*-n*uh* s]

Meaning: bulky; occupying much space; large in volume; loose and ample

Usage 1: The *voluminous* bridal gown took up the width of the aisle.

Usage 2: Her *voluminous* eyelashes brushed his cheek unexpectedly.

Usage 3: After using the shampoo her stylist recommended, Mindy's hair was shiny and *voluminous*.

VOLUPTUOUS (adj)   [v*uh*-LUHP-choo-*uh* s]

Meaning: gratifying the senses; characterized by luxury or sensual pleasure; curvaceous

Usage 1: The *voluptuous* dress moved suggestively every time she took a step.

Usage 2: Lilly is a *voluptuous* woman who always attracts male attention.

Usage 3: Though culture idealizes thinness, it is the *voluptuous* women who are the most beautiful in my eyes.

Usage 4: The *voluptuous* actress was criticized for her weight, but she made a good living out of being a role model for average-sized women.

Usage 5: The *voluptuous* curves of the sports car made it one of the top five most-desired vehicles of the decade.

VORTEX (n)   [VAWR-teks]

Meaning: whirlwind; whirlpool; center of turbulence; predicament into which one is inexorably plunged; mass of whirling fluid or air

Usage 1: Betty should have known better than to get involved with a married man, for now she is in a *vortex* of secrecy and denial.

Usage 2: My friend and I were suddenly caught in a *vortex* in the ocean, and could not swim to shore.

Usage 3: I had a nightmare last night that a *vortex* burst through the roof and carried us all straight up to the sky.

Usage 4: My brother and his friend are such daredevils; the last time a tornado came through they headed straight for the *vortex*.

Usage 5: It is physics at work when you notice that finer materials gravitate toward the center of a *vortex*, and heavier items stay on the outside.

VOTARY (n)   [VOH-t*uh*-ree]

Meaning: eager admirer or supporter of some idea; person who has made vows of dedication to a religious service; a dedicated follower

Usage 1: As a *votary*, the monk took vows of silence and lived simply.

Usage 2: My sister, a *votary* in the Roman Catholic Church, has lived in a convent for ten years.

Usage 3: I've always been religious, but never inclined to become a *votary*.

Usage 4: A *votary* of Abraham Lincoln, my husband reads every book written by and about him that exists.

VOYEUR (n)   [vwah-YUR]

Meaning: Peeping Tom; person who enjoys seeing others when they are naked or engaging in sexual activity

Usage 1: After many sightings, the *voyeur* was finally caught and sentenced.

Usage 2: The *voyeur* was so experienced he watched people for years before they became aware of it.

Usage 3: That *voyeur* is peeping through the keyhole again!

Usage 4: Don't be such a *voyeur*, just come on in and ask us what we're talking about.

WARRANT (v)   [WAWR-*uh* nt]

Meaning: authorize; to justify or necessitate; to require or deserve; to make a legal promise that a statement is true; to give a guarantee for a product

Usage 1: Don't worry; I'll *warrant* that she will be here right on time.

Usage 2: Some people thought the burglar's offense was serious enough to *warrant* years in prison.

Usage 3: If you feel bad enough to *warrant* a trip to the doctor, I don't think you need to be going shopping.

Usage 4: The car salesman *warranted* that every vehicle he sells gets over 30 miles per gallon.

Usage 5: What has he done that is serious enough to *warrant* a divorce?

WASTREL (n)   [WEY-str*uh* l]

Meaning: profligate; a wasteful or good for nothing person; a waif; a neglected child

Usage 1: The sad face of the *wastrel* who appeared at our door on Christmas Eve was impossible to turn away.

Usage 2: The upper-class *wastrel* was kind and meant well, but was ultimately pretty useless.

Usage 3: The irritable, disgruntled *wastrel* somehow ended up becoming mayor of our town.

Usage 4: The novel revolves around a selfish, mean *wastrel* who becomes stranded on a desert island with all his ex-girlfriends.

Usage 5: Humans are energy *wastrels* when compared to other animals, who consume all the parts of their prey.

WEAN (v)   [ween]

Meaning: accustom an infant or other young mammal to food other than its mother's milk; to be strongly influenced by something, especially from an early age

Usage 1: Kittens are usually *weaned* by their mothers by three or four months, though the mothers still bring back food for the babies for a time.

Usage 2: Most pediatricians recommend *weaning* infants after at least a year to reap all the benefits of breast milk.

Usage 3: Sheila's doctor unsuccessfully tried to *wean* her off the sleeping pills, but she found reasons to continue taking them.

Usage 4: As a child, I was *weaned* on a diet of meatloaf and mashed potatoes, so it's hard for my mother to understand the vegetarian diet I picked up in college.

WINSOME (adj)   [WIN-s*uh* m]

Meaning: agreeable; gracious; engaging; attractive or appealing in appearance or character

Usage 1: Her *winsome* smile captured the hearts of all adults who met her.

Usage 2: Nora's *winsome* charm was contagious, and she made friends wherever she went.

Usage 3: His *winsome* face was constantly laughing, and his eyes were always sparkling.

Usage 4: The public will miss that *winsome* man who has been on the radio for fifty years.

WITHSTAND (v)   [with-STAND]

Meaning: stand up against; successfully resist; remain undamaged or affected by

Usage 1: Even the brick homes on my street could not *withstand* the great gusts of wind that blew trees down left and right.

Usage 2: The little girl could not *withstand* the pressure of the performance and burst into tears right before she went on stage.

Usage 3: If you can *withstand* the Vermont winters, then you will love living here.

WONT (n)   [wawnt]

Meaning: custom; habitual procedure; one's customary behavior in a particular situation

Usage 1: Brad, as was his *wont*, was charming and delightful over lunch today with customers.

Usage 2: Though she doesn't regularly attend Mass, Claire would never deny her family the *wont* of baptizing her little girl.

Usage 3: Chad's *wont* is to go for a run every day after work, and the days he is not able to do so he gets quite irritable.

Usage 4: Dolly's *wont* is to visit the same hairdresser every other month, even though it is an hour out of her way.

Usage 5: It was their *wont* to dine at 6 o'clock every evening.

WRATH (n)   [rath]

Meaning: fury; strong, stern, or fierce anger; deeply resentful indignation

Usage 1: The teenager quickly hid his cigarette for fear of his father's *wrath*.

Usage 2: The tiger's *wrath* was targeted toward the small monkey cowering behind the bush.

Usage 3: Even though she never even got a speeding ticket, Preslee lived in terror of the *wrath* of law enforcement.

Usage 4: Mary wasn't completely ready to face her husband's *wrath*, but unlocked the door and went inside anyway.

WRITHE (v)   [rahyth]

Meaning: twist in coils; contort in pain; to twist or turn the body from side to side due to pain or discomfort; to shrink back due to emotional or physical discomfort

Usage 1: Jared *writhed* in pain on the ground after being hit in the foot with a stray bullet.

Usage 2: Olivia bit her lip and *writhed* in contained anger throughout the politician's speech.

Usage 3: After getting an electric shock, the apprentice *writhed* on the ground for several minutes before calming down.

XENOPHOBIA (n)   [zen-*uh*-FOH-bee-*uh*]

Meaning: an irrational fear of foreigners or anything foreign

Usage 1: Rod's *xenophobia* is hard to understand, as he grew up in a diverse neighborhood and his best friend is Korean.

Usage 2: Racial *xenophobia* is still prevalent in parts of the South, where residents are terribly cautious about socializing with others different from themselves.

Usage 3: Xenophobia against immigrants is an issue that always arises during election years but never seems to be discussed at other times.

YEN (n)   [yen]

Meaning: strong desire; a longing or yearning; Japanese currency

Usage 1: In preparation for his trip to Tokyo, Clark exchanged his dollars for *yen* so he would have cash on hand.

Usage 2: Sherri always had a *yen* to be an artist, but was never able to make enough money to sustain herself.

Usage 3: After a few days on a no-sugar diet, my *yen* for chocolate has become unbearable.

Usage 4: Mark's *yen* for a relationship with Cora was clear to everyone who spent time with both of them.

Usage 5: Her *yen* for a mother was palpable during her teenage years, even though her father tended to her every need and want.

ZEAL (n)   [zeel]

Meaning: keenness; great energy or enthusiasm in pursuit of a cause or objective

Usage 1: Leroy's *zeal* for making money gets in the way of family requests, such as attending his daughter's first dance recital.

Usage 2: Sonya's *zeal* for homeless persons' rights was the reason she went to law school.

Usage 3: Spencer's *zeal* for propriety gets irritating as he annoys everyone about their lack of adherence to policy.

Usage 4: If you pay attention to the books he reads, you can tell that Jonathan has a *zeal* for American history.

Made in United States
Orlando, FL
09 September 2022

22196328R00196